MENTAL DISABILITY, VIOLENCE, AND FUTURE DANGEROUSNESS

MENTAL DISABILITY, VIOLENCE, AND FUTURE DANGEROUSNESS

Myths Behind the Presumption of Guilt

John Weston Parry

ROWMAN & LITTLEFIELD
Lanham • Boulder • New York • Toronto • Plymouth, UK

Published by Rowman & Littlefield
4501 Forbes Boulevard, Suite 200, Lanham, Maryland 20706
www.rowman.com

10 Thornbury Road, Plymouth PL6 7PP, United Kingdom

British Library Cataloguing in Publication Information Available

Library of Congress Cataloging-in-Publication Data

Parry, John Weston, 1948–
Mental disability, violence, and future dangerousness : myths behind the presumption of guilt / John
Weston Parry.
pages cm.
Includes bibliographical references and index.
ISBN 978-1-4422-2404-9 (cloth : alk. paper) — ISBN 978-1-4422-2405-6 (electronic)
1. People with mental disabilities—United States. 2. People with mental disabilities—Legal status,
laws, etc.—United States. 3. People with mental disabilities—Mental health services—United States.
I. Title.
HV3004.P377 2013
303.6087'40973—dc23
2013020045

∞™ The paper used in this publication meets the minimum requirements of
American National Standard for Information Sciences Permanence of Paper for
Printed Library Materials, ANSI/NISO Z39.48-1992.

Printed in the United States of America

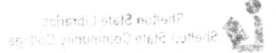

To Elissa and Jennifer Lauren, the best writers in our nuclear family.

CONTENTS

PREFACE

A critical measure of every society is how the most vulnerable and isolated members are treated. America is failing miserably with regard to persons with serious mental disabilities who need public assistance, particularly if they are deemed to be dangerous to others, themselves, or the community. We not only allow our vulnerable children and adults with mental disabilities to be neglected and abused while barely lifting a finger to help, but we use our legal system to deprive them of their liberty, fundamental rights, and opportunities for consensual care and treatment when they act out due to such neglect and abuse. This is not a recent problem. Such widespread deprivations were present for many years even before I began law school in the early 1970s. They have continued unabated in somewhat different forms during the forty years that I have been involved in mental disability law and the rights of persons with mental disabilities. In many ways, the situation for people with serious mental impairments, who are unable to care for themselves without public assistance, has grown even worse, from both a legal and a public health standpoint.

This book is an expression of what I believe is wrong with our legal system and public health policies as they affect persons with serious mental disabilities. It also provides a multidisciplinary analysis of why this has occurred in America and offers initial recommendations to address the travesties of justice that have resulted. I recognize that what I have written may meet with strong resistance in some quarters because it upsets the status quo and assigns a measure of responsibility to all of the key participants. Yet, I strongly believe this not only needs to be stated, but also openly discussed, particularly amongst lawyers, judges, mental health professionals, legislators, policymakers, and public health officials who have the power to initiate reforms.

Many people have helped me with this book and the research and writing that led up to it, not all of whom I can mention here, and none of whom are responsible for its opinions or flaws. Writing this manuscript was a learning process that required many revisions and restarts over a number of years as people whom I respect provided critical feedback, I gained new insights, and new information became available. What I began with is very different from what will be published now. In alphabetical order, these are the key individuals who, at different junctures in this process, took considerable time to provide me with their insights and gentle, and not so gentle, critiques.

- Amy L. Allbright, director of the ABA Commission on Disability Rights.

- Roberta Brawer, coauthor of *Origins: The Lives and Worlds of Modern Cosmologists*; former lecturer of physics and cultural anthropology at the Massachusetts Institute of Technology; and my sister.

- Eric Y. Drogin, lawyer and forensic and clinical psychologist; faculty at Harvard Medical School; and for many years an ABA colleague.

- John Monahan, University of Virginia professor of law, psychology, and psychiatric medicine.

- Michael L. Perlin, New York Law School professor; director, Mental Disability Law Program.

- Ronald J. Tabak, special counsel at Skadden, Arps; chair of the ABA Section of Individual Rights and Responsibilities Task Force on Mental Disability and the Death Penalty.

- David B. Wexler, University of Arizona School of Law distinguished research professor emeritus; director, International Network on Therapeutic Jurisprudence.

I also would like to thank Harold Bursztajn and Kenneth Pope for providing access to the rich online resources available from the Program in Psychiatry and Law (PIPAL) at Harvard Medical School. This information proved invaluable time and again. In addition, I want to thank the late Bruce Ennis, who was a mentor to me after law school at the Mental Health Law Project and later became chair of the ABA's Commission on the Mentally Disabled when I was its director. In addition, I am in debt to both Samuel Jan Brakel and Barbara A. Weiner, who were my coauthors in writing *The Mentally Disabled and the Law* (1985), which in 1987 received the Manfred Guttmacher Award from the American Psychiatric Association and the American Academy of Psychiatry and Law.

Finally, I am grateful to so many thoughtful and talented staff at the American Bar Association who worked with me in producing the *Mental and Physical Disability Law Reporter* from 1979 to 2011 along with many books on mental disability law, which provided me with considerable historical, judicial, and legislative information for this current book. In particular, I want to thank Amy L. Allbright, Ann H. Britton, and F. Phillips Gilliam, Jr.

INTRODUCTION

"[C]ivil rights [in America] have barely made a dent in today's most severe and persistent social injustices."[1] This is especially true for persons with mental disabilities, who remain the most oppressed minority group in our society. The United States, through its legal system—supported by many judges, lawyers, psychiatrists, and psychologists—is engaging in invidious discrimination against persons with mental disorders, conditions, or aberrations who, explicitly or implicitly, are deemed to be a future danger to others, the community, or themselves. Ultimately, there needs to be new state and federal laws to govern when, how, and to what extent the fundamental rights and liberties of persons with mental disabilities may be withheld, restricted, or diluted when those individuals are proven to be dangerous based on their actions, rather than what we believe their future behaviors might be.[2] Collectively, the laws we have now are inhumane, unjust, counterproductive, and irrational.

Unfortunately, the legal, psychiatric, psychological, and governmental structures and public opinion that enable the continuation of these injustices are well-entrenched. Even overwhelming evidence that these predictions or impressions about future dangerousness or harmfulness, particularly as applied in the legal system, are unreliable and discriminatory will be met with skepticism and broad-based resistance. Influential people in the legal system and mental health professions need to make the case as strongly as possible that such travesties of justice are wrong and against our best interests as a society. Ultimately, a reasonably unified legal and mental health voice is the only way that policymakers and judges will listen and respond in a more rational and compassionate manner to people with mental disabilities deemed dangerous whose rights, liberties, and freedoms are being improperly denied and infringed in many different ways. To paraphrase theoretical physicist Lawrence Krauss, "unless science, [empirical evidence] and data become central to informing our public policies, our [nation] will [continue to] be hamstrung."[3]

Pretexual and heuristic assumptions about dangerousness are part of a long and regrettable history of unfair and unequal treatment against persons with mental disabilities. In recent decades, this type of discriminatory official conduct toward persons with mental disabilities has been substantially inflamed and intensified by our country's obsession with violence. Violence and our exaggerated fear of violence have encouraged and empowered federal, state, and local governments to take even more extreme and biased actions against people with mental disorders, conditions, or aberrations, who, due to stigma and prejudice, are generally assumed or believed—in the absence of substantial or reliable proof—to be among the most dangerous people in our society. As a result, we now have in place a system of discriminatory and generally inhumane civil, quasi-civil, and criminal laws that only target as being potentially dangerous—and thus subject to special deprivations of their fundamental rights, liberties, and freedoms—persons with loosely and inadequately defined mental disorders, conditions, or aberrations based on psychiatric diagnoses that themselves lack—and very likely will continue to lack—validity and scientific credibility.[4]

How this *Brave New World* for persons with mental disabilities deemed to be dangerous or harmful has come to pass and endure involves a transformation—somewhat similar to, yet clearly distinguishable from, what happened in Russia and China during the Cold War[5] (and unfortunately still persists in those countries today)[6]—in which governments curtail individual rights and freedoms relying in part on the false expertise of mental health professionals. In the United States, many other factors have coalesced to create a plethora of misguided and inflammatory public policies and courtroom principles that are applied only to persons with mental disabilities.

At the center of these legal responses and policies are three fundamental yet continually changing "psycho-legal" constructs—criminal responsibility, mental incompetency, and most prominently, dangerousness to self or others, including "community" safety. The first two concepts, in one form or another, have been essential components of Anglo-American criminal law for centuries, while "dangerousness to self or others" is a more modern legal construct that has had increasingly dire implications for our rights, freedoms, and liberties in both our criminal and civil laws.

Until the early 1980s, most defendants who were not mentally responsible in whole or in part for their crimes were entitled, by law—although clearly not by practice—either to be excused from all criminal penalties and to be "hospitalized" for treatment in secure surroundings until they were cured, or to be partially excused and imprisoned for a reduced period of time, while also receiving needed treatment.[7] Two of the most important concepts in this regard are known as the insanity defense and diminished capacity. In addition, during sentencing a defendant's diminished culpability due to a mental condition was supposed to mitigate punishment and thus reduce that person's sentence.

Today, relatively few defendants even with severe mental disabilities are found "not guilty by reason of insanity" or have their charges or sentences reduced due to "diminished capacity"[8] or mitigation. Instead, defendants who are psychotic or otherwise severely cognitively impaired, mentally retarded, or emotionally disturbed typically are either sent to prison without any special dispensations given to their diminished culpability, or, in a number of jurisdictions, are found "guilty but mentally ill." This latter verdict makes defendants with significant mental disabilities completely responsible for their crimes, yet generally does not obligate governments to provide them with humane care and treatment or to reduce their sentences, even allowing them to be executed on occasion. Moreover, because of the extremely over-generalized and often misplaced associations in our society between mental disability and violence and other dangerous-like or harmful behaviors, during sentencing defendants with mental disabilities are much more apt to have their confinements in prison or prison-like circumstances, as well as any subsequent conditions of release, increased or extended than they are to have them reduced.[9]

Throughout American legal history, defendants found to be mentally incompetent to make trial and posttrial decisions and to communicate effectively with counsel have been temporarily or permanently excused, based on notions of fundamental fairness and due process, from participating in key criminal proceedings—such as making pleas, standing trial, being sentenced, or being executed.[10] However, for those who are deemed mentally unfit to be tried, sentenced, or executed, the circumstances surrounding their confinements have raised questions and due process concerns in two significant ways. First, state and federal officials, often facilitated by judges and mental health professionals, have established legally permissible avenues to forcibly administer powerful antipsychotic medications to such defendants against their wills, too often using excessive dosages with seriously harmful and even deadly side effects. Second, legislatures, aided by courts and state-retained mental health professionals, increasingly are implementing policies to ensure that defendants who are found unfit to stand trial but are unlikely to recover within a reasonable amount of time are "civilly" incarcerated indefinitely, rather than released, even though they have never been found guilty of their alleged crime(s) and could and should receive better and less restrictive care and treatment in the community.

The most egregious miscarriages of justice, however—and by far the more numerous—are various courtroom determinations about individuals' dangerousness to self, others, or the community. This once-innovative American human rights concept stood for the proposition that involuntary civil commitment of persons with mental disabilities—typically to large, isolated, inhumane institutions—should only be based on specific findings by clear and convincing evidence that those being forcibly confined for treatment, that was rarely provided, were an immediate and substantial danger to others or themselves.[11]

Today, new and far more vague and imprecise legal standards and procedures based explicitly or implicitly on future dangerousness or harmfulness have multiplied. They now dominate civil and quasi-civil criminal commitment and criminal sentencing matters—including the death penalty—and heavily influence pretrial detention, the decision to try juveniles as adults, and all sorts of civil and criminal conditional release mechanisms and other intrusions into these individuals' daily lives. In the 1970s, dangerousness standards were intended to help ensure individual rights to freedom and liberty; today, because of the ways in which they have been altered, expanded, and enforced to satisfy our distorted fears and beliefs, dangerousness standards are much more likely to legally deprive individuals with mental disabilities of their fundamental constitutional rights, freedoms, and liberties, and these deprivations continue to increase in both number and scope.

Hundreds of thousands of Americans are presently incarcerated, involuntarily medicated, mistreated, and/or deprived of other fundamental rights, liberties, and freedoms under such standards, and a significant few are waiting to be executed. This is occurring even though persuasive empirical evidence is lacking that within the many constraints of our legal system anyone—even the most knowledgeable and competent forensic psychiatrists and psychologists using the most highly structured risk assessment tools, much less juries and judges based on their own subjective impressions—can reliably and validly predict whether a specific individual is going to engage in dangerous or harmful acts in the future consistent with the legal standards and procedures at issue.

The weight of the evidence today strongly suggests that, despite significant advances over the past twenty-five years in risk assessments in clinical settings targeted at a few well-defined categories of people with specified mental disorders, there exists few, if any, reliable and valid predictive abilities within our legal system with regard to specific individuals. Furthermore, overtly violent people with mental disabilities who cause harm to others can be dealt with much more fairly and effectively under traditional principles of Anglo-American criminal law, including principles of diminished culpability and humane custodial care and treatment for those with mental impairments.

In order to meet the applicable standards of proof and other due process criteria, which are constitutionally required in most dangerousness cases, it would be reasonable to assume that clinical opinions and risk assessments—if they ever should be allowed in court in these cases—would only be based on a finding that an individual is presently dangerous because he or she has engaged in violent criminal acts, and thus requires specified care and treatment. Dangerousness in these cases would be a factual determination made by juries or judges about what the subjects of such proceedings have actually done recently that is violent and for which they have not been punished already; not the dubious and predominantly unreliable dangerousness predictions about what could happen in the future that are made by mental health "experts" or much less-informed juries and judges in a legal system in which the key decision-makers tend to presume that persons with mental disabilities are dangerous to begin with.

Also, many criminal defendants are subject to lengthy detentions before they are tried because they are found to be a danger to the community due to their mental disabilities. Sometimes these findings are based on the opinions of mental health experts regarding the detainee's future dangerousness; in other cases judges decide in a couple of minutes—or less—based on their legal impressions and secondhand reports about the defendant's dangerousness. In addition, an increasing number of adolescents, and children even younger than that, are tried as adults based on expert predictions that it is likely that these youthful offenders will continue to be dangerous in the future; thus it would be a waste of resources to even try to rehabilitate them and salvage the rest of their lives. Remarkably, even the U.S. Supreme Court in deciding to limit which children may be sentenced to life in prison without parole still ruled that certain of these young offenders, despite their psychological immaturity, may receive life sentences without parole if they have killed someone.[12] In that decision, the majority declined to establish a chronological or developmental minimum age in which these sentences could be applied, leaving the door open for state and federal governments to sentence adolescents and children, even if they have mental disabilities, to life in prison with only a minimal possibility of parole.

Dangerousness-based discrimination against persons with perceived mental disabilities continues to be on the rise, as are the number of potential subjects of such inappropriate discriminations. A substantial percentage of a large and growing cohort of persons with mental disabilities who have been trained in lethal combat, yet have experienced some of the worst forms of post-traumatic stress syndrome (PTSD), brain injuries, and other mental disorders, are being—or likely will be—dumped back into our society without adequate treatment, rehabilitation, and essential social services. Making matters worse, it has been estimated, based on Department of Veterans Affairs data, that of the 1.5 million U.S. troops who were deployed to Iraq or Afghanistan between 2002 and 2008, about 37 percent (over half a million) have returned with post-traumatic stress disorder and 17 percent (over 250,000) with depression.[13] Since then the numbers of soldiers with PTSD and other mental disorders has increased, as will the total number of potentially dangerous behaviors that might result—or be predicted to result—from those mental conditions, including self-harm.[14]

Thus, based on this new, expanding reality, sooner than we would like to think more and more severely traumatized and/or depressed combat veterans and currently active soldiers are likely to end up in our jails, prisons, military stockades, and secure detention facilities.[15] Under our current legal standards, these soldiers and ex-soldiers will be viewed as a future danger to society based on their mental conditions, combat experiences, and intensive training to be efficient at killing our enemies. Moreover, the few special courts that have been established to help veterans when they run afoul of the law specifically exclude those defendants who commit violent crimes or are viewed as being dangerous to the community.[16]

Within the strictures of the law, most dangerousness determinations are based on past acts or threats of violence or harm, coupled with subjective predictions by juries and judges, that criminal-like or other types of broadly defined antisocial or harmful behaviors are likely to be repeated sometime in the future. As a practical matter, though, psychiatrists and psychologists when they are called to participate—and not the courts— generally have the greatest impact on the outcome of most of these dangerousness decisions through their testimony. Juries and judges consistently choose to believe that government-retained mental health forensic professionals can clearly and convincingly—or without any standards at all—determine whether someone will be dangerous in the future, even though most of those opinions are typically challenged by similarly qualified experts retained by the respondents or defendants involved. Most of the time such expert evidence is less than persuasive, much less clear and convincing—and it frequently favors the subjects of such proceedings. Yet, juries and judges still tend to embrace outcomes that result in longer periods of confinement and more restrictions on the individual rights, freedoms, and liberties of persons with mental disabilities based on an understandable—but entirely misguided and discriminatory—expectation that they will be able to substantially diminish the risks of violence and other antisocial behaviors in our society by doing so.

Unfortunately, overwhelming empirical evidence, logic, statistics, a long history of abuses against persons with mental disabilities, and inherent deficiencies in the legal system strongly support the view that such "expertise" in predicting dangerous behaviors rarely—if ever—exists in our courtrooms. In fact, such expert testimony may never improve enough in a vast majority of these cases to be relied on if due process, fairness, and equality are to be achieved and preserved. Moreover, when mental health experts are not heavily influencing these dangerousness decisions, the process of deciding depends largely on jurors and judges, whose involvement typically makes those decisions even worse. In our courtrooms, laypeople tend to base their verdicts and rulings on: psychiatric and psychological evidence that they typically understand less than the experts; and/or their own subjective, often biased impressions about persons with mental disabilities, the most common of which is the misperception or tautological belief that these individuals are inherently dangerous. Thus, while the misuse or misapplication of psychiatry and psychology is a significant factor in sustaining and expanding these discriminatory policies against persons with mental disabilities who are deemed to be dangerous, it is our legal systems and the governments that run them that are ultimately responsible.

Various "legal fictions" prevent the best social science evidence from being used to inform dangerousness decisions, while discredited evidence is typically embraced. In these circumstances, the law is much more likely to inhibit the truth than to ensure that the truth is being revealed. As John La Fond and Mary Durham demonstrated in the early 1990s,[17] if the psychiatric, psychological, or other social science evidence at issue will facilitate or lengthen the individual's confinement and the state's control over their lives or otherwise worsens the deprivations of rights, courts are much more likely to deem such mental status evidence admissible, even where there is little or no empirical foundation in fact. However, if similar evidence dealing with diminished culpability will prevent defendants with mental disabilities from being incarcerated or executed, or reduce their length of incarceration, courts are much more likely to strictly limit such evidence or deem it inadmissible. This unfairness and inequality has grown much worse since then. What we revere as due process in other circumstances is often manipulated or dispensed with in order to prevent inconvenient social science evidence—which might limit or preclude these incarcerations or other rights deprivations—to be heard in the courtroom.[18]

At the same time, our courts and legal systems permit some of the worst prejudices that exist against persons with mental disabilities to be reflected in the decisions judges and juries make about whether someone is a danger to self, others, or the community. Furthermore, there is very little chance that such inequities will be corrected on appeal.[19] Even if the appellate judges are earnestly trying to be just and objective, which is made much more unlikely when dangerousness to the community is the issue, lower courts enjoy considerable discretion to ignore facts. In order to prevail, these appellants with mental disabilities—assuming they are one of the lucky few who are able to obtain competent legal representation—must demonstrate that a "clear error" was made by the lower court and it negatively affected the outcome of the ultimate disposition being decided. As the U.S. Supreme Court concluded in a 2011 case involving a controversial conviction based on shaken baby syndrome, "[d]oubts about whether [this defendant] is guilty are understandable. But it is not the job of this Court [nor the Court of Appeals] . . . to decide whether the state's theory was correct. The jury decided that question."[20]

How this accumulating injustice and lack of fairness arose in our legal system—as applied only to persons with mental disabilities deemed to be dangerous—is part of a long and often deplorable history of discrimination in the United States. Although there have been momentary and incremental improvements along the way, for over two centuries now most Americans with serious mental disabilities have been subjected to stigma, prejudice, abuse, neglect, and/or inadequate or nonexistent treatment, particularly if they are perceived to be dangerous. Typically, the worst offenses against these vulnerable and devalued members of our society have occurred while they have been confined in publicly run institutions—which once were referred to as asylums, warehouses, or mental hospitals, and now have become secure treatment or detention facilities. Mistreatment also has been rampant when these individuals have been dumped onto the streets or into dilapidated housing without access to proper health care, housing, and social services. Such callousness toward people with serious mental disabilities has been a product of an insidious form of bias, prejudice, and stereotyping called "sanism," which in the United States today is no less, and often even more, pernicious than racism.[21]

Instrumental in the evolution of sanism has been the incendiary ingredient of violence, and the fear mongering that has been engendered in our society by inundating people with images of violence from the cradle to the grave. Whether America is the most violent industrialized nation in the world is questionable, but there can be little doubt that through our media, news, sports, and entertainment, we subject our children and adult citizens and residents to more images and exaggerated impressions of violence than any other society in modern history. Yet, we also are unwilling to take—and constitutionally constrained from taking—meaningful steps to reduce either the root causes of this violence in our society or the constant creation of an overwhelming number of violent images.

Instead, we have built more prisons, jails, and secure treatment facilities per capita than any other society in the world and have continued to fill them to such an extent that widespread overcrowding and inhumane conditions remain no matter how many new cells and locked wards we add. Most of the people we involuntarily confine have been convicted of crimes and are serving sentences based on those crimes. Nevertheless, imprisoning nearly 2.5 million Americans in the traditional manner has not been enough to make us feel secure in a society that is inundated with violence and images of violence. Even though actual criminal violence has been steadily decreasing for many years now, the images of violence have continued to increase, as have our fears and our draconian actions based on those fears. Thus, we have adopted, adapted, and vastly expanded a legal construct—dangerousness to self or others—to address one of our most prominent societal fears, and we have applied special legal standards and procedures in innovative ways to confine and otherwise control many more people with mental disabilities, who we choose to believe—despite substantial evidence to the contrary—are the most dangerous group of Americans.

For many policymakers and politicians, dangerousness standards and related procedures represent a path of least resistance in responding to violence. We refuse to take administratively difficult and politically unpopular actions to prevent violence or reduce the images of violence that as a society we appear to crave. It is much easier to use unreliable and invalid predictions to pretend that we can accurately determine which people with mental disorders, conditions, or aberrations are likely to act violently in the future. Based on this mythology we can "justifiably" sequester these individuals and deprive them of their rights, making it appear that we are significantly controlling violent behaviors that we fear the most.

The public and most policymakers are convinced that there exists the "expertise" or "insights" to know who these violent people are and will be because it seems apparent—given our sanist tendencies—that as a group persons with serious mental disabilities are obviously more dangerous than anyone else. Also, generally these individuals are less able to protect themselves when they are being discriminated against. Even known gang members, people who stockpile weapons and explosives and drug- or alcohol-impaired people who drive recklessly are treated much more fairly in our legal system than persons with mental disabilities who are perceived to be dangerous.

Unfortunately, in addition to the discrimination and unfairness involved, there are several overwhelming, socially debilitating problems with dangerousness-based legal standards and procedures. First, there is no compelling evidence that experts, much less judges and juries, can make such predictions or determinations of future dangerousness or harmfulness with anywhere near the validity and reliability that our legal system should demand in meeting the applicable legal standards of proof or other legal thresholds that justify these rights deprivations. In fact, the available empirical evidence, logic, statistics, and the near infinite number of variables involved in making such predictions and determinations—particularly within the context of our flawed legal system— strongly indicate that the opposite is true: such evidence, if reviewed critically and fairly, would fail to meet existing legal standards of proof or other applicable legal thresholds by a substantial margin in a vast majority of those cases.

It is conceivable that someday predictions of dangerousness made using highly structured actuarial methods as applied to a few discrete groups of people—with and without mental disabilities—in empirically verifiable situations, could be legally justified.[22] At best, however, that day appears to be far in the future with respect to using such actuarial methods to provide persuasive evidence and testimony in a vast majority of the cases in which individuals are being deprived of their fundamental rights, freedoms, and liberties under current dangerousness-related standards and procedures. Moreover, clinically and, more so, lay-based predictions of—or impressions about—dangerousness or harmfulness, which are used in a vast majority of these cases, are considerably worse. Both are inherently unreliable and should never be used to make legal determinations.

Second, the rationale for allowing various incarnations of future dangerousness or harmfulness to be used as the bases for indefinitely incarcerating, executing, or otherwise depriving people with mental disabilities of their fundamental rights, liberties, and freedoms is nothing more than a bad legal fiction gone wild. We pretend that these people are not being punished for a crime or their antisocial behaviors, but rather are being civilly or quasi-civilly committed—or otherwise having their fundamental constitutional rights, freedoms, and liberties restricted—in order to provide them with treatment and otherwise help them, while protecting society. However, once these "patients," "detainees," or "involuntary recipients of powerful medications" are in the custody of federal, state, or local governments, as a practical matter their rights to treatment, rehabilitation, and humane care all but disappear. Instead, these so-called dangerous inmates and detained patients with mental disabilities tend to be subjected to conditions of custodial confinement and release that usually are no better, and oftentimes even worse, than the notoriously poor conditions that we provide for prison and jail inmates more generally. Tragically, because these individuals with mental disabilities are particularly vulnerable and susceptible to abuse, neglect, and mistreatment, their prognoses in these dire circumstances are correspondingly dire.

Finally, through our words, and the legal actions we take based on those words, our society dehumanizes persons with mental disabilities and subjects them to blatant injustices. This is especially true with regard to the legal language we use to describe and define dangerousness and the right to treatment. Unlike racism and sexism, which generally are condemned when made public and subjected to heightened constitutional scrutiny in our courts, sanism is practiced rather openly and its manifestations are actually subject to reduced judicial scrutiny.[23] As a result, our legal system has adopted special rules for the admission of unreliable psychiatric and psychological evidence that unfairly favor federal and state governments over individuals with mental disabilities who are on trial, particularly with regard to dangerousness.[24]

All future dangerousness standards—as well as the hollow right or entitlement to treatment that justifies those standards—depend on these or other legal inequities and fictions in order to function as efficient social control mechanisms; otherwise these standards would have very little social utility. As a result, no group in our society is more in need of—yet less likely to receive—special legal protections than persons with mental disabilities who are perceived to be dangerous. They are, as established in the chapters that follow, the epitome of what should be deemed a suspect classification under our Constitution.

I

PERSONS WITH MENTAL DISABILITIES AND THE AMERICAN LEGAL SYSTEM

A History of Discrimination, Abuse, and Mistreatment

[Laws are suspect] when they place categorical disqualifications and restrictions on persons [with mental disabilities]. Each person's capacities must be judged individually before he [or she] can be denied rights of citizenship and humanity. (Patricia Wald 1976) [1]

INTRODUCTION

Mental disability law is a broadly defined and continually changing field of study that encompasses the legalities that govern human behaviors, including what restrictions, if any, should be placed on the individual rights of persons with mental disorders, conditions, or aberrations in order to attempt to ensure that they receive needed care, treatment, and other essential social services, and do not create what have been deemed burdensome social problems. This area of law is and has been a fundamental component of American jurisprudence, combining the principles of law with psychology, medicine, disability, and social science.

Despite—or arguably because of—its multidisciplinary nature, in the courtroom mental disability law has been dominated by two professions: (1) psychiatrists, who typically are the most influential and powerful experts, as well as the authors, revisers, and keepers of the *Diagnostic and Statistical Manual of Mental Disorders*—which is generally accepted by courts as the bible of mental disorders; and (2) judges, who manage our courtrooms and are supposed to be the informed "gatekeepers" for ensuring justice, including the admission of expert and other mental status evidence and testimony. Lawyers, jurors, psychologists, other mental health professionals, and social scientists all may have important—and often even determinative—roles to play in courtroom proceedings. However, what is and may be presented as psychiatric, psychological, or other mental status evidence and testimony and how it is to be legally evaluated, are primarily determined or influenced by psychiatrists and judges within increasingly flexible and often arbitrary parameters established by court interpretations of our Constitution, statutes, regulations, and judicial precedents as applied to persons with mental disabilities.

While law, psychiatry, and psychology may be viewed as three essential components of one field of study, the legal, psychiatric, and psychological professions are separate, and often vigorously disagree with each other. Spanning many years, representatives of these three disciplines have been involved in numerous turf disputes to obtain, retain, or expand power, status, influence, and income streams within the legal system. When these professions do come together for a shared legal purpose, however, the arguments and rationales that they mutually espouse may be particularly convincing, more often than not—but certainly not always—with good reason.

At one time beginning in the 1950s, psychiatry and law—as it was commonly referred to then—was a vibrant scholarly pursuit, which seemed to have a limitless supply of innovative ideas and reasonable empirical avenues for improving both civil and criminal jurisprudence. Some of the most esteemed psychiatrists, psychologists, judges, legal practitioners, social scientists, and professors of law became an integral part of an often contentious series of policy debates on how to properly balance needed care, treatment, and social services with basic rights of citizenship, in order to bring an end to a long and deplorable litany of abuses perpetrated against many people with mental disabilities, particularly in mental institutions. In those days, lobotomies, sterilizations, human experimentations, assaults, wanton neglect, murders, wrongful deaths, and mayhems were all part of the custodial care and treatment package.[2] The debates over these disgraceful conditions were frequently heated and the policy implications often profound.

By the late 1970s, the horrific and widespread human rights violations toward people with mental disabilities were largely extinguished in the large state "hospitals" that had characterized psychiatric "care" through the 1960s,[3] because those institutions were largely extinguished. Relatively soon, however, similar and different abuses were reconstituted primarily in the inhumane institutions that dominate our criminal justice system, and in the shadows of our urban—and later our suburban—communities. Furthermore, in recent years, involuntary civil "hospitalization" has been making a sustained comeback, while consensual care has seen only a few lasting systemic improvements, and many disappointments and regressions. Moreover, what were widely recognized by most scholars and knowledgeable professionals in the 1960s as intolerable conditions that had to be remedied[4] were eventually recast and repackaged in our state and federal correctional systems, so that today similar and different types of abuses and inhumane circumstances have become readily accepted as a cost of protecting our society from its worst fears, some real, but most exaggerated and distorted.[5]

Of all the groups in American history that have faced overwhelming societal oppression, people with severe mental disabilities—especially those who are deemed to be dangerous—deserve to be at or near the top of any list of plaintiffs, along with slaves and Native Americans. In 1942, for example, the *American Journal of Psychiatry* in an editorial, which seemed to reflect the prevailing view of psychiatrists and society at that time, went so far as to recommend "that kids reaching the age of 5 who showed that they were 'feebleminded' should be euthanized so that they could be spared 'the agony of living.'"[6] Also, the insensitive and demeaning vocabulary that was widely used by lawmakers well into the 1970s—which still lingers on today[7]—to refer to people with mental disabilities is indicative of how American society has almost always devalued members of this vulnerable group of people. Our statutes and case law were then, and in many instances continue to be, infected by powerful, derogatory terms such as: "the feeble-minded," "the insane," "idiots," "morons," "imbeciles," "mentally deficient," and "mental defectives."[8]

What made the lives of people with mental disabilities so awful was that to a large extent American law allowed states to involuntarily confine citizens and take away most of their basic civil rights simply because those individuals had been identified, through subjective and often incorrect psychiatric and psychological assessment criteria, or frequently no formal criteria at all, as having a mental disability or various physical or developmental impairments that were treated like mental disabilities. Once people were sent to civil or criminal mental institutions their legal status generally became permanent or lengthy and indefinite, and most of their individual rights of citizenship were taken away in the process, including their fundamental decision-making rights.[9]

Unfortunately, similar and different—albeit somewhat less outrageous—civil rights deprivations occur today, only the labels and locations of the abuses have changed and, as a result, our society pretends that travesties of justice no longer exist on a widespread basis. Today, our popular culture is still littered with terms like "retards, "crazed killers," "mental defectives," "predators," "going postal," and other derogatory, stigmatizing, inflammatory, and alarming references targeted exclusively at persons with various broadly defined mental disabilities. Moreover, we continue to categorically refer to persons with mental disabilities as "the mentally ill," "the retarded," or "the autistic"—rather than as individual persons with mental illness, mental retardation, or autism—and then we often ascribe criminal or other antisocial behaviors to the entire group. While polite society scrupulously avoids such discriminatory references for other categories of people, so that today we rarely see in court opinions or newspaper articles terms such as "the blacks" or "the Jews," these types of derogatory general references continue to be commonly used to improperly describe or categorize people with mental disabilities.[10]

PERSONS WITH MENTAL DISABILITIES IN CIVIL INSTITUTIONS

Until the late 1970s, many people with mental disabilities—or conditions or impairments that were wrongly thought to be mental disabilities—endured tragic human rights abuses in this country, including: involuntary civil commitment to large, inhumane institutions without due process; the deprivation of their most basic human rights to care and treatment while confined in those institutions; and deprivations of fundamental rights of citizenship, again without due process, simply because they were or had been institutionalized.[11] Like descendants of slaves and Native Americans, people with mental disabilities tended to be treated much differently and inevitably in awful ways, by virtue of their deeply diminished status within our society and the "special" laws that governed this class of people, particularly when they were in the custody of the states or federal government.

Involuntary Confinement

Through the end of the nineteenth century, there were only marginal differences in the types of procedures that most jurisdictions employed in order to effectuate the indefinite, and often permanent, confinement of people with alleged mental disabilities in large state institutions, or in private facilities for those relatives who could afford to send their "loved ones" there. Typically, if a judge and/or the facility administrator, often without any prior medical exam being made, concurred with the petitioner or proponent of incarceration—usually a husband, father, or male guardian—that the proposed mental patient—often a wife, infant, or child— needed treatment, there was little that the patient could do to contest the confinement that was almost certain to be authorized.[12]

As a result of these and other obvious abuses that led to the commitment of wives by their husbands for little more than disobeying them, or of infants and children for appearing to be different, being defiant, or simply being unwanted, states began enacting statutes "during the latter part of the nineteenth century [that] constitute[d] the basic legislative patterns" that existed through much of the 1970s.[13] While this legislation purportedly addressed many of the worst commitment abuses, there remained widespread problems both in the statutes themselves and in their implementations that led to hundreds of thousands of people being confined in substandard conditions, year after year after year, without basic due process protections being mandated or observed. Reportedly, the zenith year in terms of the number of involuntary civil commitments was 1956, when "state and local public mental hospitals had almost 559,000 resident patients."[14] Most of these mental patients were confined in large state institutions that were variously described by critics, reformers, and humanists as snake pits and human warehouses.[15]

Abuses in the Institutions

Once they were inside these facilities that were euphemistically called "hospitals," the patients or residents were often at the mercy of underpaid, poorly trained custodial caregivers, who did what they could or what they pleased with inadequate resources and very little supervision. Almost nothing was beyond the pale, including some of the very same types of eugenics, human experiments, and other crimes against humanity that characterized Nazi "medical care" for prisoners with disabilities. Abuse and neglect were rampant, substandard health and safety conditions were the norm, and release was extremely unlikely because the laws then, like today, consistently favored the state and federal governments over the so-called patients.[16]

Until the 1970s, state and federal courts had what "in effect [was] a hands-off policy towards institutions and institutionalization laws."[17] Once the courts were willing to take a closer look, however, they found fundamental flaws with these commitment statutes and the horrific conditions in the civil institutions to which inmates were being incarcerated. "Whole sections of state mental health codes were struck down as unconstitutional—sometimes repeatedly—and treatment facilities were ordered to upgrade general conditions and operations or in some instances to begin a phased process of depopulation, when not ordered to close outright."[18]

The catalog of institutional deficiencies that were commonplace, which spanned many decades of public ignorance and disinterest with only an occasional organized outcry, went far beyond invidious discrimination, and on many occasions actually resembled concentration camp–like abuses. In fact, historical analyses make comparisons between certain types of mistreatment of prisoners by the Nazis and the mistreatment of persons with mental disabilities in American institutions.[19] The abuses that were perpetrated in many of our hospitals and civil facilities for persons with mental illnesses, mental retardation, developmental disabilities, and drug and alcohol addictions included: the absence of basic standards of custodial care, treatment, health, and safety; compelled administration of noxious and primitive treatments, such as rudimentary forms of electroshock therapy, sterilizations, lobotomies, painful restraints, negligent seclusions, and various "experimental" medical procedures that injured, maimed, and even killed the patients; arbitrary and sometimes absolute restrictions on receiving and sending mail, having visitors, voting, and viewing one's records; and indefinite confinement without meaningful treatment, or even after a patient's symptoms had largely abated.[20] "Patients" also were deprived of the panoply of basic due process rights that Americans had come to expect, such as a right to a competent lawyer and hearings in front of a court or judicial tribunal using traditional rules of evidence, when fundamental liberty and related rights are at risk.[21]

Rights of Citizenship Lost

One of the most pernicious aspects of institutionalization was the loss of basic rights of citizenship that accompanied the commitment process. Involuntary commitment established a largely irrebuttable legal presumption that those confined as individuals with mental disabilities were incapable of making any decisions for themselves about their persons or their property. This was equivalent to having been adjudicated incompetent with a "plenary" guardian being appointed to make all their personal and financial decisions for them, while at the same time losing their rights and privileges of citizenship, such as voting, holding elected office, and driving.[22]

Moreover, those who served informally as the patients' substitute decision-makers often made decisions that were far different from what the patient would have wanted, including many that conflicted with the patient's best interests or expressed preferences. Greedy, ill-informed, and/ or unprincipled relatives, friends, caregivers, institution directors, bankers, and lawyers could, and often did, deplete the patients' estates, steal their possessions, or consent to highly questionable medical procedures and treatments, such as rudimentary forms of electroshock therapy, experimental brain surgeries, or highly intrusive bodily restraints.[23] From the 1930s well into the 1960s, for example, "thousands of psychiatric patients" reportedly were subjected to "crude and destructive" lobotomies after doctors became convinced that "sticking an ice pick through a patient's upper eye sockets and twirling it like a swizzle stick through brain matter would cure psychosis, depression, or troublesome behavior."[24]

Today, more sophisticated psychosurgery has made a comeback. "In the last decade or so, more than 500 people have undergone brain surgery for problems like depression, anxiety, Tourette's syndrome, even obesity, most as part of medical studies."[25] This type of human experimentation worries "some psychiatrists and medical ethicists [who] say, doctors still do not know much about the circuits they are tampering with, and the results are unpredictable."[26]

For similar reasons, an FDA panel has raised serious questions about the growing use of modern electroshock devices, finding that generally the risks—memory loss and other serious side effects—were high, as compared to the potential benefits. The only time the FDA found the risk to be medically acceptable was in the treatment of catatonia because there were no other treatment alternatives.[27] Also, aversive therapies, including painful and uncomfortable electric shocks on children with "severe autism or emotional problems"—based on the behavior modification principles of B. F. Skinner—have continued to be administered at the Judge Rotenberg Center in Boston, even though they were termed "cruel" and even "torture" by critics of the program and "universally condemned" by disability rights advocates.[28] In November 2011, after many years of criticism and several lawsuits, the Boston facility agreed not to use such "therapies" on new admissions.[29]

Perhaps the most notable and morally offensive misuse of substitute decision-making was the relatively widespread practice of sterilizing women who had been institutionalized, to prevent them from having children because they were thought to be "mental defectives" or "imbeciles."[30] This was part of the eugenics movement that began in the second half of the nineteenth century to improve the genetic characteristics of the human race by promoting good breeding practices. The first statute in the United States to compel sterilization was Pennsylvania's bill "for the prevention of idiocy," that was vetoed by that commonwealth's governor, who explained, sardonically, that a much better way to prevent "idiocy . . . is . . . to cut the heads off the inmates."[31] Two years later, however, Indiana "enacted the first compulsory sterilization law," which was followed by similar measures in a number of other states.[32] Various state supreme courts differed as to whether these intrusive laws were constitutional under the equal protection clause, which in 1927 brought the matter to the U.S. Supreme Court.

In *Buck v. Bell*,[33] the much-admired Justice Oliver Wendell Holmes, writing for the Court, not only ruled that such statutes were constitutional, but opined that they were highly desirable. In his words, the "principle that sustains compulsory vaccination is broad enough to cover cutting the Fallopian tubes. . . . Three generations of imbeciles is enough."[34] Thereafter, "20 states passed sterilization laws . . . [and] in all, 32 states . . . had [these] statutes."[35] Those laws that called for mandatory sterilization were joined by schemes that allowed sterilization upon the consent of a responsible third party, such as a parent or institution administrator, or as a condition of admission to a facility. In North Carolina, these laws also applied to men and boys who resided in facilities for persons with "mental and emotional problems."[36] Between 1933 and 1977, "an estimated 7,600" people were sterilized under this eugenics program, variations of which reportedly were found in "[t]hirty-one other states."[37]

Tragically, it was not until the early 1980s that most of these statutes had been repealed or amended,[38] and that courts began to insist that any legal decisions to authorize such surgeries incorporate strict due process protections.[39] Yet even today there are reports of other types of sterilization abuses, such as in Arkansas, where an obstetrician was reprimanded for "secretly tying the fallopian tubes of a patient with learning difficulties during a Caesarian section."[40] Also, certain judges have ordered inmates with mental disabilities not to "become pregnant as a condition of . . . [their] probation."[41]

THE RIGHTS OF PEOPLE IN MENTAL INSTITUTIONS

The Right to Treatment

The center of the mental disability rights movement beginning in the late 1950s focused on adults and children who were being warehoused in large, isolated state institutions in inhumane conditions with little or no treatment beyond custodial care. The issue that most defined that period was the "right to treatment." This seminal legal concept was based on the work of Morton Birnbaum, a civil rights lawyer who also was trained as a physician. In a 1960 issue of the *American Bar Association Journal*, he argued for a constitutional right to treatment based on substantive due process guarantees for mental patients who were about to lose or had lost their liberty to involuntary commitment.[42]

Birnbaum contended that the logical *quid pro quo* (justification) for this type of compelled civil confinement should be the provision of minimally adequate treatment that would guarantee patients a "realistic opportunity to be cured or improve [their] mental condition."[43] He was convinced that widespread litigation asserting this constitutional right would change public opinion sufficiently that state legislatures would increase appropriations to address the dismal conditions in these state institutions.[44] As Birnbaum recognized, the root of the problem for most persons with mental disabilities who were being subjected to inhumane institutionalization and other rights abuses was—and continues to be today—the unwillingness of our society to allocate sufficient financial, staffing, and other resources to minimally address their basic needs in the community.

The right to treatment (and later the analogous right to habilitation for persons with mental retardation or other developmental disabilities, which today are called intellectual disabilities) did not begin to gain traction until 1966. That year the distinguished jurist, David L. Bazelon, as chief judge of the U.S. Court of Appeals for the District of Columbia Circuit, wrote an opinion in *Rouse v. Cameron*,[45] which for the first time favorably mentioned this right in a court decision, although without actually using it to decide that case. Months later Judge Bazelon authored the opinion in *Lake v. Cameron*, which introduced the principle of the least restrictive alternative to disability law in the context of involuntary civil commitment. He reasoned that "[d]eprivations of liberty solely because of dangers to the [mentally] ill persons themselves should not go beyond what is necessary for their protection."[46] This was a logically compelling variation of the U.S. Supreme Court's prior ruling in *Shelton v. Tucker*[47] that even legitimate governmental purposes may not be pursued in ways that intrude upon fundamental personal liberties, when the same purposes can be achieved using less restrictive means.

Typically, the law moves slowly, cautiously, and incrementally when embracing new legal concepts, and the right to treatment—although arguably almost revolutionary in its eventual outcome in another form—was a classic example of this deliberative process. The first tribunal to find a constitutional deprivation of rights based on the lack of treatment was an Alabama federal court, presided over by Judge Frank M. Johnson, who in

1971 and 1972 issued a trio of opinions in the landmark case of *Wyatt v. Stickney*.[48] Birnbaum's original concept of a right to treatment was joined, and substantially modified in *Wyatt*, by a very different human rights concern: abolishing involuntary civil commitment and closing these large, inhumane state mental institutions forever. Bruce Ennis, who was a driving force behind what became known as the "mental health bar," as well as the deinstitutionalization movement, subscribed to and developed this later view, but realized—albeit grudgingly to begin with— that the right to treatment could provide the leverage and momentum that would be needed to close these human warehouses forever.[49]

Early in the *Wyatt* litigation, however, Ennis opposed the right to treatment as a legal strategy because he was concerned—quite presciently as it turned out years later—that "successful [suits] . . . would become a legitimizing stamp on involuntary confinement, another basis for depriving people of their liberty."[50] Soon, Birnbaum quit the case after failing to persuade his fellow litigators that the best outcome possible would be to challenge "the constitutionality of the 1965 Medicaid legislation that excluded state mental hospital patients under sixty-five from Medicaid benefits."[51]

Nevertheless, Judge Johnson quoted Birnbaum directly in finding that the residents of Alabama's mental institutions "unquestionably have a constitutional right to receive such individual treatment as will give each of them a realistic opportunity to be cured or to improve his or her mental condition."[52] Alabama had violated the residents' constitutional due process rights to liberty by basing their confinements on the need for humane care, and then "failing to provide adequate treatment."[53] Judge Johnson defined what the right to treatment minimally required with specific objective measures that are still relevant and useful today, and ordered the state to meet those requirements. In doing so, he expanded the notion of a right to treatment for persons with mental illnesses (and habilitation for persons with mental retardation and related developmental disabilities) to also include a humane environment, adequate staffing, individualized plans for each resident, and protection from harm, which established a broad legal framework for rights within institutions for those who remained.

Rights in Involuntary Commitment Hearings

If *Wyatt* was the case that used the rights to treatment and habilitation to introduce an array of other rights for involuntary patients into the law in order to improve the institutional milieu for everyone inside, then it was *Lessard v. Schmidt*,[54] decided around the same time, which for the first time established substantial due process protections for those facing involuntary civil commitment. This case opened the door for a flurry of similar due process challenges in other jurisdictions.[55]

The *Lessard* ruling established substantive and procedural protections for people facing involuntary civil commitment that were similar to and in many ways followed closely the protections that were required in order to imprison criminal defendants.[56] First, commitment could no longer be based on a vague notion that it was in the patients' best interest to be confined and "treated." There had to be a finding that the respondent, due to his or her mental condition, was an actual danger to self or others. Dangerousness was defined narrowly to mean "an extreme likelihood that if the person is not confined he will do immediate harm to himself or others." Second, respondents in these criminal-like proceedings were entitled to the rights to counsel, to remain silent, to exclusion of hearsay evidence, and to a beyond-a-reasonable-doubt standard of proof. These courts understood the serious rights deprivations that civil commitment could engender.

The combined legal weight of *Wyatt* and *Lessard* was a clear signal that litigation could produce positive results even though policymaking efforts had failed to change the lives of institutionalized persons for the better. Thus, the creative energies of a multitude of keen legal minds were all focused on helping the most vulnerable, stigmatized, and abused segment of society: residents of mental institutions.[57] In addition to persons with mental disabilities, this population also included residents who had been confined because they had severe physical and/or other socially stigmatized impairments—for example, epilepsy, deafness, speech impediments, cerebral palsy, and blindness—that were ignorantly or misleadingly equated with mental disabilities by the public, family members, mental health professionals, lawyers, and judges.

Around this time, the plight of persons with mental disabilities also received a big boost in the media. In 1972, a young Geraldo Rivera opened the public's eyes to the horrors of our mental institutions with his critically acclaimed documentary about New York's infamous Willow-brook State School for persons with mental retardation and developmental disabilities. Rivera and his crew filmed the horrific conditions inside the institution, which Robert Kennedy had described earlier as a "snake pit."[58] Rivera's televised news stories about Willowbrook, with raw footage of the residents being degraded and mistreated, shocked policymakers and helped launch a national effort to reform the care and treatment of people in mental institutions.[59]

DEINSTITUTIONALIZATION

Deinstitutionalization was a necessary and rational response to wide-spread, intolerable institutional abuses, but later was badly flawed in much of its neglectful implementation. By most humane and progressive measures of the time, deinstitutionalization was the correct policy to pursue, and nobody did it more effectively than the public interest–minded "mental health bar" led by Bruce Ennis and others.[60] A compelling question at the time was whether the right to treatment, even if it was coerced, should precede in importance the right to self-determination, because without forced treatment the ability of people with severe mental illnesses to make rational decisions for themselves and enjoy their freedoms could be severely compromised.

The answer to that important question for an overwhelming majority of the mental health bar was formed by three critical considerations. First, by the early 1950s the reformer Mary Switzer and others already had convinced many, if not most, involved scholars and policymakers that institution-centered care and treatment, even if it was administered competently, could not come close to meeting the needs of the entire person; a more holistic approach in the community would be far more humane and effective.[61] Second, Robert Kennedy, Geraldo Rivera, the American Bar Association's Commission on the Mentally Disabled, the Mental Health Law Project, and a slew of public interest lawyers had revealed that these large, isolated institutions were places where crimes against humanity were being perpetrated.[62] Third, the esteemed sociologist Erving Goffman and other scholars had argued convincingly that these hospitalization horrors were due, at least in substantial part, to the inherently destructive and stigmatizing nature and characteristics of large institutions themselves, and how their dysfunctional milieus negatively affect the human beings inside, patients and staff alike.[63] Thus, there was very little reason to think then that these institutions could be successfully reformed in meaningful ways, and much evidence indicating that they should cease to exist.

Also, on the fringe of these discussions were certain influential academics, led by Thomas Szasz, who essentially argued that in reality there was no such thing as mental illness in a medical sense, and thus no one should be confined, involuntarily, based on these highly dubious diagnoses.[64] While Szasz and others like him seemed extreme in their points of view, they focused attention on the fact that psychiatric and psychological diagnoses were hardly scientific, and often were little more than impressionistic opinions that had grave negative consequences on the liberty and related rights and interests of citizens with mental disabilities.

The ingenuity of the mental health bar, however, was its ability to transform the right to treatment into a potent legal weapon for the closure of these failed institutions. This strategy began with *Wyatt* and *Lessard*, but it did not bear much fruit in terms of depopulating human warehouses until later. With regard to deinstitutionalization, the *Wyatt* decision adopted Judge Bazelon's least restrictive alternative and required the State of Alabama to create a system that would move its mental institution residents from:

(1) more to less structured living; (2) larger to smaller facilities; (3) larger to smaller living units; (4) group to individual residence; (5) segregated from the community to integrated into the community living; [and] (6) dependent to independent living.[65]

Lessard, in turn, gave lawyers in Wisconsin—and many other jurisdictions throughout the United States—new legal tools with which to slow involuntary admission rates.

However, it was not until Kenneth Donaldson successfully sued his doctors at Florida's Chattahoochee State Hospital for refusing to release him into a supervised halfway house, that the U.S. Supreme Court became involved in 1975. Morton Birnbaum represented Donaldson, initially, and based on the legal arguments that were presented, Birnbaum apparently believed that the case was a golden opportunity to gain further recognition for the constitutional right to treatment, which he had conceived. A lower federal court had ruled in Donaldson's favor based on a jury instruction that the plaintiff should prevail if it was shown that he was deprived of necessary treatment.[66] The U.S. Court of Appeals for the Fifth Circuit affirmed, reasoning persuasively and humanely that Donaldson "had a constitutional right to such treatment as would help him to be cured or to improve his mental condition."[67]

Ironically, this litigation could just as easily have been positioned as a right-to-refuse-treatment case, since what Donaldson really had wanted was to be released, to be left alone, and not subjected to any more intrusive treatments. He did not believe that he was mentally ill, at least not in a way that could be helped by coercive psychiatry. When his treating physicians appealed the case to the U.S. Supreme Court and certiorari was granted, this irony was not lost on Donaldson's new counsel, Bruce Ennis, or apparently a majority of the justices themselves. Ennis was most concerned with the fact that Donaldson had been incarcerated against his will, and less concerned that his client had been deprived of his right to treatment, which was rarely provided for in these circumstances anyway.[68] Moreover, the chief justice at that time was Warren Burger, who, as Judge Bazelon's nemesis on the D.C. Court of Appeals, had often opined that there was nothing in the Constitution about a right to treatment. Burger firmly believed that such a right did not and should not exist.[69]

It was Potter Stewart, however, who wrote the unanimous opinion in *O'Connor v. Donaldson*,[70] which established a new right of nondangerous, mentally ill individuals to live in the community. The Court elected not to decide whether "mentally ill persons dangerous to themselves or to others have a right to treatment upon compulsory confinement by the State, or whether the State may compulsorily confine a nondangerous, mentally ill individual for the purpose of treatment."[71] Instead, the majority ruled that a "State cannot constitutionally confine without more a nondangerous individual who is capable of surviving safely in freedom by himself with the help of willing and responsible family members or friends."[72]

Although *O'Connor v. Donaldson* was a carefully crafted ruling that ostensibly went no further than was necessary to affirm that the plaintiff's rights had been violated and that he might be entitled to damages from the doctors who were responsible, Ennis led the Court far enough to revamp the ways in which involuntary mental patients would be dealt with in the future. To begin with, no matter how one parsed the Court's words, the impact on state involuntary civil commitment laws was dramatic and relatively immediate, as dangerousness to self or others became the predominant legally recognized standard, and almost all of those states that employed criteria that diverged from this specific language incorporated terms such as "gravely disabled" or harm to a respondent's health and safety that loosely approximated and was equated with dangerousness to self.[73]

Furthermore, the Court's emphasis on the right of individuals to live without confinement, if they could do so safely with the help of others, initially seemed to pave the path to community-based care. As a result of this historic decision, far fewer people were going into institutions, and far more were being released into the community, which should have led to groundbreaking, widespread, and enduring improvements in the care, support, and treatment of persons with mental disabilities. As it turned out, however, the improvements that did occur were groundbreaking, but they were not widespread, and clearly most were not enduring.

DANGEROUSNESS TO SELF OR OTHERS AND THE FAILURE TO PROVIDE TREATMENT AND OTHER ESSENTIAL SOCIAL SERVICES

Unfortunately, while the deinstitutionalization of abused residents of large, isolated, inhumane state institutions was needed and justified, in most instances implementation of this new policy failed to meet its promise of humane and effective care in community-based residential settings. There were numerous examples in which deinstitutionalization worked as well, or nearly as well, as it should have,[74] but in too many instances similar types of abuses that had been associated with institutions were transferred into the community, some residents never were released, and homelessness, poverty, and extreme community intolerance became commonplace.[75] Nevertheless, the primary source of the problem with community-based care was largely the same as what had characterized the era of large, isolated civil institutions: American society was unwilling to take the administrative steps and spend the money that was necessary to ensure that people with mental disabilities were placed in decent living conditions, and received proper support services with humane care and treatment. [76] In addition, much of the funding that was available, including virtually all Medicaid funds for essential mental health care, continued to go to institutions and medical-like facilities. [77] In other words, for the most part, this desperately needed money did not follow former institution residents into the community.

Moreover, the dangerousness to self or others standards, which had been the foundation of the deinstitutionalization movement, had a conceptual flaw that the initial path to liberty and freedom tended to mask. The definition of dangerousness meant very different things to different legislators and policymakers, and this lack of certainty and consensus was incorporated into the variety of state statutes that governed involuntary civil commitments. From a civil liberties–constitutional Bill of Rights perspective, dangerousness should have been a limited and precise construct, which encompassed only overt acts of actual bodily self-destruction or violence against others that had occurred in the very recent past.

This type of "current" immediate bodily harm was what Bruce Ennis and others [78] had envisioned and the *Lessard* case had required. This type of dangerousness also was something that could be determined by juries of laypeople because the two determinative questions were relatively straightforward: (1) had the respondent, meaning the person subject to commitment, acted violently toward self or others; and (2) if so, had that violence occurred recently, meaning days and weeks, not months or years. There would be minimal need for expert testimony regarding dangerousness per se, although such expertise would continue to be relevant in determining whether the respondent had a mental disorder or impairment, whether that condition was responsible for his or her current dangerousness, and what type of care and treatment would be best.

From the perspectives of those who believed many more people should be confined because either they needed treatment or they might pose a danger to society, however, the dangerousness to self or others standard became something that should be and was expanded beyond recognition. The right to compel treatment faction, which was represented by substantial segments of the mental health community, particularly psychiatrists, was uncomfortable with or opposed to the dangerousness standard to begin with, but realized that the only way to incorporate compelled treatment into the leading commitment standards of the day was incrementally, by expanding and redefining what constituted dangerousness to self or others.

The noted psychiatrist and Harvard law professor, Alan Stone, who soon would become president of the American Psychiatric Association, and others focused their attentions on the potential future danger posed by those people with mental disorders who did not receive adequate psychiatric treatment and whose conditions, as a result, were deemed likely to deteriorate, psychologically, over time.[79] While it was virtually impossible to clearly demonstrate that these proposed patients were currently dangerous, otherwise they already would have been involuntarily committed, many psychiatrists and psychologists were willing to testify that, based on their presumed clinical expertise, it appeared "likely" that these respondents would be dangerous in the future, unless they were compelled to receive the treatment that these experts felt was necessary.

At the same time, the President Ronald Reagan–John Hinckley inspired "we need at all costs to protect our loved ones from any perceived risks of violence" faction of society saw dangerousness very differently from the individual rights or the "right to compelled treatment" professionals. Many Americans who were particularly risk averse wanted, and soon insisted, that society be protected from any future dangerousness that people with mental disorders might pose, and they were frequently alarmed by constant references in the media that linked dangerousness to mental patients and other people with mental disabilities.[80] Moreover, this faction was a far larger and more politically significant voting bloc than either individual-rights or right-to-compel-treatment adherents because the perceived danger posed by mental patients represented the often sanist sentiments of the average American.

Nevertheless, many policymakers representing concerned citizens also readily embraced the right-to-compel-treatment perspective, at least to the limited extent that without treatment in an institutional setting it appeared that these people with mental disabilities would pose a future danger to others. As a result, the dangerousness standards were stretched to incorporate behaviors further in the future, and behaviors that were more threatening, bizarre, disgusting, or socially offensive than actually violent. Dangerousness to self or others was still the dominant standard, but its meaning was being expanded in many different directions to incor-

porate far more people and situations than was originally intended by
those who had promoted deinstitutionalization from a civil rights perspective.[81]

One of the major challenges that future dangerousness posed initially
was that it depended on establishing by clear and convincing evidence—
the minimum standard of proof the Constitution, as interpreted by the
U.S. Supreme Court, requires for involuntary civil commitment[82]—that a
proposed patient would commit dangerous acts in the future. This standard was considerably less rigorous than proof beyond a reasonable doubt
required for criminal-like incarcerations, but significantly more substantial than a mere preponderance of the evidence. At first this evidentiary
problem was solved because psychiatrists and psychologists claimed, and
the courts and the public readily believed and presumed, that due to their
specialized expertise in human behavior, these mental health experts
could accurately predict who was or was not dangerous. Such a heuristic
and pretextual conclusion certainly appealed to the common sense of the
time; it made the public feel more secure and initially no substantial body
of evidence had been generated to demonstrate that the belief was untrue.

Yet, there were substantial inklings that no such expertise in predicting human behavior, particularly dangerousness, existed.[83] There was
little empirical evidence supporting this assertion and most of the limited
empirical and fast-accumulating anecdotal evidence that began to appear
suggested the opposite: mental health professionals had no such special
expertise. Still, the need for the legal system to believe in these clinical
powers, despite the obvious uncertainties and limitations inherent in predicting human behaviors, was overwhelming because the entire civil
commitment system was based on this legal and social science fiction.
Moreover, the predictions of dangerousness had become essential components of death penalty statutes, since the single most important factor in
deciding whether to execute someone was their future dangerousness.
Dangerousness in a different form also was an essential component in
justifying the preventive detention of defendants accused of crimes.[84]

In 1974, the same Bruce Ennis, who a year later would have such a
critical role in providing the legal justification for deinstitutionalization
based on the absence of dangerousness, published a groundbreaking law
review article with psychologist Thomas Litwack directly challenging the
ability of anyone, including mental health professionals, to accurately
predict dangerousness. The title of their piece was "Psychiatry and the

Presumption of Expertise: Flipping Coins in the Courtroom,"[85] which cleverly equated so-called psychiatric expertise in predicting dangerousness with a coin flip. This analogy between clinical expertise and a coin flip actually turned out to be overly generous in suggesting that psychiatrists and clinical psychologists were correct 50 percent of the time in predicting dangerousness based on their clinical expertise. In a vast majority of legal circumstances, it turned out to be much less than that, both then and today.

Still, it was not until a distinguished psychologist, John Monahan, compiled and reviewed all the relevant data on predictions of dangerousness in a 1981 federal government publication that the tide really began to turn on this issue.[86] He concluded that the empirical literature indicated that psychiatrists and psychologists were accurate in no more than one in three of their clinical predictions of violent behavior amongst mental patients who already had committed violent acts.[87] In 1983, the American Psychiatric Association, largely agreeing with these findings, submitted a friend of the court brief to the U.S. Supreme Court in *Barefoot v. Estelle*,[88] a landmark death penalty case, advising the justices that these highly questionable predictions of dangerousness should not form the basis for deciding whether someone should live or die.

Amazingly, the Court's majority, led by Justice White and joined by Chief Justice Burger, simply shrugged off this inconvenient news. Those justices ruled that because occasionally such predictions were or might be correct, they were potentially useful in making death penalty and presumably other sentencing decisions.[89] Jurors, the use of cross-examination, and the adversary system itself would ensure that any mistakes that these so-called forensic behavioral experts made would be corrected in the courtroom. Making matters worse, as death penalty expert Ronald J. Tabak and others have noted, "the sentencer (most often the jury) is usually able to take its fears about the defendant into account, regardless of what the statute says about aggravating and mitigating factors."[90] Not surprisingly, the most conspicuous fear is the defendant's presumed dangerousness.

Barefoot v. Estelle created an unreasonable and illogical exception to the normal rules of evidence that applies only to admitting expert testimony on dangerousness. For other types of expert testimony, the evidence not only was supposed to be generally accepted within the professional community from which it had originated, but particularly after *Daubert*[91] was decided in 1993, also relevant, valid, and reliable before it would be admissible. What the justices were saying in *Estelle* was that despite the fact that the empirical evidence demonstrated, and psychiatrists themselves had agreed, that they cannot predict future dangerousness accurately, such testimony would be allowed anyway under the legal fiction that somehow—through the alchemy of "common" sense as opposed to empirical evidence and sound reasoning—juries and the adversary system would turn inadequate evidence into testimony that would be reliable and accurate enough to impose the ultimate punishment, the death penalty.

Subsequently, this tortured legal logic was extended to encompass the use of future dangerousness in involuntary civil and quasi-civil commitment and other proceedings as well. Courts soon allowed this highly dubious expert testimony to form the primary basis upon which a jury or other trier of fact would find that by clear and convincing evidence respondents were dangerous, even though statistically and empirically such predictions could not possibly be clear and convincing. Today, courts widely embrace this patently unreasonable legal construct nationwide to allow evidence or impressions of future dangerousness to be used as the primary legal justification for initial and continued indeterminate incarcerations, involuntary inpatient and outpatient commitments, the death penalty, preventive detention, trying children as adults, overly restrictive and intrusive conditional releases, and other deprivations of fundamental rights involving several hundred thousand American citizens and residents annually.[92]

The U.S. Supreme Court in a 2011 decision upholding the depopulation of the California prison system, for example, warned that inmates with mental disorders, who were being subjected to conditions that were "incompatible with the concept of human dignity [which] has no place in civilized society," should not be freed from those unconstitutional conditions of confinement. Their release "[would be] likely to create special dangers because of their recidivism rates."[93] Yet, there was no persuasive statistical or other empirical evidence presented that the recidivism rates of inmates with mental disorders were higher than those of the general prison population or any effort to differentiate amongst various types of mental impairments. One broad and misleading legal presumption fit all.

JOHN HINCKLEY, THE INSANITY DEFENSE, AND INCREASED CULPABILITY OF DEFENDANTS DUE TO THEIR MENTAL DISABILITIES AND PERCEIVED DANGEROUSNESS

The History of the Insanity Defense in the United States, Until Hinckley

From the fourteenth century through most of the twentieth century, Anglo-American law embraced the notion that certain criminal defendants should be excused from punishment for crimes that they committed while "mad" or "insane."[94] The exact standards have varied, although jurisdictions that were once a part of the British Commonwealth, including those in Australia, Canada, and the United States, have incorporated versions of the famous M'Naghten test, which was established by the British House of Lords in 1843, and/or standards that are more encompassing than that. Under the original M'Naghten Rule, in order to establish insanity defense, it had to be

> clearly proved that, at the time of the committing of the act, the party accused was laboring under such a defect of reason, from disease of the mind, as not to know the nature and quality of the act he was doing; or, if he did know it, that he did not know he was doing what was wrong.[95]

Two critically important rationales supported the notion that persons who committed crimes while their thoughts and perceptions about what they were about to do were severely distorted due to a mental disability should not be punished or at least punished less, and should be cared for and treated in reasonably secure but humane environments until they recovered their sanity. First, a fundamental principle of Anglo-American criminal law is that in order to hold someone responsible for a crime, and thus criminally culpable, those who are accused must have what is called *mens rea*, the state of mind necessary to intend the criminal act that they have been charged with. "Since the very concept of *mens rea* or the 'guilty mind' assumes rational choice, persons deprived of this capacity do not come within the concept,"[96] and thus should not be criminally responsible for their actions.

A second fundamental principle of Anglo-American criminal law is that punishment by the state is justified in substantial part because it will deter those who are punished from committing other crimes.[97] People who have mental disabilities accompanied by delusions, other psychoses, or intellectual or cognitive deficits that prevent them from making rational choices, exercising control of their emotions and desires, or perceiving the world as it really is are unlikely to be deterred by such punishment.[98] Furthermore punishing these individuals "does not help deter other persons in the community from behaving similarly."[99]

At the same time, there also has been a strong public and scholarly sentiment in America, going back to the late nineteenth century, to abolish or limit the insanity defense, primarily because much of the public does not trust the legal system to properly determine who is or is not insane, or believe, as did Thomas Szasz, that those who have mental disabilities and commit crimes should be punished, regardless of their cognitive conditions.[100] Also, there has been a group of academics and lawyers opposing the insanity defense, including Thomas Szasz, in order to protect the rights of those defendants who are incarcerated longer as insanity acquittees than they would have been if they had been sentenced to prison for a specified period of time.[101] For most of these critics—along with most Western European nations and Canada—making sincere efforts to rehabilitate offenders, regardless of their mental status, had been a primary objective. There was an understanding that prolonged institutionalization would rarely provide a successful path toward rehabilitation, particularly for persons with mental disabilities.

Largely similar sentiments, pro and con, had attached themselves to the related but far less utilized notion of "diminished capacity." This often confusing concept was supposed to be an intermediate mental status disposition that is somewhere between a complete excuse—the insanity defense—and full responsibility. The rationale behind diminished capacity, which a vast majority of American jurisdictions never implemented—and now only exists in some diluted forms in a few states[102]—is that criminal charges should be reduced if the defendants' mental status significantly contributed to their committing the crimes charged. The affirmative diminished capacity defense, which occurs during the guilt phase of a trial, should be distinguished from: (1) diminished capacity due to a lack of *mens rea*, which is an essential element of a crime; or (2) diminished responsibility due to mitigation, in which punishment is reduced at sentencing.[103]

In the first half of the nineteenth century, the insanity defense emerged as an important part of our legal culture. There is some evidence that what is called the "irresistible-impulse" insanity test actually predated M'Naghten because it reportedly was first utilized in an 1834 Ohio decision.[104] Regardless, the 1843 knowing right from wrong and not knowing the nature and quality of the act standard from the M'Naghten decision were the first insanity defense criteria to have widespread support in the British Commonwealth nations and the United States. Beginning in the early 1960s, though, M'Naghten was eclipsed in popularity and influence in the United States by a more expansive formulation drawn up by a committee of legal experts appointed through the American Law Institute.[105]

Until the 1950s, when the American Law Institute's Model Penal Code insanity defense provision was drafted to "respond to criticism of both the M'Naghten and Durham Rules,"[106] there were no new insanity defense standards of any consequence. Relatively soon after it was adopted, however, ALI's two-pronged formulation[107] became the leading standard, applying language that was a compromise between what had been perceived as the overly restrictive M'Naghten test and the overly broad Durham rule. The first prong of the ALI test—a defendant's "substantial capacity to appreciate the criminality [wrongfulness] of his conduct"—was an updated and somewhat more expansive version of the M'Naghten capacity to know right from wrong standard, while the second prong focused on the defendant's "substantial capacity to conform his conduct to the requirements of the law."[108]

In order to satisfy either ALI prong, the defendant's incapacity must be due to a "mental disease or defect." However, any abnormality that is "manifested only by repeated criminal or otherwise anti-social conduct"—such as the behavior of a defendant with what is now called antisocial personality disorder—is excluded.[109] In its heyday—from the early 1960s until the early 1980s—the ALI formulation was adopted in about half the states[110] and most notably was applied in every federal jurisdiction throughout the United States. It remained the predominant standard for some twenty years.

Despite the fact that the ALI formulation was thriving, there was no shortage of criticism by those who found it too forgiving or not punitive enough toward defendants with mental disabilities or too difficult to implement due to deficiencies in mental status evidence and testimony. In addition, there were others, including U.S. Supreme Court Chief Justice Warren Burger, who thought any type of mental status defense was a poor idea, and thus all such defenses should be abolished.[111] The first significant statutory manifestation of this dissatisfaction—an enactment that went against the trend of expanding beyond the M'Naghten rule—was the guilty but mentally ill formulation that Michigan first adopted in 1975.[112]

Under this scheme, defendants could be found guilty but mentally ill if it were proven, beyond a reasonable doubt, that they were guilty of the offense charged and were mentally ill when the offense was committed, but they were not legally insane. This new verdict reflected a thinly veiled legal strategy to convince juries and judges that they had a supposedly humane and enlightened alternative to finding persons with severe mental disabilities not guilty by reason of insanity.[113] Instead, those states that had this verdict tended to encourage juries through their prosecutors to find these defendants fully culpable, when they clearly were not, by pretending that if defendants were convicted, they would receive needed mental health care and humane treatment. Thus, the American Bar Association, the American Psychiatric Association, and the American Psychological Association have strongly opposed such a verdict since the early 1980s, and the history of this insincere formulation has demonstrated that their collective opposition was and continues to be well-founded.[114]

On the surface this special verdict might have seemed like a humane response to the treatment needs of defendants with mental illnesses who were not acquitted by reason of insanity. It certainly was intended to create that impression, but such a conclusion ignored the practical implications of the law itself and those who were supporting its enactment. Critics of the insanity defense believed that by providing juries with an alternative verdict, this would help reduce the number of insanity verdicts by muddling the issue for juries and judges.[115] Yet, the very notion of having a special verdict to provide needed treatment to inmates with mental disorders made little sense when examined critically. It would have been far more humane, logical, and efficient to provide such treatment to all inmates who needed it as part of their rehabilitation and care after they were imprisoned. This law, however, was serving a very different, nontreatment, incarceration-driven purpose.[116]

That purpose was magnified when Ronald Reagan became president of the United States in 1981. One of his presidential themes was to enact measures to deal more harshly with criminals at a time when the murder and violent crime rates—and correspondingly the public's fears—would soon reach their apex.[117] As part of this intense scrutiny of laws that supposedly favored criminals, the insanity defense was a natural target, since it excused what otherwise would be criminal behaviors. Tragically, in March 1981, two months into his presidency—just as his get-tough-on-crime movement was gaining momentum—Ronald Reagan and three others, including Press Secretary James Brady, were shot. The perpetrator was John Hinckley, a former mental patient who, as part of a readily apparent psychotic delusion, had carried out this assassination attempt in order to impress movie actress Jodie Foster, whom he had never met. Fifteen months later, a District of Columbia federal jury found that under the federal ALI test Hinckley was not guilty by reason of insanity.[118]

The Insanity Defense Post-Hinckley

The reaction of the public, media, and federal government to the Hinckley verdict was immediate, far-reaching, unrestrained, and often irrational.[119] This clamor was similar in tone to the public reaction following the Columbine, Virginia Tech, Tucson, Aurora, and Sandy Hook killings, but much greater in terms of its intensity, longevity, and scope. The insanity defense and people with mental disabilities became targets of a siege that came from many different directions, but particularly federal and state governments, which were influenced by the public uprising. The fact that the verdict had been rendered appropriately, given the circumstances, only made the public's outrage more intense. The criminal laws affecting persons with mental disabilities were going to be changed in many different ways that favored retribution, long-term incarceration, deprivation of rights, and inadequate care over proportion, rehabilitation, meaningful treatment, and community reintegration.

Between 1975 and 1982, only three other states—Georgia, Illinois, and Indiana—had joined Michigan in enacting guilty but mentally ill verdicts.[120] In the years after the Hinckley decision, nine more jurisdictions passed such laws, although Nevada repealed the law after its attempt to abolish the insanity defense had been ruled unconstitutional in 2001,[121] but then reinstated the GBMI verdict in 2007.[122] Furthermore, Montana, Idaho, Utah, and Kansas, in addition to Nevada, abolished their insanity defenses altogether, leaving in their place a narrow constitutionally re-quired window allowing defendants only to introduce evidence of their mental state to show that they lack *mens rea*, the minimum state of mind necessary to commit the crime charged.[123]

More importantly, though, most states and the federal government amended the standards and/or due process protections underlying their insanity and related mental status defenses, all in ways that made it far more difficult for individuals using such defenses to be successful.[124] Before the Hinckley verdict, the ALI test was the most common standard, with the more limited M'Naghten standard being a reasonably close sec-ond.[125] A few years later, M'Naghten strictly construed became the gov-erning standard in a large majority of jurisdictions, including under feder-al law, and ALI became a distant second. In addition, the federal govern-ment and many states changed the critically important burden and stan-dards of proof, requiring defendants, rather than the government, to show by clear and convincing evidence[126] or a preponderance of the evidence that the applicable insanity standard had been met. These changes were deemed constitutional because the U.S. Supreme Court had upheld a proof beyond a reasonable doubt standard for defendants claiming insan-ity in a 1952 case that had never been overruled.[127] As a result of these statutory amendments, successful insanity defenses for serious felonies, which were never common to begin with, became rare, even including "the PTSD defense for Vietnam veterans."[128]

For nearly twenty-five years the Supreme Court was relatively silent about mental status defenses. In *Clark v. Arizona*,[129] however, a majority of the Court ruled that states and the federal government have wide con-stitutional latitude in implementing statutory schemes that prevent defen-dants from prevailing when they try to use any type of mental status defense. Those justices invited jurisdictions to substantially constrict their current schemes by opining that as long as the states and federal govern-ment do not preclude all mental status evidence, there are few other limits on what they may do. Stated another way, under this rationale, "jurisdic-tions . . . may 'channel' the evidence with their own preferred procedures and choose to enact narrow substantive standards related to *mens rea* and the insanity defense that all but eliminate the possibility that the sanity issue will be seriously considered by the jury (or judge)."[130] Given such broad legislative discretion and the public's overwhelming fear of persons with mental disabilities, a number of jurisdictions continued to make it increasingly more difficult—and sometimes virtually impossible—for defendants to prevail with any type of mental status defense, even those who have very severe mental disabilities. [131]

CRIMINALIZATION OF PERSONS WITH MENTAL DISABILITIES

Another society-changing, historical development—which in part resulted from the aftereffects of poorly implemented deinstitutionalization, but even more from stigma, prejudice, fear, neglect, and anger—has been the criminalization of persons with mental disabilities. [132] Since the late 1970s, the total population of large, state civil institutions has been substantially reduced, along with the average length of each civil inpatient commitment. Thereafter, the number of people identified with severe mental disabilities in prisons, jails, and other correctional facilities increased substantially and has continued to increase, [133] much more than the reduction of involuntary commitments to our civil institutions. Today, it would be misleading to suggest that the populations of prisoners and jail inmates with mental disabilities are primarily former residents of civil mental institutions. However, most of these inmates—then and today—either had diagnosed mental disabilities or untreated symptoms before they were first imprisoned, or developed new symptoms that were, or soon would be, aggravated by the inhumane conditions in those correctional facilities. [134]

In the 1980s and thereafter, deinstitutionalization became linked—often unfairly—to homelessness and the overwrought perception fed by the media that many people living on the streets were engaging in serious antisocial behaviors and otherwise creating threats and nuisances in the mostly urban communities where such people tended to be dumped. [135] While failed deinstitutionalization implementation policies certainly contributed to the criminalization of persons with mental disabilities, by far the greatest factor was a shift in attitudes toward crime in general and persons with severe mental disabilities in particular.

During the Reagan years, beginning in the early 1980s, prosecutors were encouraged to become tough on crime and to reject rehabilitation

and treatment as effective means of reducing crime and promoting justice.[136] There also was a common misperception that many defendants
were not being punished for serious felonies, including murder, because
lawyers and forensic experts were manipulating mental status defenses,
such as not guilty by reason of insanity and diminished capacity. This
view was due in no small measure to John Hinckley being found not
guilty by reason of insanity in the near assassination of President Reagan
and the devastating injuries to people in the Reagan entourage.[137] Increasingly, antisocial behaviors due to mental disabilities—particularly if such
behaviors involved what were loosely deemed to be dangerous acts or
threats to the public—were subjected to criminal prosecutions, rather than
diversion into the mental health or related social service systems for care
and treatment. Also, the "war on drugs," which President Nixon had
launched in 1971, already had undermined the notion of rehabilitation
and treatment for drug users and replaced it with "one of the biggest,
most expensive, most destructive social policy experiments in American
history," which led to the imprisonment of addicts and other drug users
for unconscionably long periods of time,[138] typically without adequate
treatment.

Unfortunately, this also created a situation in which there were considerably more desperate people with mental disabilities in communities
without proper housing, income, treatment, and supportive services, and
many of them acted in ways that were, or seemed to be, antisocial, offensive, bizarre, and occasionally criminal. Moreover, the liberating idea that
only those who were truly "dangerous" should be compelled to receive
custodial care and treatment in large state institutions also helped to fuel
the misperception—typically generated and inflamed by the media—that
persons with mental disabilities were much more likely to commit acts of
violence than other groups of people.[139] This misleading and discriminatory stereotype has become even more pervasive today. As noted already,
the U.S. Supreme Court recently accepted without scrutiny the conclusion that inmates with serious mental illnesses are "likely to create special
dangers because of their recidivism rates."[140] Yet, in truth "overall rates
of violence among people with mental illnesses are much lower than
popular stereotypes would suggest," and where violence rates exceed
what is found in the general population, this is due mostly to "co-occurring substance abuse disorders,"[141] particularly the misuse of alcohol.

Until the 1980s, it was common for persons with mental disabilities who were detained for committing serious antisocial acts, including felonies, to be diverted into state mental health systems, and then civilly committed to large state facilities for custodial care.[142] Since then, this civil institutionalization trend has been reversed, but it is clear now that persons with mental disabilities have been jailed and imprisoned at rates much higher than those of the general population.[143] Today, a variety of secure correctional facilities, especially jails and prisons, have many more persons with mental disabilities in their custody than do mental hospitals and other civil facilities.[144]

The most cited study is a 1999 report by the Bureau of Justice Statistics of the Department of Justice that concluded 7 percent of federal prisoners and 16 percent of state prisoners have significant mental illnesses.[145] Even more alarming, these figures appear to substantially underestimate the current problem. A 2009 review notes that "epidemiologic studies show that 15% to 24% of U.S. inmates have a severe mental illness" and concludes that the "epidemic of psychiatric disorders in the U.S. prison system represents a national public health crisis."[146] Other "studies and clinical experience indicate that somewhere between 8 and 19 percent have significant psychiatric or functional disabilities and another 15 to 20 percent will require some sort of psychiatric intervention during their incarceration."[147] Furthermore, it has been estimated that over 6 percent of these inmates are actively psychotic, which is close to four times the rate found in the general population.[148]

Typically, these surveys have not counted many federal and state prisoners, who were not formally classified or diagnosed with mental disorders, but have undiagnosed disabilities or will develop mental impairments while enduring the harsh and often inhumane conditions of imprisonment.[149] Due to stigma, many inmates conceal their conditions. Others do not "present symptoms . . . until they have been incarcerated for some time."[150] In addition, a significant number of inmates may have mental disorders that are masked by medications or substance abuse.[151] Also, these surveys do not include inmates with other mental disabilities, such as intellectual disabilities including mental retardation,[152] cognitive disabilities, organic brain injuries, and certain dementias. Thus, it may not be so surprising that a September 2006 Bureau of Justice Statistics survey of inmates in federal and state prisons and jails revealed that close to 50 percent of those surveyed reported having a recent history or current symptoms of a serious mental disorder.[153] How many of these reported symptoms were due to cruel and inhumane prison conditions are unknown, but the overall percentage is remarkable nonetheless.

To put these estimates in perspective based on the conservative 1999 Bureau of Justice Statistics report, over 237,000 prison and jail inmates would be incarcerated with serious mental disorders. Again this estimate is probably quite low. According to the Subcommittee on Criminal Justice of the New Freedom Commission on Mental Health, which issued a comprehensive report in 2006, perhaps as many as two million persons with serious mental disorders are admitted into the criminal justice system each year; and on any given day, 323,500 will be found in our jails and prisons.[154] Also, it is estimated that 75 percent of those prisoners with mental disorders have "a co-occurring substance abuse disorder."[155] In addition, if a 2006 Bureau of Justice Statistics study presented an accurate reflection of the incidence of serious mental disorders in the prison and jail populations, the number of individuals affected was about one million.[156]

At the same time, the number of adult patients in state mental hospitals at any given time is now only about 80,000 when it used to be more than 550,000 in the 1950s.[157] Similarly, the average daily population of persons with intellectual and related developmental disabilities—which includes what was and is still known as mental retardation—living in large state institutions (excluding psychiatric facilities) has dropped from a high of 194,650 in 1967 to 43,289 in 2003.[158] Yet, there also are large numbers of people with intellectual disabilities in jails and prisons, in part because one of the prominent characteristics of their disorder is that they are easily influenced and want to please others, including by committing crimes for those they associate with.

As a result of these various phenomenons, which collectively have been termed the "criminalizing of the mentally ill"[159]—but more accurately should be called the criminalization of persons with mental disabilities—correctional institutions and detention facilities have become the most popular placements for persons with serious mental disabilities, particularly when other social service systems fail to provide needed income, housing, care, treatment, and habilitation. For most poor persons with severe mental disabilities—and most persons with severe mental disabilities are poor—the alternatives our society normally provides are disturbing and disheartening: homelessness; transient housing with inade-

quate social services; involuntary inpatient and outpatient civil or quasi-
civil commitments; or most commonly, imprisonment. By comparison,
voluntary, community-based options are relatively few and far between,
and due to severe fiscal problems of federal, state, and local governments,
have been decreasing.

The behaviors, which we perceive as being dangerous or offensive,
are triggers that we use to transform homelessness and the need for humane voluntary care and treatment into incarceration and other forms of
extreme coercion. The National Alliance of the Mentally Ill has concluded, quite correctly, that the staggering number of inmates with mental
disorders is "an indictment of the nation's mental healthcare system," and
a clear indication that it is "failing—long before people enter the criminal
justice system and after they leave it."[160] Offenders with mental disabilities, who in the past often were ignored by or passed through the criminal justice system, have become subjects of harsh prosecutions for nui-
sance and nonviolent crimes and misdemeanors, which often result in
enhanced sentences and dispositions because the offenders have mental
disabilities.

Pursuant to these social and attitudinal changes, there has been a dramatic shift in the way in which persons with mental disabilities are perceived and "handled" when they are engaging, thought to be engaging, or
"predicted" to be engaging in crimes and other objectionable antisocial
behaviors. A 2006 federal court decision reflects how popular fears in our
society about persons with mental disabilities affect public perceptions,
such as when individuals with such impairments try to live more normally in our residential neighborhoods. After a regional health-care provider
indicated its intention of establishing a home-like, residential living environment for a group of people with mental disabilities in a Pennsylvania
township, the "good people" of that town packed the zoning board hearing to express their concerns that these individuals might be "child molesters, fire bugs, or drug addicts" and were likely to go "beserk."[161]
These town residents promised that if this "type of people" were allowed
to move in, their neighbors would have to "get on guard, go buy guns, get
great big dogs" in order to protect themselves.[162] Reportedly, the same
type of community opposition exists in many other places as well, including throughout Vermont, where "individuals with mental illness still face
blatant discrimination when they attempt to create a home to meet their
needs in a community of their choice."[163] "Not in my backyard" has been

a familiar theme for many years whenever efforts have been made to integrate people with mental disabilities into residential communities.

Inevitably, given our current attitudes and policies, incarceration and other sanctions have become the standard operating procedure for dealing with persons with severe behavioral disorders and mental disabilities of all kinds. Many people with mental disabilities, for example, are criminally confined because the mental health and related systems have failed to meet their basic needs and, not surprisingly, their mental conditions or impairments deteriorate under the stress of being ignored, abused, and mistreated.[164] Mental health experts often differ on the best response to these failures, particularly whether patients should be coerced into accepting hospitalization and other promises of humane mental health treatments, or whether, as recommended later, comprehensive community programs, preventive services, and support should be available instead. The truth is (as is discussed in chapter 6) that neither response is being implemented on a widespread basis because, as has been the case throughout our history, the amount of money and resources our society has allocated to address severe mental health problems has been inadequate, and the resulting response has been deficient, inconsistent, and fragmented.

Sooner or later a disproportionately high percentage of persons with severe mental disabilities, who are denied proper housing, care, and treatment, act—or are provoked to act—antisocially or make nuisances of themselves in ways that now constitute nonviolent criminal misdemeanors or less serious felonies. Occasionally, they also will commit violent crimes. Yet, the greatest risk is to persons with serious mental disabilities trying to survive in inhospitable communities. One risk factor is encounters with police. There are increasing reports of persons with mental disabilities being killed or permanently injured by police, who often lack the knowledge, training, sensitivity, and special procedures to deal with these individuals without using deadly force, when their actions are perceived or often misperceived to be life threatening.[165]

Even if these vulnerable defendants with mental disabilities are only arrested and not seriously injured, abuses of their rights are common. The police often use defendants' mental disabilities against them in obtaining confessions, or interrogate them inappropriately because they do not actually know about a defendant's mental status. Moreover, many prosecutors, as a trial strategy, intentionally try to alarm judges and juries by perpetuating the misperception that persons with these impairments are inherently more violent and dangerous than other people. Instead of being viewed as a mitigating factor that should reduce the sentence or other punishments or sanctions that are imposed, mental impairments, when linked to the perception of dangerousness, are much more apt to be used as aggravating circumstances to justify or mandate longer sentences, longer periods of supervision and restrictions when inmates are released, and even the imposition of the death penalty. [166]

Also, once they are in prison, inmates with mental disabilities are much more likely to be denied parole and "serve the maximum sentence allowed by law." [167] While in prison, they typically receive substandard mental health care and treatment, or no such treatment at all. Those inmates who are released usually fail to meet the conditions of their paroles or probations, unless they have the necessary support services in the community, which are rarely available. [168] Being dropped off on a street corner with several days of medication, a few dollars in their pockets, and no realistic hope of finding employment is a far more likely scenario for inmates with mental disabilities than being placed in a community living situation with adequate treatment, proper care, and decent prospects for a steady income. [169]

"QUASI-CIVIL" COMMITMENT OF DISORDERED CRIMINALS AND THOSE CHARGED WITH CRIMES

Beginning in the 1930s with laws to provide indeterminate detention and treatment for sexual and other "psychopaths," [170] quasi-civil involuntary commitments frequently have been used as a clever and public-pleasing ploy to extend incarceration of persons with mental disabilities who have been charged with or convicted of crimes, by promising them treatment. Today, this has become a commonplace legislative objective with overwhelming public support, except the legal rules have changed. Terms of incarceration and other rights deprivations have been extended indefinitely for offenders with sexual and other mental disorders, insanity acquittees, and persons found incompetent to stand trial. Modern constitutional due process requirements have been revised to accommodate these new more restrictive and punitive statutory provisions by utilizing the legal fiction that these forms of imprisonment are essentially civil public health detentions for humane care and treatment in secure surroundings, rather than extended incarcerations and rights deprivations without criminal due process protections. Moreover, if these inmates and respondents are released, highly intrusive, punitive, and lengthy conditions—often covering a lifetime—are imposed with the promise of immediate re-incarceration even for relatively minor infractions.

Sexually Violent Predators

A good illustration of the legal axiom that the most heinous offenses make the worst laws is the use of what we euphemistically call "civil" commitment in order to extend, when their criminal sentences are about to expire, the incarceration of inmates who have committed sexually based crimes. Until sexually violent predator (also called sexually dangerous persons) laws—and similar laws for certain other offenders with mental disorders—became acceptable and then popular, the commitment of criminal defendants with mental and related sexual disorders generally was limited to those charged with criminal offenses to reduce their punishments. This would occur as an alternative to imprisonment where the defendant was diverted from the criminal justice system into the mental health system to receive promised treatment rather than imprisonment; after an insanity acquittal; or on a temporary basis to restore a defendant's competency to stand trial.

During the 1970s, however, in response to public safety concerns and outrage regarding relatively rare homicidal and other violent serial sexual offenders, state legislatures began to enact different types of statutory provisions to commit "sexually violent predators" indefinitely after they had served their maximum criminal sentences.[171] "In contrast with the original [sexual offender] laws that identified treatment as an alternative to criminal incarceration, these statutes permit[ed] involuntary commitment after completion of the criminal sentence if the offender is found to have a mental abnormality and to be dangerous."[172] Thereafter, to secure their release, sexually violent offenders had to prove a negative: that they were no longer dangerous where their dangerousness was presumed; or no longer had a mental abnormality or aberration of any kind—whether or not it was the same abnormality for which they were confined originally.

These laws represented an entirely new way to view civil commitment, and like the guilty but mentally ill statutes discussed earlier, they used a deception—in the form of largely unfulfilled promises of treatment—to justify extended incarceration. Moreover, because treatment was vaguely promised or intended, few of the additional due process protections that had to be provided to criminal defendants—but need not be provided to persons subjected to involuntary civil commitment for care and treatment—were available to sexually violent predators (or sexually dangerous persons). For all intents and purposes, these special formulations extended imprisonment indefinitely, yet they were not considered criminal penalties for the purpose of deciding what basic due protections are required.[173] Therefore, since the mid-1980s, the American Bar Association has called for the repeal of these sexually violent predator laws, along with similar post-imprisonment statutes targeting "psychopaths and defective delinquents."[174]

Early on many legal observers were convinced that such an obviously unfair and contrived law could not withstand constitutional scrutiny. Nevertheless, despite a few litigation successes by the lawyers representing these offenders—along with many defeats—when the matter finally reached the U.S. Supreme Court in 1997, a narrow majority of the justices upheld these statutes in *Kansas v. Hendricks*.[175] Those justices ruled that the existence of any mental abnormality or personality disorder—including pedophilia or antisocial personality—would be enough to justify the indefinite commitment of these inmates where it also was shown that they were "likely" to be sexually dangerous in the future.[176] What made these schemes even more unfair was the fact that "likely" typically meant whatever a jury or judge said it means, rather than more likely than not, which logic and common sense dictated and should have been required.

Four years later, the Court concluded that criminal due process protections were not constitutionally required in these types of cases because such incarcerations were considered civil detentions—and not criminal sentences—even though the promise of treatment was only meaningful for those who respond to known, readily available treatments.[177] For other "sexual predators," who appeared to be the significant majority, their dangerousness and the absence of any recognized effective treatments for their particular disorders would be enough to hold them indefinitely.[178] As a practical matter, this meant that for some unknown percentage of sexually violent offenders—probably a majority—permanent

incarceration would be tolerated under our Constitution, even if the offenders had never committed crimes that would justify such a lengthy
punishment in the first place. Thereafter, the Supreme Court added the
requirement that to establish sexual violence, the state or federal government also had to prove that the person to be committed has "serious
difficulty in controlling his behavior."[179] This was not much of a protection, however, since it was generally presumed that people with mental
disorders could not control their behaviors, including violence.

In recent years, the number of statutes that are based on the sexually
violent predator model that was upheld in *Kansas v. Hendricks* has been
growing. By 2010, well over a third of the states had such laws,[180] as well
as all federal jurisdictions,[181] and other states were considering such legislation. Furthermore, these popular legal strategies of committing criminals with mental abnormalities after they have served their sentences and
of utilizing expanded definitions of mental conditions—including disorders and impairments that had been ruled insufficient to justify traditional
involuntary civil commitments or insanity defenses—also have had the
implied imprimatur of the U.S. Supreme Court. Since 2006, a majority of
the justices have encouraged legislators to think of new, creative ways to
incarcerate more people with mental disabilities who are deemed to be
dangerous.[182] Moreover, in 2010 the Supreme Court upheld the federal
sexual predator/mentally disordered offender legislative scheme, even
though the Court had consistently held over many years that, as a constitutional matter, "civil" commitment was supposed to be exclusively a
state function.[183]

Legislation and court decisions with regard to sexual offenders have
relatively few limitations that prevent serious violations of fundamental
rights and liberties from occurring. The legal system has responded re-
flexively to the public's growing desire to enact measures to incarcerate
these offenders for a very long time and to prevent them from being
released and mainstreamed back into society.[184] In addition to extremely
harsh sentences and post-imprisonment "civil" commitments, sexual offenders are subjected to other unique post-confinement penalties, including: permanent monitoring and supervision by the states and federal
government; gross intrusions into their personal and bodily privacy; residency restrictions; community harassment and other actions taken against
them by virtue of their being placed on sex offender registries; limitations
on the jobs that they may take; and being barred from receiving essential

social services, a ban which also may be applied to anyone who is dependent on them, including their wives, their domestic partners, and their children. [185]

This American phenomenon of making sexual offenders of any type social pariahs and the overgeneralized unfairness it has caused has been aptly described in the *Journal of Justice and International Studies* as being based on highly exaggerated fear. "The mainstream media, together with politicians in both parties, is pressing for these measures and the public generally supports these efforts." [186] As a result, "individuals (including juveniles) accused of even minor sex crimes are subject to a rush to judgment, an inability to get a fair trial, and harsh, long-term penalties that can be disproportionate to the severity of the crime." [187]

As of 2009, there were an "estimated 674,000" sex offenders who were on state registries, [188] and this number continues to steadily increase. Because the definition of what constitutes a sex offense worthy of this type of attention is so broad, however, the monitoring and follow-up for the small core of truly dangerous sexually violent predators is inconsistent at best, and "little more than an offender mailing a postcard with his address to a police department once a year" at its worst. [189] At the same time, many adults who have viewed or downloaded pornography online, masturbated in public, had sex with non-objecting older adolescents, or committed other nonviolent sexual offenses—or even children who have had inappropriate sex with other children or texted sexually explicit images of themselves—have been jailed and then indiscriminately labeled on these registries as sexual predators, as they become grouped in the same general, overinclusive category as homicidal offenders and serial rapists. Furthermore, even in the rare situation in which they later are proven innocent of the sexual crimes for which they have been convicted, it may be difficult to get off these registries because there are no specific mechanisms for doing so. [190]

Insanity Commitments

While insanity defenses have been severely curtailed, those who have been acquitted under such verdicts face much longer terms of incarceration in secure, penitentiary-like surroundings with fewer opportunities for treatment in less restrictive settings. The beginning of the period of legal

retrenchment on the freedom and treatment rights of insanity acquittees
can be traced back to1983, two years after the Hinckley verdict, when the
Supreme Court decided *Jones v. United States*[191] and broadened commitment standards as they apply to persons who have committed criminal
acts. In that decision, a majority of the justices ruled that a finding of
mental illness and dangerousness during a criminal trial was enough,
without further formal proceedings, to commit insanity acquittees indefinitely, which increasingly meant decades or a lifetime, not just years.

Moreover, the commission of almost any crime—in that particular
case, the relatively minor, nonviolent act of shoplifting a jacket—was
enough to establish the acquittee's per se dangerousness.[192] This immediately expanded the scope of dangerousness to others. Also, as a practical
matter, it created in most jurisdictions a virtually irrefutable presumption
that insanity acquittees continue to be mentally disordered and dangerous; thus for them, this type of criminally based "civil" commitment
became mandatory. In addition, this opinion encouraged legislatures and
courts to embrace the notion that dangerousness to others should include
antisocial behaviors that may be categorized as criminal, but clearly are
not violent.

Once it became constitutionally acceptable to expand the incarceration
of insanity acquittees, those states that already had such laws kept them in
place and additional jurisdictions, including the federal government—the
largest jurisdiction of all[193]—enacted new laws and adopted new practices that would keep insanity acquittees confined longer by making them
prove two negatives: that they were no longer mentally ill, nor dangerous.
Nine years later, a divided Supreme Court addressed the related issue of
how far states could go in continuing to confine insanity acquittees.

At first blush, *Foucha v. Louisiana*[194] seemed to uphold the logically
compelling dictate that states must release these inmates, even if they are
found to be dangerous, if they no longer have the mental condition or
disorder for which they had been confined. A plurality of the Court reasoned that without proof of an acquittee's continuing mental disorder, the
basis for confinement no longer existed. However, in a concurring opinion that was needed to obtain the critical fifth vote required to form a
majority, Justice O'Connor, in her familiar role as the Court's swing vote
in major individual rights cases, stated that an exception existed if the
acquittees had committed a violent offense and the state could merely
show "some justification" for continued commitment. In her opinion,

"Louisiana evidently . . . determined that the inference of dangerousness drawn from a verdict of not guilty by reason of insanity continues even after a clinical finding of sanity, and that judgment merits judicial deference."[195]

Deference to the states in insanity and related mental status matters, including implementing the bar against executing persons with mental retardation,[196] has been an often-repeated judicial theme in recent years, which has permitted states and other jurisdictions to be even more punitive in their actions toward inmates with mental disabilities than the Constitution would otherwise seem to allow. Thus, governments have been given the benefit of the doubt even where serious due process and equal protection concerns have been raised about how inmates and other respondents with mental disabilities are treated in our state and federal correction systems. Criminal defendants may be presumed innocent until proven guilty beyond a reasonable doubt, but if they have a mental disability, particularly if they use that condition to excuse or reduce their culpability, federal or state governments are given great constitutional leeway with regard to incarcerating them afterward. Furthermore, almost anything a state or the federal government chooses to do legislatively to prevent defendants from raising such mental status defenses is being given the presumption of constitutional correctness as well.[197]

Incompetent to Stand Trial or Participate in Other Criminal Proceedings

Defendants who are found incompetent to stand trial or participate in other criminal proceedings are proper subjects for indefinite commitment and the involuntary administration of medication to restore their competency with only certain modest restrictions. The Supreme Court first addressed this indefinite commitment issue in *Jackson v. Indiana*,[198] a historic 1972 case involving a defendant found incompetent to stand trial for petty theft, who was unlikely to be restored to competency because of his profound mental retardation. He also was deaf and mute, which made the symptoms of his retardation appear much worse, since little had been done for him throughout his life to mitigate his aural and speech impairments. The justices declared that if a defendant, like Jackson, is incapable of proceeding to trial, he may be held no longer "than the reasonable

period of time necessary to determine whether there is a substantial probability that he will attain that capacity in the foreseeable future." If it is
probable that the defendant will never become competent, as it was with
Jackson, "the State must either institute the customary civil commitment
proceeding that would be required to commit indefinitely any other citizen, or release the defendant."[199]

In other words, incompetent defendants were to be restored to competency within a reasonable period of time, or be released from criminal
incarceration as soon as it became apparent that restoration was unlikely.
In deciding what standards and procedures should be used in making such
determinations, considerable discretion has been given to the states,
which today are almost always as a matter of policy working hard to
incarcerate the accused offender for as long as the law, psychiatry,
psychology, and government finances will permit, particularly if he or
she has a mental disability. Typically, states have been reluctant to provide mental health care and treatment to inmates with mental disabilities
when they have been in the criminal justice system, even after they have
been found guilty but mentally ill in order to receive needed treatment.

When it comes to defendants found incompetent to stand trial or to
participate in other criminal proceedings, however, states have been more
than willing to spend a great deal of resources and money and establish
elaborate—albeit deceptive—procedural mechanisms to compel those defendants to take powerful antipsychotic medications that will restore their
competency, so that they may be tried and/or sentenced for their alleged
crimes. This treatment largesse also is true in capital crimes involving the
death penalty. When a defendant with a mental disability resists the administration of such medications, the legal question focuses on a weighing of the self-determination and privacy rights of that individual versus
the rights of the state or federal government to obtain justice and retribution by trying and sentencing the defendant, or carrying out a sentence. If
the defendant consents to the administration of such medications, particularly in capital cases, the issue focuses on whether the defendant was
really competent to do so.

Two U.S. Supreme Court cases established the broad constitutional
parameters under which medication may be administered to defendants or
inmates without their consent, and often against their liberty, freedom,
and personal interests. In 1990, *Washington v. Harper*[200] created the
broad precedent that the constitutional right to refuse medication is sub-

stantially limited for any prisoner with a mental disability. A divided Court ruled that the state's compelling concerns about safety and prison administration outweigh privacy and self-determination interests for inmates who have mental disabilities, were dangerous to themselves or others (or gravely disabled), and for whom the proposed medication was viewed by the governments' medical providers as being medically beneficial.[201] Moreover, the decision as to whether this standard was being met could be made administratively by a committee of prison hospital staff all employed by the state, as long as the members of that committee were not directly involved in the inmate's treatment.[202] While the *Harper* decision did not involve an inmate who was being medicated because he was incompetent to stand trial, it established the precedent that in the context of corrections systems, compelling governmental interests in maintaining a prison milieu would generally override the individual's fundamental constitutional right to self-determination.

Thirteen years later in *Sell v. United States*,[203] the Supreme Court established the minimum constitutional standards that should be used for determining when incompetent defendants may be administered medications over their objections. A majority of the justices ruled that in order to compel drugs in these circumstances, the state had to prove that the defendant would receive a fair trial while medicated, the medication would significantly enhance the state's interest in a fair trial, involuntary medication was the least restrictive alternative available to further those interests, and the medication was medically appropriate.[204] In addition, the charges against the defendant had to be serious enough to justify this type of burdensome intervention, particularly if the defendant already had been confined for a substantial period of time. However, the Court offered the states two alternative ways to circumvent this ostensibly rigorous test, altogether, by creating standards in which defendants could be medicated involuntarily on other grounds. Compulsory medication also was justified if the state demonstrated that the defendants were a danger to themselves or others as broadly defined by the states, or were civilly incompetent and a guardian or other substitute decision-maker was legally appointed to make decisions for them.[205]

Logic compelled that standards at least as rigorous as those established in *Sell* would apply in the far less common situation in which defendants were charged with a capital offense, and thus might be facing the death penalty. However, whether, constitutionally, those standards had to be higher remained—and continues to remain—unresolved. In 1990, the Supreme Court ruled in *Perry v. Louisiana*[206] that the Louisiana courts, in light of *Washington v. Harper*, should balance the constitutional rights of a prisoner on death row to determine whether he could be forcibly medicated in order to make him competent to be executed.[207] On remand, the Louisiana Supreme Court held that the inmate could not be medicated without his consent, even though it seemed evident that he would not be competent to be executed unless he was on such medication.[208]

Nevertheless, the U.S. Court of Appeals for the Eighth Circuit decided the same issue differently, finding that the standards for determining whether a defendant should be medicated to make him competent to be executed should be the same as the standards for determining whether the defendant may be medicated to make him competent to stand trial.[209] Furthermore, the Supreme Court decided not to remand the Eighth Circuit's decision in light of *Sell*, suggesting that the justices, based on what they knew then, did not strongly disagree with the Court of Appeal's reasoning. Whether this also suggested that states may circumvent the *Sell* requirements in death penalty cases by finding the defendant dangerous or incompetent was unclear, but there was nothing in the Supreme Court's opinions to preclude such a view, even though it could lead to the morally repugnant situation in which an incompetent defendant would be medicated to protect his or her medical best interests, only to be executed by the state thereafter as a result. The American Medical Association in its Ethics Code strongly discourages doctors from participating in such inhumane practices,[210] but such executions are carried out anyway, often using psychologists or renegade psychiatrists to make these legally permitted clinical assessments.

Sometimes even with the use of involuntary medication, however, incompetent defendants convicted of capital crimes have not been executed because they were unable to assist defense counsel in their appeals. The proposed solution—which the U.S. Supreme Court has agreed to review but has not yet ruled on—is to allow such appeals to be held even if the federal judges hearing those appeals have concluded that these proceedings should be delayed until defendants are able to assist counsel.[211] Not surprisingly, the concern amongst prosecutors representing the states and federal government has been that defense counsels may be using their defendants' incompetency as a tactic to indefinitely delay those executions. Yet this push to expedite these executions has ignored a practical reality: If incompetent defendants may not be executed anyway, what harm could there be in a delay to ensure that their appellate rights are preserved? Logically, the circumstances in which a defendant, who is found incompetent to assist counsel, would be competent to be promptly executed—while not impossible—should be very rare. It will be instructive to see how the justices rule.

CONCLUSION

"Therapeutic jurisprudence" and what lawyer and forensic psychologist Eric Drogin has termed "jurisprudent therapy" are essential components of multidisciplinary analytical frameworks intended to promote the overall welfare of individuals with mental disabilities in our legal and mental health and related social service systems.[212] These frameworks are used to demonstrate the "extent to which substantive rules, legal procedures, and the roles of lawyers and judges produce therapeutic or antitherapeutic consequences."[213] These concepts "encourage all participants in the legal process to make the overall welfare of individuals with mental disabilities a major concern."[214] As U.S Court of Appeals judge Patricia Wald observed in 1976 before she became an esteemed jurist, "[Laws are suspect] when they place categorical disqualifications and restrictions on persons [with mental disabilities]. Each person's capacities must be judged individually before he [or she] can be denied rights of citizenship and humanity."[215]

Despite the promise of these and other humanistic and rehabilitative perspectives, the overwhelming evidence suggests that in recent decades, state and federal governments—at almost every opportunity—have applied law, psychiatry, and psychology to extend the detention and control of persons with mental disabilities, or even to promote their executions. Therapeutic jurisprudence principles have been ignored, omitted, or replaced in favor of "legal coercion [to mandate] . . . intensive treatment."[216] The overriding governmental objective has been to place these often extremely vulnerable individuals with mental, cognitive, emotional, or developmental impairments in secure prisons or prison-like detention facilities for as long as possible with little or no special care or treatment, except the excessive, involuntary administration of powerful antipsychotic drugs to make them compliant with institution rules, or to restore their competency to be tried, sentenced, or executed. In the process, mental health and other service professionals increasingly have become agents of social control, rather than treatment providers.

These antitherapeutic policies have become so ingrained in our culture that the public and most policymakers, lawyers, judges, and mental health professionals simply accept this type of unfairness, inequality, abuse, and neglect as the way things are done in this country. These inequities are particularly prominent in our criminal justice system because most Americans too easily reject rehabilitation and adequate care and treatment for offenders with mental disabilities as being part of a failed experiment. As a nation, we presume that being humane and compassionate to anyone who commits, or is charged with committing, a crime is counterproductive and wasteful.[217] As one law professor has accurately observed, "[a]ny reform agenda that does not acknowledge the ingrained nature of [America's] punitive impulses will surely fail."[218] Unfortunately, this punitive mindset has produced deplorable conditions of detention for inmates and other detainees with mental disabilities that are reminiscent of the awful conditions inside the large, isolated, civil mental institutions that we depopulated beginning in the 1970s. Moreover, we have implemented many new laws and policies that in various innovative and sometimes ingenious ways improperly deprive persons with mental disabilities deemed to be dangerous of their fundamental rights, liberties, and freedoms.

2

SANISM AND AMERICA'S EXAGGERATED FEAR OF VIOLENCE

The discrimination and stigma associated with mental illnesses largely stem from the [greatly exaggerated] link between mental illness and violence in the minds of the general public. (United States Government—SAMHSA)[1]

Among the consequences of failing to [involuntarily] treat individuals with severe mental illnesses living in the community, violent behavior and homicides are the most alarming. (E. Fuller Torrey, MD)[2]

Violence and the fear of violence are potent social concerns in the United States, particularly in the context of persons with mental disabilities, who most Americans incorrectly believe are substantially more dangerous than other people. Even some influential psychiatrists, who are supposed to calm our fears, deliberately stoke the flames of irrationality with regard to our perceptions about violence and persons with mental disabilities. These societal misperceptions are part of a larger set of stigmatizing beliefs called "sanism," which historically has contributed to widespread incarceration, mistreatment, and other deprivations of rights of individuals with mental disabilities—including even their executions—based in substantial part on a social animus toward this particular group of people.

This animus has become particularly widespread in the United States due to the "greatly exaggerated" link between mental disabilities—particularly mental illnesses—and violence, which has been "promoted by the entertainment and news media,"[3] certain involuntary treatment advocates, and others. "Members of the public exaggerate both the strength of the association between mental illness and violence and their own personal risk."[4] Thus, "the vast majority of Americans believe that persons with mental illnesses pose a threat for violence towards others and themselves," even though there is "little reason for such fears."[5]

These exaggerated fears also have become intensely felt by many therapists and other mental health professionals who increasingly view the "possibility of being stalked, threatened or attacked by a patient [as] . . . an occupational risk."[6] Nearly 20 percent of psychologists, for example, have reported being "physically attacked" sometime during their careers, more than "80% . . . reported having been afraid that a client would attack them," and "over half reported having fantasies that a client would attack [them]."[7] Therapists acknowledge that many of their fears are imagined or exaggerated due to countertransference,[8] in which they experience "repressed feelings in reaction to the emotions, experiences, or problems of a person undergoing treatment."[9]

Too many Americans simultaneously embrace, exaggerate, and fear violence, and then use people with various mental disorders, conditions, and aberrations as scapegoats to appease those fears. Due to sanism, we are willing—and often eager—to take draconian actions against our citizens and residents with mental disabilities based on subjective and unreliable predictions that they are "likely" to be dangerous. Yet, most of us would recoil at the idea of taking comparable actions based on similar predictions against members of other supposedly dangerous populations, such as gang members, people who possess assault rifles, gay coaches, Catholic priests, African-American adolescent males, Caucasian men, professional football players, or soldiers who have served in combat.

STIGMA AND SANISM

Stigma is a social phenomenon in which members of a particular group—based on certain human characteristics that they share—are devalued and discriminated against by the larger society in which they live due to bias, prejudice, misperception, ignorance, and/or fear of those characteristics and the human beings who possess them. These intense feelings may be conscious, or unconscious and thus partially—or mostly—beyond the awareness of the biased individuals.[10] According to one emerging view, all people have "unconscious prejudices against outside groups [which] exists at a basic [human] level" that seems to be reflected in their "brain activity."[11] Conversely, they have a natural affinity toward members of their own group.

Stigma based on mental disability has been a part of most cultures, including ours, for centuries.[12] Often stigmas are culture- or even community-specific, but certain ones appear to exist globally and across cultures, including those attributed to race, gender, religion, and mental disability. Yet even those stigmas that seem to resonate globally are strongly influenced in their manifestations by the particular societies or groups in which they exist. In England, for example, a national campaign was initiated in 2009 to eliminate stigma based on mental illness. One of the core messages was that "mental illness is [England's] last taboo . . . that the accompanying discrimination and exclusion can affect people in a way that many describe as worse than the illness itself."[13] This stigma, which extends to persons with all different types of mental disabilities, appears to be even more prevalent and ingrained in American culture and our legal system. Tragically, we do not appear to be ready as a nation to acknowledge these prejudices, much less take serious steps to address them.

Sanism is a concept that originated with New York Law School professor Michael Perlin in order to add dimension to the study of stigma based on mental disability. He made it comparable to racism and sexism, but linked it directly to the American legal system. Perlin defined "sanism as an irrational prejudice, due to a person's mental or emotional disability, that is 'based predominantly upon stereotype, myth, superstition, and deindividualization,' which 'infects both our jurisprudence and lawyering practices.'" Because sanism produces stigma and certain specific forms of stigma lead to sanism, these terms are inextricably bound together.[14] In the United States, sanism has become a particularly pernicious form of stigma and improper discrimination.

Sanism has had a direct and penetrating impact on our laws and their implementation.[15] Due to sanism, persons with severe mental disabilities tend to be subjected to extreme restrictions on their rights, freedoms, and liberties—including the risk of indefinite confinement, extended or permanent monitoring and supervision, other rights deprivations, and even execution—and to be further stigmatized in the legal process. The key courtroom participants—including jurors, judges, lawyers, and even many mental health experts—are much more likely to demonstrate bias, prejudice, and hostility toward people with mental disabilities because of sanism, which makes a fair trial difficult—and oftentimes impossible—when these systematically devalued individuals are the respondents or defendants in such proceedings. This socialized prejudice within the legal system is so ingrained, concludes Professor Perlin, that many lawyers with mental disabilities who need help are deliberately ignored,[16] and the "dismal track record [nationwide] of counsel providing" representation to criminal defendants with mental impairments is rarely addressed.[17] Instead of being judged as individuals, these respondents and defendants are viewed as members of a devalued group who all share similar devalued characteristics, especially a proclivity for violence.

With regard to legal proceedings that involve serious deprivations of the rights, freedoms, and liberties of persons with mental disabilities, three sanist stereotypes or prejudices are particularly prominent. First, there has been a long history in America of using highly "[p]ejorative terms to describe people with mental conditions (e.g. 'mental deficiency,' 'insane,' 'depraved,' 'idiot,' and 'lunatic' were common in the past…)."[18] Other sanist terms such as "psycho," "sexually violent predator," "mentally disordered," "retarded," "going postal," and "extreme behavioral disorder" are used today, and many of the older terms linger on. Such language communicates that those negatively labeled individuals are somehow less worthy as human beings, and thus should be kept apart and treated differently from the rest of society to their detriment.

Second, a misconception has been perpetuated, repeated, and accepted in America, including within the legal establishment, that persons with mental disabilities are particularly violent "and are generally dangerous to themselves or others."[19] To make matters worse, the American Psychiatric Association in revising the current *Diagnostic and Statistical Manual of Mental Disorders* (*DSM-IV-TR*) appears intent on expanding the numbers of people who will be labeled as having psychiatrically defined mental pathologies,[20] and thus stigmatized as being potentially dangerous. Damning social prejudices due to various forms of sanism have rendered most legal proceedings involving persons with mental disabilities facing indefinite incarceration, the death penalty, and other deprivations of rights patently unfair because the assumption is ever-present that "these" people will be a threat to society if they are allowed to be in the community, unmonitored, unmedicated, and uncontrolled. Some form of future dangerousness linked to having a mental disorder, condition, or aberration are the primary criteria for almost all of these rights deprivations.

A third widespread belief in our society is that people who use the legal system to allege that they have a mental disability "are manufacturing mental impairments to benefit themselves."[21] This substantial overgeneralization applies to both civil and criminal legal matters, even though the stigma in our society related to sanism is so great that some capital defendants, including "unabomber" Ted Kaczynski, would rather be put to death than claim that they have a severe mental impairment. Moreover, the leading psychological assessment tool used to draw conclusions that people with alleged mental disabilities are "malingering" and thus faking appears to be biased, discriminatory, and inaccurate even when it is properly administered in a clinical setting,[22] much less if it is vetted subjectively in an advocacy-based courtroom.

Fairness and individualized decision-making in many different types of criminal proceedings—including incompetency to stand trial, not guilty by reason of insanity, sentencing, probation, and parole dispositions—are negatively affected by widespread prejudice, suspicion, and fear involving defendants with mental disabilities. Many lawyers, judges, jurors, and expert witnesses for the government, like the rest of our society, are too easily convinced—or automatically assume—that defendants who allege they have a mental disorder, condition, or aberration which may seem to benefit them legally, are—at the urgings of their counsel— faking or exaggerating their symptoms or conditions in order to receive preferential treatment. Unfortunately, this biased perspective is enhanced when certain comparatively sane, but typically famous and wealthy individuals, invoke far-fetched alleged mental disorders in the media and the courtroom to try to excuse their bad behaviors.[23]

The concept of "sanism" is a valuable and powerful construct for understanding why Americans who are thought to have a mental disability and to be dangerous are subjected to less fair and unfair legal proceedings, which as a general rule result in harsher or much harsher penalties and deprivations, including indefinite and often permanent periods of custodial confinement, lifetime supervision and restrictions, other rights' denials, and even death. Yet, when Americans with similar types of impairments attempt to use their mental statuses in ways that would reduce their culpability, it is increasingly likely that they will be ignored or dismissed as being liars and fakers, and their comparative culpability will be increased because of the presumption that they are inherently dangerous. As La Fond and Durham convincingly argued in the early 1990s,[24] in one situation the legal system supports a presumption that persons subject to quasi-civil commitment or the death penalty have a mental disability that makes them inherently more dangerous, and in the other situation the presumption is made that even if defendants have a mental disability, it should not reduce their culpability. This double standard in the law has persisted and been expanded, in large measure because we have been taught repeatedly through various informational venues, particularly the popular media, to be afraid of and to devalue persons with mental disabilities.

As with other forms of stigma, considerable incremental progress was beginning to be made with regard to exposing and controlling sanism in the late 1960s as part of the larger civil rights movement. By 1980, even the normally cautious U.S. Supreme Court had recognized that the presence or absence of stigma based on mental disability has substantial constitutional implications in terms of individual rights, both civilly with regard to involuntary commitment,[25] and criminally with regard to forced transfers from prisons to mental health and other secure treatment facilities.[26] In each of these decisions, a majority of the justices ruled that because the actions of governments related to incarcerating or hospitalizing the respondents based on their mental illnesses would likely stigmatize those individuals, their constitutional liberty interests were negatively affected. Thus, the respondents were entitled to significant due process protections measured by the extent to which their liberty interests were being negatively affected. Furthermore, during that same period there was a movement to expand the grounds for mental status defenses, particularly with the adoption of the American Law Institute's broader insanity standards in all federal jurisdictions and nearly half of the states.[27]

In those days, many legal scholars, sociologists, and social scientists, based in part on the two aforementioned Supreme Court opinions, were convinced or becoming so that stigma attributed to mental disability might be substantially reduced. Unfortunately, the notion of linking dangerousness to civil commitment and the death penalty—and thus people with mental disabilities to dangerousness—also was increasing, along with the extreme fear of violent crime in our society. Time and time again, mass killers who made national headlines became indelibly etched into America's subconscious as crazed and dangerous psychopaths. Since then, even significant segments of the psychiatric community—notably E. Fuller Torrey and other allied mental health professionals who support the Treatment Advocacy Center—have helped perpetuate and inflame this association by deliberately linking persons with mental disabilities to highly publicized massacres, and the killings of police officers and little children.[28] Not surprisingly, sanism reestablished itself even more strongly and pervasively as our nation's exaggerated fear of violence became directly linked to people with mental disorders, conditions, and aberrations.

Because we have been unwilling to implement more effective, more humane, and less intrusive policies to prevent and address violence and our excessive fears of violence—in part due to legitimate First Amendment constraints—we have embraced two extreme and ultimately counterproductive solutions: (1) imprisoning more persons per capita—a high percentage of whom appear to have or will develop mental disorders—than any other nation in the world; and (2) unfairly depriving persons with mental disabilities—whom we believe are the most dangerous people in our society—of their fundamental rights. In this context, the close association between sanism and dangerousness may be viewed as a pervasive manifestation of the exaggerated fear of violence in American society more generally.

VIOLENCE

Violence is defined in *Webster's Dictionary* as a "physical force that is employed so as to damage or injure." In the United States, violent crime, as measured by federal and state governments, generally is focused on serious bodily harm, rather than damage to property or other antisocial behaviors that are viewed as offensive or immoral. Yet, when the media, politicians, policymakers, certain mental health professionals, and various special interest groups martial evidence to justify extreme governmental interventions to "control" and punish dangerousness as it applies to persons with mental disabilities, many different types of offensive, antisocial, sexual, or nonviolent criminal behaviors and threats may be—and often are—lumped together with actual bodily harm, often indiscriminately.

The same laws intended to register, incarcerate, or monitor truly violent habitual offenders with sexual or other mental disorders also are applied to persons with nonviolent, yet socially or morally offensive habits and behaviors like masturbating in public, having consensual sex with mature adolescents, viewing or exchanging child pornography (as opposed to actually producing it), defecating in public because there are no public toilets, or physically resisting those who are trying to force them to move from their makeshift homes on the streets. Almost any crime committed by a person with a mental disability is likely to be equated with dangerousness, regardless of whether it is violent. Moreover, in predicting dangerousness in the legal system, what might happen—or is mistakenly thought "likely" to happen—often is considered equally determinative as what actually has happened.

Both the reality and specter of violence envelops us. Violence is woven through the fabric of our everyday lives, social institutions, and most forms of American news and entertainment, particularly television, video games, music, and sports. Furthermore, violence is made to appear to be much worse than it really is through the media's ingrained habit of over-reporting and sensationalizing deaths, sexual crimes, mayhems, injuries, disasters, and the threat that any or all of these calamities might occur, in order to increase ratings and profits. At the same time, corporations, politicians, and special interest groups continually exploit the fear of violence to enhance their financial and/or political interests and/or increase memberships in various organizations. It is in this nearly hysterical, violence-dominated atmosphere that decisions about incarcerating, executing, and otherwise restricting and controlling people with mental disabilities who are deemed dangerous to others or themselves are made under the guise of due process and legal objectivity.

This fearful and fear-mongering atmosphere largely explains why violent crime—and many nonviolent crimes and antisocial behaviors loosely associated with violence—are viewed so alarmingly in our society and generate such widespread and exaggerated concerns, even though the relevant statistical evidence indicates that violent and other crimes have been steadily decreasing.[29] At the same time, because of the sanism and stigma that attaches to all disabilities, one of the only sectors of our society that has experienced dramatic increases in being victimized by violent crimes is persons with disabilities.[30] In particular, "[p]eople with psychiatric disabilities are far more likely to be victims than perpetrators of violent crime."[31] Nevertheless, our criminal and civil laws continue to be revamped and amped up based on a misguided view that draconian governmental actions against persons with mental disabilities perceived to be a future danger to others, themselves, or the community will be the most effective means to prevent and control violent behaviors in our society. We have embraced extreme deprivations of liberty that unnecessarily curtail civil rights by indefinitely imprisoning and/or effectively quarantining—in many instances for the rest of their lives—people with mental disabilities who we predict without proper empirical, scientific, or logical foundation will engage in dangerous antisocial behaviors in the unforeseeable future.

There is little appetite or support for prevention, rehabilitation, consensual treatment, humane living conditions, and other types of enlightened interventions that countless American reformers have urged over many years since the late eighteenth century.[32] We have largely lost our compassion and sense of justice in clouds of fear and retribution that have enveloped and distorted our ability to reason and to make objective assessments. Due to sanism and their perceived and presumed dangerousness, people with mental disabilities have become primary targets for the fear and rage associated with violence that is manifested throughout our society. Individuals with mental disabilities, including sexual disorders, are convenient and popular scapegoats for our collective inability to control violence, our willingness to perpetuate and inflate it, and the exaggerated fears that result from our collective failures and shortsightedness.

EXAGGERATED FEAR OF VIOLENCE

Violent crime remains a persistent and undeniably serious problem in the United States. Yet its magnitude and severity are considerably less than what our collective perceptions—and our overreactions to those perceptions—would indicate. Until 2003, when violent crime rates nudged upward slightly,[33] there has been a sustained period of improvement as rates steadily declined from the early 1980s. At the same time, our society's reactions and responses to violence and perceived dangerousness have become less rational and more punitive as the images of violence in our society continue to grow more numerous and intense.

One of the main reasons why our view of violence has become so distorted is that collectively the media, entertainment, and sports industries inflate our society's perceptions of imminent threats of violence in two penetrating and enduring ways. First, we are regularly saturated with depictions of violence and exaggerated images of violence from a variety of sources. Second, these images are "packaged" and enhanced audiovisually and digitally in ways that encourage us to think that our distorted perceptions about violence accurately represent the world we live in. Moreover, as was noted earlier, certain mental health professionals and advocates who believe government should be forcibly "treating" and controlling many more people with mental disorders, conditions, and aberrations than what occurs already have initiated a media campaign to publicly link the worst examples of violence to persons with severe mental disabilities.[34]

Inflating the Reality of Violence

"Violence has a stranglehold on our nation" warns the National Mental Health Association.[35] "Americans have what sometimes seems to be an insatiable appetite for it. "Depictions and descriptions of violence saturate our culture" concludes an article in the *Journal of Law, Medicine and Ethics*.[36] Every day Americans are peppered with graphic images of violence and violent crime. These images influence kids—mostly boys—in the early years of their cognitive development when they are most likely to be affected[37]; that initial exposure is constantly reinforced throughout their childhoods and during their adult years. While everyone is affected differently by such exposures, very few people in our society escape those effects entirely. Generally, these mass exposures to violent images increase violence and aggression in our society as a whole,[38] make the reality of violence appear even worse than it actually is, amplify our fears of violence, and contribute to policy decisions to implement unrealistic, discriminatory, overly severe, and ineffective punishments, sanctions, and controls—particularly aimed at persons with mental disabilities—to deal with our distorted perceptions about violence.

How much violence each individual is exposed to remains unknowable. Nor are we able to measure accurately how and to what extent such exposures will affect a given individual. What is theorized and what the available empirical evidence and common sense all strongly support is that high exposures to images of violence and actual violence in any population—particularly when they occur with great intensity during childhood—will increase the amount of aggression and violence in that population.[39] Thus, it is more than reasonable—based on the existing evidence—to conclude that as a society Americans are substantially more violent and commit considerably more violent crimes because of this excessive exposure. This would be true even if, as some continue to argue but many others dispute, viewing certain types of violence or engaging in certain simulated violent actions in controlled circumstances could produce a cathartic release for some people.[40]

As with any assessments of future human behaviors, what remains unknown—and most probably unknowable—is the extent to which such exposures are responsible for specific incidents of violence, which individuals are going to be so affected that they will actively engage in what could be considered violent behaviors, and of those who will actually commit violent crimes. There are no accurate and reliable scientific means at hand to determine which particular individuals will be violent. What empirical studies provide is "substantial evidence that an individual's repeated exposure to portrayals of violence is associated with significantly increased likelihood that the individual will commit aggressive acts against others."[41] Nevertheless, any such increase would fall well short of the significant likelihood that should be required to meet even the lowest applicable standard of proof for taking intrusive legal actions against particular defendants or respondents to deprive them of their fundamental rights, which should be no less than clear and convincing evidence.

On the other hand, it is difficult to dispute that we live in a culture that produces a multiplicity of sources of violent images and actual violence that are experienced, to a greater or lesser extent, by almost everyone—but particularly our children. Reportedly, "[h]undreds of studies have been conducted on this topic . . . and all have come to the same conclusion: that [just] viewing violence increases aggression," which is why the "American Psychological Association (APA), the American Academy of Pediatrics, the American Academy of Child and Adolescent Psychiatry, the American Medical Association, the American Academy of Family Physicians, and the American Psychiatric Association signed a joint statement on the hazards of exposing children to media violence."[42] Moreover, it appears that most children directly experience some form of violence or serious physical harm. A 2008 federally funded study—based on a randomized national sample of 4,549 children—found that 60 percent of those children were exposed to actual violence, crime, or abuse, and more than half of them were physically or sexually assaulted.[43]

At the same time, it is important to remember that the vast majority of Americans who have been exposed to violence or images of violence never commit violent crimes or otherwise attack or harm others, although, not surprisingly, the low risk that they will do so increases substantially if as children they grew up in an extremely violent environment, particularly if they were abused themselves[44] and/or they are currently abusing alcohol.[45] Yet even these substantially greater risks would almost always fall well short of the levels of certainty that should be required in our legal system in order to conclude that particular individuals are going to carry out serious acts of violence in the immediate future.

Although there are many places in our culture where visual and audio images of violence originate, entertainment, sports, and news appear to be the most substantial. Each of these cultural outlets is somewhat different in what it disseminates, who is targeted, and the dissemination methods that are used. However, with regard to increasing violence and the perception of violence, the combined effects of all these cultural inputs on our society have been profound, yet widely accepted as a necessary part of free expression, which protects certain types of antisocial behaviors and tries to crush others. While the freedom of businesses and corporations to express themselves through words or images of violence is effectively insulated from most government restrictions, the freedom of American citizens and other residents to behave bizarrely or antisocially may be intrusively and indefinitely restricted, controlled, and monitored, but only if those individuals have mental disabilities and are perceived to be dangerous.

Entertainment

Television, music, movies, radio, and video games, among other media, lead the entertainment parade of simulated violence. While there is no actual violence involved, there is an overabundance of penetrating violent images that strongly affect our emotions. Apparently, "[w]e are hunter warriors and need a little brutality in our entertainment."[46] Unfortunately, we get much more than a "little brutality" and those exposures have social consequences.

Because television has played such a major role in the daily lives of Americans for many decades, much has been written—including articles and reports by journalists, social scientists, mental health professionals, lawyers, and Congress—about how this particular type of media programming is closely associated with violence. The American Psychiatric Association,[47] the American Psychological Association,[48] and the National Mental Health Association[49] all have asserted that the best evidence indicates that television teaches and precipitates aggressive behaviors including actual violence, especially in boys.

In 1999, the Senate Committee on the Judiciary concluded that "[c]ountless studies have shown that a steady diet of television, movie, music, video game, and Internet violence plays a significant role in the disheartening number of violent acts committed by America's youth."[50] According to the American Psychiatric Association, "the typical American child watches 28 hours of television a week, and by the age of 18 will have seen 16,000 simulated murders and 200,000 acts of violence."[51] In particular, younger children and youth, mostly boys, including many who are developmentally immature, learn to be aggressive and sometimes violent without separating the consequences of actual violence from the violence of make-believe characters; older and more mature kids, who can make such distinctions, have been shown to be more negatively affected by "realistic portrayals of violence."[52]

Despite all the public attention that has been focused on television violence, not much is being done to rectify the obvious and abundant excesses, in part because there are important First Amendment and practical limitations on regulators and advocates for change. At the same time, because the companies that own the networks and local stations must obtain licenses in order to use the public airways, they may be subjected to more government interventions than would otherwise be permitted under the First Amendment.[53] In the end, though, regulators are confronted by well-organized special interests supporting the broadcast industry. Studies show, for example, that news broadcasts that emanate from television networks and local stations, which "have a substantial impact on public opinion," tend to ignore, consistently understate, or dispute the scientific evidence that links media violence to aggression and violence in society.[54]

Furthermore, as the empirical evidence has grown much stronger to support a substantial connection between violence in the media and aggression and violence in our society, studies also indicate that the news media has treated such evidence with heightened—and arguably unjustified and self-interested—skepticism.[55] In addition, Congress, fueled by its own public image concerns, understands that that there is an underlying reason why most Americans have chosen to be steeped in violence and to let it trickle down to our youth. We enjoy viewing—and do not prevent our children from watching—programs in which violence is a prominent and often dominant theme, whether they are more critically acclaimed shows such as "Dexter," "Breaking Bad," "The Wire," "Southland," "The Sopranos," "Law and Order," "Homicide: Life on the Streets," and "NYPD Blue," or a broad array of other violent programs including "The Following," Criminal Minds," "Sons of Anarchy," and "Walking Dead." As a society, we like to be entertained by violence and images of violence. Thus, "TV dramas, good and bad, have become addicted to blood."[56]

Ultimately, there is only minimal impetus for change. A clash of forces—between those who want violence curbed legislatively and those who either support or facilitate a laissez faire approach or recognize that aggressive regulation may be too great a risk to the First Amendment—has resulted in a virtual stalemate. There have been many hearings and repeated scolding of the television industry, but in the end Congress "has employed a limited range of strategies and taken few legislative actions to deal with television violence."[57] Even though the first congressional hearings on television violence were held in 1952, no national legislation was passed until the 1980s, when an embarrassingly weak law was enacted to give television broadcasters a time-limited antitrust exemption in order to allow the industry to develop its own standards for curbing television violence.[58] After the law "expired in 1993, it was clear that [the exemption] had had little effect,"[59] which is exactly what one would expect where the fox is guarding the hen house.

Since then, the only significant congressional enactment to regulate violence on television has been a law put forward to mandate that V-chips be used to let parents and children know the age appropriateness of television programs and to block out programs accordingly.[60] This buyer beware, free market, diluted regulatory approach to the problem—which has been similarly unsuccessful in regulating our financial institutions, mortgages, food, and oil drilling operations—places the onus on parents, rather than on society or broadcasters. Not surprisingly, according to surveys by both the Kaiser Family Foundation and the Annenberg Center for Communication, relatively few parents and families even make an attempt to use this resource.[61]

Typically, most parents or guardians—assuming the child even has involved parents or guardians—have either been apathetic to this approach, or found it too technically or emotionally difficult to enforce the voluntary guidelines within their own households, much less the households and other places that their children visit. Even if some parents are reasonably conscientious about monitoring their children's viewing habits, there are many situations in which those children are exposed to images of violence and encouraged to ignore or disobey their parents' wishes. It is difficult for parents to manage their children's television watching and, even if a significant percentage of parents are ultimately successful, the vast majority of children continue to be exposed without any meaningful progress being made within our society to reduce that exposure. Nevertheless, voluntary compliance is better than nothing, as long as it does not continue to be a deterrent to doing something more meaningful.

In the long run, however, the pressure to do more than what is being done now is relatively small and the current responses are largely ineffectual. Beyond the fairness doctrine for political "messages," the type of television content that is substantially regulated—and that to the extent it can only be shown during "late night hours"—is sexual content, when it is characterized as being either "indecent" or mischaracterized as being "obscene."[62] Moreover, this dichotomy is now protected by the Constitution. The U.S. Supreme Court has upheld First Amendment restrictions on "sexual images" in magazines, yet struck down comparable restrictions on violence in video games.[63]

Similar problems also characterize restrictions on other types of entertainment that prominently disseminate violent images to children and young adults. Since the 1990s, for example, the music industry has generated a great deal of heat, but little in the way of legislative action, for their violence-laced lyrics and videos. "Songs urge us to rape women, kill police officers, and commit suicide,"[64] warned concerned citizens—including Tipper Gore—as well as many medical and related professionals. In 1997, representatives of the American Academy of Pediatrics testified to a Senate committee about the Academy's long-standing policy position that music violence has a destructive social impact on children and youth.[65] In its testimony, the Academy was particularly alarmed by the lyrics found in heavy metal and rap songs about "drugs, sex, violence and even of greater concern, sexual violence."[66] The Academy reaffirmed its views in 2009 by releasing an updated statement that reiterates its profound concerns about the negative impact of violent and sexually explicit lyrics and videos on the normal development of children and adolescents.[67]

Despite such lyrics and their effects on children, which they deemed alarming, the national organization of pediatricians, both then and now, decided that its members were even more concerned about the inappropriateness of censorship and government interference. Accordingly, the Academy continues to recommend that the onus for reform should be placed not on governments, but rather—through the use of "specific content-labeling"—on the *voluntary* actions of the music industry itself, the performers, the parents, and health-care providers. Like television programs, songs and videos are now rated in terms of their violence and sexual content. Unfortunately, the ratings do not seem to matter much in determining whether teenagers will obtain and listen to content that they are not supposed to have because the music is widely available on the Internet and from one's friends and acquaintances. In fact, since many— and arguably most teenagers—are inclined to challenge authority, the existence of such warnings often makes the music even more desirable.

Concerns about heavy metal and rap have been extended in more recent times to include hip-hop, particularly its evolution into "gangsta rap," because of the message this genre conveys to society, particularly African-American youth, by embracing "violence . . . as 'authentically' black."[68] Even the genre's most able defenders have described this form of music in ways that should raise red flags. Violence and mysoginistic sexual aggression toward women is a foundation of its appeal and popularity.[69] Not coincidentally, a number of different rap and hip-hop music artists, promoters, and executives have been shot at, wounded, or killed in violent displays of jealousy and territoriality.

A third major form of media entertainment is movies, which for a long time now have been protected from any meaningful sanctions in a cocoon of self-regulation in which films are rated and admissions limited (unless an adult is present) based on the perceived content of those films. Despite these ratings (or, more cynically, perhaps because of them), many—and perhaps most—of the movies targeted at boys and young men "glorify violence as an intrinsic element of every imaginable plot line."[70] Also, since most movies are no longer watched in theaters, but rather are ordered online to be watched in homes, apartments, and dorm rooms, and on computers, iPads, and other electronic devices, these weak sanctions are increasingly pointless and ineffectual.

Arguably, the most disturbing type of violent entertainment is video games in which kids of all ages, but mainly boys and young men, are taught to simulate acts of violence against people generally, and often authority figures and the most vulnerable in society more specifically. These games teach users how to kill more easily, applying the same type of incremental desensitization methods that are used to train soldiers to take lives without moral qualms or hesitation.[71] Many of the mass killings in this country carried out by male adolescents and young men, including those in Columbine and Virginia Tech, involved perpetrators who played, and may well have used as practice, video games that improve an individual's efficiency in murdering many people in confined spaces, such as *Manhunt 2*, "which features a mentally ill patient on a killing spree"[72] or *Grand Theft Auto*, which encourages players to kill police officers. Reportedly, the "grisly murders of 31 people at Virginia Tech eerily matched the stalking targets in video programs sometimes called 'first person shooter' (FPS) games."[73]

With regard to all types of entertainment aimed at children and youth which exploit violence in penetrating ways, our society's response has been limited to self-regulation of content by the industry involved and to encourage parents to take responsibility for their children's entertainment choices. In the end, legislators have not taken stronger actions for two main reasons: the lack of scientific evidence of actual harm to specific individuals, and a reluctance to limit First Amendment freedoms.[74] As one author explained, "[d]espite the distaste—even perhaps the revulsion—we might experience at much of the violent content that the media produces today, the plain fact is that we do not know enough with the requisite degree of certainty that it actually causes [specific] people to commit crimes."[75] Furthermore, the U.S. Supreme Court has found a First Amendment right to direct violent images at our children "[b]ecause speech [including video games] about violence is not obscene," and thus may not be abridged by government.[76]

Sports and Athletics

Sports are a microcosm of society,[77] mirroring our social values, good and bad. Today, winning by overly aggressive and even violent means is too often—and arguably most of the time—more important than fair and safe play. This should be a major concern since "[e]ach year millions of Americans participate in sporting competitions on some level."[78]

Scholars and sports commentators have observed that "violence in sports has become commonplace"[79] and "an epidemic plaguing our nation,"[80] so much so that there have been frequent calls in recent years for federal regulation of sports violence.[81] Violent incidents involving athletics have filled the sports pages and, on too many occasions, spilled over onto the front page and national news, where high-profile crimes are covered. A headline in the *Christian Science Monitor* exclaimed: "For sports news, see . . . crime pages."[82]

This close association between our most popular sports and violent crime goes back at least twenty years. The *Los Angeles Times*, noting a substantial increase in news stories "about athletes and crime," conducted a "study of 1995 court documents and wire-service reports [which] found 252 incidents involving [345] active American or Canadian sports figures and the criminal justice system."[83] The most prominent violent criminal offenses identified in that study included murder, sexual assault, and spousal battery. Of particular significance was "violence against women," and the most likely offenders were professional and collegiate athletes who "played" football,[84] the most popular American sport.

Depending on the circumstances, sports violence may involve the athletes themselves, their fans, or parents of athletes. Many kids who play organized sports become particularly aggressive in order to be successful, and, as the aforementioned *Los Angeles Times* study indicated, this largely directed and controlled aggression on the field sometimes may explode into uncontrolled aggression and violence, both on and off the field, especially when alcohol or performance-enhancing or other drugs are involved. Moreover, a number of these contact sports, especially football, boxing, lacrosse, and hockey, promote a "culture of violence among their athletes,"[85] which also rubs off on their fans, particularly boys and young men.

Prominent examples of famous and near-famous male athletes acting violently have become commonplace. In the world of professional football, for example, O. J. Simpson obtained a controversial acquittal to the charges of brutally murdering his ex-wife and her close male friend.[86] Years later he was convicted and sentenced to a prison term of over thirty years for stealing his own sports memorabilia from two dealers chiefly because one of his associates had brandished a gun.[87]

Rae Carruth, once a high draft pick of the Carolina Panthers professional football team, with tens of millions of dollars in his future, is serving eighteen to twenty-four years in prison—with time off for "good behavior"—after hiring a hit man who murdered Carruth's pregnant girlfriend.[88] Reportedly, she became a liability to his professional career after becoming pregnant with their child. Also, perennial and much-admired All-Pro and likely Hall of Fame linebacker Ray Lewis pled guilty to covering up a murder that he at least witnessed and did nothing about, and for which he may have been an accomplice or even the perpetrator.[89] The white suit that Lewis was wearing when the blood began to splatter mysteriously disappeared and was never recovered. In exchange for murder charges being dropped against him, he received probation with no prison time and agreed to testify in the subsequent trial.

Pro Bowl quarterback Michael Vick served less than two years in prison after he was convicted of being the money man and an active participant in a "sport" and business enterprise that included dog fighting, dog torture, and dog killing for entertainment and profit.[90] After being released early for good behavior, Vick returned to professional football with the Philadelphia Eagles. In December 2009—his first year back—Vick, even though he rarely played, was unanimously honored by his Eagle teammates as being their most courageous player, apparently for weathering the bad publicity.[91]

Superbowl-winning quarterback Ben Roethlisberger was accused of sexually assaulting a twenty-year-old girl in the back room of a nightclub. Although charges were dropped, the district attorney took the unusual step of stating publicly that he believed Roethlisberger was guilty, but could not prove rape "beyond a reasonable doubt." A year earlier, another woman had accused Roethlisberger of sexually assaulting her in Lake Tahoe, Nevada.[92]

Football is not the only major professional sport with serious problems related to violence. Troubled boxer Mike Tyson was imprisoned for three years after being found guilty of forcible rape; then after being released on parole, he deliberately bit off part of the ear of an opponent in the boxing ring without any further legal sanctions being imposed.[93] Superstar professional basketball player Kobe Bryant was charged with rape, but avoided the looming likelihood of a criminal trial by convincing the alleged victim to accept a financial settlement.[94] In addition, Vancouver hockey star Todd Bertuzzi broke the neck of an opponent by striking him from behind with a closed fist and then slamming his victim's limp body into the hard ice, head first. Bertuzzi received conditional release with no prison time, leaving him with only a several-month suspension by the National Hockey League[95] and possible civil liability. His victim, however, was permanently injured and never played professional hockey again.

Furthermore, in college sports former Baylor University basketball player Carlton Dotson pled guilty to second-degree murder of his teammate,[96] and a lacrosse player at the University of Virginia was charged with brutally murdering his ex-girlfriend after admitting that he killed her in a fit of rage.[97] Also, a former coach and defensive coordinator for the Penn State football team, Jerry Sandusky, was convicted on multiple counts of sexually abusing boys, which included his "raping a boy in the locker-room shower—and the university [Penn State] appeared to have covered it up."[98]

Sometimes it is spectators who engage in violent confrontations. Soccer contests involving England and South American nations have received the most unsavory publicity in this regard, but fan violence occurs regularly in the United States as well. In 2011, for example, one or more Los Angeles Dodgers baseball fans beat a San Francisco Giants fan so severely that the injured man was placed in a "medically induced coma"[99] and very likely sustained permanent brain damage. Previously, a father and son, both of whom were Chicago White Sox baseball fans, attacked a coach on the Kansas City Royals, causing him permanent injuries.[100] Also, when New York Giant football fans started throwing snowballs toward the end of a game with the San Diego Chargers, the Chargers' equipment manager was struck in the face and knocked unconscious. By the time the violence was quelled, there were 14 other injuries from snowballs, 14 arrests, and 175 fan ejections.[101] Furthermore, multiple fights broke out in the "stands" between Indiana Pacer basketball players and Detroit Piston fans that led to criminal assault charges being brought against players and fans alike.[102]

Parents who watch their children compete in sports often become carried away rooting for their children and their children's teams, which sometimes precipitates ugly incidents, including actual violence. "Overbearing parents creat[e] dangerous situations on the field," was a 2004 headline of an Associated Press article on violence in youth sports.[103] As examples of what was described as "an epidemic of parental rage sweeping through youth sports," it was reported that a father beat another "father . . . to death at a hockey game in Massachusetts," and eight boys on a youth football team were deliberately "poisoned."[104] In California a father who pummeled a coach for taking his son out of a little league baseball game was sentenced to forty-five days in jail.[105] As a result of these types of attacks, experts from around the country convened a summit in Chicago to devise ways "to control violence in youth sports," and at least sixteen states deemed it necessary to pass laws that make it a criminal offense to assault those who umpire and referee athletic contests between children.[106]

A number of the most popular spectator sports intentionally promote or countenance extreme aggression or the possibility of injury and even death to maximize their player and fan appeal. The number one American sport in terms of spectator popularity is football—professional, intercollegiate, and high school. In professional football, it reportedly has been a frequent practice for coaches to encourage and even offer sizable bounties to players for seriously injuring opponents with "kill shots."[107] Deliberating injuring players on the other team has been viewed as being a part of the "game" at all levels of football competition. As one professional football player who recently retired from the NFL observed about such deliberate violence: "No doubt it can be downright disgusting. . . . It's a fundamental part of the NFL's culture that isn't talked about outside of team facilities."[108] Moreover, medical studies indicate that even the normal aggression and violence in football makes the sport inherently unsafe, particularly for preteens and adolescents whose bodies are more vulnerable to injuries than adults.[109] Yet football continues to be America's most popular sport in large part because it is violent and war-like.

Other popular sports in which violence and danger of death or serious injury are important elements, include race-car driving, boxing, ultimate fighting, and hockey. In those sports, as well as football, violence is viewed as an essential element and, from that perspective, often glorified as a rite of passage for male and now female athletes and spectators alike. The race-car industry has tried to minimize deaths—of its drivers and fans—from spectacular, vehicle-disintegrating crashes, but all involved accept a certain level of risk of death or serious injury from the very high speeds and the violent crashes, which are viewed as necessary to grow the sport. In 2010, because ratings were trending down, Nascar reportedly encouraged its drivers to put each other at more risk by driving more aggressively "to draw fans back to the sport."[110] Even our most pastoral national pastime, baseball, has its share of player-to-player violence and confrontations between athletes and fans.

All of the aforementioned sports are particularly effective in inculcating aggression and violence because they involve actual, on-the-field-of-play contact, as compared to other forms of entertainment in which violent images are directed toward the audience. Football features bruising, bone-crushing, and concussion-causing intensity on every play. Broken and seriously damaged necks, brains, and central nervous systems are increasing as the size and speed of the athletes increase through new training methods, better nutrition, and performance-enhancing drugs, vitamins, and other "supplements." Boxing celebrates the bashing of participants' skulls and bodies above the waist—and sometimes just below—including intense shaking of the brain that often leads to permanent neurological damage. Hockey is an extremely fast-moving contact sport that can result in the players' heads and other vulnerable body parts being bounced off the hard ice or smashed into Plexiglas siding. Moreover, hockey players carry and frequently use their large "sticks" as weapons to attack or defend their territory.

Car racing involves the threat of death or bodily injury whenever drivers occupy the same space at the same time, or their vehicles explode into restraining walls when racers lose control, even for an instant, or they are not so "gently" nudged or slammed out of control by a competitor at speeds well over 150 miles an hour. In 2011, IndyCar racer Dan Wheldon "died after his car became ensnared in a fiery 15-car pileup, flew over another vehicle and hit the catch fence."[111] As one lawyer who specializes in motor sports law commented, no one can be held liable for Wheldon's death because it is "an inherently dangerous sport."[112]

Even baseball too often is characterized by pitchers throwing fastballs at batters' heads, on-the-field brawls, and base runners crashing into often vulnerable infielders or catchers, hoping to cause whatever harm is necessary to jar loose the baseball and avoid an out. In 2011, San Francisco Giants star catcher and World Series hero Buster Posey had his leg severely broken in what was described as an unnecessarily reckless collision at home plate.[113]

Today, these spectator sports attempt to insulate—with varying degrees of dedication and success—the participating athletes from harm by providing protective gear and equipment and new procedures that generally continue to improve over time. However, none of the protections are perfect, and sometimes they are less than adequate, particularly since the athletes are becoming bigger, faster, stronger, and more aggressive. Nonetheless, athletes in these dangerous sports are still expected to play and overcome—by pain management, rehabilitation, and drug enhancements—whatever injuries they may incur. Broken bones, head injuries, drug addictions and other drug side effects, serious cuts, large and deep bruises, expansive abrasions, post-athletic-career disabilities, profound dementia, brain-damage, and shortened life spans are all relatively common occurrences; and paralysis and death, while still comparatively rare, represent the ultimate sacrifices athletes can make playing particularly violent contact sports.

An extremely serious problem that has existed for many decades related to aggression and violence in sports has only become a national issue of concern with the publication of several neurological studies. These medical reports have shown active brain deterioration and serious to devastating, permanent brain damage to athletes from repeated concussions and other concussive incidents that are primarily caused by the excessive aggression and violence in various contact sports, particularly football, hockey, and boxing.[114] At the same time, this level of violence has become so engrained in these sports and viewed as such an essential element of playing them that overwhelming evidence of frequent brain damage has been squelched for years, not only by the owners and leagues that run these sports, but by many of the affected athletes themselves.[115]

Moreover, while most of the studies have focused on professional athletes, even more serious brain damage occurs when children and adolescents sustain repeated shocks to their developing brains while playing organized contact sports.[116] Unfortunately, "[s]port-related concussions are common in youth and high school sports."[117] Yet, they are underdiagnosed and often neglected because such violence has been an accepted part of youth and scholastic sports.

As a group, athletes who play particularly violent contact sports appear to be responsible for a disproportionate number of violent incidents off the field as well. As indicated earlier, arrests and prosecutions for assault, sexual assault, and even murder are no longer rare occurrences in the worlds of football and boxing, and they are occurring more regularly in hockey and other contact sports as well. In addition, studies indicate that adolescents who engage in these sports, along with their friends and close peers, are "significantly more likely" to engage in violence, especially serious fighting.[118]

Furthermore, the spectators who follow these sports and admire the star athletes, or are friends of these athletes, are inculcated in a value system that glorifies high levels of aggression, levels which not infrequently cross the line and result in violence on and off the field.[119] The traditional ideal that athletics build "good" men and now good women has been polluted in many sports by the reality that many "good" athletes are highly skilled, but highly aggressive, and in many sports—as compared to the rest of the population—disproportionately violent. Even women's team sports, including soccer and various forms of hockey (field and ice), are far more aggressive and violent than ever before, and our culture increasingly celebrates this trend as an indication of greater sexual equality.[120]

News Media

Much of the news that we watch and read is deliberately populated with powerful, emotion-laden images of violence, death, pain, and calamity. "Television news is filled with violence and suffering," especially local coverage, which tends "to overemphasize brutal crime and to rely heavily on sensational presentations of violence."[121] In watching and listening to television and radio presentations, viewers are immersed in stories featuring descriptions and depictions of murders, rapes, and other violent crimes, extreme weather, and sports violence that are often repeated multiple times. War, death, serious accidents, and other human tragedies are the staples of this myopic and profitable coverage. According to surveys, such tragedies account for as much as "42% . . . of local news," with serious crime by itself serving as the lead story in about 30 percent of these broadcasts.[122] In addition, "signs of the symbiotic nature of sports violence and media are increasingly abundant."[123]

Like other forms of visual entertainment, television news bombards society with still another layer of violence. Such images, however, are of real events, so they appear to have an even greater impact on more mature minds than similarly intense and graphic simulated images would have. "Studies have shown that more realistic portrayals of violence may heighten levels of involvement with aggression . . . particularly in older, school-aged children [and adults], who are able to distinguish the real from the unreal on television."[124]

Only "a handful of studies" have focused on the "harmful effects that violence portrayed in news broadcasts may have on children,"[125] which is a small number compared to the studies on media and television violence more generally.[126] The dearth of studies on the effects of violent broadcasts on minors is unfortunate because children have been shown to be the most susceptible. Not surprisingly, though, the few empirical studies that have been done indicate that kids have "fairly strong and enduring emotional reactions" to violence on television news broadcasts.[127] This suggests that the same type of "short-term aggressive behavior, which is fostered by arousal processes and imitation of violence" that result when children watch television programs "could be encouraged by violent news portrayals, especially when news pictures show sensational images of weapons and actually occurring violence."[128] Furthermore, watching broadcasts that "overemphasize crime, terror, and war" may encourage children "to believe that the world is a hostile place" and create for them "the impression that violence is a justified means to protect oneself or to resolve conflict."[129]

Exaggerating the Perception of Violence

Generally

As socially devastating as the realities of violence—including violent crime and terrorism—are, the exaggerated perception of violence creates a host of additional problems for our society, particularly from overreactions and other counterproductive responses. While actual violence in America—particularly violent crime—appears to be steadily decreasing, perceived violence continues to grow, particularly as associated with mental disorders, conditions, and aberrations. The media, entertainment, and sports industries have thrived by embracing violence and violent images, a problem which is compounded because the news media report exaggerated and distorted views of violence as supposedly accurate reflections of reality. Through constant exposure to images, depictions, and news of violence, people are led to believe that violence is significantly more prevalent and more severe than what the facts demonstrate. Our lasting impressions about violence tend to be based on images of the most extreme types of behaviors and events that are pushed into our minds by various media. Too often those penetrating images involve extreme violence committed by persons with mental disabilities.

In this atmosphere of sustained violence inflation, it is hardly surprising that a few years ago the Florida legislature passed a law which established the right of state residents to use overwhelming force in self-defense based on a subjective judgment—which need not be correct or even reasonable—that they are in imminent danger, even if such force is not actually needed to deal with the perceived threat.[130] "If you feel threatened, just shoot"[131]—particularly if they are young, black, and male, or have a mental disability and are acting differently. This National Rifle Association–promoted, "stand your ground" statute—which many other states also have enacted in various forms—takes us back to the "good old days" of the Wild West, when gun owners enjoyed state-sanctioned licenses to kill in "self-defense" with few meaningful legal constraints. Furthermore, because of an archaic nineteenth-century U.S. Supreme Court decision,[132] which has never been overruled, bounty hunters and bail bondsmen are substantially insulated from prosecution and liability when they use violence and excessive force to arrest those who skip bail or are charged with crimes. The violent deeds of such individuals have been glorified on television dramas for years now, dating back to the late 1950s, when Steve McQueen starred in the aptly named "Wanted Dead or Alive," and more recently in docudrama reality shows like "Bounty Hunter."

Even without such ill-advised statutes, courts often excuse excessive violent force when used by citizens who assert that they are protecting themselves, their homes, or their valuables. In Laredo, Texas, for example, a "jury acquitted a man accused of killing a 13-year-old boy who broke in his home looking for a snack. . . . A medical examiner testified that [the boy] was shot in the back at close range."[133] Similarly, state and federal governments often encourage, sanction, or ignore the use of excessive force by the police—even where relatively minor infractions, misdemeanors, or nonviolent felonies are involved—by allowing police to repeatedly beat or shoot suspects until they stop struggling, or to recklessly endanger citizens who happen to get in the way of high-speed car chases between the police and their suspects.

Police violence is particularly common against people with mental disabilities who may be perceived as creating threats,[134] even when those threats are relatively minor and unlikely. Suburban Denver police, for instance, "use[d] . . . pepper spray on an 8-year-old boy they say was throwing a violent tantrum at school. . . . Police sa[id] it was the safest option."[135] Moreover, this type of police violence generally, and against persons with mental disabilities more specifically, is encouraged on television, in movies, and in video games.

As a result of all these different negative influences, our country is overwhelmed by images of violence. Unfortunately, in America, the current options for reducing the amount and intensity of those images—beyond changing the channel, using channel blockers, or reading, viewing, or listening to something else—are constrained by other important social concerns, particularly the First Amendment. Thus, instead of preventing and controlling those exposures, we continue to allow violent images to be freely disseminated in ways that are almost impossible to avoid, while making it relatively easy for violence-saturated children, juveniles, and young and older adults to obtain firearms and munitions.

News Media

Whether a person's source of news is network television, local television, newspapers, magazines, radio, the Internet, social media, or more commonly some combination of media, it is likely that that the news will be filtered through a selection and packaging process that is intended, above all else, to increase audience ratings and advertising dollars. Depending on the news medium, the particular media outlet, and the individuals who are reporting the news, the coverage is influenced, to a greater or lesser extent, by a tendency to report on what audiences want to see and hear. This news bias is exacerbated by increasingly flexible journalistic standards,[136] which tend to become particularly distorted and ineffective when the news media covers violence, dangerousness, and persons with mental disabilities, including sexual disorders.

Violence entertains and news of violence helps to boost ratings. Television and radio news shows tend to "hype" violence, some unconscionably so. A substantial proportion of network newscasts, and an even higher proportion of local news, feature violence in some form as the lead stories, and often have violence-dominated stories throughout each newscast.[137] Murders, violent crimes, and the crimes and whereabouts of offenders with various mental disorders are among the most frequently reported news stories. The importance of proportion and depth in the search for truth and objectivity is pushed aside by the emphasis on representations and points of view that grab, move, involve, please, shock, or entertain the viewer or listener.

Furthermore, the news media often lower already diminished journalistic standards when covering social issues in which the public's sentiments are overwhelmingly aligned on one side or the other. This is the media equivalent of DeTocqueville's "tyranny of the majority." Too many journalists advocate a particular point of view, as opposed to trying to be objective, balanced, and thorough. Too many of the most blatant examples of distorted coverage involve news stories on violent crimes or actions attributed to persons with mental disabilities. Because current journalistic standards equate the reporting of a particular point of view or representation of reality as legitimate news, stories about violent crimes attributed to persons with mental disabilities do not have to be "fair" or in proportion to reality.

Journalistically, persons with mental disabilities may be indiscriminately and unfairly represented as being violent as a group, as long as the particular subjects selected for each story acted—or were perceived by others to have acted—dangerously. At the same time, when a person has committed awful antisocial acts, the ratings and sales-pleasing assumption often is made that the person must be "crazy." The fact that an overwhelming majority of people with mental disabilities are not violent is rarely, if ever, mentioned in these news reports. In fact, such information may well be scrupulously omitted or downplayed because it would undermine the "point of view" or "perspective" the "journalist" wishes to portray.

The coverage of offenders with sexual mental disorders is often even worse. In part this is because of government-mandated online sexual offender registries. They lump persons with socially unacceptable sexual aberrations—adults who have had sex with older teenagers,[138] people who like to view or exchange pornography,[139] family members who commit incest,[140] juveniles who convey naked images of themselves or their friends on their cell phones, and many persons who are mistakenly identified as sexual offenders[141] —in the same sexual offender category as persons who have repeatedly murdered, attempted to murder, or used or threatened to use weapons or extreme physical force on their victims.

Critical distinctions among individual sexual offenders are rarely made. All of these offenders tend to be portrayed and treated as dangerous predators who are continuing threats to commit crimes of sexual violence.

Because of the imprecise and disorganized ways that these sex offender registries are compiled and the information is controlled, governments and thus journalists—even if they wanted to—would find it difficult and usually impractical to verify whether persons on these registries have been listed correctly or fairly. The fact that someone has been listed as a sexual offender does not mean that the listing is accurate or, even if it is accurate, that such sanctions are justified for each of the listed individuals involved. As of 2009, it was estimated that there were nearly 700,000 sex offenders on these registries [142] and that number is steadily increasing.

At the same time, more and more reported sex offenders once they are released face retaliatory actions, including mob violence, and sometimes those actions are based on false reports. [143] As these registries become more widespread and using them a universal requirement within the United States, the number of such abuses may well increase, including attacks on people who never committed a sexual offense, or committed a sexual crime that may be viewed as bizarre, socially offensive, pathetic, pornographic, or disgusting, but are not violent. Moreover, anyone who is publicly identified as being on such a list is likely to be viewed as a social pariah and given few, if any, meaningful options to live a productive life and be rehabilitated. [144]

CONCLUSION

Violence has become a highly visible and dominant component of American culture. Our obsession with violence and images of violence is extreme and divisive. We repeatedly inculcate aggression and violence in our children from an early age, particularly boys, and such exposures typically continue for the rest of their lives through news media, entertainment, and sports. As a society, we have become extremely fearful of violence and constantly exaggerate both its presence and its likelihood, especially when it involves persons with mental disabilities, who due to stigma and sanism we fear the most.

Nevertheless, we have few effective programs in place to ameliorate violence or images of violence, or the exaggerated fears that they create.

Many mental health professionals, who should be providing a salve to dampen our exaggerated fears of violence, are themselves overly concerned with such threats from persons with mental disorders. A number of psychiatrists and other mental health professionals have been provoking such fears in our society to promote coerced mental health treatments, particularly the use of powerful and profitable antipsychotic drugs, sometimes because they are concerned that they may be attacked by their patients.

Due to sanism and a presumption that they are inherently dangerous, people with mental disabilities have become the most prominent—and too often the exclusive—scapegoats for our preoccupation with violence. The news and entertainment media deliberately and painstakingly search for examples of dangerousness attributed to persons with mental disorders, conditions, and aberrations and portray these individuals using inflammatory and distorted words and images. These sensationalized depictions are based on the highly exaggerated and misleading assumption that persons with mental impairments are inherently violent.

This belief is supported by anecdotal and illustrative "evidence" in the form of extreme examples that are packaged, "hyped," and then repeated or re-created on television or radio, and in newspapers, books, magazines, movies, and video games. As a result, our nation has become fixated with exaggerated images of persons with mental, intellectual, and sexual disorders acting dangerously. In response, we have created and implemented highly flawed, discriminatory, and extreme legal means to punish, incarcerate, monitor, restrict, limit, and control adults and children with mental disabilities whom we deem—typically without reliable proof—to be dangerous.

3

SANIST WORDS AND LANGUAGE

Dangerousness, the Right to Treatment, and Civil versus Criminal

There was a time when judges routinely deployed legal fictions . . . in order to temper the disruptive effect of changes in legal doctrine. . . . [Mostly] they have been replaced by new legal fictions . . . [based on] judicial ignorance . . . [and] false factual suppositions in the service of other goals. (Peter J. Smith)[1]

INTRODUCTION

As Harvard University psychologist and linguist Steven Pinker explains, "language [is] a window into human nature,"[2] and "[s]emantics is . . . about the relation of words to . . . human concerns."[3] Through words "[h]umans don't just entertain ideas but steep them with emotion," such as the terror they experience when confronted with "disease, death, and infirmity."[4] Moreover, the "human mind can construe a particular scenario in multiple ways,"[5] which may convince us that our false beliefs closely correspond to reality. Increasingly, it appears likely that even our most vivid memories may be manipulated by our future recollections, so that what we think we remember may replace what we originally remembered, which then becomes our revised version of truth and reality.[6] Humans also experience what is known as cognitive dissonance, which occurs when facts and knowledge conflict with our beliefs, creating a psychological imperative that pushes us to discount and distort reality.[7]

Language both captures and affects the shared conceptual meanings and base emotions of any society, especially in their legal systems. With words that are steeped in strong feelings and emotions, individuals, groups, and nations frame social and political issues, make and enforce laws, and carry out public policies. Sometimes in the context of actions inflamed by words and language, these collective behaviors become irrational and even pathological, which has contributed to such awful human excesses as slavery, genocide, and indiscriminate use of lobotomies, sterilizations, inhumane incarcerations, and other unconscionable deprivations of human rights perpetrated against persons with mental disabilities.[8] In this way, language can be the catalyst for various tyrannies in which the controlling "majority," composed of those who exert the most influence over the legal and political systems, compel and enforce popular beliefs, even within an otherwise democratic society. At the core of such influence are judges and lawyers who by virtue of their status and training exert great influence over policymaking and the legal system with their words and beliefs, and their actions and decisions based on those words and beliefs.

Our language, through the words we create and use, reflects how we think. At their symbolic core and emotional essence, these words affect our thoughts and the actions we choose to take, both individually and collectively. In the United States, we still have much too much violence as well as a greatly exaggerated fear of that violence, which, through our language and words, pervade our beliefs, our emotions, our views of morality, and our actions. With respect to our legal definitions of "dangerousness" and the "right to treatment," as these constructs are applied to persons with mental disabilities, we have allowed our sanist beliefs and emotions to trump facts, logic, statistics, and empirical knowledge. We use the legal system, psychiatrists, and psychologists to make it seem as if our shared beliefs constitute due process, justice, and fairness. Under the umbrella of dangerousness and the right to treatment in particular, our society has created illusions constructed from words that frame and bypass reality in order to respond to our worst fears and prejudices about violence and persons with mental disabilities.

The awful ways Americans treat and care for people with mental disabilities, who they view as being dangerous, exemplify how language can evoke strong emotions that overcome objectivity, fair judgments, and even fundamental constitutional rights. In our legal system, dangerousness is conceptualized and then interpreted in ways that correspond most closely to the exaggerated fear, hostility, and underlying revulsion we often feel toward those with mental, sexual, and other related behavioral disorders. Our legal definitions of dangerousness, along with the rules and procedures that are invoked in the legal system to implement those standards, promote societal values and emotional responses to those labeled as dangerous that objectivity, fairness, and good judgment would never countenance otherwise.

More like our beliefs in religious and political doctrines, mysticism, faith healing, or superstitions, our acceptance of predictions of dangerousness usually are based on leaps of faith—not science, not logic, not empirical knowledge, not mathematics, not statistics[9]—which is understandable given human nature, albeit no less regrettable. "Many psychological experiments have shown that when people have a pet theory of how things work . . . they will swear that they can see those correlations in the world, even when the numbers show that the correlations don't exist and never did."[10] Moreover, through cognitive dissonance, too often people will embrace a pet theory more fervently when it is attacked, criticized, or even largely or completely disproved,[11] which is what has happened with predictions of dangerousness in the legal system as those predictions have been shown to lack reliability, validity, and accuracy.[12]

A "pet theory" of our legal system (and apparently of many mental health professionals) is that experts can predict dangerousness accurately enough to justify intrusive legal interventions, including extended incarceration, lifetimes of supervision, monitoring, coerced treatment, other deprivations of rights, and even the death penalty—dispositions that should be based on clearly defined legal standards and procedures that are applied to actual evidence of an individual's present status. This particular pet theory has been framed and accepted as valid in substantial part because of the misleading words that we use in the law. Unfortunately, our views about dangerousness related to persons with mental disabilities often have little basis in fact, but these beliefs have been elevated to the status of minimally sufficient constitutional legal principles, nonetheless, in large part because of misdirected emotions, sanism, and legal sophistry. Moreover, the more we should have learned and understood that these predictions of dangerousness typically are invalid and unreliable, the more legal means we have devised to expand their reach to new populations and new circumstances,[13] which—not coincidentally—is what the theory of cognitive dissonance would predict.

LANGUAGE, WORDS, AND EMOTIONS

The connotation of a word—as distinguished from its denotation—is the linguistic vehicle in which its "emotional meanings" are expressed. Such meanings may range "from attractive to neutral to offensive"[14] and may "take on awesome powers" particularly where various social taboos or prejudices are involved,[15] such as those meanings that are associated with obscenity, slavery, or persons with mental disabilities who are thought to be dangerous. Human beings have a singular ability as the most intelligent known species "to combine [words and their constructions] into bigger assemblies and to extend them to new domains. . . . But [these words and their constructions] can also clash with the nature of things, and when they do, the result can be paradox, folly, and even tragedy."[16] In very real and pragmatic ways the language we use substantially influences what and how we think about things and what we do. In this context, our legal definitions of "dangerousness" and "treatment" and their courtroom constructions provide very clear and persuasive illustrations of the resulting social problems that the misuse of words and language can engender.

The notion of being able to accurately forecast the actual dangerousness of individual human beings, like other questionable and discredited beliefs, "has distinctively human quirks that make it useful for reasoning about certain things"—in this instance related to controlling human behaviors—but it also has led "to fallacies and confusions when we try to apply it more broadly"[17] to our laws. In the courtroom, we accept, as specialized knowledge and proper evidence for making ultimate judicial decisions, vague predictions about dangerousness based on unreliable and inaccurate risk assessments, and, far more commonly, even less reliable and less accurate clinical and judicial judgments. We allow so-called dangerousness experts and judicial decision-makers, through a process of induction disguised as empiricism, to "go beyond their data and put forward laws [theories or impressions to] . . . make predictions about cases they haven't observed."[18] Instead of requiring experts and courts to base their opinions entirely on what the respondents or defendants have actually done, the legal system allows dangerousness experts to testify, or courts to draw conclusions, based on impressions about what they think the subject of such an inquiry might do in the future.

Leading philosophers of science view such loose applications of the inductive method of scientific inquiry as a "'scandal' because there are an infinite number of generalizations that are consistent with any set of observations, and no strictly logical basis for choosing among them."[19] This is an especially apt criticism of dangerousness experts (or worse, lay juries and judges) who often make predictions about such human behaviors in the guise of making legal determinations based on substantial evidence. The essential "difference between past and future . . . [is that the] past has taken place and is knowable . . . , whereas the future is up for grabs and is inscrutable, as if it were out of view."[20] In the science fiction movie *Minority Report*, people are imprisoned or executed for antisocial acts that "tribunals" think they will commit based on the outputs of a device that appears to reveal what is going to happen in the future. Today, rather than relying on a device, we continue to rely on future dangerousness predictions by so-called experts and laypeople in order to justify depriving Americans with mental disabilities of their fundamental rights and freedoms.

Our use of words and language also helps determine how we apply causation within the legal system, which can and does produce arbitrary and scientifically sloppy and unsophisticated results. The main problem is that "[p]eople somehow distinguish just one of the necessary conditions for an event as its *cause* and the others are mere *enablers* or helpers, even when all are equally necessary"[21] for the event to take place. In other words, instead of accounting for all the main causative factors, we tend to choose just one and assign it all the responsibility because it is more convenient and sustaining of the status quo to do so.

This conceptual shortsightedness and incompleteness in our notions of causation is reflected in our legal system in a number of ways, but especially when people with mental disabilities are defendants or respondents in legal proceedings in which they must rebut grave allegations that they are dangerous to others, the community, or themselves. Once a certain arbitrary threshold is attained, our courts assign total responsibility to one individual through the veil of proximate causation, even if the responsibility may be (or certainly is) divided. By using a flawed method of framing reality to match our words with our beliefs, as well as what our minds want us to perceive, the law can appear to be rationally and reasonably assigning total responsibility to individuals for illegal or socially inappropriate actions, whether or not the persons involved are only partially to blame or responsible, and/or external intervening forces significantly influenced their actions or culpability.

There is little doubt that the infamous Andrea Yates killed her children, but to try to hold her fully culpable for those actions when her severe depression intervened underscores how unforgiving and arbitrary causality can be in our legal system. If it had not been revealed—more by good fortune than anything else—that the key psychiatric expert for the state of Texas had manufactured evidence based on what he falsely remembered about a television show—*Law and Order*, for which he was a consultant—as opposed to what he actually knew, this obviously impaired defendant could have been sent to prison for life. In reality, though, there is not *that much* practical difference between preparing a diagnosis from one's false memories of a television show and preparing it based on predictions about the unknowable future. Both types of "evidence" have little or no basis in fact and undermine the resulting legal conclusions, even though such faulty opinions may be accurate because of random selection and chance.

In both situations a faulty diagnosis is being used to support the expert's opinion, unless a judge as the evidentiary gatekeeper says no, which rarely happens because one of the threshold legal standards is whether such evidence is generally accepted by psychiatry and psychology as something mental health professionals should be allowed to use,[22] not whether it actually would help or hinder the ultimate legal determination consistent with the legal standards and procedures that are supposed to be required. As a practical matter, the admissibility of dangerousness evidence does not even have to meet minimal legal standards of relevancy, reliability, and validity. In making predictions about future dangerousness in the legal system actual causality is ignored and suppressed.

Instead we simply assume that such human actions or behaviors may be conceptualized as a single event when in fact legal standards of dangerousness normally require more than one event to take place. If calculated properly, this would mean that the actual probability of the dangerous behavior occurring would be substantially reduced, since the probabilities of each event occurring would have to be multiplied as fractions in order to obtain an accurate overall risk assessment. This statistical blind spot helps explain why judges are willing to find respondents dangerous, even if it is much more likely that the respondents are not dangerous,[23] and supports those studies that demonstrate Americans (and much of the rest of the world) are statistically illiterate.[24]

PEOPLE WITH MENTAL DISABILITIES, DANGEROUSNESS, AND THE RIGHT TO TREATMENT

With regard to persons who are thought to be dangerous due to a mental disability, our society tends to frame their criminal and other antisocial actions in words that make those events appear to be entirely deliberate or intentional, even if it is clear that these individuals are substantially limited in their abilities to comprehend or control those actions due to mental illnesses, intellectual and cognitive deficits, and/or horrible abuses, traumas, and deprivations they may have endured in the womb, as infants, as children, or as young adults. We ignore actual culpability and causality by using words that only focus on the result of the defendant's actions—he shot, he raped, she assaulted, he maimed, she robbed, or he harmed the victim—rather than focusing on all the significant circumstances and factors that led up to, contributed to, or compelled those actions.

For example, as a society we continue to believe that a child who commits an adult crime should be tried and punished like an adult, even though social science has persuasively demonstrated—and belatedly even the U.S. Supreme Court has twice acknowledged—that children are not adults and lack the mental and cognitive development, skills, and awareness that characterize adulthood.[25] The justification for this legal non sequitur of equating children with adults is a patently absurd syllogism:

> Only adult-like people can commit adult crimes.
> Children who commit such crimes must be adult-like people.
> Therefore, it is reasonable and moral to try and punish children as adults should they commit adult crimes.

Using similarly faulty logic, we continue to believe that persons with mental disabilities should be tried and punished as if they have no mental disorders or impairments—or worse, that they should be treated even more harshly because we believe—typically without substantial proof—

their disorders or impairments make them more dangerous and thus somehow more blameworthy.[26] Only in a relatively few circumstances does the legal system take the extenuating factors and circumstances related to mental disabilities into account by excusing or reducing criminal culpability through the use of not guilty by reason of insanity and diminished capacity verdicts, or by mitigating sentences.[27] When one of these relatively rare events occurs, however, the defendants involved face indefinite incarceration by involuntary civil commitment, extended monitoring and supervision, and other restrictions on their fundamental rights, which frequently produce harsher and more inhumane results than if they had been found guilty and sentenced to a full prison term.[28]

Even in the vast majority of cases in which the legal system refuses to take any extenuating mental status circumstances into account in determining defendants' culpability at trial, those same factors may be used against those persons with mental disabilities who are convicted of crimes to demonstrate that they should be dealt with more harshly and indeterminately based on their presumed dangerousness. When this happens they may receive longer sentences, lifelong supervision and monitoring, coerced treatments, and/or other intrusive restrictions on their lives, including even the death penalty. Furthermore, after these defendants finish serving their criminal sentences, they alone—because they have some sort of loosely defined mental disability—may be involuntarily committed indefinitely if they are deemed dangerous because they are perceived to be more likely to commit future crimes or other antisocial actions due to their impairments.[29]

Sanist Language and People with Mental Disabilities

Through stigma and sanism our use of words and language can determine whether a group of people is viewed as being a part of, or apart from, society, as in "us versus them" constructions that often are used to describe persons with racial or ethnic characteristics, gender or sexual identity differences, or mental disabilities.[30] "Metonyms" in particular are used to stereotype an individual or group of individuals based on a single physical or behavioral characteristic.[31] The negative power of the derogatory terms that we choose to use when we refer to persons with mental disabilities, such as "retard," "mentally deficient," and "crazy"—or to their dangerousness—"psycho," "sexual predator," "whacko vet," "going postal," and "crazed killer"—isolate and dehumanize these individuals. Such extreme negativity contributes to a collective willingness and desire within our society to monitor, restrict, incarcerate, and even execute these individuals, or more commonly to simply sit by without protesting when arbitrary and invidious discrimination and mistreatment occurs. Why should we as individuals or members of communities assume any perceived additional risk for someone whom we believe is less than human, or is viewed as inhuman?

Conversely, more enlightened appellations called "hypernyms" tend to elevate the way we view people by relying on terminology that recognizes that a particular characteristic—in this instance a disability or disorder—is only one aspect of who a person is as a human being.[32] Terminology such as a "person with Down Syndrome," a "person who uses a wheelchair," or "person with pedophilia," for example, is far superior linguistically—in terms of enhancing the worth of humanity, reducing stigma, and being more accurate and descriptive—than "mongoloid," "cripple," or "sexual predator."

DANGEROUSNESS

Because as a society we want to ensure that people with mental disabilities deemed to be dangerous—whom we generally fear and frequently loathe and distrust—are segregated from us, we use clever words to manipulate and sometimes subvert the legal system, psychiatry, and psychology in order to bring about the result(s) that the popular majority desires. In particular, the law has established special rules of evidence that only apply to people with mental disabilities thought to be dangerous. These rules distort the usual meanings of key words and concepts—such as dangerousness, treatment, and civil versus criminal—in order to make it much easier for the state and federal governments to incarcerate, permanently monitor, supervise, restrict, forcibly medicate, or even execute people who have mental disabilities.

Moreover, many psychiatrists and psychologists, despite—or in many instances because of—their professional training, accept without meaningful protest or actively participate in such legal proceedings. As a result, they implicitly embrace or tolerate as being relevant and reasonably accurate expert mental health evidence and testimony about dangerousness in the legal system that is generally unreliable, inaccurate, and empirically deficient for the purposes that they are being used. A significant number of psychiatrists and psychologists are paid—well[33]—to provide this highly flawed "expert" information to the courts, and in doing so, they are pushed and encouraged by the lawyers who hire them and our advocacy system to skirt—and too often clearly violate—their ethical responsibilities.

As a society, we have established legal definitions of dangerousness that are without logical boundaries in the sense that all sorts of different types of people who commit antisocial acts are grouped under various legal definitions that are supposed to protect us against truly violent individuals. We rarely make meaningful distinctions regarding the extent to which we should allow the states and federal government to impose extremely intrusive and typically punitive-like "public health" measures on those for whom these very broad definitions of dangerousness have been applied. Unlike science, where terms are defined "more loosely" to begin with and then over time "the meanings of words gradually become more precise as the scientists come to understand the phenomenon more thoroughly,"[34] legal definitions of dangerousness have become less and less precise in capturing actual violence in order to respond to the public's exaggerated fears and misconceptions about persons with mental disabilities.

Dangerousness has devolved into a loose, mixed metaphor for future violent, nonviolent, and non-criminal antisocial behaviors, which state and federal governments describe or define in circular terms: people who have mental disabilities appear to be more likely to behave in ways that make them dangerous to themselves or others; thus they should be viewed as presently violent and likely to continue to be violent for the unforeseeable future. Rather than reflecting the social science of actual violence, dangerousness has become a largely arbitrary legal definition that is more akin to "words that refer to whatever we say they mean when we stipulate their meanings in a system of rules."[35] Concluding that someone with a mental disability is dangerous, legally, is little more than a tautology that has been elevated to the status of objective legal truth supported by legal fictions and the imprimaturs of the courts, lawyers, psychiatrists, and psychologists.

Dangerousness has become a threshold concept in which persons with mental disabilities—and only persons with mental disabilities—who fall within its expansive and still expanding parameters may be deprived of their fundamental rights, freedoms, and liberties. This is true even though the U.S. Supreme Court has made it clear that people should not be punished for the status of having a mental disorder, including being addicted[36] or being drunk.[37] Such individuals are only supposed to be "punished" for illegal behaviors that accompany such a status.

With dangerousness, however, the legal question is framed differently, so that the types of punishments and deprivations that we normally think of as being criminal are conveniently termed civil treatments or public health interventions. As a result, the heightened due process standards and procedures that these defendants should be entitled to are magically whisked away under the deceptive rubric that these individuals with mental disabilities facing incarceration and other fundamental deprivations of freedoms and liberty within the criminal justice and civil systems are civil respondents.[38] In addition, we allow persons with mental disabilities— and only persons with these disorders—to be fully punished criminally and then we attach further extreme deprivations of liberties and freedoms on top of that in the guise of supervision, forced treatment, and monitoring, which can last indefinitely, often meaning decades or, increasingly, a lifetime.[39]

Moreover, in our civil and quasi-civil commitment schemes, the word dangerousness is used indiscriminately so that those who are deemed dangerous to themselves are often subject to the same types of intrusive restrictions as those who are deemed dangerous to others; those who shoplift or who choose to live and act antisocially on our streets may be placed in the same loose dangerousness category as violent serial rapists and murderers; and within our "civil" or quasi-civil legal systems, those who are considered to be dangerous based on highly unreliable predictions of their future dangerous behaviors may be treated similarly to persons who have just been tried and convicted of committing violent crimes.

If all of this were not bad enough, a new construct has been proposed, which would differentiate between extended "temporary [civil] detention" and "[involuntary] civil commitment."[40] Under this well-intentioned proposal, extended detentions would be applied without additional due process protections in hopes of reducing the number and/or duration of the more traditional involuntary civil commitments. Unfortunately, in the absence of additional due process safeguards, there would be only words and little substance to prevent this new approach from becoming a legal mechanism that would increase the length of time patients deemed to be dangerous could be detained, with or without effective and humane care and treatment.

Treatment as a Right and Entitlement

"Treatment" in the legal vernacular surrounding dangerousness proceedings has meanings that confound logic and common sense. The right—or more accurately the entitlement—to treatment that has been used as the prime justification for incarceration and other intrusive deprivations of freedoms and liberty imposed upon persons with mental disabilities has always been a contorted legal concept. Adequate, effective, or even humane care usually has not been provided. Even with its promising beginnings when the constitutional right to treatment for persons with mental disabilities was first presented in a scholarly way in 1960, plain English was eschewed for a legal fiction.[41] This right to treatment never meant that people with mental conditions should be entitled to humane care that would ameliorate their symptoms and allow them to be more productive human beings. Instead, it was proposed that if the state were to forcibly incarcerate respondents because they supposedly needed treatment, then those who were confined should be entitled to receive minimally adequate treatment to resolve the particular mental condition that was the basis of their involuntary "hospitalization."[42]

Yet even that diluted concept of treatment rarely passed legal muster. Instead, the U.S. Supreme Court diluted the right even further so that for involuntary mental patients it cryptically devolved into an entitlement to *something more than humane custodial care*.[43] What was "more" has always remained vague, but it also was illusory for respondents who were deemed dangerous because it soon became apparent that they were only entitled to humane custodial care, and nothing more, and often much less than that in practice. Thus, the right to something more than humane custodial care, which was masquerading as some kind of right to treatment, only applied to those who were vaguely deemed nondangerous.

Worse, the law's evolution, pushed by increasing popular demands for more security and punishment, continued on the path of entitling persons with mental disabilities to less and less in the way of humane care, treatment, and habilitation. This massive injustice was made possible in large part because of the artificial distinction that was and continues to be made between civil and criminal with regard to incarceration, detention, and other deprivations. It also has occurred because within our legal system most individuals have been at a severe disadvantage when they attempt to enforce laws and entitlements against state and federal governments. This is particularly true when those individuals are poor or isolated—which people with mental disabilities who are perceived to be dangerous tend to be—and vulnerable due to their mental conditions or impairments.

The distinction between what our laws consider civil and what they consider criminal has many legal ramifications, almost all of which go against the liberty, freedom, care, and treatment interests of persons with mental disabilities. For example, based on what is termed a need for civil treatment, criminal offenders with mental disabilities and those who are found not guilty by reason of insanity or incompetent to stand trial may be incarcerated, monitored, restricted, and closely supervised indefinitely—which increasingly may be permanently. These intrusive governmental actions are justified because the respondents have been diagnosed with a mental disorder or condition that requires "treatment" to prevent them from committing the type of criminal or antisocial behaviors that they were convicted of—or accused of committing—in the first place.[44] In addition, their confinements may be continued because they have an entirely different mental disorder, which may be due in large part to the poor custodial care and treatment they have received.

Our laws create a popular but highly deceptive and grossly unfair dichotomy regarding the due process protections that are required based on this civil-versus-criminal distinction. The distinction allows—and largely ensures—that individuals with mental disabilities who are presumed to be dangerous remain confined and/or under control of the state. We justify using civil due process guarantees—which are considerably less protective of the individual's rights than those that the Constitution demands for criminal prosecutions—for a type of incarceration with other accompanying rights deprivations that are practically indistinguishable from criminal imprisonment, probation, and parole. In many circumstances, quasi-civil—and even civil—confinement and release conditions are actually worse, and sometimes much worse than criminal dispositions.

The rationale for making this highly arbitrary, yet extremely consequential, civil versus criminal distinction is that the respondents involved are being subjected to a public health intervention, which promises meaningful treatment rather than punishment. The implication is that these quasi-civil patients will receive treatment and humane care comparable or similar to that which people confined in a traditional manner to our civil mental health facilities are supposed to receive. This is why the American Bar Association's Criminal Justice Mental Health Standards specify that insanity acquittees should be legally entitled to receive such care and treatment.[45]

Once a person is indefinitely in the custody of a correctional system as a so-called civil patient, however, the meaning of treatment—with its implied entitlement to humane care—is transformed into an amorphous concept filled with "ifs," "ands," and "buts" that allow most of these inmates to be treated no better, and oftentimes worse, than prisoners who received full criminal due process protections. To begin with, the law creates a gaping loophole by allowing treatment to be denied to inmates who are considered to be a future danger to themselves or others, unless the jurisdiction has promised—in a legally binding manner—to provide such treatment,[46] which rarely happens. Furthermore, the law equates any type of crime, whether it involves actual violence or not, with definitive proof of dangerousness.[47] Thus, based on this overly broad and thus faulty equivalence between crime and violence, almost all of these so-called quasi-civil committees are found to be dangerous, and thus rarely are constitutionally entitled to adequate treatment.

In addition, once dangerousness is established initially, it normally is up to the respondent to overcome the presumption that he or she remains dangerous. This occurs because the presumption is codified in a legal standard and/or courts discount any proof that a respondent has engaged in no further violent behaviors while confined, in favor of unreliable predictions by "experts" or juries or judges that if released inmates are likely to act dangerously or will become dangerous because they fail to take their medications.[48]

Relatively few jurisdictions actually promise to provide treatment to those who are quasi-civilly confined, and for those few our justice system has provided governments with two major loopholes. First, certain mental disabilities that apply to persons who are confined civilly rather than criminally, particularly many types of sexual and other types of behavioral compulsions, do not respond well to treatment, or only seem to respond to what are viewed as "unreasonably" expensive treatments. In both situations, the law generally holds that no treatment is required.[49] Even if treatment was implicitly or explicitly promised as a justification for incarceration or other intrusive deprivations of rights, there would be no due process violation. Second, only clear and unambiguous promises to provide treatment are normally considered to be legally binding.[50] Thus, the only circumstances in which treatment would be required is if there was an explicit promise made and the inmate has a condition that will respond positively to reasonably affordable treatments.

Moreover, where some kind of entitlement to treatment exists for those inmates or patients, there may be no practical way for them to enforce it or any other rights and entitlements, such as humane care and freedom from bodily harm, abuse, and neglect. To begin with, those officials and staff who manage these inpatient (or outpatient) civil and quasi-civil programs, institutions, or detention facilities are endowed with considerable discretion to take measures that may limit treatment opportunities or result in inhumane care and other abuses, if those measures are required to keep order and security within a facility or program. The benefit of the doubt almost always resides with the facility and facility staff who manage the inmates.[51] As the Supreme Court has explained, "in the absence of clear evidence to the contrary, courts presume that [public officers] have properly discharged their duties."[52]

Second, involuntary civil or quasi-civil inpatient and outpatient commitments or conditional release programs are insulated from legal remedies when abuses do occur. Various legal obstacles make it difficult or impossible for inmates with mental disabilities to successfully bring actions against local, state, and federal governments: constitutional immunities;[53] statutes that limit remedies;[54] statutes that cap damages;[55] statutes of limitations that substantially narrow the time frames for redress;[56] statutes that require plaintiffs to exhaust their administrative remedies;[57] and, most of all, a scarcity of lawyers willing to provide this type of legal representation, and even fewer who are properly trained and adequately paid to do so.[58] Also, remedies do not exist for plaintiffs in outpatient or conditional release programs, unless they can prove that they were in government custody when the alleged violations of their rights occurred.[59]

CONCLUSION

Words and language have such powers of influence and deception that they can "severely skew how scientists look at the world, time, space, and causality."[60] Therefore, it should come as no surprise that the words and language legislatures and courts use can—and often do—skew legal determinations involving people with mental disabilities, about whom we share a common belief that they are likely to be dangerous. Using legal semantics and linguistic obfuscation to justify unreliable predictions about their future actions, we have created systems of involuntary confinement, compelled mental health supervision, monitoring, and treatment, inhumane care and other intrusive and abusive measures that deprive people with mental disabilities of their fundamental rights.

We also have embraced the linguistic deception that when they are confined and deprived of their rights and freedoms, as a result of so-called civil public health interventions, their constitutional right to treatment should be extremely limited: something more than the mere warehousing of individuals in state institutions, but little else. Like obscenity, something more has never been defined with any precision, but we continue to assume judges and juries will know what it should be by shared societal or judicial values, rather than by specified standards. Whatever this custodial care may mean, however, our legal system does not require that meaningful treatment actually be provided. For as long as we have had coerced mental health interventions—a period that has spanned multiple centuries[61]—individuals who have been subjected to this governmental coercion generally have not received humane care.

Typically, such treatment has lacked proper funding and has been abusive and poorly administered. The more recent default solution has been to coercively administer powerful, mind-calming drugs, which have potentially debilitating and even fatal side effects—frequently using excessive dosages and providing inadequate follow-up. Furthermore, government-supported consensual treatment for persons with severe mental disabilities has been either practically nonexistent, inadequate, or— from the points of view of many of these potential patients themselves— worse than homelessness.

What allows these travesties of justice to occur is our collective mindset—a tyranny of the majority—that is reflected in the language we use to define dangerousness, the right to treatment, and what constitutes civil versus criminal due process protections. Collectively, our involuntary "civil" and "quasi-civil" inpatient and outpatient commitment and conditional release schemes exemplify how words and language can be used to distort legal principles in favor of our subjective beliefs.

Regrettably, the inhumane actions that we have authorized—or at least tolerated—based on these linguistic distortions have been expanding rather than contracting, especially as the media-inflamed horrors of Columbine, Virginia Tech, Northern Illinois, Tucson, and Sandy Hook have "informed" public opinions about "deranged killers." As thinking beings we have the cognitive skills to "entertain new ideas and new ways of managing our affairs."[62] Yet, whether we have the will to change our language and mind-set with regard to how we should view and treat persons with serious mental disabilities, who we believe are dangerous, is very much in doubt.

4

PREDICTIONS OF DANGEROUSNESS IN THE COURTROOM

Unreliable, Inaccurate, and Misleading

[I]t is possible to identify the approximately 400,000 most problematic and 40,000 most dangerous individuals with severe psychiatric disorders . . . and provide [coerced] treatment for the most problematic and dangerous individuals. (E. Fuller Torrey, M.D.)[1]

The essential "difference between past and future . . . [is that the] past has taken place and is knowable . . . whereas the future is up for grabs and is inscrutable, as if it were out of view." (Steven Pinker, psychologist and linguist)[2]

[P]redictions offered with great certainty and voluminous justification prove, when evaluated later, to [be] . . . the equivalent of monkeys tossing darts. (paraphrasing Nate Silver)[3]

Economic forecasters divide into two groups: those who cannot know the future but think they can, and those who recognize their inability to know the future. (Lawrence Summers, economist)[4]

If I take a putrid body part, douse it in perfume, delicately place it inside an expensive gift box, wrap the box in fancy paper, and place a large bow on the top, the box appears to be a nice gift. If I use calligraphy to write my wife's name on the box and then place it under the Christmas tree, she is likely to believe that she is going to receive a lovely gift, as will most

everyone else who passes the tree and sees the gift with her name on it. If
I paid them well, I could probably convince several gift box "experts" to
certify that in their opinions, based on their experience closely examining
gift boxes, there is going to be a very nice gift inside. That collective
perception would continue indefinitely, as long as my wife did not actual-
ly open the box. Moreover, I could make my wife's expectations of a nice
gift increase substantially, if on Christmas Eve, I gave her a copy of the
"beautiful gift" certification form signed by my gift experts. Yet, when
Christmas morning arrives, she carefully removes the bow and the fancy
paper and views what is inside, her perception will be changed by reality.

INTRODUCTION

Risk Assessments and Clinical Predictions of Dangerousness

During the past thirty years, there have been significant—albeit modest—
advances in the use of risk assessment tools to predict dangerousness and
dangerous-like behaviors more reliably and more accurately in clinical
settings.[5] Unfortunately, being significantly better than in the past, clinically, is not nearly equivalent to being reliable, relevant, or accurate
enough to reasonably satisfy required legal standards of proof and due
process. "Two generations of researchers . . . have detailed, with much
empirical support, that psychiatrists lack the ability to assess danger pro-
ficiently, [which] . . . has resulted in mental health professionals over-
predicting instances of harmful behavior."[6] This encompasses not only
harm to others, but also harm to oneself, including suicidal behaviors.[7]

Dangerousness overpredictions by experts occur for numerous reasons, but two are most compelling. First, mental health professionals are
strongly encouraged, either implicitly or explicitly, to avoid liability and
the personal responsibility that might result should they authorize a person with a mental disorder to live in the community, who then causes
harm to others or him- or herself.[8] Second, mental health professionals,
particularly psychiatrists, through their training have understandable "biases towards treatment," which for many of them justifies finding persons
with severe mental disorders to be legally dangerous so that treatment
may be mandated.[9]

Regardless of the actual motivations or incentives involved, however, the notion that there are "experts" who can validly and reliably predict an individual's dangerousness with any legally relevant degree of certainty directly contradicts human experience and empirical evidence to date. The best these behavioral "experts" have been able to do—and even that is unlikely to be achieved consistently in the courtroom—is to guess or estimate more accurately than non-experts or than chance. [10] As a group, even well-trained and reasonably objective experts, even in clinical environments, will be wrong in predicting dangerousness most of the time until: (1) the environments in which their predictions apply can be controlled so that all of the significant variables become manageable; (2) highly structured and empirically validated actuarial methods replace clinical judgments as the primary basis for making dangerousness assessments; and (3) those structured methods are only applied to discrete situations using very selective, empirically-based criteria. [11] In a courtroom environment applying diverse dangerousness standards, these challenges are overwhelming and other serious problems emerge as well.

Overwhelming Challenges in Using Dangerousness Assessments in the Courtroom

Even if these stiff clinical and empirical challenges are met, our legal system presents numerous other obstacles that also need to be overcome in order to make future dangerousness proceedings fair and just. To begin with, there is a plethora of significantly different dangerousness standards and procedures that exist, depending on the jurisdictions involved and the antisocial, offensive, or criminal behaviors that are being "controlled," "treated," or "punished," and new standards and procedures are being implemented. This means that in order to draw meaningful empirical conclusions about their reliability and accuracy, these risk-assessment tools must be tested and validated for each dangerousness standard and procedure (or type of standard and procedure, assuming all the standards and procedures within a given type are reasonably equivalent) with which they would be used.

Even today, this process has just barely begun, if it has begun at all. [12] Moreover, there is little reason to believe that sufficient testing and validation will be completed anytime soon, since these actuarial methods are rarely used in the legal system anyway. [13] Theoretically, possible exceptions may be certain specific actuarial tools intended to identify certain types of sexually dangerous persons, which currently have not been proven to be reliable or accurate enough to satisfy due process, but are used anyway.[14]

Second, too often dangerousness determinations—whether primarily actuarial, clinical, or impressionistic—are misused in our courtrooms in order to confirm pretexual and heuristic presumptions that either people with mental disabilities are dangerous and thus should be detained, or they should be deemed dangerous because they "need" to be treated involuntarily. Third, our advocacy system, as applied in these dangerousness proceedings, tends to further undermine and distort the potential accuracy and relevancy of any actuarial or clinical tools or methods that are being used.

As a result, whatever social science risk assessment advances have been made—even if they were widely and rationally implemented in our legal system—still would not allow courts to make predictions of dangerousness with anywhere near the reliability and validity that would be necessary for justice and fairness to prevail. Furthermore, the outcomes are much worse when using clinical methods or, even worse than that, allowing juries and judges to make dangerousness decisions on their own. Collectively, these flawed proceedings continue to: invidiously discriminate by focusing almost exclusively on persons with mental disorders, conditions, or aberrations as being legally dangerous; depend—at least to a significant extent—on judges and jurors, who like most people tend to be statistically and scientifically deficient, to make relatively complex social science decisions; tend to embrace the "sanist" presumption that persons with mental disabilities are inherently more dangerous than other people; and generally use experts in ways and circumstances that make them perform more as "hired guns" than as competent, independent-minded mental health professionals.

Despite all of these flaws and deficiencies, the law accepts these highly unreliable predictions of dangerousness as sufficient to meet due process, and as relevant and valuable in making the ultimate dangerousness determinations. This legal fiction is problematic using any legal standards of proof, but especially so when clear and convincing evidence is supposed to be used to justify civil incarcerations and other deprivations of fundamental rights, and much more problematic with proof beyond a reasonable doubt, which arguably should be used whenever fundamental rights are at risk.[15] The law's reliance on dubious dangerousness evidence is unreasonable in most circumstances, and usually depends on misusing and distorting basic professional principles of law, psychiatry, and psychology in order to be successful.

Predictions of dangerousness are permitted in our courtrooms primarily for two reasons. First, these assessments are presumed to be necessary in order to protect our communities from violence, antisocial behaviors, and self-harms. Second, the harsh results that flow from these assessments only apply to persons with mental disorders, conditions, or aberrations, who are devalued as human beings in our society and thus have very little leverage to protest. Unfortunately, no matter what legal procedures are used to hide their lack of validity, lack of reliability, lack of relevance, and lack of accuracy in the courtroom—and in today's legal systems there are plenty of ingenious disguises and legal fictions—in a vast majority of the legal situations in which they are used today, the admissibility of assessments of future dangerousness typically make fair and just determinations less likely or practically impossible.

Neither distorted due process nor the legal vetting of such flawed testimony by lawyers, judges, and juries can mystically transform statistically, empirically, and logically unreliable future dangerousness assessments into the persuasive evidence which should be required to deprive individuals of their fundamental rights. Moreover, where dangerousness predictions are used against persons with mental disabilities without such expert assessments—relying instead on the inherently subjective and often sanist opinions or impressions of judges and juries—travesties of justice are even more likely. Our legal system, due in no small part to "endemic" statistical and quantitative illiteracy[16] and to engrained societal prejudices against persons with mental disabilities, inevitably make these expert assessments—and even more so the subjective lay opinions of judges and juries—far less reliable and accurate, and their uses in the courtroom particularly discriminatory.

As social scientist and law professor, John Monahan—and many others—has concluded that as a society our views and beliefs about violence and persons with mental disorders are overinflated and misapplied. The overall risk for them is "trivial [even for] . . . 'major' mental disorders such as schizophrenia . . . [and is much less than] the magnitude of risk associated with the combination of male gender, young age, and lower socioeconomic status . . . [or] alcoholism and other drug abuse."[17]

It is conceivable that for some people who are violent emerging evidence will demonstrate that their "repetitive acts of aggression are grounded in an underlying neurobiological susceptibility"[18] or "genetic mutations"[19] that may respond positively in a therapeutic sense to certain specific "psychosocial interventions."[20] However, what is known now is insufficient to conclude that such susceptibility can be applied meaningfully to specific categories of persons with mental disabilities, or that we will ever have any reliable means for identifying people who pose a future danger to themselves or others consistent with legal notions of due process. Nevertheless, our laws continue to unfairly, obsessively, and almost exclusively target persons with mental disorders, conditions, and aberrations as being dangerous; and our courts continue to implement various legal fictions to justify incarcerating and otherwise depriving these individuals of their fundamental rights based on flawed predictions of dangerousness.

PREDICTIONS OF DANGEROUSNESS

As a Practical Matter in Courtrooms

From a social science perspective dangerousness is a concept that is used to measure the likelihood of acts of violence being carried out by individuals or groups of individuals at a future time, which, by definition, means that these so-called predictions actually involve only threats of violence. Violence typically encompasses serious harm to persons, and may also include serious harm to property, although this later type of violence is— and should be viewed as being—of lesser legal and social importance. Harm to persons or property may be directed at others or oneself. Self-harm is generally conceptualized as a public health matter, rather than a crime. Also, harm to others may come into play if either someone else is injured in the process of harming oneself or the state is using the illusion of civil commitment for *care and treatment* to extend the incarceration of a criminal inmate with a mental or sexual disorder after that person has served his or her prison sentence.

In the legal system, there are many different criminal, quasi-civil, and civil dangerousness standards, usually explicit, but sometimes implicit. As discussed in chapter 5, legal definitions of dangerousness change de-

pending on their specific law-related contexts and the different legal procedures that are used to impose those standards. The sound legal application of future dangerousness, however, depends on the specific circumstances in which the violent act or threat is presented. Even if someone
commits a violent crime, this does not necessarily mean that the person is
a significant future danger to others a day later. For instance, a woman
who kills her husband because he torments and abuses her arguably may
be guilty of manslaughter or even second-degree murder for what she has
done today, but it could well be that she would no longer be a significant
danger to anyone else, even if she were set free tomorrow.

In most situations, dangerousness also should be dependent to a substantial extent on the timeliness of the violent act or threat. Unfortunately,
no sound scientific or legal bases exist for determining how long an
individual will continue to be dangerous or when they will act dangerously, beyond subjective impressions that typically have little or no empirical
bases in fact. Virtually always, the further away in time the violent act or
behavior is that forms the basis for attempting to determine whether a
person is sufficiently likely to be dangerous: (1) the more likely it is that
the threat level from that particular predictor will have subsided; and/or
(2) the more difficult it will be to accurately assess how dangerous that
person is—assuming, for the purpose of comparison, that the dangerous
act or behavior that is being measured remains the same. In other words,
the reliability, validity, and accuracy of any such prediction continually
diminish over time because the behavioral and environmental variables
involved in making such predictions continually increase over time. Only
at the very instant that actual violence occurs can one be absolutely certain that someone is dangerous; thereafter as time intervenes that certainty tends to decrease unless and until that individual actually commits
another violent act or threat. (Threats of violence by their nature always
lack such absolute certainty, although arguably certain types of immediate threats should be used as persuasive indications of current dangerousness.)

In addition, dangerousness may lessen or subside after a violent act
has occurred, as the perpetrators mature from one stage of life to another,
and typically, but certainly not always, gain insight, understanding, and
control over their actions during that process. For example, if sixteen-
year-old Juan Valdez shoots a gun in the air several times in the middle of
a large crowd at a New Year's celebration while inebriated, at that mo-

ment he is a clear and present danger to everyone around him. However, five years from now, as a responsible parent who no longer drinks, Juan's dangerousness to others as a result of that prior shooting probably has been reduced substantially, quite possibly to almost nothing.

Conversely, while most human beings in our society tend to mature during adulthood, some may devolve, temporarily or more permanently, into states of less maturity, less insight, and less control, often brought on by social or environmental factors, psychological stress, addictions, and/ or illness or disease. Yet, while we generally expect more maturity and less maturity to affect decision-making regarding violence either positively or negatively, we really have very little substantial basis for determining how the intricate and ever-changing social and environmental factors affecting maturity and stability are likely to "play out" collectively with respect to individual human beings in their particular milieus. Also, depending on the mental, behavioral, physical, environmental, or social conditions that are thought to be most responsible for a person's potentially violent behavior, that individual's level of dangerousness may spike, recede, or stabilize over time, as a result of myriad social, emotional, and environmental factors, medication, treatment, stress, and the apparent progress or regression of that person's mental condition. Thus our judgments need to be individualized, rather than generalized to various populations or groups.

Furthermore, whether alleged violence presents itself as overt acts, perceived threats, or annoying, disgusting, or criminal behaviors or threats that are not really violent at all—or some combination of those acts, threats, or behaviors—may be crucial in being able to determine actual dangerousness more accurately, yet as a practical matter critical distinctions tend not to be made for acts or behaviors that are antisocial or threatening, but not actually violent. In addition, there is a significant difference, for example, between hitting a person with a shovel and threatening to hit someone with a shovel. Moreover, if a person hits someone with a shovel and then a day later hits another person with a shovel, conceptually that is a third distinct type of dangerousness based on the same violent behavior being repeated in a relatively short period of time.

What makes predictions of future dangerousness so difficult for those forensic "experts," who are asked by governments to conclude that the subject involved is dangerous, is the number of variables involved, as well as the inadequacies of the information being utilized. Most of the information that dangerousness experts use in their assessments, including those retained by the government, is not subject to meaningful objective standards and typically it is not based on direct observations of the respondent living in the community. These behavioral experts frequently, and arguably most of the time, are basing their assessments, at least in part, on second-, third-, and fourthhand reports about a respondent's behaviors, some or many of which may be inaccurate, distorted, self-serving, or simply false.[21]

Experts in dangerousness proceedings usually lack the time and the means to confirm the accuracy and reliability of that type of evidence, beyond their faith in the process used to collect social service, medical, or other official records in very demanding circumstances.[22] The rest of an expert's evidence typically is based on three or four hours, or often less, of observing and speaking with a respondent or defendant in contrived, highly stressful, and unrepresentative circumstances in which indefinite inpatient or outpatient commitment, the death penalty, or other deprivations of rights, freedoms, and liberties may be imposed once such an exam is completed and admitted as evidence against the respondent.[23] Sometimes these experts give their opinions without ever having met the defendant/respondent.

As a Statistical Matter

An additional and even more daunting problem in rationally establishing and using dangerousness in the legal system is the applicable burdens and standards of proof, which normally are supposed to protect the subjects of such proceedings over the governments who are trying to diminish their rights. Where personal liberty and/or fundamental freedoms are at risk, the legal standard is and should be no less than clear and convincing evidence, and even that standard is probably insufficient for extended or indeterminate involuntary commitments, which involve "severe deprivations of liberty" based on mental status evidence that has "such a high rate of inconsistency" from one expert to another.[24] As a matter of logic, statistics, fairness, and common sense, it should be much more difficult to prove in a courtroom that clear and convincing evidence of dangerousness exists than that clear and convincing evidence is lacking. Thus, the proffered testimony of experts who are opining that a subject is dangerous, where a clear and convincing standard of proof (or higher) is required, should be held to a correspondingly higher admissibility standard than that of those who are taking the opposite position.

Such an approach would reflect the conclusions of a comprehensive study published in the *British Medical Journal* in 2012.[25] There the authors found that, based on samples involving 24,827 people, the use of risk assessment instruments to predict violence are unreliable in trying to establish that a particular individual has a high risk of being violent or antisocial; but such instruments may have substantial utility in identifying low risk individuals. Unfortunately, in our legal system the admissibility standards and procedures typically favor the state or federal governments over the individuals with mental disabilities in deciding whether to admit expert evidence to prove future dangerousness.

Legally, there is no actual standard or rule that mandates how accurate clear and convincing evidence (or proof beyond a reasonable doubt) must be, mathematically, although now that we are well into the twenty-first century, one would hope that there could be specific guidance to help triers of fact make legal determinations that are both logical and rational. Logic and the deconstruction of language used in court cases have led legal scholars to recognize that if a preponderance of the evidence means being correct more often than not (more than 50 percent), then clear and convincing evidence should be substantially more than 50 percent, but substantially less than a virtual certainty, which would be close to 100 percent. Thus, 75 percent (70 to 80 percent) is an approximation that those legal scholars who have assigned clear and convincing with a percentage have embraced, with 90 percent, 95 percent, or higher being used to approximate proof beyond a reasonable doubt.[26]

Conversely, this indicates that one would expect even clear and convincing evidence, if applied rationally and logically, would be wrong around 25 percent of the time, which is a frightening percentage to begin with if you happen to be the individual whose fundamental rights, liberties, and freedoms are at risk, especially if you are amongst the 25 percent. Unfortunately, a 25 percent error rate represents a best-case scenario in these types of proceedings. As a practical matter, due to sanism, fear, and basic inequities in the legal system, the odds are very likely to be considerably worse than that for most people with mental disabilities when they are "accused" by state or federal governments of being dangerous to themselves, others, or the community. In fact, it may be as high as a 74 percent error rate.

A survey by two respected social scientists demonstrates that as a group even judges, who are supposed to be trained to be objective, will institute short-term civil commitment where the likelihood that a given respondent will carry out a violent act is only 26 percent.[27] Collectively those judges would be wrong 74 percent of the time, or nearly three times out of four, which is almost exactly the reverse of what it should be— approximately 25 percent wrong—even if one accepts clear and convincing evidence, rather than proof beyond a reasonable doubt, as being minimally appropriate. In this legal context, "likely" means whatever the judge—or more commonly the jury—says it means even if that meaning is illogical, irrational, and biased. The existence of this judicial pretexual flaw should not be surprising, however, since, for a long time now, other studies and commentaries have observed or demonstrated that highly trained mental health professionals, due to similar social, economic, and professional incentives, also tend to overpredict by substantial margins the dangerousness of persons with mental disabilities.[28]

Court decisions buttressed by empirical evidence strongly suggest that when dangerousness is at issue, jurors and judges view "clear and convincing" as being much less than what should be required logically and rationally, if these terms are to bear any reasonable relationship to how they are intended or described, legally.[29] If all the respondents must have mental disorders, conditions, or aberrations in order to meet the applicable legal criteria and jurors and/or judges tend to believe people with mental disabilities are considerably more dangerous than other people, then what is supposed to be clear and convincing evidence (or even a preponderance of the evidence) in theory, becomes much less convincing in practice. In these circumstances, the possibility that the triers of fact will use poor judgment or deliberately ignore the applicable legal standards is substantial and arguably likely, given the depth of sanism and pretexuality involved in such determinations.

With any expert prediction of dangerousness based on a legal standard, there are at least two separate events (and often more)—not even factoring in the threshold calculation as to whether the subject involved actually has a mental disorder, condition, or aberration—which should be considered: (1) the violent or harmful acts or threatening behaviors that the subject of the proceeding is supposed to have committed or engaged in; and (2) the expert's prediction based on those reports being accurate. Thus, as a statistical matter, even if only one-quarter of the violent or harmful events attributed to dangerous people do not actually take place or are not really violent due to mistaken, exaggerated, or misleading reports or records, then in order to reliably meet a clear and convincing threshold of being accurate approximately 75 percent of the time, the predictions themselves would have to be accurate 100 percent of the time (infallibility). This is because in order to be statistically accurate on a consistent basis, the predictive chain requires that the two separate probabilities of each of these separate events being accurate—the record and the prediction based on that record or other evidence—must be multiplied as fractions. (Even if one used 70 percent as the statistical equivalent of clear and convincing—which would seem to be a stretch—the fundamental statistical problem would only improve marginally, and if one used 80 percent, it would become statistically more difficult.)

Using a 75 percent clear and convincing standard, if the reports being applied are based on bad information *more than one-quarter of the time*, it would be impossible to reliably meet that standard; and even if those reports and records were correct 90 percent of the time, the prediction would have to be accurate well over 80 percent of the time. Moreover, because the predicative chain in the applicable legal standards generally involves more than two causative factors—including in particular whether the respondent actually has a covered mental disorder and can be successfully treated in the community voluntarily—meeting the clear and convincing equivalence threshold is even less likely, statistically, and arguably almost impossible with any satisfactory degree of reliability in the courtroom.

This statistical fallacy, as discussed in chapter 3, is due to the improper use of causality (proximate causation) in our legal system, which typically assigns total responsibility for an event to the most prominent factor involved, rather than assessing the relative and relevant statistical probability to each significant contributing factor. Every independent factor—whether known or unknown—that could significantly contribute to the predicted outcome—in these cases an imprecise or often vague legal standard or notion of dangerousness—should be accounted for if the prediction is to have acceptable statistical validity and reliability. This is very difficult to accomplish in a clinical setting, but immeasurably more difficult to achieve in advocacy-oriented proceedings in which: (a) the

definitions of dangerousness change substantially depending on the jurisdiction and type of proceedings involved; (b) due process favors the
government over the subject involved; (c) typically winning is more important than establishing truth; (d) protecting community safety is the
preeminent concern of most decision-makers; and (e) sanism and pretexuality tends to substantially affect those who are making the ultimate decisions.

Courtroom rules further muddle already questionable clinical outcomes. The legal system, however, easily overcomes any mathematical,
empirical, or logical hurdles by employing various "legal fictions," which
tend to discount, ignore, or distort the statistical, logical, and empirical
realities of predictions of dangerousness in the courtroom. These fictions
include the following: (1) reports of violence normally are presumed to
be true and accurate if they come from an "official" source or are testified
to in court; (2) each prediction normally is considered to be one event—
whether or not there is a chain of events that all need to be factored in for
that prediction to be accurate; and, (3) as a practical matter, in most of
these dangerousness cases the threshold for meeting the applicable standard of proof is reduced to such an extent that juries and judges will be
deemed to have met the standard even if they are likely to be wrong most
of the time. In other words, our legal system will tend to involuntarily
commit, otherwise detain or constrain, deprive, mistreat, or, on rare occasions, execute an individual with a mental disability, as long as there
appears to be a significant possibility—which usually is a misleading
perception of such a possibility—that he or she might commit a violent or
harmful act in the future.

Furthermore, legitimate questions about the validity, reliability, and
accuracy of the diagnoses of mental disorders, conditions, or aberrations—which logically are essential elements with regard to most predictions of dangerousness—are rarely if ever factored into dangerousness
assessments when they are applied in the courtroom to meet the required
legal standards. The existence of a mental disorder, condition, or aberration generally is accepted in the legal system, if a qualified mental health
professional makes a diagnosis using the criteria found in the latest version of the *Diagnostic and Statistical Manual of Mental Disorders* (*DSM-
V*). Yet, there is a "high rate of inconsistency" in these diagnoses from
one mental health professional or physician to another, which "are often
mistaken" and "often yield false positives . . . which can lead to unneces-

sary treatments."[30] No one really knows the percentage of mistakes that are made in diagnosing individuals as having various mental disorders, but logically, based on all that is known about how the *DSM* is currently structured and was being revised, it has to be a significant percentage, which would vary substantially depending on the disorder, condition, or aberration under consideration, the training and perspective of the mental health professional involved, and the legal circumstances in which the diagnosis is being made.

We know, for example, as is discussed later, that mental health professionals, including psychiatrists, often strongly disagree about the utility of the *DSM* in diagnosing different mental conditions, the *DSM* recently underwent major and controversial revisions to bring it up to date, and the legal system usually dismisses or minimizes the same diagnoses when they are used to attempt to excuse, diminish, or mitigate criminal responsibility. In addition, we know that mental health professionals often confuse mental disorders with undiagnosed "medical ailments," particularly in elderly patients.[31] We also know that the *DSM* has been used inappropriately to make race-based diagnoses, which among other things, has resulted in African-American men being assessed as having schizophrenia five times more often than other patients,[32] and immigrants being diagnosed with psychotic symptoms that reflect "aberrant behavior" due to critical cultural differences that psychiatric diagnoses fail to consider.[33] These race-based and ageist diagnoses demonstrate that social prejudices can and do negatively affect how psychiatric and psychological assessments involving members of devalued groups are made. In our society today, no group of individuals is more devalued than people with mental disorders, conditions, and aberrations who are deemed to be dangerous.

Ultimately, it should not be up to respondents or defendants in the legal system to demonstrate that a mental diagnosis is faulty, but rather the burden should be on the government or other person or entity proposing to deprive someone of their fundamental rights, freedoms, or liberties based on alleged dangerousness to at least prove clearly and convincingly that the mental disorder diagnosis is accurate, relevant, and reliable. Yet, as a practical matter, this vital element of proof is largely ignored in our courtrooms in the sense that a *DSM* diagnosis by a qualified mental health professional is implicitly presumed to be accurate and relevant. The primary focus is on so-called evidence of future dangerousness and whether it is linked to a mental disorder. The diagnosis itself is rarely scrutinized by the courts in these subjective dangerousness proceedings,[34] much less rigorously taken into account as an essential element of a predictive chain in an actuarial dangerousness assessment that forms the basis for a legal decision. This uncritical reliance on DSM-based diagnoses is an unjustifiable and irresponsible flaw in our legal system, given the lack of validity and scientific verification of the disorders that are contained in the DSM.[35]

The Social Science of Dangerousness

Since at least the mid-1950s, psychiatry and psychology have been enticed—like Tantalus to his reflection—by the presumed abilities of trained clinicians to accurately predict socially significant individual human behaviors. Many psychiatrists, psychologists, and other mental health professionals have professed a special ability to make such predictions. This has been particularly true with regard to so-called violent behaviors that are grouped together under the expanding and increasingly imprecise umbrella that is known as dangerousness.

Experience over many years has revealed, however, that psychiatrists, psychologists, and other mental health professionals tend to overestimate their abilities to predict these human behaviors by wide margins when such claims are tested empirically. This also has proven to be true with all sorts of forecasting, from elections to the weather to the stock market. Yet predicting future dangerousness typically involves many possible behaviors—and innumerable shades of behaviors—of the individual being assessed, as well as an unmanageable number of social, environmental, and psychological variables that can influence those behaviors and that change over time. Even assuming one is able to isolate a majority of the key behaviors and other factors that most contribute to the occurrence of the particular type of dangerousness that is being considered—which is usually extremely difficult to do in any circumstance—the ultimate prediction usually—and arguably almost always—will involve a probability that cannot be precisely and reliably determined in our legal system with regard to any one human being within a specified time frame.

In a science as precise as physics can be, the "experts" may be able to determine with a relatively high degree of accuracy the probability of whether a particular type of particle is likely to appear in a defined space in a precise time frame. In the far less precise world of social science, it is possible to determine, with a modest degree of accuracy and reliability, what many or most people who share certain general characteristics will likely do in the future with regard to a particular type of behavior, but validity, reliability, and ultimately overall accuracy are substantially diminished when a particular individual is involved. Validity, reliability, and overall accuracy are further diminished if an imprecise range of possible behaviors of a particular individual are being assessed in subjective and distorted circumstances, which is typically the situation when legal standards of dangerousness are being applied in advocacy-oriented, courtroom proceedings.

There was a time in the 1950s and 1960s when psychiatrists, who dominated the mental health professions even more than they do now, generally seemed to think that they could predict dangerousness with reasonable accuracy, even though the empirical evidence suggested that such predictions could not be made with much greater accuracy than pure chance.[36] By the 1980s, however, even the American Psychiatric Association had taken the position before the U.S. Supreme Court that testimony regarding future dangerousness should not be permitted in death penalty cases because of its inherent unreliability.[37] Today, psychiatrists and clinical and forensic psychologists appear to have improved their dangerousness predictive abilities considerably by using various types of risk assessment tools that are similar in concept to the actuarial charts that are used by life insurance companies.[38]

Yet even with these notable but inconsistent advances, predictions of dangerousness for a specific individual in the legal system are still highly questionable at best, unless many factors and conditions are controlled. In terms of accuracy, such predictions rarely would meet even a preponderance of the evidence legal standard—which in theory would require that these predictions be correct more often than they are wrong—much less the considerably more demanding clear and convincing or proof beyond a reasonable doubt standards that are required for involuntary civil and criminal incarcerations and other deprivations of fundamental rights, freedoms, and liberties. In these circumstances, an expert's prediction of dangerousness will tend to mislead the triers of fact or to provide them with a justification for arriving at a preconceived conclusion consistent with their belief that persons with mental disabilities are dangerous.

Until recently when internal politics intervened,[39] even the American Psychiatric Association acknowledged that "the vast majority of people who are violent do not suffer from mental illnesses. However, there is a certain small subgroup of people with severe and persistent mental illnesses who are at risk of becoming violent, with violence defined as threatening, hitting, fighting or otherwise hurting another person."[40] Here, it is important not to lose sight of the fact that this relatively careful characterization overstates the actual violence problem from a legal perspective because by including threats and less serious assaults that fall well short of what would constitute substantial bodily harm or a violent crime, psychiatry's violence threshold is relatively low, and thus overly broad if applied within the legal system, as opposed to managing patients and protecting staff in a hospital ward, for example. Moreover, our current concept of dangerousness, which has many different legal definitions that are often changing, encompasses many antisocial behaviors that are not violent—or differently violent.

Generally, persons with mental disabilities are not significantly more likely to be violent than anyone else in society without substance abuse being involved. The additional risk for mental illness alone is small. Even people with schizophrenia, who constantly are portrayed as particularly dangerous in the media, are at most marginally more likely to be violent than anyone else.[41] This has been confirmed in an international study, which concluded that random murders by someone who has schizophrenia are "rare and unpredictable events."[42]

There are three notable, but limited, possible exceptions to the general rule that persons with mental disabilities are not significantly more dangerous, clinically, than people in general. (Here it is important to remember that being significantly more dangerous is not equivalent to being dangerous as a legal, much less a scientific, matter if the initial risk is low.) First and foremost in terms of relative risk are persons with substance abuse problems or persons with severe mental illnesses aggravated by substance abuse.[43] Contrary to what most people seem to think, it appears that alcohol rather than drugs is the more significant substance abuse factor.[44] Much—and arguably most—drug-related violence, while obviously quite prevalent in our society, tends to be carried out deliberately based on economic or lifestyle considerations,[45] rather than on cognitive or volitional impairments due to drug abuse.

The close association between alcohol and violence and other antisocial behaviors should not be particularly surprising, however, since alcohol consistently has been shown to reduce a person's inhibitions and precipitate aggression.[46] A comprehensive study published in 1998 concluded that while there was "substantial evidence to suggest that alcohol use is significantly associated with violence of all kinds," there was "no significant evidence suggesting that drug use is associated with violence."[47] This distinction between alcohol and drug use in measuring violence is particularly true with regard to homicides, the ultimate expression of violence.[48] Nevertheless, even that enhanced risk has not been shown empirically to come close to meeting minimum legal standards of proof. Moreover, whatever risk substances abuse adds to the potential for violence, it does so "whether it occurs in the context of a concurrent mental illness or not."[49]

Second, people who are *actively* psychotic are at a somewhat greater—but usually not a legally significant—risk of becoming violent if their psychosis involves delusional or extremely paranoid behaviors.[50] According to one relatively recent study examining schizophrenia in particular, this increased risk "does not appear to add any additional risk to that conferred by substance abuse alone."[51] Similarly, with regard to psychoses more generally, a meta-analysis of all the leading studies to date is only "sufficient to conclude that psychosis *may* elevate a person's risk"[52] (emphasis added).

Moreover, whatever increased risk there is, most—and arguably virtually all—individuals with severe mental disorders would be far less psychotic, both in degree and in duration, if they could obtain proper care, treatment, housing, and other necessary services in their respective communities. "Major determinants of violence continue to be socio-demographic and economic factors."[53] As demonstrated in chapter 6, typically federal and state programs do not provide these individuals with adequate income, housing, care, treatment, and other supportive services that they need to avoid mental deterioration due to the substantial environmental and health stressors that are likely to aggravate their illnesses and disabilities.

In addition, many psychotic (or potentially psychotic) individuals refuse institutional mental health care because they prefer voluntary treatments in the community and/or assert their rights to refuse medications because the drugs that are available have what are perceived to be, and often are, seriously unpleasant, debilitating, and/or deadly side effects.[54] A 2009 study published in the *New England Journal of Medicine* indicates that patients using modern antipsychotic medications, as well as those using the more traditional antipsychotic drugs, generally double their risk of "sudden cardiac death,"[55] which admittedly is still a relatively low risk, but it is nonetheless significant, particularly if you are the one who is being coerced to take those drugs. Moreover, it is reasonable to conclude, based on many recent reports, that the drug companies may have deliberately minimized the reported frequency and seriousness of many or most of those negative side effects in two ways: by ignoring or reducing the significance of unfavorable research data; and/or contributing substantial sums of money to influence the researchers and journals that write and publish the studies, which are supposed to objectively assess the impact of such side effects, but appear to be biased in their conclusions in order to promote a drug's usage and acceptance.[56]

Third, persons with severe neurological impairments "usually stemming from diseases . . . or head injuries which damage the brain . . . [who] have psychological effects, interfering [with their] . . . ability to interpret what is real, and to act or relate to others appropriately" also are at a somewhat greater, but still legally insignificant, risk of violence.[57] Understanding that the actual risk in terms of potential dangerousness is still relatively low for this group of people is particularly important for soldiers and veterans. Reportedly, soldiers in modern-day combat sustain brain damage at much higher rates than in past wars, including 150,000 American troops with such injuries from the Iraq and Afghanistan conflicts alone.[58]

Dangerousness, from a legal point of view, encompasses three primary elements: severity of the risk (how much harm will be done), its imminence (how soon or far in the future will it occur), and its probability (likelihood).[59] The first two elements—severity and imminence—are based in large part on a person's history of violence or patterns of violence, and, of course, are directly influenced by that person's environment and personality. The probability of the dangerous event(s) occurring is the element that risk-assessment tools attempt to ascertain.[60]

The use of actuarial models underscores an important conceptual distinction between clinicians' abilities to predict dangerousness and their abilities to identify factors that increase the potential risk of violence.[61] The American Psychiatric Association—many of whose members earn some portion of their livelihoods by making such predictions in the legal system—currently takes the position that while mental health experts "can often identify risk factors associated with an increased likelihood of violent behavior" that are found in groups of people, they "cannot predict dangerousness with definitive accuracy" for a particular individual even using risk assessment tools. [62]

Consequently, there has been renewed optimism that well-trained clinicians using highly structured actuarial methods applied to very structured settings can or will eventually be able to identify those who over the relatively *short term* (a few weeks) may have an increased risk of being violent, as well as those who may best respond to remediation and treatment to reduce any risk that might be present. [63] Yet it is widely conceded by social scientists that clinicians in most situations cannot now reliably predict with a degree of certainty that should be required in the legal system—no matter what assessment tools they use or choose not to use— which individuals will commit a violent act or when it might occur. [64] As a 2006 study of risk-assessment factors clinicians use to make predictions of dangerousness revealed that even those most commonly relied on and widely thought to have the highest predictive potential—such as past assaults, non-compliance with medication, history of substance abuse, presence of psychosis or violent thoughts, or previous admission to a psychiatric hospital—were unreliable in allowing clinicians to determine who would act violently in the next two years. [65] Furthermore, the aforementioned 2012 "systematic review and meta-analysis" of methods of "risk assessment to predict violence and antisocial behaviour" reached the conclusion that "even after 30 years of development, the view that violence, sexual, or criminal risk can be predicted in most cases is not evidence based." [66]

Not surprisingly, actuarial methods vary considerably with regard to how much human subjectivity is allowed in these assessments. All of them, to a greater or lesser extent, rely on subjective clinical judgments. [67] Only the most "structured" tools, which "specify a risk factor's operational definition and quantification" in advance, even have the potential to provide a convincing degree of "predictive validity." [68] Nevertheless, mental health professionals when using any such tools still must "generate a final risk estimate" based on "additional (unstructured) information the clinician has gathered . . . information not included on the structured risk assessment instrument." [69] Also, there is no "consensus . . . as to which form of structured violence risk assessment has the greatest predicative validity" and, in any case, "relatively few practicing mental health professionals employ any form of structured violence risk assessment." [70]

More importantly, though, estimates of predictive validity are based on relatively controlled clinical circumstances that are unlikely to be replicated by experts who are hired to provide testimony in adversarial courtroom proceedings that apply to a wide assortment of legal definitions of dangerousness that are substantially different from clinical violence.

Even the most optimistic empirically based sentiments fall far short of asserting that within the limitations of our legal system, even the best-trained mental health professionals are able to apply risk assessments to predict an individual's dangerous behavior with a degree of reliability and accuracy that should be necessary to satisfy any of our legal standards of proof and due process. In fact, no such empirically based claim is even being made. What is being asserted is that well-trained, competent, *and intellectually honest* clinicians will make fewer mistakes if they utilize highly structured risk-assessment tools than if they rely on their subjective clinical judgments alone.

Unfortunately, making fewer mistakes is hardly a substitute for being reliably accurate to the degree that should be required under the legal system's applicable standards proof and due process. In most courtroom circumstances involving dangerousness, this should mean that the assessments need to be consistently correct no less than about three times out of four (clear and convincing evidence). While there are circumstances involving dangerousness in which the law only requires a preponderance of the evidence—being correct more often than not—even that low standard generally is not met in our courtrooms if judged objectively. In addition, there are compelling reasons to complain that using that lower standard violates due process where important individual rights are in jeopardy.

Both risk assessment and dangerousness are imprecise constructs. As one team of social scientists explained, even in clinical settings risk assessments involve "a multitude of contributing and interacting variables. . . . Dangerousness is the product of a multitude of complex variables, whose relative weight and interaction is inadequately known."[71]

One of the major obstacles in making accurate dangerousness predictions continues to be what is known as "the base-rate problem of predicting statistically rare events, such as murder"[72] or any or all violent crimes, for that matter. If, for example, the average annual murder rate in the general population is one in one thousand, even if a clinician were able to forecast with reasonable accuracy (which has never been demonstrated) that a defendant is one hundred times more likely than the average person to commit a murder, that clinician still could not conclude that there is anywhere even close to a reasonable likelihood that the defendant will commit a murder in the next two years. Statistically, the likelihood of that event occurring would approximate 10 percent. As it turns out, however, there is no identified group of people with mental disabilities using sound empirical data that presents even a 10 percent risk. The highest empirically verified risk of committing a clinically violent act in the past year (9.4 percent)—as opposed to actually committing a violent crime, which would be much lower—are persons with severe mental illness who also have drug or alcohol problems. [73]

Moreover, the accuracy of any such risk assessment assumes that the evaluator has all the necessary information available, has enough time to make a proper assessment, has competently considered all the relevant factors, has made no significant errors, and has honestly and objectively reported the results. In the legal world of civil and quasi-civil commitments, conditional releases, criminal prosecutions, sentencing, and other dangerous matters, where typically funds and time are scarce and the economic, social, and professional pressures and incentives to "win" are high, each of these assumptions is questionable at best. Thus, it becomes far more doubtful—even though it is certainly possible—that all of these assumptions will be true with regard to any single evaluation.

At the same time, even if all those assumptions are true, there are many other reasons why a prediction that a person is dangerous may be and probably is unreliable. To begin with, "legal definitions of dangerousness often are not well defined and predictions based on those definitions are not likely to be 'highly accurate.'"[74] Also, the accuracy of such assessments is dependent upon a host of variables, including the "offender's gender; the clinician's training; the type of dangerousness involved . . . and the particular environment in which the assessment is made."[75] Ultimately, though, even the best of these predictions are not likely to be reliable enough because "there is a sharp difference between risk assessments and legal decision-making."[76] The fundamental weakness of the actuarial approach is that because of the large number of variables involved, the "aggregate determination does not wholly account for the individual,"[77] much less the most prominent vagaries and counterproductive incentives of the legal system.

In addition, violence risk-assessment methodologies often—and probably most of the time—are based at least in part on social service and police records[78] that inevitably inflate the incidence for persons with mental disabilities. This is because, as a group, they are much more likely to come in contact with the social service agencies and police departments from which those records are drawn. Also, risk-assessment methods which are not based on official records tend to be even less reliable and less accurate than those that are.[79] In addition, statistically, a dangerousness finding is only one element of most of these dangerousness legal standards. Usually, those standards are supposed to require a separate finding that dangerousness is due to the existence of a mental disorder or condition, which is usually simply presumed based on the existence of a clinical diagnosis, rather than being made as a separate and necessary component of any statistically valid and reliable dangerousness actuarial calculation.

As one respected psychiatrist warned his colleagues, for all of these reasons and others as well, dangerousness is a "failed paradigm" that probably cannot be fixed because "future research is unlikely to give clinicians and judicial decision-makers prediction instruments with much practical utility."[80] None of the key risk factors that clinicians rely on to predict violence—such as an individual's past assaults, noncompliance with medications, history of substance abuse, or the presence of psychosis—enabled clinicians to accurately predict violence over the next two years in patients with those given characteristics.[81]

That study also showed that the cues and factors clinicians rely on to make their assessments differ significantly, depending on their professional training.[82] In other words, mental health professionals often perceive the same behavioral evidence differently based on the professional training they receive, which is not accounted for in making dangerousness assessments either clinically or actuarially. Moreover, all medical and related diagnoses are subject to substantial errors, and those involving human behaviors are subject to the most errors.

In diagnosing diseases, for instance, doctors often make blatant mistakes, even in assessing the most deadly physical medical conditions. According to the *New York Times*, "[s]tudies of autopsies have shown that doctors seriously misdiagnose fatal illnesses about 20 percent of the time."[83] Medicine is an art more than a science, and psychiatry (and by extension psychology) is recognized as one of the least, if not the least, scientific of all the medical arts. More importantly, in allowing states to apply their own individualized standards to reject or strictly limit psychiatric testimony—when it is to be used on behalf of criminal defendants—even the U.S. Supreme Court has concluded that such evidence is "controversial . . . [and has] the potential . . . to mislead jurors."[84]

Assuming that a future dangerousness determination in the legal system will be accurate, and thus fair and just, is like betting on the outcome of a series of coin flips, and thinking that there is a higher probability of being successful in guessing the outcome because four people in succession, rather than one, are making the prediction, and the last person to guess must have learned something that improves the odds by watching and listening to all the others. The fallacy is that the probability of being correct can only be as high as the quality of the information upon which the prediction is actually based. Since the quality of the information behind a prediction of dangerousness is typically poor, the prediction will be typically poor no matter how many people are involved in the legal translation, unless, of course, luck intervenes. Having experts, lawyers, judges, and jurors all involved in the determination is not likely to make a poor prediction a good one. Our advocacy system can only eliminate from consideration, or lessen the weight of, a prediction that was based on particularly faulty data that can and actually is identified as such. With dangerousness predictions this is unlikely to happen, particularly if such an intervention will favor respondents or defendants who have mental disabilities.

More likely, inserting juries, judges, and the advocacy system into the risk assessment mix is going to make the ultimate legal determinations less valid, less reliable, and less accurate. If the persons who make the ultimate dangerousness assessment—which is normally the jury (or judge acting as the trier of fact)—typically possess incomplete diagnostic information, understand the information less than the experts, usually are statistically deficient, already believe persons with mental disabilities are dangerous, and have no particular assessment skills, the probability of their being correct—which generally is relatively low for the experts—would likely decrease significantly. It would be better (or more precisely not as bad) in terms of validity, reliability, and accuracy to allow a reasonably objective expert or board of experts to make the predictions, than it would be to filter these decisions through the vagaries and biased incentives of the legal system in hopes of improving the outcomes. Each subsequent deficiency in the legal process that is part of a future dangerousness determination is likely to magnify the determination's fundamental unfairness and weakness: most, and arguable almost all, such opinions of future dangerousness, even those of the experts, are going to have particularly low validity and reliability when they are applied in the courtroom with regard to the many different legal definitions of dangerousness that are used.

Despite these problems in making accurate dangerousness assessments for legal purposes, we continue to rely on them in death penalty cases, in a variety of civil and quasi-civil involuntary commitment situations, and in a growing number of other types of cases in which fundamental individual rights, freedoms, and liberties are at risk. This paradox exists because in the particular contexts in which these dangerousness predictions are used, even minimum legal standards of proof do not apply in practice. Instead, these highly complex decisions are left to the subjective discretion of judges and juries. There is a conceptual and practical disconnect between the low validity, reliability, and accuracy—and lack of relevance—dangerousness assessments actually have, and their admissibility in the courtroom. Admissibility in these cases is founded on a tortured legal leap of faith (*bad legal fiction*) that juries and judges will understand and properly weigh the opinions of the experts, or, in many death penalty or pretrial detention cases, will make valid and reliable decisions about a defendant's future dangerousness without expert assistance.

In one set of circumstances involving involuntary commitments, civil and criminal conditional releases, certain death penalty cases, and certain other rights deprivations involving dangerousness, the legal system assumes that unreliable expert evidence will be made reliable by the subjective decision-making of juries and judges based on their lay interpretations of the experts' highly technical and flawed opinions. In the other set of circumstances, such as those involving pretrial detention and certain other death penalty cases, juries and judges often simply make dangerousness judgments based on little more than their common sense. These other determinations tend to be mostly "nonsense" after they have been filtered through feelings of anger and rage, bias, stereotypes, and prejudices that are intense in any criminal circumstance, but particularly so when the crime involves these highly stigmatized respondents or defendants who have mental disorders, conditions, or aberrations.

With all the independent and interdependent variables, intervening events, distortions of time, and changing circumstances to account for—

not to mention the extreme difficulty presented by having to account for imprecise dangerous standards and procedures the legal system has to offer—even the best forensic experts are usually confronted with an over-whelming challenge in making an assessment as to whether a particular person will be violent in an established time frame. Within the constraints and inherent distortions of the legal system, a reliable prediction of any future dangerous behavior is going to be improbable most of the time. At the very least these predictions should be based on: (1) a highly structured actuarial methodology; (2) sound statistical evidence that this particular methodology can validly and reliably satisfy the specific legal standard of proof that is being employed in the courtroom; *and* (3) assurances that the assessment based on that methodology was done properly and competent-ly. Furthermore, even if these basic social science thresholds could be met in particular types of proceedings using specified dangerousness defi-nitions, there are other extremely serious practical and systemic deficien-cies within the legal system that need to be addressed and overcome for any future dangerousness determinations to be fundamentally fair and just.

BATTLE OF THE EXPERTS: "HIRED GUNS," DSM, PROFITS, AND OTHER CORRUPTING INFLUENCES

Substantially undermining the validity, reliability, and overall accuracy of expert opinions about future dangerousness, which usually are question-able in the best of circumstances, is the "battle of the experts." While the injustices perpetuated by the "hired gun" syndrome have been recognized for many years, particularly with regard to psychiatric and psychological experts,[85] it has become progressively worse, even after 1993 when the U.S. Supreme Court established the "modern" rules to govern the admis-sibility of expert testimony.[86] The negative aspects of these unseemly competitions between experts are especially troublesome when danger-ousness predictions are involved.

In far too many—and arguably most—dangerousness proceedings, mental health professionals representing the state and those representing the defendant or respondent draw divergent—and sometimes directly contrary—conclusions that support the side they are representing at rates of agreement that cannot be explained by honest differences of opinion.

These predictions, and how judges and juries view them, tend to be infused with our society's prejudice and bias against persons with mental disabilities generally and persons with psychiatric diagnoses more specifically,[87] including the presumption that they are dangerous. Moreover, as will be discussed later, the normal limitations which apply to the admissibility of expert evidence, which are not particularly rigorous to begin with, do not apply to dangerousness predictions.

A former psychiatrist describes these courtroom battles as the "farce of the dueling psychiatrists [and psychologists]," which in large measure he attributes to the fact that psychiatric diagnoses, as reflected in the American Psychiatric Association's *Diagnostic and Statistical Manual of Mental Disorders* (*DSM*), are based on "cultural [and] historical norms" that are variable and subjective, rather than on "hard numbers."[88] Currently, psychiatrists and psychologists, both nationally and internationally, have been in disagreement about how the next version of the *DSM* (V) should have been organized, what disorders should have been included, and how expansively these disorders should have been defined.[89] Four psychiatrists and four psychologists, for example, in an article published in the *American Journal of Psychiatry*, concluded that the proposed revisions for the major category of personality disorders were "an unwieldy conglomeration of disparate models that cannot happily coexist and raises the likelihood that many clinicians will not have the patience and persistence to make use of it in their practices."[90] While this vetting process was necessary, it also underscores the logical flaw and injustice of relying on the *DSM* in the courtroom as the primary—and generally the only— basis for establishing the existence of legally significant mental disorders and conditions without giving the *DSM* much closer scrutiny than is done now.

There also was a widespread concern by psychiatrists, psychologists, and other mental health professionals that the American Psychiatric Association was being overly secretive and intellectually disingenuous in the process it was using to revise the *DSM*, particularly the corrupting influences of the drug companies.[91] Allen Francis, the chairman of the task force that oversaw the revisions to *DSM-IV*, has been highly critical of the process being used for *DSM-V*. He believes that "publishing profits clearly trumped concern for the quality and integrity of the product."[92] He characterizes the field trials to test the proposed changes as a "pure disaster from start to finish."[93] He also is concerned that the new version "will continue to contribute to the already rampant diagnostic inflation in psychiatry, especially . . . even greater overuse of psychotropic drugs."[94]

Whatever their disagreements about the *DSM* may be, and they appear to be substantial, psychiatrists and other mental health professionals were united in the conclusion that the *DSM* should be revised. In the interim, the admittedly outdated version of the *DSM* typically was being used in the legal system without questioning its reliability and validity with respect to each different type of disorder that is being diagnosed. Unfortunately, the revised version may be no more reliable or valid, and according to many critics less so, particularly if *DSM-V* is relied upon in the courtroom without substantial scrutiny.

At the same time, both in the United States[95] and Great Britain, numerous public concerns have been raised about the frequency of "miscarriages of justice based on discredited expert witnesses"[96] in a variety of cases in which medical and other types of scientific evidence was later proven to be false or misleading. According to the Mathematical Association of America, even something as seemingly "objective" and verifiable as mathematics frequently has been misused and misapplied in the courtroom.[97] As one legal scholar wrote more than twenty years ago, "[t]he worst that can be said about an expert opinion is not that it is a lie—that criticism is often beside the point—but that it is unreasonable, that no competent expert in the field would hold it."[98]

Today, the ethical confusion—and sometimes even blatant hypocrisy—governing expert psychological and psychiatric testimony has produced many extreme results that help illustrate the unseemly nature of the "hired gun" problem. For example, in a Kentucky case involving harm to a woman who had been "strip searched and sexually assaulted in a McDonald's restaurant," the company's forensic psychologist, who had never personally examined the plaintiff, testified that the victim's damages should be mitigated because, although the woman had "suffered major depression and post-traumatic stress . . . she seemed more assertive and self-reliant than she was before the incident."[99]

Also, in the much-publicized Andrea Yates case, in which a severely depressed mother drowned her children, the prosecution's psychiatric expert testified that the defendant had made up her story about having hallucinations based on an episode of "Law and Order," which the psychiatrist had testified that he recalled because he was a consultant for the show. Later, when the defense fortuitously discovered no such episode had ever been aired, Yates' conviction was reversed, she received a new trial, and, in a relatively rare event, she was eventually acquitted by reason of insanity.[100]

This "hired gun" syndrome, in which many—and probably most—experts generally advocate the position of the party that is paying them, at an agreement rate that cannot possibly be attributed to coincidence or a statistical anomaly, continues to raise fundamental questions. First, when, if ever, should expert assessments be allowed to be used to satisfy any legal standards of proof, particularly if the assessments in a given case are divergent and/or contradictory? Second, if in typical cases, at most one expert or set of experts is correct and the other side is substantially or entirely wrong, how can experts as a group be trusted to give reliable and unbiased results?

Given these otherwise inexplicable differences of opinion based on which party is paying them, it appears evident that many of these experts are shading, ignoring, or distorting their professional and ethical training in order to arrive at preconceived, lawyer-orchestrated results, particularly when predicting dangerousness, in which the information being conveyed lacks reliability and validity to begin with. Such bias can be easily camouflaged because difficult to detect logical and statistical fallacies are commonly found in dangerousness assessments and testing anyway,[101] especially in courtrooms where judges and jurors, who must reach ultimate conclusions based on that dangerousness evidence, generally are far less able than the experts to understand such fallacies. How much of this "bad science" may be unintentional is unknown, but whether deliberate or not, the resulting "confirmation bias" more than likely will support the party that has retained that expert.

Making such matters even worse, unprofessional, incompetent, and unethical behavior has spread beyond the experts themselves to those who are responsible for conducting and publishing the studies upon which expert opinions are based, including even the federal Food and Drug Administration.[102] Not only the forensic experts, but also the researchers and professional journals that largely determine whether a theory or concept is generally accepted in the field from which it comes—and thus is admissible as evidence—have been subject to manipulation, bias, and lack of accountability.[103] "A large and growing literature details the many ways in which research and the subsequent record can be inappropriately influenced."[104] Moreover, "[m]uch of what medical researchers conclude in their studies is misleading, exaggerated, or flat-out wrong."[105] In particular, articles published in major medical journals about drug trials have been distorted by the apparently prevalent practice of authors only reporting those outcomes which are favorable and hiding or ignoring those outcomes that are unfavorable.[106] This is the scientific equivalent of plausible deniability. Thus, what is generally accepted by mental health professionals is no longer a reliable means of separating what should be accepted in the courtroom from what should be ruled inadmissible.

In medicine generally, as well as psychiatry more specifically, the opinions of doctors are for sale, whether it is to parties in legal proceedings[107] or to drug companies.[108] Expert testimony regarding the side effects of psychiatric medications is undermined, for example, because—as a former president of the American Psychiatric Association and law professor, Allan Stone, complained—the pharmaceutical companies often "distort the results of clinical trials and mislead psychiatrists about the relative merits of their products."[109] Furthermore, the inspector general of the U.S. Department of Health and Human Services found that "90 percent of universities [which typically employ the researchers who conduct these studies] relied solely on the researchers themselves to decide whether the money they made in consulting and other relationships with drug and device makers was relevant to their government-financed research."[110] Also, drug companies have reportedly paid ghostwriters to prepare medical journal articles that are favorable to those drugs the company is selling, including antipsychotic medications, even where the safety of patients taking those drugs may be compromised.[111]

Were it possible to deal with all of these aforementioned problems in reasonably effective ways—which is doubtful—there remains the worst problem of all, which is when experts deliberately testify falsely or modify their opinions in order to arrive at a predetermined result that is consistent with the view held by the party paying the expert to testify. Social science journals now openly discuss without much impact what should be done about medical or psychological experts whose court testimony is dishonest in the sense that they know that their statements are "false or deceptive,"[112] or the research that they rely on is tainted by obvious conflicts of interest.[113]

In recent years, the state of Mississippi's medical board responded to the "hired gun" problem by approving expert witness regulations, which could result in the loss of medical licenses for doctors who testify falsely. Initially, the American Medical Association (AMA) encouraged other state medical boards to do the same thing because fraudulent testimony was deemed unprofessional conduct.[114] Similarly, the American Psychiatric Association's *Psychiatric News* warned its readers about such "heightened scrutiny" by medical boards and suggested that psychiatrists need to be better trained and prepared when they testify.[115]

Subsequently, however, based on the outcries of many of its members, the AMA reconsidered its position and passed a policy resolution intended to protect doctors from public scrutiny. State medical boards were urged to adopt a recommended policy that would make doctors' testimony part of the practice of medicine. This would mean that most such improprieties would be subject to peer review and possible internal sanctions by their colleagues, rather than external sanctions from a board or tribunal accountable to the public.[116]

The situation certainly is no better, and in some ways worse, for forensic psychologists, who are governed by ethical guidelines that are "aspirational" standards that cannot be enforced.[117] Moreover, the American Bar Association has refused to endorse standards that would provide ethical guidance about the "relationship . . . between experts and the lawyers who retain them on behalf of clients" because they were deemed unnecessary and counterproductive.[118]

For all these reasons, the foundation for determining whether an expert opinion is based on specialized knowledge that is generally accepted in the professional community from which it comes has been compromised, along with many of the experts themselves and the "generally accepted" information that they and the courts rely on, especially where predictions of dangerousness is concerned. Furthermore, there is little reason to think that this situation will improve soon. Experts generally are well-insulated from liability for what they do in the courtroom.[119] Professional licensing boards and associations rarely issue sanctions against their colleagues, and the AMA has implemented measures intended to reduce the number of external sanctions. There is even serious debate whether any sanctions would be beneficial,[120] although a few states, like Mississippi, have concluded that sanctions are necessary to protect the public.[121] As one law professor explained, "there appears to be a fair degree of resigned acceptance of the status quo. In large measure this is because of a lack of agreed upon ethical standards,"[122] as demonstrated by the ABA's inability to reach a consensus on this topic.

Overwhelmingly, respondents and defendants with perceived mental disabilities who are deemed to be dangerous ultimately lose in the courtroom. Time and time again, appellate courts uphold lower court decisions based, at least in part, on the conclusion that the jury (or judge) is able to weigh the expert evidence and reach a fair dangerousness determination, even when the expert evidence is at best divided or even favors the losing side. These judicial leaps of faith occur in death penalty cases, involuntary commitments of all types, and other critical legal decisions involving incarceration and the deprivation of fundamental civil rights, liberties, and freedoms of persons with mental disabilities.

Thus, an admittedly "failed paradigm"—presented as being reliable by often biased, misleading, or sometimes even dishonest or incompetent experts—is now the most important factor justifying incarceration and other extreme deprivations of rights and freedoms for hundreds of thousands of Americans with mental disabilities annually, including, on occasion, their execution. This situation, as bad as it has become, begs two questions: How is such misleading or corrupt expert evidence allowed into the courtroom in the first place? Why is it so much worse when expert evidence of dangerousness is involved?

JUDGES AS THE COURTROOM GATEKEEPERS

In theory, judges are supposed to act as gatekeepers in the courtroom to ensure that jurors—or judges if they are the triers of fact—consider only relevant and reasonably valid and reliable expert testimony, which will aid the court in making its ultimate determination.[123] Whether this actually occurs is subject to much debate—and substantial doubts—by social scientists and legal scholars alike.[124] When the admissibility of dangerousness expert evidence is the ultimate issue to be decided, however, there is little question that the judicial gatekeeper role typically breaks down. "Judges routinely defer to psychiatric assessments of danger,"[125] so much so that reportedly judicial fact finders agree with the experts "between ninety and one hundred percent" of the time.[126] Courts have all but conceded that the failed dangerousness paradigm and the unseemly "battle of the experts" are necessary evils that should be permitted in the courtroom because the high—and often overwhelming—potential for injustice will somehow be negated by our adversary system. A judge's main focus as a gatekeeper is not on the relative truthfulness or value of the testimony itself, nor the truthfulness of those who testify. Rather, the court's focus is on the increasingly flexible rules of evidence and courtroom procedures that apply to the admissibility of that evidence, which favor those with the most resources and influence.

Typically, these particular courtroom rules and procedures are supposed to be governed or substantially directed by the *Daubert/Frye* collection of admissibility standards, although there is a unique and extremely troubling exception that is made for expert evidence of dangerousness, which effectively undermines even these already-flexible admissibility standards. Furthermore, in deciding whether to admit dangerousness evidence of experts as relevant, valid, and reliable, judges, like most people in our society—even those who otherwise are well-educated—tend to be statistically and empirically deficient, which makes them less able and less likely to properly understand and weigh the actual significance of the dangerousness evidence.[127]

A substantial minority of states largely follow the rules that were established in 1923 in *Frye v. United States*.[128] Initially, the primary admissibility consideration was whether expert evidence or testimony was founded on a well-recognized scientific principle or discovery that had "gained general acceptance in the particular field in which it belongs."[129] Since then, all of the *Frye* jurisdictions have added the requirement that the "scientific, technical, or other specialized knowledge [must] assist the trier of fact to understand the evidence or to determine the fact in issue."[130] Thus, even if the specialized knowledge is generally accepted, it may be excluded if a judge concludes that it will mislead the jury. As a practical matter, though, this rarely happens with dangerousness evidence or testimony.

A clear majority of jurisdictions generally follow, with certain wrinkles, the U.S. Supreme Court's 1993 ruling in *Daubert v. Merrell Dow Pharmaceuticals, Inc.*,[131] which applies to all federal courts through the Federal Rules of Evidence, and to courts in the many states that have adopted the federal rules, or close variations thereof.[132] Under *Daubert*, the judge is the "gatekeeper for the admissibility of scientific, technical, or other specialized knowledge, including psychiatric, psychological, and other disability-related expert evidence and testimony."[133] In theory, the judge's role is to decide whether expert evidence or testimony "is suffi-ciently trustworthy . . . to prove or disprove" the ultimate legal issue in dispute.[134] The key factors in determining trustworthiness are the evi-dence's relevance to the issue being decided, and its accuracy, validity, and reliability.

Whether a jurisdiction follows *Daubert* or *Frye*, ultimately the admis-sibility decision is placed in the discretion of judges, who, despite their judicial training, are still prone to bias, prejudice, outside influence and pressure, and mistakes because they are human beings who represent the communities from which they come. What judges feel and think—and the communities or constituencies to whom they are accountable or beholden to feel and think—about persons who have mental disabilities often influ-ences judicial decisions, especially if the judges are elected, which most of them are. Negative pretexual thoughts and feelings about persons with mental disabilities are referred to as "sanism," which, as discussed else-where, is comparable in its intensity to extreme racism, but is not widely viewed as being socially unacceptable. Thus, sanism continues to be ex-pressed and practiced rather openly throughout our society, including within the American legal system.[135]

In addition, most judges, whether they are supposed to follow *Daubert* or *Frye*, give considerable weight to the legal principle that specialized knowledge that has been generally accepted in the field from which it comes should be admissible in court. Unfortunately, generally accepted does not mean that the evidence has been validated scientifically, empiri-cally, or even objectively, or that it is reliable. Rather, the standard can be—and often is—met based on the opinions of the most influential people in a profession. What is most influential is reflected in the articles published in professional journals, which may be—and apparently often are—negatively influenced by professional politics, personal and profes-sional self-interests, what is currently in vogue academically, and, as discussed earlier, by money and other corrupting influences.[136] Thus, the validity and reliability of expert evidence and testimony often are ques-tionable to begin with.[137] These questions are magnified considerably when the ultimate issue involves psychiatric and psychological evidence, and magnified much more with regard to expert evidence about danger-ousness.

Even without the overwhelming prejudice toward people with mental disorders, conditions, and aberrations that our society practices and that courts tend to reflect in their rulings, empirical observations reveal that judges often "rely on intuition" at least in part when they make their decisions.[138] This "intuitive system appears to have a powerful effect on the judges' decision making. The intuitive approach . . . can lead to erroneous and unjust outcomes."[139] Especially when sanism influences and informs such intuition, the potential for error and injustice increases substantially because, as one law professor has written, "judges rely with surprising frequency on false, debatable, or untested factual premises . . . in the service of other goals."[140]

The other goal in dangerousness legal proceedings is that judges are trying to protect their communities, their reputations, and their career aspirations from: (1) the unknown—and typically highly exaggerated and inflated—possibility that a respondent or defendant with a mental disability who is released will act criminally or antisocially in the future with potentially harmful and even catastrophic results; or (2) the increasingly likely prospect that people and the media in the community will roundly criticize or try to remove the judge for releasing such an individual, whether or not something bad happens, and whether or not there was reasonable justification for the release.

The Dangerousness Exception to the Admissibility of Expert Evidence and Testimony

For many years, there has been a fundamentally inequitable legal exception that applies only to dangerousness, which has made this type of expert evidence and testimony particularly unfair. In the 1983 U.S. Supreme Court decision *Barefoot v. Estelle*,[141] a majority of the justices ruled that expert testimony on future dangerousness should be allowed in death penalty cases, even though the American Psychiatric Association had submitted an *amicus curiae* brief explaining that such evidence was unreliable,[142] and thus not generally accepted in the field from which it came. Incredibly, the Court decided that such evidence should not be excluded because the defense was unable to prove that "psychiatrists are always wrong with respect to future dangerousness," even though the existing empirical evidence showed that psychiatrists were wrong "most of the time."[143] The majority said it believed that because of the adversary process, juries would properly "sort out the reliable from the unreliable evidence and opinion about future dangerousness."[144]

Justices Blackmun, Brennan, and Marshall strongly dissented from such spurious reasoning, pointing out that the empirical evidence indicated that at best psychiatrists were able to predict dangerousness accurately in only one of three attempts, and thus such evidence should never be admitted.[145] As it has turned out, the dissent was correct. Unfortunately, unreliable evidence of dangerousness continues to be admitted with very little judicial scrutiny. The *Barefoot* decision and its progeny have created a dangerousness exception to the prevailing admissibility standards for specialized knowledge that has carried over to all types of dangerousness cases in which such evidence and testimony is proffered. As one federal court judge observed a number of years ago, "the U.S. Supreme Court should reconsider the question of whether evidence of future dangerousness should ever be admitted into evidence because it is both "unreliable and unscientific."[146] Yet nothing has ever been done to remedy this miscarriage of justice.

Despite the fact that these predictions rarely meet basic admissibility standards, dangerousness—either based on the subjective impressions of jurors (or judges) alone or, more typically, opinions of experts as interpreted by juries (or judges)—continues to be routinely and uncritically relied upon as the primary consideration in death penalty and other sentencing, conditional releases, civil and quasi-civil involuntary commitment cases, and various other types of cases involving the deprivation of fundamental individual rights.[147] As long as the specialized knowledge regarding dangerousness is generally used by "experts" in that field, it does not seem to matter how unreliable and inaccurate those predictions may be. Nor does it matter that the experts who rely on such evidence are paid well for doing so and generally shade—and many even deliberately distort or manipulate—their testimony to comply with the advocacy needs of the parties who retain them.[148]

On top of all the questions and doubts about psychiatric, psychological, and other mental health evidence, juries and judges tend to accept the reliability and overall accuracy of such evidence if it supports a dangerousness finding in order to incarcerate, otherwise control, or even execute a person with a mental disorder, condition, or aberration.[149] Not surprisingly in these proceedings involving respondents with mental disabilities, who generally are presumed to be dangerous to begin with, jurors and judges tend to be heavily swayed by credentialed professionals representing the governments' positions. These pretextual decisions confirm our society's sanist predispositions and establish a modern tyranny of the majority.

Not surprisingly, there is a serious judicial double standard at play in these proceedings that involve persons with mental disabilities. The widely acknowledged problems with behavioral evidence tend to be rigorously taken into account by courts—often at the direction of legislatures—to make such evidence inadmissible when it would benefit the person who is to be subjected to incarceration, execution, or other deprivations of rights. Conversely, such evidence is largely left to jurors or judges to sort out when it may lead to incarceration, execution, or other deprivations of rights. The applicable due process rules and procedures consistently favor governments over these individuals with mental disabilities who are the subjects of these proceedings.

For instance, whereas it is a relatively rare event for mental health professionals to be allowed to use their expertise in the courtroom to challenge the reliability of eyewitness testimony[150] or to prove a defendant's lack of criminal responsibility,[151] experts generally are allowed, with minimal judicial scrutiny, to testify as to a defendant's or respondent's future dangerousness, even though the social science data indicates that these assessments of human behavior are highly unreliable. These experts even are allowed to testify that defendants are likely to be lying, not because they told a lie, but because they have been diagnosed with a mental disorder associated with lying.[152] As John La Fond and Mary Durham astutely observed nearly twenty years ago—in explaining why they believed that our nation would soon return to using "asylums" (secure detention centers) to confine persons with mental disabilities—the legal system values psychiatric expertise that contributes to the social control functions of the law and disparages the same type of expertise when it is used to show that individuals lack the culpability to be punished to the full extent the law allows.[153]

This double standard also applies to psychiatric and psychological evidence more generally. Mental health law scholar Christopher Slobogin has opined that: "If juries can be trusted to treat highly prejudicial prediction testimony [of dangerousness] with appropriate caution in deciding whether to put someone to death, it is hard to see why states should be able to keep from the jury psychiatric evidence on mens rea" that might reduce the charge.[154] While it is difficult to dispute the basic logic of Slobogin's conclusion, the overwhelming evidence suggests that his premise is misplaced. The far more important concern for our legal system should be exactly the opposite: if jurors can be barred from considering psychiatric and psychological evidence, which might diminish a defendant's responsibility for the crime charged because such evidence is too unreliable, how can jurors be allowed to consider such evidence about dangerousness, which usually is even more unreliable?

Posing the question in this way should be more compelling based on the numbers of Americans with mental disabilities who are actually caught up in this legal double standard. While the number of defendants who use mental status defenses always has been very small—reportedly no more than 1 percent overall even in their heyday—and the number of those who are successful represents a fraction of that small total, the hundreds of thousands of people who are incarcerated, executed, or otherwise deprived of their fundamental rights, freedoms, and liberties based on the dangerousness standards are a much more significant number by any measure. Moreover, there are cries within the mental health community that many more people with mental disorders should be subjected to involuntary treatment in secure detention facilities—or under the threat that they will be sent to such a facility—if they do not comply with compelled care and treatment and other intrusive restrictions. [155]

Making the situation even more unfair for these defendants and respondents with mental disabilities, who are being targeted with indefinite incarceration, lifetimes of supervision and monitoring, inhumane treatment, other infringements on their fundamental rights—and even death— is the fact that within the legal system these individuals generally are much less likely, as compared to the government, to be able to obtain the expert testimony they need to defend themselves because hiring experts is expensive. "Poorer litigants [are] at a distinct disadvantage" in obtaining expert testimony [156] and probably no group of litigants is poorer and less able to find expert assistance than defendants, respondents, and inmates with mental disabilities.

Thus, if the only choice is between eliminating all such evidence and testimony or admitting most of it, including dangerousness, then clearly it all should be eliminated. Fortunately, the much better answer in terms of logic, statistics, social science, and legal fairness is to: eliminate all expert evidence supporting an individual's future dangerousness until it can be shown to be persuasive in the courtroom based on objective standards of relevance, reliability, and validity consistent with the applicable burden of proof and other due process standards.

At the same time, such psychiatric and psychological evidence and testimony should be admitted to shed light on a defendant's present or past mental status if it meets applicable standards of relevance, reliability, and validity in the context of the legal standards that apply to the party proposing to introduce such evidence. In other words, the admissibility of mental status expert evidence of any kind should be assessed, taking into consideration the burden and standard of proof and other due process standards that the party seeking to introduce or consider such evidence is supposed to meet. As noted earlier, for example, risk assessment "in most cases" is unreliable when it is used to predict a high risk of violence or antisocial behaviors attributed to specific individuals, but may be quite useful in demonstrating that those same individuals have a low risk of acting violently or antisocially.[157] Also, where the standard of proof to rebut an assertion of dangerousness is much lower, the legal threshold of admissibility should be lower as well.

CONCLUSION

The two leading mental health professions—the American Psychiatric Association and the American Psychological Association—have largely looked the other way when future dangerousness evidence and testimony has been misused. Empirical studies demonstrate that such evidence lacks validity and reliability in clinical environments, much less in the uncontrolled and even more subjective context of our advocacy-oriented courtrooms using diverse legal standards and procedures. A significant number of psychiatrists and psychologists are retained to testify in these contrived dangerousness proceedings, and many of them do so in ways that disrespect themselves and their professions. Moving in line for their share of the relatively lucrative courtroom compensation in dangerousness cases are neuroscientists, who profess a new expertise in uncovering violent tendencies based on computer-rendered neuroimaging. Down the road there may even be mental health professionals who measure the "degrees of empathy" that respondents exhibit.[158] Also in line are so-called sex offender experts, who have convinced courts that they are able to assess dangerousness based on blood flow in the penises of respondents who are compelled to view images that are sexually inappropriate.

None of these questionable, often discredited, and sometimes unethical forensic practices would occur, however, without our flawed legal system. It has established and countenanced, and continues to expand dangerousness-based standards in order to incarcerate, execute, and otherwise restrict the fundamental rights, liberties, and freedoms of more and more people with mental disabilities who are deemed "likely" to be violent, harmful, or antisocial. Legislatures and the courts encourage and facilitate the use of such unreliable future dangerousness testimony by creating and applying special rules of evidence that allow this testimony to be admissible. As a result, miscarriages of justice have become commonplace whenever courts order involuntary commitments, executions, or other intrusive restrictions against people with mental disorders, conditions, or aberrations based on flawed findings of or impressions about future dangerousness. Sadly, relatively few people seem to care what happens to these individuals in our legal system, as long as members of the public perceive themselves, their families and their friends to be safer and more secure.

5

ASSUMPTIONS BASED ON THE UNKNOWABLE

Predictions of Dangerousness in Civil and Criminal Proceedings

While sanism and various evidentiary, procedural, logical, statistical, and professional problems generally undermine outcomes in a vast majority of cases in which predictions of dangerousness are allowed, important distinctions exist based on the type of legal proceedings at issue and how they are characterized. Some may be deemed civil, some quasi-civil, and others criminal. The due process rules, procedures, and safeguards change significantly depending on these broad characterizations. In addition, while expert dangerousness evidence and testimony is admissible in most of these proceedings, some dangerousness determinations are left entirely to the judge and/or the jury. What unites all of these proceedings, however, is that the fundamental rights, liberties, and freedoms of persons with mental disabilities may be substantially diminished because they have been "accused" of being dangerous based on socially harmful acts that they might commit in the unknowable future.

INVOLUNTARY CIVIL COMMITMENT AND RELATED RIGHTS INTRUSIONS

Increasingly, jurisdictions have been employing a variety of legal tactics to justify—and in many instances mandate—prolonged incarceration, supervision monitoring, and/or other rights deprivations of persons with mental disabilities through the use of involuntary civil inpatient and outpatient commitments and detentions. In the past, civil involuntary commitment abuses—which were even more prevalent, unreasonable, and harmful—centered on mental patients and other persons thought to have mental disabilities who were indefinitely confined in large, isolated state institutions. Ostensibly they were there to receive humane care and treatment, which typically turned out to be custodial and substandard, and too often cruel, degrading, and abusive as well.[1] Similar types of abuses against persons with mental disabilities are more common today in secure detention facilities for those who are quasi-civilly committed or in jails and prisons where even more persons with mental disabilities actually reside.[2]

Numerous examples of mistreatment or unfairness also occur today with regard to the more modern types of civil involuntary commitments,[3] but as compared to the horrific past, these abuses are less common and less blatant, and the periods of confinement tend to be considerably shorter. At the same time, the number of civil involuntary commitments has been increasing in recent years, along with the social pressures to involuntarily "treat" and coercively control more people with mental disabilities. Court decisions are increasing nationwide as new legal schemes are being passed and new legal inequities are being litigated.[4] Most states, for example, have enacted commitment schemes that use indeterminate outpatient monitoring, supervision, and other restrictions in order to coerce patients into taking powerful antipsychotic medications based on threats of prolonged confinement if they do not.[5] There also is building pressure—much of it well-intentioned—to lengthen "temporary involuntary detentions," which would substantially reduce due process requirements as compared to having to initiate formal commitment proceedings.[6]

One of the main reasons inpatient civil commitments are shorter today than in the past—other than the widespread use of antipsychotic medications—is that confining patients and other residents is expensive, and normally states and counties must pay for those costs. Fiscal realities, more than due process, contribute substantially to a revolving door in which many adult mental patients experience multiple commitments over many years, rather than one lengthy period of involuntary commitment.[7] Ultimately, though, if a state or county pushes for release, it most probably will be approved, and if release is opposed, it most probably will be denied.

Moreover, once these particularly vulnerable patients are dumped back into their communities, typically there are very limited resources available to provide them with the comprehensive services they need to survive, much less thrive, including the absence of basic essentials such as decent housing, sufficient food, transportation, basic medical care, and non-coercive psychiatric treatments.[8] Even antipsychotic medications for those who want to take them voluntarily are not always guaranteed and may be unavailable until the person is involuntarily committed;[9] then a very common risk becomes excessive and/or inappropriate medication(s) in order to help ensure that the person is easy to manage and obeys the many rules that are established to govern that person's life in these structured inpatient and outpatient settings.[10] This type of coercion and medication abuse occurs not only in traditional involuntary civil mental health settings for adults, but apparently much more so in residential and nursing home settings where particularly vulnerable populations with mental disabilities are forced to live, including children, adolescents, racial and ethnic minorities, and older Americans.[11]

Despite fiscal constraints, there has been a growing movement to try to substantially increase the number of people who are forcibly treated using inpatient or outpatient commitment, or the threat of such commitments. There are several reasons why this is happening.[12] To begin with, segments within the psychiatric and mental health communities, as well as many parents and relatives of persons with mental disorders, are pushing for more involuntary and coercive treatments. These are last resort solutions—as opposed to planned remedies—to potentially improve the lives of the proposed patients, but also to improve the lives and work situations of the parents, the relatives, and the mental health professionals who tire of caring for and trying to control difficult-to-manage and sometimes aggressive patients in the community without adequate resources.

Yet ultimately this involuntary, coercive approach has proven to be extremely shortsighted. Coercion and incarceration are not humane or effective answers for the vast majority of people with severe mental disabilities, and probably is not be the best answer for any of these individuals. For many years reformers have counseled that nothing less than a holistic approach is going to work well.[13] As law professor Richard Bonnie has observed, broadening the commitment criteria will not have much impact on "the overall problem [of violence] because the issue is getting people . . . services voluntarily before they get to a point where civil commitment is a possibility."[14] He believes convincing them "to voluntarily agree to treatment and improving . . . [their] access to services are the best approaches to ensuring success."[15]

Second, the federal government and others have documented that the system of voluntary community mental health treatment throughout the United States is grossly inadequate, especially for those persons with the most serious mental impairments.[16] Medicaid in particular—which has been the primary mechanism for delivering health care to poor people, including those with serious mental disabilities—continues to have a strong institutional bias, which even today more often than not impedes or actually prevents funding for voluntary community programs.[17] Recently more states have been experimenting with various types of Medicaid waiver programs that provide improved community care for a significant but relatively small percentage of people with mental disabilities. Unfortunately, the available alternatives for most of these patients—and proposed patients—has been inadequate care and treatment in the community, involuntary treatment, or arrest and imprisonment.[18] Furthermore, with the precipitous downturn in our economy, particularly for state and local governments, even these modest Medicaid waiver programs are being reduced or eliminated, along with other essential complementary social service programs, particularly housing and income maintenance.[19]

Third, the public—fueled by views like those of psychiatrist E. Fuller Torrey,[20] the Treatment Advocacy Center, the media generally, certain groups representing the parents and relatives of persons with serious mental disabilities, certain politicians, and others[21] —is being frightened into believing that forcibly treating persons with mental disorders, conditions, or aberrations based on unreliable predictions of their future dangerousness will substantially lower the homicide rate, and prevent police officers, students, and other citizens from being killed by emotionally disturbed individuals.[22] The type of catastrophic tragedies that happened at Columbine, Virginia Tech, Northern Illinois University, Tucson, Aurora, Sandy Hook and other sites of mass killings have fueled such beliefs and speculations. In turn, legislatures have acted and been pressured to act, demonstratively, in order to convince the public that they are actually doing something meaningful to prevent such tragedies from occurring.

What news reports rarely reveal is that the main reasons that people with mental disabilities as a group *appear* to be particularly violent have much more to do with media coverage, their dire economic circumstances, other social problems that have been neglected, and the grossly misleading information that is being used to draw the conclusion that persons with mental disabilities are more violent than almost any other group. To begin with, individuals with severe mental disabilities are far more likely to reside in high crime environments; to lack the basic necessities of life; to be vilified, stigmatized, isolated, and feared by society and their neighbors; and to be victims of crime.[23] As a result, many people with mental disabilities are under extreme and sustained stress that could be prevented, and still their rates of violence—with the exception of a very few types of mental conditions or disorders exacerbated by severe substance abuse—are only slightly higher than those of everybody else in our society.[24]

When all the various social and environmental stresses upon them become uncomfortably intense, people with serious mental disabilities— like any other persons under extreme stress—are more likely to act out in antisocial and bizarre ways; a few even act violently; and a very few extremely alienated and emotionally fragile, but often intelligent and highly capable and organized individuals become so disassociated from themselves and society that they decide to end everything, including themselves. Unfortunately, our society provides them with relatively easy access to the arms, munitions, instruction videos and manuals, and other supports they need for carrying out such massacres. The reality is that only a small minority of these extremely alienated and emotionally fragile, but often intelligent and highly capable and organized individuals, resort to extreme violence. It does not make sense to coercively detain and treat individuals with perceived mental health problems, who are not currently acting violently, out of a fear that some of them may do so in the future. The much better solution is to focus our resources on prevention, holistic community-based care, and changing public attitudes about persons with mental disabilities and violence.

Nevertheless, as our involuntary civil commitment standards continue to be broadened, the number of people who are involuntarily detained and treated will increase significantly, even though such schemes are based on two legal fictions. First, the resulting deprivations of liberty due to commitments are euphemistically characterized as paternalistic actions by the state to provide care and treatment to persons in need, and public health measures to protect our communities. As a consequence, heightened, criminal-like due process protections are rarely mandated or used, even though, if certain criteria are met, the lengths of incarceration or other forms of intrusive state controls may be longer than criminal sanctions for the same acts[25] and the conditions of confinement can be even worse than in traditional jails and prisons.[26]

Second, the clear and convincing standard of proof that the Constitution mandates in such "civil" proceedings, instead of proof beyond a reasonable doubt, is further diluted in practice because juries and/or judges are charged with making the ultimate legal decisions. These courtroom arbiters of fact and fiction, like most other people in our society, tend to be swayed by pretextual assumptions that persons with mental disabilities are inherently dangerous. Those assumptions are very likely to be confirmed by the opinions of state-retained experts, who probably will not be retained in future cases if their opinions lead to respondents being released more than rarely. The incentives that line up on the side of ensuring community safety will normally overwhelm the incentives for protecting individual rights of respondents and defendants with mental disabilities.

The centerpiece of modern involuntary civil commitment is its reliance on mental health experts to predict dangerousness—or some future behavior that is somewhat similar or seemingly related to dangerousness to self, others, or the community. The experts representing the state typically provide the courts with assessments, and testimony based on those assessments, which almost always support and justify confinement or the use of other coercive measures. The risks of liability and other disincentives for state-employed treatment providers for incarcerating mental patients inappropriately are considerably less than for failing to incarcerate them if those patients should ever do serious harm. This is what is known as a "black swan" type of scenario, in which an unlikely event, if it should occur, has the potential for social or personal catastrophe[27]—in this instance for the careers of those treatment providers who are willing to testify that a given patient is unlikely to be dangerous in the future. For this reason, it has long been advocated that mental health professionals be substantially immune from civil liability for harm to third parties in recommending that patients be released.[28] Unfortunately, this type of liability has been expanded, which has had an even greater chilling effect on the objectivity of those professionals.

Also, in civil and quasi-civil commitment proceedings of all types, due process is further undermined because the "quality of counsel assigned to represent [these] individuals . . . is, in most jurisdictions, mediocre or worse."[29] According to law professor Michael Perlin, one "constant in modern mental disability law . . . is the near-universal reality that counsel assigned to represent individuals at involuntary civil commitment cases is likely to be ineffective."[30] Furthermore, the right to independent expert assistance is limited in these cases at best,[31] and typically there are insufficient funds available for respondents to hire their own experts to assist their lawyers in preparing for these commitment hearings and related proceedings.[32] "[P]atients are significantly disadvantaged because judges will inevitably defer to expert testimony in deciding whether to authorize the confinement of the civil committee."[33] Also, "psychiatrists [and other mental health professionals] have a well-recognized bias toward treatment [even if it means 'certifying a patient as dangerous']."[34]

By employing mental health experts as social agents to do our governments'—and often their own—biddings in the courtroom in ways that make little scientific, empirical, logical, medical, or psychological sense, care and treatment for patients has been compromised and corrupted and individual rights denigrated.[35] Many, and perhaps most, mental patients with severe conditions who could benefit from consensual treatment or habilitation fail to receive—or refuse—needed care, for a variety of reasons: the lack of public resources devoted to voluntary mental health care; the decision to spend most of the limited public funds that exist in order to arrest, try, commit, and care for those who are deemed dangerous, rather than to provide effective voluntary care in the community for those individuals; patients' reasonable fear that if they accept voluntary care, it can easily become coerced care; overreliance on antipsychotic medications—with their unwanted and often physically harmful side effects, including, on rare occasions, death; patients' poor insight into their treatment needs and options for care; and patients' perceptions and feelings that mental health care and treatment in this country is too often ineffective, counterproductive, abusive, and even dangerous to them.

Our mental health systems focus on coercing so-called dangerous patients into accepting care, even though the reality is that this cohort of patients—even if the individual members could be reliably identified, which is unlikely in most cases—includes a relatively significant percentage of people who have conditions that are untreatable in traditional ways with medications, do not require involuntary treatment, and/or refuse to be treated. At the same time, most people with severe mental disabilities who want and could benefit from voluntary, adequate mental health and related care and treatment or habilitation go without because they cannot afford it on their own. Thus, a significant number of these untreated or improperly treated and cared for individuals eventually act out and become part of the expanding cohort of persons with severe mental disabilities who are deemed dangerous, whether or not they really are. The following conclusion by a Canadian psychiatrist about his country's mental health system may be even more applicable to the United States, where forced hospitalization is more common and publicly funded mental health less available than in Canada. "[H]aving untreatable features can . . . lead to hospitalization, [while] having a treatable mental illness . . . has the potential to lead to chronic, partially treated illness . . . where potentially effective treatment modalities exist."[36]

Consensual care and treatment can make a substantial difference if it is implemented in a comprehensive way, nationally. In fact, it is far more likely to be effective than our current fragmented and inhumane, coercive programs. New York City, for example, has "pioneered the strategy of providing [certain] homeless people not just with housing but with drug treatment, psychiatric care and other services they need to live successfully on their own," an approach that is "many times less expensive than jails or beds in psychiatric hospitals."[37] Providing largely voluntary, subsidized mental health and related services to persons with severe mental disabilities will be far more effective in controlling dangerousness, and far less inhumane, than trying to lock up everyone who is deemed to have a mental disorder, condition, or aberration and thought to be dangerous.[38] As *Olmstead v. L.C.*[39] and cases interpreting that landmark U.S. Supreme Court decision counsel in interpreting the Americans with Disabilities Act,[40] we can help many more people with severe mental disabilities and better protect society's interests for less cost if we have widely available, integrated, consensual care, treatment, and supportive services in the community.

Predictions of Dangerousness Related to Involuntary Civil Commitment

Generally

Involuntary civil commitment of adults and older juveniles—whether it is to a facility that houses persons with mental illnesses, intellectual disabilities, developmental disabilities, or addictions—is largely based on findings of dangerousness to self or others, although the definition of dangerousness has been systematically expanded over time to include many different harmful acts or omissions that are not directly connected with any actual violence or bodily harm. In a vast majority of civil involuntary commitment proceedings, proof of likely dangerousness (or harmful or aggressive behavior) by clear and convincing evidence is determinative.[41] Unfortunately, because there is a presumption in our legal system that mental health experts can reliably predict dangerousness—a presumption that in an overwhelming percentage of cases cannot be demonstrated empirically—too often there are no effective means for the affected individuals to successfully challenge courtroom opinions about their dangerousness made by government experts, which juries and judges tend to accept.[42] Thus, even in these involuntary civil commitment proceedings—which tend to be somewhat less arbitrary and unfair than quasi-civil commitments and conditional releases in the criminal justice system—due process, both in terms of fundamental fairness and equal protection, is flawed. More often than not, legal representation for the respondents is nonexistent or less than adequate and the stereotypical presumption of dangerousness is difficult to overcome even with adequate legal representation.

Dangerousness in the civil commitment context has its own set of meanings. These legal determinations largely depend on the opinions of mental health experts as to whether the respondents have a mental disorder or condition that makes that person a broadly defined danger to themselves or others if they were allowed to live in the community with whatever resources are likely to be available, which tend to be inadequate. The applicable legal standards, with only a few exceptions, require predictions of dangerousness to be made. Broadly construed, that includes antisocial behaviors that are considered harmful to others or harmful to oneself, such as grave disability, a deteriorating mental condition, or an inability to survive safely in the community.[43]

Whether the governing civil involuntary commitment standards involve persons with mental illnesses, intellectual disabilities, developmental disabilities, substance abuse (either drugs or alcohol), or other disabilities, the formula almost always has two key elements: the existence of diagnosed mental, developmental, or intellectual impairment; and a link between a diagnosed impairment and past, present, or future behaviors that supposedly make the person a likely future threat to others or themselves.[44] In addition, many jurisdictions add a third element: that the respondent needs inpatient treatment or habilitation,[45] although most courts have ruled that adequate treatment or habilitation does not have to be provided as a constitutional matter, unless the state clearly and unambiguously promises to do so, which rarely happens. Even when the promise of treatment is made, plenty of legal arguments exist that allow governments to dilute or renege on those treatment promises.[46]

Also, most—but not all—minors may be forcibly committed to an institution or facility by their parents or legal guardians, if the admitting mental health professional(s) at the facility—who may well be influenced by economic pressures to fill facility beds—agrees that involuntary commitment is warranted[47] or because there is no other place for the child to go. Furthermore, many teens and emancipated minors are subject to the same flawed commitment criteria as adults: a mental impairment loosely linked to broadly defined notions of dangerousness.[48] In addition, individuals who are viewed as frail or elderly may be involuntarily dumped into various nursing or rehabilitation facilities by their loved ones, guardians, or state and local governments when they are perceived to be mentally incompetent or too frail to make their own care and treatment decisions.[49]

The mental health expert's role in the adult or adult-like involuntary commitment process is to establish or refute the proposition that the respondent has a mental impairment that is covered by the governing statute, and that the impairment has resulted in some type of dangerous behavior—or a behavior that resembles dangerousness in that it appears to place the respondent, others, or the community at an increased risk of physical, mental, or financial harm. Generally, both clinically and legally, whether a person has a covered mental impairment appears to be a much less scrutinized determination—although not necessarily more valid, reliable, and accurate—than whether that impairment is likely to result in dangerousness.[50] If experts base their diagnoses on a condition contained in the American Psychiatric Association's *Diagnostic and Statistical Manual* (*DSM*) and apply established diagnostic criteria, then—as a practical matter—it normally is presumed to be correct, even though the U.S. Supreme Court[51] has observed, along with many mental health experts and social scientists, that "the history of diagnostic classification in psychology and psychiatry is fraught with the problem of unreliability."[52]

Involuntary inpatient commitment typically turns on whether broadly defined dangerousness is established and usually, but not always,[53] whether the mental impairment is linked to that dangerous-like behavior. Dangerousness—or a behavior that resembles dangerousness—is constitutionally required to justify involuntary civil commitment, unless the state can demonstrate that it will provide the respondent with something more than custodial care,[54] such as a promise of treatment or rehabilitation. Statutorily, however, an overwhelming number of state jurisdictions require dangerousness or something akin to dangerousness.[55] The federal government is not directly involved in this type of civil incarceration because traditionally it has lacked the authority to commit individuals to civil mental health facilities. Involuntary civil commitment has been an exclusively state function, although there is now a gray area after the U.S. Supreme Court upheld the federal government's limited role in quasi-civil commitments of federal inmates through the Bureau of Prisons.[56]

Dangerousness to Others or to Self

Most involuntary civil commitments are based on harm to others or self, although the precise legal criteria may differ significantly—and even fundamentally—from jurisdiction to jurisdiction. Generally, the legal definition of what constitutes a legally significant harm continues to expand under both branches of dangerousness. If respondents have been diagnosed with a mental disorder or impairment that has resulted in their having committed recent overt acts of serious violence against others or themselves, it is likely that there will be minimal opposition to incarcerating those respondents for a short period of time. Nevertheless, such clearcut circumstances are the exceptions, rather than the general rule. In most civil involuntary commitment cases there are legal complexities, variations, and ambiguities, which make assessments of dangerousness far more tenuous and less reliable. Typically, clinical assessments and judgments based on those assessments are unreliable predictions that harmful behavior will occur sometime in the future, or that past harmful behavior continues to affect how the respondent will behave now and in the future.

The ultimate question that the judicial trier of fact—the judge or jury—should be answering in involuntary civil and for that matter quasi-civil commitment cases is not whether the court believes a respondent is or continues to be potentially dangerous, but whether the respondent is or continues to be currently dangerous based on the applicable standard of proof. Being a danger to others is a criterion that exists in all adult involuntary civil and quasi-civil commitment schemes.[57] Depending on the jurisdiction, however, the evidence that may be used to establish dangerousness to others may differ substantially, depending on how the governing jurisdiction's statutory scheme and court interpretations address three factors: bodily harm versus other types of harm, such as economic or psychological injuries; actual harm versus threats of harm; and immediate harm versus less foreseeable future harm.

Regardless of the standard, however, what is needed to establish harm to others has been expanding nationwide since 1997 when the U.S. Supreme Court determined, in a case involving the commitment of so-called sexual predators, that the "likelihood of such [dangerous] conduct in the future . . . is sufficient to satisfy constitutional *minima*"[58] Arkansas, for instance, broadened its commitment criteria to include dangerousness to self or others based on recent behavior or behavior history, as indicated by a respondent's declarations, the observations of others, or records about the respondent."[59] Utah amended its criteria to eliminate the requirement that a respondent pose an "immediate danger" to self or others, as long as the danger is "substantial."[60] And Virginia now allows involuntary commitments where a substantial likelihood exists that the respondent will cause "serious physical harm" to self or others without having to demonstrate the time frame within which such future harm is likely to occur.[61]

Danger to self is the second major category. It also exists in some form in every jurisdiction.[62] Originally, it was viewed as bodily injury to oneself, particularly suicide and the threat of imminent suicide. However, there have been many variations over the years that many jurisdictions have adopted—such as gravely disabled, unable to provide for basic needs, and the likelihood of future physical or mental harm due to a deteriorating mental condition, which have significantly stretched the notion of dangerousness to self, so that it may encompass—particularly as judicially interpreted—a broad range of potentially harmful behaviors or conditions.[63]

In addition, there are statutory schemes that allow for extended involuntary outpatient commitments that further dilute the dangerousness requirement, but they do not necessarily involve extended incarceration, unless the person fails to meet increasingly intrusive outpatient commitment conditions.[64] These schemes are primarily used to coerce patients to take prescribed antipsychotic medications and accept other intrusive treatments and restrictions on their personal rights. Outpatient commitment also may result in temporary involuntary inpatient commitment, so that the respondent may be evaluated for involuntary "care" in a secure facility pursuant to an involuntary inpatient commitment hearing, a process that may take a week or two, or more.

Like dangerousness to others, dangerousness to self has been expanding to include a much wider range of future harmful behaviors.[65] Harm to one's own property, for example, may justify involuntary commitment if it results in a threat of harm to self or others, or a substantial decrease in the person's financial assets. In many jurisdictions, dangerousness to self has been expanded by criteria that are intended to make the applicable commitment standards more sensitive to functional and psychological deterioration that might cause some broadly defined future self-harm, particularly if the respondent's decision-making capacities appear to be compromised.[66] A number of states, beginning with California in the 1960s, adopted "gravely disabled" as a standard, which is similar in many ways to the "unable to provide for one's basic needs" standard that certain other jurisdictions had embraced previously. Both of these criteria require that respondents present a serious risk of harm to themselves, which may include threats to their lives, health, or safety; or an inability to live in the community safely even with the assistance of others.[67]

A growing number of states employ language that permits inpatient commitment of those who are in need of care and/or treatment, but most of those statutes require something in addition, which makes the standard resemble dangerousness to self, while still being considerably more expansive than the traditional criteria.[68] Arizona, for example, mandates involuntary civil commitments based on proof that there is a substantial probability that respondents will incur a severe and abnormal mental, emotional, or physical harm that significantly impairs their judgment, reason, behavior, or capacity to recognize reality.[69] Furthermore, Alaska commits individuals who, if not treated, will "suffer severe and abnormal stress . . . associated with significant impairment of judgment, reason, or behavior causing a substantial impairment of the person's previous ability to function independently."[70]

The Timing of Dangerous Behaviors

One factor that inevitably decreases prediction reliability and overall accuracy is increasing the amount of time that separates the dangerous-like actions or behaviors and the period of confinement or custodial care that is permitted with the proposed involuntary commitment. Predictions of dangerousness cannot be validated empirically without specifying the time period. Unfortunately, there is no available method to determine where on the time continuum a line should be drawn demarking an acceptable versus an unacceptable time interval because there are too many variables that need to be accounted for. Time produces change and change means increased uncertainty. Should the acceptable duration be a day, a week, a month, or several months? All that we know is that if all other factors are the same, the longer the time interval, the less reliable the dangerousness prediction becomes. Time frames that extend beyond what would be commonly viewed as immediate—days or perhaps a couple of weeks—substantially increase the likelihood that the prediction will be wrong thereafter, and that likelihood increases rapidly as the time interval widens because new variables are introduced or existing variables become more difficult to control and assess.

Jurisdictions differ significantly as to the amount of time that may be allowed to elapse between the dangerous behavior and commitment in order for the alleged behavior to be legally determinative. These subjective calculations of time usually are based on the impressions of the judge or jury as to what is meant by "recent" or "imminent," which are the two most common criteria. Furthermore, an increasing number of jurisdictions do not have any substantive limitations related to timeliness,[71] and so far the U.S. Supreme Court has not applied any constitutional limitations in that regard. The only conclusion that one can draw with any reasonable degree of certainty is that generally, even where substantive limitations continue to exist, the maximum amount of time that will satisfy the recent or imminent criteria has been increasing in all different types of civil and quasi-civil commitments. As a result, the predicate dangerousness predictions have become increasingly less reliable and thus collectively more likely to be inaccurate.

Only some states even require that the evidence of dangerous behavior be recent or imminent, and what is considered to be imminent or recent has been expanded in many—and maybe most—of those jurisdictions to include actions, behaviors, or events that occurred months or even years ago.[72] Typically, the dimension of time has been left to the judge or jury to weigh without much guidance. As with other factors involved in making a dangerousness prediction, juries and judges are even less apt to properly assess the impact of time than the mental health experts upon whom they tend to rely. Moreover, there is little reason to think that juries, judges, or the experts will be able to come close to maximizing their assessment capabilities in an advocacy-oriented legal environment in which the key participants tend to be overtaxed and highly stressed.

Recommitments and Release

The potential for time to negatively impact the reliability of a dangerousness assessment—whether it involves civil or quasi-civil commitments—becomes more problematic for respondents who currently are being confined or placed in the custody of the state. If they are petitioning to be released from government custody, and often even if they are being given a statutorily mandated periodic review, the burden—either as a legal or practical matter—is on them to prove a negative by demonstrating that they are no longer dangerous.[73] Because the respondents are in the custody of the government in a controlled environment, courts generally assume that the absence of any incidents of violence or other harmful behaviors is due to their secure environment rather than any signs of improvement on the part of the respondents. Courts also assume that if the respondent were released or placed in an environment in which there is less supervision and control, they would become dangerous again. These assumptions beg the question of whether the respondent still meets the legal criteria for dangerousness.

The problem is that even if this presumption about increased recidivism in the community were true for specific individuals seeking release, it probably is not particularly relevant—much less meaningful—because being more likely to occur does not have much predictive significance if the likelihood of violence or other legally harmful behaviors is low to begin with, which normally it would be. This logical and statistical fallacy is analogous to a doctor saying that a highly invasive cancer treatment should be used because it is 50 percent more likely to prevent death than no treatment at all, where there is only a 5 percent chance of dying without having that treatment in the first place.[74] It also is similar to a researcher claiming that involuntary commitment standards should be broadened because those proposed provisions would significantly decrease the homicide rate where the measured decrease is only "1.42 less homicides per 100,000 [people]."[75]

Being more or even much more likely to be dangerous than other people should only be legally significant if that likelihood—assuming it can even be assessed reliably and accurately—would be sufficient to meet the applicable burden of proof or other legal standards being used. Otherwise, this information will tend to sway, confuse, or mislead the trier of fact by supporting the widespread socially accepted bias that persons with mental disabilities are inherently dangerous, particularly if they already have been adjudicated as being dangerous. Logically, such expert evidence, if it is to be used at all, should only be admitted to refute dangerousness, including expert testimony that the respondent is dangerous. It should not be used to establish continuing dangerousness.

Furthermore, the dangerous behavior that was used to justify the original commitment often is reused or recycled to justify continued commitment, even if respondents have not engaged in any substantially dangerous acts since they were committed.[76] Typically, respondents must show that they are no longer dangerous in a proceeding in which the absence of dangerous behavior since the person was first involuntarily committed is rarely deemed persuasive. Instead, a relatively minor threat to harm oneself or others based on the opinion of a facility physician or psychologist that the respondent remains dangerous may be combined with the original dangerous behavior to allegedly "prove" continuing dangerousness, when in fact there has been no substantial proof presented at all.

Also, courts often decide to recommit if an expert predicts that patients *probably* (more than 50 percent) are not going to take their medications once they are in the community, and this failure is *likely*—more than 50 percent, but considerably lower than that if the court has the more common view of what "likely" means to judges in such cases—to make them dangerous to themselves or others.[77] Even if it could be determined reliably that it was likely that these patients are not going to take their medications *and* that such a failure would place others or themselves in danger, one cannot rationally conclude that these patients are more likely than not to be dangerous. Statistically, these are two separate events, which both have to be measured independently. If each is likely to occur 51 percent of the time, then only about 26 percent of them would be dangerous due to medication noncompliance. Unfortunately, these statistical realities are beyond the purview of most judges and juries, whose primary concern is protecting the community or their reputations within that community over the rights of the respondents. Not surprisingly, given our social attitudes about dangerousness, two esteemed social scientists found that in our courtrooms being correct 26 percent of the time—which would mean being wrong 74 percent of the time—is sufficient for the judges they surveyed to order a commitment.[78]

No Duty to Prevent or Mitigate Dangerousness

At the same time, the governing authority that orders those involuntary civil or quasi-civil commitments typically has no legal responsibility or even perceived moral duty to provide the necessary placements, care, treatment, and support services that would prevent or mitigate respondents' dangerousness due to their mental disabilities. In fact the opposite appears to be true since the absence of a suitable placement in the community often is used to show that respondents are more "likely" to be dangerous should they be released.[79] Moreover, once a person is committed often considerably less evidence is required to justify recommitment than was required originally. This paradox is particularly significant if the person is seeking release—as opposed to receiving a required periodic review—because respondents seeking release generally bear the burden of demonstrating that they no longer meet the commitment criteria by a preponderance of the evidence, rather than the state being obliged to prove continued dangerousness by clear and convincing evidence.[80] Even if the government has the proof burden in theory, however, as a practical matter the respondents still have to convince the trier of fact that they are no longer dangerous in order to secure their release.

Nonviolent or Less Violent Forms of Dangerousness

Another factor that undermines involuntary civil and quasi-civil commitment determinations is definitional: the many types of nonviolent or less violent harmful behaviors that may be used to prove dangerousness to self or others. While there is a split of authority as to whether dangerous behavior must be overt, more often than not even perceived threats of harm—as opposed to actual harm—may be used to establish future dangerousness based on overt behavior,[81] which has led—and will continue to lead—to injustices due to overreaching in order to protect the community from perceived harm. For example, a man who drove his van in the direction of a police officer when told to halt, but never came close to hitting anyone and the government provided no evidence that he intended to hit the officer, satisfied the dangerousness to others standard.[82] Also, certain so-called threats may involve non-overt behaviors, particularly a predicted failure to take antipsychotic medications, which are presumed to lead to dangerous behaviors that satisfy the commitment standard. An expert's prediction that a respondent will fail to take his or her medication often creates—without anything more—a presumption that there is a significantly higher risk that this respondent will harm others or him- or herself. This can become the most compelling evidence supporting those types of involuntary commitments and recommitments.[83]

In addition, while most jurisdictions appear to require harm to others to be bodily, many states allow dangerousness to be established by harm to property.[84] In North Dakota, for instance, a woman who twice started fires in the cement bathroom of a state hospital was committed as having created a "serious" risk of harm to property, presumably because the government did not believe it could prove that she had created the requisite risk of harm to other persons.[85] Also, certain courts have found emotional harm or mental injuries to others constitute dangerousness.[86] More significantly, the U.S. Supreme Court, in the context of committing defendants acquitted of crimes by reason of insanity, ruled that virtually any crime may be used to prove dangerousness to others, including in that case shoplifting a jacket.[87] As a result of this flawed reasoning, legal dangerousness may include almost any type of criminal behavior, whether violent or not.

A Flawed Concept of Dangerousness

Dangerousness has a long history of being applied to achieve questionable and discriminatory purposes in the legal system. In 1974, Harvard law professor Alan Dershowitz made his groundbreaking observations about "predicted harms," which remain true today. No "systematic effort" is made to determine "what . . . harms warrant preventive confinement," the "degree of likelihood [that] should be required," the "duration of preventive confinement [that] should be permitted," or the "relationship [that] should exist between the harm, the likelihood, or the duration."[88]

Even though significant incremental progress has been made in making risk assessments using actuarial methods, all of these prior definitional problems persist. "Most state statutes and court decisions simply have not incorporated all of the components of a dangerousness determination . . . which would limit the [biased and pretexual] discretion of the civil commitment evaluators."[89] Also, the same person in similar circumstances may be involuntarily committed in one jurisdiction and remain free in another, depending on how the civil or quasi-civil commitment scheme in a particular jurisdiction is established and implemented. Furthermore, even if the same standards and procedures were used to commit respondents, serious deficiencies involving the reliability of expert testimony are likely to continue to exist unless the legal system itself is improved; testifying experts are required to base their opinions that a respondent is dangerous on very recent acts or overt threats of violence to self or others; and the duration of each commitment is strictly limited to days rather than weeks, months, or years.

The Number of Involuntary Civil Patients Is Still Significant and Increasing

Substantially fewer individuals are involuntarily committed by traditional civil means than in the more distant past and, on average, those who are committed to mental health facilities remain confined for shorter stays. Nevertheless, today hundreds of thousands of Americans with mental disabilities are coercively hospitalized or otherwise detained in various civil facilities over the course of a year. One estimate indicated that as of the late 1990s, there were nearly a million people being involuntarily confined in public and private mental hospitals over the course of a year.[90] This does not include a disproportionately high percentage of children and older Americans with mental, intellectual, or developmental disabilities coercively confined or dumped in detention, nursing, and other facilities, which are more like the human warehouses of yesterday. Their terms of confinement tend to be more indefinite and considerably longer. Also, many other patients are coerced into accepting specified treatments and other intrusive restrictions in the community using the threat of involuntary inpatient commitment as the penalty for not complying.

Another more discrete group of involuntarily patients are adults who are committed primarily as a result of their addictions. Again, an exact number is not available nationally, but related figures provide estimates of the approximate minimum size of the populations involved. According to the 2002 National Survey of Substance Abuse Treatment Services (N-SSATS), 27,358 "clients" were confined in hospitals as inpatients for substance abuse.[91] Of those, 5,736 were in state and local government-run facilities that are primarily intended for involuntary patients. More importantly, according to the federal government, 36 percent of all substance abuse treatment admissions are "coerced" in the sense that the patients were receiving treatment through a mandatory referral from the criminal justice system, primarily as part of probation or parole, or a state or federal court order.[92]

An even greater number of juveniles and other children are being forced by the criminal or juvenile justice systems or their parents to accept civil inpatient substance abuse treatment, and that number is increasing.[93] In 1998, when the most recent national data was compiled, 138,000 juveniles were admitted for treatment, which was more than a 46 percent increase compared to 1993, when the number was "only" 95,000.[94] That trend, when combined with news reports and other anecdotal evidence, suggests that these numbers are considerably higher today than they were in 1998.

Dangerousness Restrictions on the Right of Persons with Mental Disabilities to Bear Arms

Another significant area of the law in which their presumed dangerousness is used to unfairly restrict the fundamental rights of many persons with mental disabilities is gun possession and ownership. No doubt this is a difficult and delicate problem. Certainly there are convincing arguments to be made that our society should more actively restrict gun ownership and possession—particularly armaments that allow people to shoot off many rounds of bullets in seconds—based on reasonable criteria that would apply to everyone. Unfortunately, the national debate about gun restrictions evokes great emotion and controversy, but not much progress.

In recent years, the only serious national efforts to comprehensively control guns have arisen in the days following a mass, single-event killing and then those efforts seem to peter out, become watered down, or focus almost exclusively on persons with mental impairments. Given our biases and misconceptions about dangerousness, we find it politically and morally convenient to enact gun laws that place restrictions, including criminal penalties, on people who have received treatment for mental disorders, even if they have never misused a gun before and are not legally dangerous. Politicians on both sides of the political aisle support these laws.

Liberals and progressives—recognizing that comprehensive gun reform is politically unlikely, if not impossible—believe that incremental gun restrictions that apply only to persons with mental disabilities are better than no restrictions at all because those who are negatively affected are presumed to be dangerous. As New York Governor Cuomo has concluded, "[p]eople who have mental health issues should not have guns."[95] Similarly, Mayors Against Illegal Guns believe that "[e]very mental-health record that isn't in the system—the National Instant Criminal Background Check System (NICS)—is a ticking time bomb waiting to go off in another community."[96] The National Rifle Association (NRA) and its supporters, on the other hand, pretend that gun restrictions do not violate their otherwise all-encompassing view of the Second Amendment, if and only if such laws are applied to persons with mental disabilities.[97]

Liberals, progressives, and gun owners are united over two false beliefs about persons with mental disabilities that have consistently guided our gun laws. The first is that everyone who has been treated for a serious mental impairment is unable to possess or use guns safely because those individuals are inherently dangerous. This broad overgeneralization is joined by another misconception that anyone who could commit a mass, single-event killing must be deranged due to a mental impairment. This second belief ignores the fact that what has defined these mass killers is not illness per se. What all of them seem to have in common is that they are highly intelligent and organized individuals who have easy access to rapid-fire weaponry and training materials on how to kill many people quickly, *and* they have made what Camus and William Styron have referred to as the most fundamental human decision: their life is no longer worth living. These killers are social outcasts who blame others for their extreme psychic pain. Thus, shortly before they kill themselves or allow themselves to be killed, they choose a confined space—typically a school, theater, or office—to murder as many people as they can. These individuals tend to be disturbed, calculating, evil, and fatalistic, rather than psychotic, delusional, or lacking in self-control.

When these two popular misconceptions are combined into one mythology, they create an unreasonable political mandate about guns and persons with mental disabilities that is difficult—and sometimes impossible—to counter with facts and reasonable arguments. This mandate has resulted in a federal law, for example, which prohibits the sale of guns and other arms and munitions to certain classes of persons with mental disabilities[98] and makes it a federal crime for persons who have been involuntarily committed to possess firearms or munitions.[99] That statute also requires states and federal agencies to report to the NICS any person who has been "adjudicated as a mental defective" or "committed to a mental institution."[100] As the Seventh Circuit Court of Appeals opined in upholding its constitutionality, such a federal law is justified based on the common belief that persons with mental disabilities are more likely to have difficulty exercising the self-control needed to use guns safely.[101] That presumption by itself—without any further evidence—is sufficient to make it illegal for those individuals to possess firearms.[102] In this respect, our federal gun control law is little different from the many other laws that broadly restrict the rights of persons with mental disabilities based on their presumed dangerousness, rather than on specific evidence presented in a due process hearing that clearly and convincingly proves them to be currently dangerous.

Litigation involving gun ownership laws has centered on the meaning of involuntary commitment, which courts—not surprisingly—have interpreted broadly against the interests of the ex-patients involved. The Second Circuit, for example, agreed that the federal law should be applied to an individual who had been committed based on a two-physician certificate, even though there had been no judicial proceeding and he had been almost immediately converted to voluntary status.[103] Also, the First Circuit concluded that a defendant, who had been involuntarily admitted as an inpatient in Maine for five days so he could be observed to determine whether he should be subject to extended commitment, was properly prosecuted for illegally possessing firearms. His commitment was deemed involuntary because, even though there had been no due process commitment hearing, a physician had signed a certificate that a judge had reviewed *ex parte* to justify the temporary hold.[104] In addition, the Fourth Circuit affirmed an arms possession conviction against a defendant, who had been committed in order to restore his competency to stand trial, because the due process that he had been afforded by a criminal court was considered to be comparable to—yet clearly distinguishable from—what the federal gun law contemplates for civil commitments more generally.[105] Furthermore, an Iowa federal court determined that anyone who has been committed for outpatient treatment is considered to be an involuntary patient, and thus subject to federal prosecution if they possess a gun or munitions.[106]

A number of states provide their own additional restrictions on persons with mental disabilities who possess or use firearms or munitions. Indiana's provision allows the police to seize firearms of individuals who are presumed dangerous where the respondents have not been taking their medications, or have a propensity for what is vaguely described as emotionally unstable conduct.[107] In California, an appeals court affirmed a ruling under state law[108] that prohibited a patient with mild to moderate depression from possessing firearms because some time in the past he had been evaluated at a psychiatric facility for allegedly threatening to shoot himself.[109] This second-hand evidence constituted proof by a preponderance of the evidence that the respondent "would not be likely to use firearms in a safe and lawful manner" for the next five years.[110]

New York, in reaction to the Sandy Hook school massacre, enacted a law that requires mental health professionals to report patients who are likely to cause harm to themselves or others—whether or not there is reason to believe those patients own guns—so that law enforcement officials can initiate investigations and confiscate any firearms those patients might have.[111] This first-of-a-kind statute is not only highly discriminatory, but counterproductive as well, because it increases stigma on patients seeking mental health treatment and undermines confidentiality and the patient-therapist relationship. As a former president of the American Psychiatric Association, Paul S. Appelbaum, observed, "the prospect of being reported to local authorities . . . may be enough to discourage patients . . . from seeking treatment or being honest about their impulses."[112]

Former mental patients have tried to challenge the permanency of these firearms bans with limited success. The Washington Supreme Court, for instance, initially found that its state gun law violated equal protection where it mandated the immediate and permanent revocation of weapons permits held by persons who had been involuntarily committed. Unlike former felons, these plaintiffs had no means to obtain weapons permits in the future.[113] Washington later amended its law to allow parties who are subject to these firearms prohibitions based on their having been involuntarily committed for mental health treatment to petition the courts for relief. In order to prevail, however, the applicants must prove by a preponderance of the evidence that they are no longer substantially dangerous to themselves or others and that their mental health symptoms are unlikely to recur.[114]

Other jurisdictions, including Florida and Iowa, have enacted provisions that allow former mental patients to have their gun rights reinstated. Similar to Washington, these jurisdictions allow persons with mental disabilities, who have lost their right to possess firearms, to have those rights restored if they can prove that doing so would not endanger the public's safety.[115] Maine's statute provides that ex-patients may submit a petition to the public safety commissioner for gun restoration, but they must wait five years after their final commitment discharge and establish with clear and convincing evidence that they are no longer likely to act dangerously.[116] Arizona's law also allows persons who have lost their right to possess firearms due to mental incapacity to petition to have that right restored.[117] Those applicants must prove by clear and convincing evidence that they no longer have the mental disorder that led to the original finding that they were dangerous or had a persistent or acute disability.

Virginia's statute permits persons who have been civilly committed involuntarily, including insanity acquittees, to petition a court after their release to restore their right to bear arms, but they must prove that their having a gun is not likely to create a danger to public safety.[118] Finally, West Virginia's law authorizes courts to issue orders that would allow petitioners who have been barred from possessing a gun after having been involuntarily committed to show by clear and convincing evidence that they are competent and capable of responsibly possessing a gun.[119]

Generally, all of these federal and state laws that restrict the right to bear arms for persons with mental disabilities—including the federal version that makes possession of a gun or munitions a felony—assume without anything more that merely because someone has been subject to some sort of broadly defined involuntary mental health treatment that person is likely to be a continuing danger to self or others. Thus, predictions of dangerousness that are part of most involuntary civil commitment proceedings to begin with are automatically extended well beyond the terms of those commitments themselves with regard to the issue of firearms or munitions possession or ownership, whether or not there is any evidence that the respondent is likely to misuse a gun now. These laws ignore the fact that these former patients had to demonstrate a lack of dangerousness in order to be released from custody. Despite these obvious legal inequities, as with other dangerousness interventions permitted by our laws, there is overwhelming public support—strongly embraced by the media—not to allow persons "with histories of mental illness [to] petition to get their gun rights back," regardless of the individual circumstances involved. [120]

QUASI-CIVIL INVOLUNTARY COMMITMENTS

Overview

There has been—and continues to be—a steady increase in the number of people with mental disabilities who are involuntarily incarcerated as a result of their contact with the criminal or juvenile justice systems. There are at least half a million inmates with mental disabilities in the custody of those federal and state correctional systems at any one time. Most of them are in our traditional prisons and jails [121] or juvenile justice detention centers. A growing number of people with mental disabilities, however, are confined in quasi-civil, secure detention facilities that look, feel, and are operated like prisons, except their incarcerations are indeterminate and the pressures to keep them confined are substantial and often overwhelming, regardless of the individual circumstances involved.

Typically, individuals with mental disabilities who are subject to these quasi-civil commitments receive considerably less substantive and procedural due process protections than criminal defendants. Often, if they are able to secure their release from our corrections systems, they are involuntarily committed and placed indefinitely in traditional "civil" mental health or related facilities, or subjected to indeterminate supervision and monitoring with the possibility of quasi-civil recommitment if they fail to meet what tend to be highly intrusive conditions of release. What all of these quasi-civil commitments have in common are dangerousness criteria, which are deemed proper justifications for highly intrusive restrictions on the respondents' rights, liberties, and freedoms in the guise of providing meaningful mental health care and treatment. In addition, before trial or as part of a plea bargain a relatively small number of criminal defendants with mental disabilities who have been charged with nonviolent crimes and are not deemed a future danger to the community may be sentenced to participate in various types of mental health care and treatment programs in lieu of going to prison.

Generally, predictions of dangerousness are used as the primary justification for keeping quasi-civil inmates confined longer and to impose intrusive restrictions on their daily lives if they are released. Their initial dangerousness is presumed because they have been charged with or convicted of crimes. These quasi-civil commitments are used to confine persons who are adjudicated incompetent to stand trial, not guilty by reason of insanity, or sexually dangerous or mentally disordered offenders.

Also, courts—often at the direction of state legislatures or Congress—use parole, probation, and other alternative dispositions to place onerous conditions on the release of offenders with mental disabilities who are thought to be a future danger to the community, even if there is no current evidence of violent behaviors. For many such offenders these alternative dispositions include very lengthy—or even a lifetime of—harsh restrictions with the promise of indefinite and lengthy confinements if any of the imposed conditions are violated.

Commitments in Lieu of Imprisonment That Arise before, during, or after a Trial

Intrusive commitments and conditions of release may be imposed as dispositions in lieu of being tried or sentenced for a nonviolent crime, or after being found incompetent to stand trial or not guilty by reason of insanity. In all of these situations, the legislative scheme in effect is based, at least in large part, on the rationale that the government is supposed to be implementing a more humane judicial response that recognizes defendants' diminished culpability or trial incompetency and their need for specialized care and treatment. In reality, however, these dispositions often are nearly as bad as—and oftentimes worse—than imprisonment for the defendants involved. Typically, because the dispositions are indeterminate, they can—and often do—last longer than traditional prison sentences, and increasingly many may last for the rest of the respondents' lives.

Alternatives to Imprisonment for Nonviolent Offenders

A relatively small but slowly increasing number of defendants—either pretrial or as part of plea bargains—make themselves the subjects of involuntary outpatient and inpatient civil commitment in lieu of imprisonment. Generally these alternative dispositions are only available in the relatively few jurisdictions that have created special courts for this purpose, which may focus on mental health, substance abuse, homelessness, veterans, or some other emerging vulnerable population, such as persons with fetal alcohol spectrum disorders.[122] In this way, a relatively few eligible defendants with mental impairments have an opportunity to avoid or delay their imprisonment, or have their prison sentences shortened, which appears to be—and sometimes is—a humane judicial response because typically adequate care and treatment and other supportive services are provided.

At the same time, typically only defendants who commit nonviolent crimes and are not otherwise viewed as being dangerous to the community are eligible to participate in these programs.[123] This is future dangerousness criteria working in reverse in the sense that defendants who are deemed dangerous may not participate. Also, increasingly, the participating defendants receive sentences that are intended to ensure that they remain under the control of the criminal justice system indefinitely, which allows courts to jail, imprison, or otherwise incarcerate these individuals with only minimal due process protections if they fail to follow the strict conditions that they must agree to in order to qualify for these alternative dispositions.[124] Since typically these defendants have to have committed nonviolent crimes in order to be eligible for these special considerations, these defendants would not be found dangerous for this limited purpose, unless additional factors were present.

Increasingly, however, strict and intrusive release conditions are imposed on these nonviolent defendants, and if they should fail to meet those conditions, harsh measures often result, including prolonged incarceration and extended monitoring and supervision, particularly for those who have committed federal crimes.[125] Instead of using the fact that they have not acted violently to diminish the actual amount of time that these defendants spend behind bars, the trend today is to create the potential for incarcerating or otherwise controlling them indefinitely should they "screw up." This can happen whether or not the release violations are due to their mental disabilities or inappropriate environments in which these defendants may have been placed. If they are found to have violated any of the conditions of their alternative dispositions—which may have nothing to do with their having acted dangerously—in proceedings with minimal due process protections, these defendants may be committed, imprisoned, or jailed for periods of time that exceed the likely terms of incarceration that they would have received had they been found guilty and served their entire prison sentences. [126]

Incompetency to Stand Trial and Not Guilty by Reason of Insanity

Most trial-related, quasi-civil commitments result from incompetency to stand trial findings, rather than insanity acquittals, which have become relatively rare events. Usually, incompetent defendants are sent to forensic detention facilities to receive treatment—typically antipsychotic drugs—to restore their competency, so that they may be tried for the crimes that they have been charged with. Normally, the necessary degree of dangerousness to justify those commitments is established by the fact that they have been charged with the commission of a crime, [127] although many jurisdictions require the state to demonstrate that it is likely that the defendants committed such a crime. [128] Virtually any type of crime—whether violent or not—is deemed sufficient. Occasionally and probably rarely, those who are charged with nonviolent crimes may be treated as outpatients. [129] Often when this happens it is because they are eligible for one of the special courts that have been established to dispose of nonviolent offenses in ways that seem more humane. Ultimately, though, these dispositions make public safety a paramount concern and thus are likely to impose many highly restrictive and intrusive conditions, which include severe penalties for noncompliance. [130]

If, after an extended period of time, defendants' competency cannot be restored, then in theory they should be released. Increasingly, however, after being released they are being civilly committed as dangerous persons, which may mean that the total length of their confinement is longer than if they had been convicted of the crime(s) they were charged with. In addition, the state does not have to show that the respondents in such commitment proceedings will even benefit from the proposed treatment. [131] Nevada enacted a law, for instance, which allows prosecutors to petition the criminal courts for a special quasi-civil commitment order within ten days of when incompetent defendants have been released from their incompetency commitments after it has been found that they are unlikely to have their competency restored in the foreseeable future.[132] These respondents may be held for up to ten years more, as long as they receive periodic reviews every twelve months.

A smaller number of defendants, who have been found not guilty by reason of insanity, are automatically committed indefinitely because they are presumed to be a future danger to others. While insanity acquittals normally involve murders or other serious felonies, the U.S. Supreme Court has ruled that virtually any crime is enough to justify an insanity commitment[133]—and increasingly other types of quasi-civil commitments as well. Moreover, once these acquittees are committed, typically a Kafkaesque catch-22 is set into motion in which they must prove a negative in order to be released: that they no longer are dangerous or have any type of mental impairment.

A Connecticut inmate, for example, was involuntarily committed to the jurisdiction of the state's psychiatric review board for forty years, even though the crimes for which he had been found not guilty by reason of insanity—first-degree harassment, threatening someone, and two counts of attempted larceny[134]—were all relatively minor offenses, which had included no actual acts of violence. Also, the Sixth Circuit upheld the continued confinement of a federal insanity acquitee who no longer had the mental condition for which he was originally committed, or any condition which could have been used to establish his legal insanity.[135] nstead, he was diagnosed with vague and controversial conditions—antisocial and other personality disorders—which were deemed to have increased his risk for being a future danger to the community.

Because of these types of commitment outcomes, defense lawyers are typically cautioned to think very carefully about raising an insanity defense even if it is justified by the facts. Unless the crime is a serious felony, and even then, there is a very real possibility or probability that their clients will serve considerably more time confined in a secure forensic facility than they would have served if they had been convicted of the crimes they were charged with.[136] Also, considerably more social stigma is associated with the "insanity acquittee-crazed offender" label than the typical "prisoner-ex-con" designation, and this heightened stigma attaches not only to the acquittees, but also to their families and significant others.

Post-imprisonment Commitment: Sexually "Violent" and Other Offenders with Broadly Defined Mental Disorders

Even after serving their entire prison sentences, offenders with what are deemed to be repetitive antisocial mental disorders, particularly of a sexual nature, may be subjected to indefinite quasi-civil inpatient commitment that can last a lifetime; compelled tests and treatments that are reminiscent of the degrading and draconian future world described in *A Clockwork Orange*; and, if they should be conditionally released, highly intrusive community-based restrictions and treatments. Also, if their offenses are of a sexual nature, they become part of a database that is disseminated to the general public online, which allows governments to enforce limitations on where such ex-offenders may live, what community facilities they may utilize, and what social services, if any, that they, their families, and their significant others may receive.[137]

The usually more enlightened state of Maryland, for instance, has enacted legislation requiring courts to impose lifetime supervision on defendants if they are convicted of a sexually violent offense and are at risk of reoffending, or, for any reason, they have been required to register as sex offenders under the laws of any other American jurisdiction, including the military, whether or not they committed a violent sexual crime.[138] Conditions for their lifetime supervision may include: global positioning satellite tracking; restrictions on living or being near schools, family day-care centers, child centers, and other places used primarily by minors; restrictions on employment or other activities where the person might have contact with minors; intrusive and degrading treatments; prohibitions on using alcohol; access to their personal computers by state officials; and regular polygraph and other sexual offender testing. Failure to comply with any of these restrictions is deemed a "misdemeanor" for the first offense, which is punishable by up to five years in prison. A second offense is a felony, which invokes punishment of up to ten years in prison for each additional infraction.[139]

In California, a series of initiatives has been enacted, which has placed intrusive restrictions on "74,000 living Californians convicted of sex crimes since 1947."[140] People on these registries have been "barred . . .

from not only schoolyards and playgrounds but also beaches, libraries, harbors and other public places."[141] As a result, local communities reportedly are building more parks so neighborhoods can prevent those offenders from living within 2,000 feet of the parks' borders.[142] In addition, as a result of a 2012 ballot initiative, sex offenders "must inform the authorities of their e-mail addresses, user names, screen names and other Internet handles, as well as report any additions or changes within 24 hours."[143] These restrictions have been challenged on First Amendment privacy grounds, but supporters of the initiative argue that the law was justified because "registered sex offenders presented a potential danger even if their crime was unrelated to the Internet."[144]

So-called sexually and mentally disordered offender laws go much further than that by permitting the states that have them and the federal government, without having to satisfy criminal due process standards, to indefinitely extend offenders' terms of incarceration, place them under the control of the state for the rest of their lives, and take punitive measures against them and often their family members and significant others. Most of these laws loosely target "sexual predators" or "sexually dangerous persons" who are deemed psychologically predisposed to re-offending, but the eligibility criteria for imposing these interventions on sexual offenders tend to be overly inclusive by wide margins. In North Dakota, for instance, the state's highest court ruled that a defendant convicted of indecent exposure was properly confined as a sexually dangerous person and thus subject to indefinite confinement.[145] While he had never been charged with—much less convicted of—a sexually violent crime, in an interview pursuant to a compelled polygraph exam that was required for his commitment proceedings and without benefit of counsel, the respondent had disclosed he had molested young girls in the distant past.

Moreover, in a number of jurisdictions—most notably California[146] and the federal government,[147] which are the two largest—this type of quasi-civil confinement and supervision may be applied to offenders with any type of mental disability, who, as a result of such conditions, are deemed likely to commit more crimes in the future. Under the federal statute, for example, inmates may be committed as their "sentence is about to expire" if they are "presently suffering from a mental disease or defect as a result of which [their] release would create a substantial risk of bodily injury to another person or *serious damage to property* of another."[148] It is important to note that a "substantial risk" does not even

require that the state prove a likelihood of injury to persons or property—
much less provide proof beyond a reasonable doubt—in order to indefinitely confine these individuals.

Many legal scholars initially reasoned that this federal law would be
found unconstitutional due to the lack of proper due process safeguards
and because, as one federal appeals court explained, there was no authority for Congress to enact commitment legislation, which traditionally has
been exclusively a state function.[149] Nevertheless, a majority of the U.S.
Supreme embraced a convoluted rationale allowing it to decide that Congress had the constitutional authority under the "necessary and proper
clause" to enact this legislation in order to facilitate the management of
quasi-civil inmates in the federal prison system.[150] In doing so, the Court
created one more double standard that favors government over the individual rights of persons with mental disabilities. For the purposes of
incarcerating persons as mentally disordered and dangerous in the criminal justice system, this type of commitment is deemed civil, so that criminal due process guarantees do not apply. Yet, in determining whether
Congress has the authority to establish a federal post-imprisonment commitment law, the Court ruled that this scheme was a necessary part of the
federal prison system, distinguishing it from civil commitment, which is
exclusively a state function.[151]

In addition to the extreme intrusions on these offenders' constitutional
liberties and freedoms, there also is much evidence to suggest that these
special laws do not work as intended to protect society or to rehabilitate
the offenders, and they are extremely costly. When New York enacted its
sexually violent predator law in 2007, the *New York Times* opined that—
based on the newspaper's comprehensive study of what has happened in
other jurisdictions—this type of "civil commitment can become a judicial
fraud . . . [that] cost[s] on average, four times more per inmate than
prison, but almost never make[s] an offender fit to rejoin society."[152] In
addition, these laws, particularly those requiring sex offenders to register
after they are released, tend to "[lump] all offenders into broad levels of
dangerousness based on the crimes for which they were convicted, allowing . . . the worst offenders to blend in with less threatening ones."[153]

According to data collected by the Washington State Institute of Public Policy in 2006,[154] 4,534 so-called sexually violent predators were
being confined nationwide, which was 80 percent more than in 2002.[155]
Undoubtedly, these numbers have continued to increase as more states—

like New York, New Hampshire, and Maryland—have enacted similar or new types of predator laws,[156] and states with existing statutes have responded to public pressures to place more sexually or mentally disordered offenders behind bars, indefinitely. In 2005, for instance, California opened a new facility to "house up to 1,500 [more] sexually violent predators and other seriously mentally ill patients" who are confined under such laws,[157] and other states have been increasing their confinement capacities as well. Furthermore, according to the National Center for Missing & Exploited Children, as of 2009 there already were more than 700,000 people who had been required to register as sex offenders nationwide.[158]

In addition, states are more predisposed than ever to treat adolescents who commit sexual offenses as sexually dangerous predators, so that once these kids complete their terms of detention in either a juvenile facility or an adult jail or prison, they too may be confined indefinitely, perhaps for the rest of their lives, or be placed on probation for life and/or permanently entered into sex offender registries.[159] These child offenders, who are viewed as deserving such unforgiving measures, include many adolescents, and even younger children, who have engaged in behaviors that were once viewed as merely inappropriate, including consensual sex, oral sex, or fondling between children not of the same age. Several jurisdictions, including Pennsylvania, have even tried to prosecute teenage girls for texting their own naked photographs to schoolmates.[160] What were once considered "boundary problems" that should be treated with better parenting, counseling, therapy, and rehabilitation, have been stigmatized and then too often handled as serious felonies.[161]

According to the Department of Justice, more than one-third of all the people who are prosecuted for sex crimes are juveniles and one-eighth of all those defendants are kids under the age of twelve.[162] In 2008, for example, a Pennsylvania appeals court affirmed the continued indefinite confinement of a juvenile sexual offender who, nine years earlier, when he was only twelve, had sex with an eight-year-old.[163] Although he had committed no further "sexually deviant" acts since then, he was deemed dangerous nonetheless, after the state's expert had predicted that the respondent would be unable to control his sexually violent behavior. The expert's conclusion was based on the fact that the respondent had become sexually aroused when he was compelled to view images of sexual humiliation, force, torture, and coercion.[164]

Post-imprisonment quasi-civil, indeterminate incarceration, supervision, and monitoring is a clever and increasingly popular means of confining—and keeping confined or under restrictive government controls—offenders with mental disabilities who are particularly reviled and feared, even though, legally, they already have been fully punished by the state or federal government for their crimes.[165] In the guise of taking care of citizens in need of treatment in order to protect the public, the federal and state governments have invented ways to extend imprisonment and other methods of supervision and control, indeterminately and often for a lifetime. All that has to be shown is that these respondents have mental impairments or aberrations—particularly of a sexual nature—that are tenuously linked, by dubious expert testimony, to future dangerousness based on their past criminal behavior(s).

Once these offenders are quasi-civilly committed, they must prove that they are no longer dangerous due to any type of mental impairments, conditions, or aberrations, if they ever hope to be released, even with extremely restrictive conditions. Their confinement may be extended based on their having mental conditions or disorders that are completely unrelated to those that formed the bases for their original commitments. This can happen even if these new disorders were precipitated in substantial part by the substandard and sometimes horrific conditions of their confinement.[166]

In most instances, the care and treatment that is needed for these inmates to recover or not to decompensate is either unavailable, or the conditions or disorders that justified their confinements do not readily respond to any available treatments.[167] As a result, these individuals may be incarcerated until they die because they have no realistic hope of proving that they are no longer dangerous. The primary reason that these offenders even have a small opportunity of being released has little to do with due process, but rather the high cost of detaining them, which in 2006 averaged $94,000 per inmate per year,[168] or more[169]—amounts that are approximately four times as much as keeping someone confined in prison[170] and which keep rising.

To make matters worse, three states which had no sexually violent predator laws—Oklahoma, Louisiana, and Montana—and two states that do—Florida and South Carolina—had amended their criminal statutes to require the execution of any offenders who were found guilty, more than once, of committing certain specified sexual crimes against children.[171] In

2008, a divided U.S. Supreme Court struck down these laws as cruel and unusual punishment because, while most—but not all—of these crimes are heinous, they do not involve the death of another human being and some do not involve actual violence.[172] Nevertheless, both presidential candidates at the time—Obama and McCain—publicly criticized that decision, knowing full well where the votes and public sentiments of most Americans were likely to be on this highly emotional issue.[173]

Predictions of Dangerousness and Indefinite Quasi-Civil Commitments

Criminal behavior—conviction of almost any crime, or merely what appears would be a "likely" conviction, if that person were tried—is sufficient to establish the dangerousness criteria for quasi-civil commitments. Typically, under existing laws dangerousness becomes a pivotal issue in these quasi-civil proceedings only after respondents are committed and then attempt to secure their release; initially their current and future dangerousness is simply presumed because crimes were involved, even if the crimes were nonviolent. In this context, the pivotal dangerousness issue almost always involves predictions that the respondents would likely be dangerous if they were released into the community, or otherwise allowed to live without intrusive restrictions on their individual rights, freedoms, and liberties. As noted earlier, the existence of a qualifying mental disorder, mental condition, or mental aberration is normally accepted by the jury or judge without further scrutiny based on the diagnosis of a qualified mental health professional, which can be staff who are paid by the state or federal government that is opposing the respondent's release.

Once these respondents have been incarcerated, they must show that they are no longer a future danger to others in order to secure their release. The state can rebut the respondents' evidence with flimsy evidence or—if respondents have the burden of proving that they are no longer dangerous—no evidence at all. Once respondents are committed based on their alleged criminal behaviors, it becomes difficult—and sometimes nearly impossible—for them to obtain their freedom, unless the government concurs, which is relatively rare. In quasi-civil commitment proceedings—particularly involving insanity acquittees and mentally disordered offenders—respondents are confronted with evidentiary obstacles that usually prevent them from disproving their dangerousness, which increasingly means that these indeterminate court dispositions become very lengthy or permanent.

The exception is that class of respondents who are found incompetent to stand trial. With these defendants the state or federal government normally has an incentive to facilitate their release from quasi-civil commitments, so that they may be tried for their crimes and imprisoned or executed. However, if these defendants cannot be tried because their competency is unlikely to be restored within the amount of time the governing statute or case law requires, increasingly jurisdictions are civilly committing these individuals indefinitely, rather than releasing them as was supposed to be done in the past.[174]

Quasi-civil Commitments in Lieu of Imprisonment

Predictions of dangerousness may not be directly involved in the initial inpatient or outpatient commitment of defendants who accept alternative court dispositions to imprisonment. Generally, defendants who commit violent crimes are ineligible for such dispositions. Nevertheless, an official perception or impression that a defendant who has been charged with committing a nonviolent crime (or crimes) may be a future danger to public safety is likely to substantially influence whether that person is viewed as being a good risk for these special programs. Furthermore, when community safety is being assessed, it is not limited to the type of nonviolent criminal behavior(s) that the defendant was charged with, but may extend to whatever behaviors a background check reveals, which is based mostly on official reports and other second-hand evidence. As stated by the Standing Master in charge of the mental health court in Missoula, Montana, "[p]ublic safety is a high priority. Participants are carefully screened prior to admission and monitored . . . throughout the program."[175]

Subsequent program monitoring—including informal court proceedings—in which these defendants may be accused of not meeting the conditions of their alternative dispositions, such as not taking their medications, or otherwise failing to follow the detailed conditions of their release, often involves assessments or perceptions about the defendants' future dangerousness. Courts—and through them special programs operated by or affiliated with the courts—typically have indeterminate jurisdiction over these individuals and open-ended discretion in deciding what further dispositions are most appropriate in the circumstances presented.

Generally, these special programs include "regular status hearings." During these informal proceedings, "treatment plans and other conditions are periodically reviewed . . . and sanctions are imposed on participants who do not adhere to the conditions of participation."[176]

Because virtually everywhere in the United States public safety is a high priority, the collective perceptions of those administering these programs about whether an individual is likely to be perceived as dangerous to the community typically determine what requirements, restrictions, and interventions, including various forms of coerced outpatient and inpatient civil commitment, are ordered. Future dangerousness, for the purpose of these court-initiated interventions, may be based on uncorroborated evidence and opinions that were compiled by program staff from a variety of potentially unreliable sources, or the defendants' failure to follow any of the conditions of their alternative dispositions. Future dangerousness also may be based on little more than the opinions of the mental health professionals who are affiliated with these court programs.

Depending on the jurisdiction, subsequent interventions may be ordered as part of regular civil involuntary commitment proceedings, in which case the evidence of dangerousness is subject to the same deficiencies and abuses described earlier with regard to involuntary civil commitments. More likely, though, such court-sanctioned interventions will be part of a post-sentencing disposition with considerably fewer due process protections than are found in regular civil commitment proceedings. In fact, there may be no constraints on the use of subjective impressions about the defendant's future dangerousness beyond the subjective determinations of the program administrators or judicial officers overseeing these programs. In Eau Claire, Wisconsin, for instance, the mental health court coordinator may order "inpatient treatment as necessary" for defendants without the further court review that normally would be required if this were a typical involuntary civil commitment.[177]

Incompetency to Stand Trial

Increasingly, due to various legislative initiatives or judicial decisions, predictions of dangerousness are becoming part of incompetency to stand trial dispositions. Such evidence may be submitted or otherwise considered with regard to two types of criminal incompetency determinations: whether the initial incompetency restoration should be in an inpatient or outpatient facility; and whether an incompetent defendant who is unlikely to regain his or her competency should be involuntarily civilly committed instead of being released. Not surprisingly, heightened civil rather than the more rigorous criminal due process protections apply in both of these situations.

Typically, defendants who are found incompetent to stand trial will not be treated on an outpatient basis to have their competency restored or be released, unless the crime they are charged with is nonviolent and the judge concludes that the defendant is unlikely to be dangerous to the community.[178] Again, because this type of determination is made as part of a pretrial disposition, which the defense typically has advocated for and in which the judge has broad discretion, it is likely that most of the dangerousness evidence will come from court-appointed or affiliated mental health professionals and will not be subject to meaningful cross-examination or other due process protections.

With regard to involuntary civil commitment proceedings that occur because the defendant's competency is not likely to be restored, dangerousness evidence will be similar to the evidence required for traditional civil commitment proceedings, except the criminal charge that originally was lodged against the defendant may be used to support the respondent's current and future dangerousness.[179] In addition, sometimes other evidence of continuing dangerousness may be needed, such as the testimony of a mental health professional that the defendant is likely to be dangerous to others or the community if released. Regardless, the original criminal charge(s) against the respondent combined with subsequent expert evidence of his or her future dangerousness is extremely difficult for the respondent to overcome, which, of course, is the purpose of these relatively recent statutes, which *mandate* and thus demand that commitment proceedings be initiated before any incompetent defendants are released.[180]

Insanity Acquittees

Over time the risk of future dangerousness should tend to dissipate for insanity acquitees, unless they have continued to commit dangerous acts while confined. Nevertheless, their dangerousness, which was initially presumed based on the crimes that they were originally charged with committing, may be extended indefinitely in several different ways. First, these acquittees must demonstrate that their original crime no longer makes them dangerous. This requirement is made more burdensome by a popular legal fiction. Judges and juries may presume—which they normally are predisposed to do—that the reason acquittees have not committed new dangerous acts is unrelated to the likelihood that their mental status has improved. Instead, triers of fact may conclude—without any further supporting evidence—that the only reason acquittees have not acted dangerously is because they have been in a secure environment and/or are being compelled to take medications and participate in other treatments.[181]

Second, normally the burden falls on the acquittees to prove that they have not committed any other dangerous acts since being committed. Almost any subsequent official accusation of a dangerous act or threat by that individual, including hearsay evidence in various treatment and corrections records, when combined with the original crime itself, may be enough to deny respondents their release.

Third, even if the original crime was committed years ago and no other dangerous acts have occurred since then, acquittees still must somehow demonstrate that they are not likely to commit any dangerous acts once they are in the community. Furthermore, subjective testimony from mental health professionals employed or retained by the government that the acquittees are unlikely to take their medications once they are outside an institutional milieu is sufficient to rebut evidence that an acquittee has not committed any dangerous acts while confined, even if the period of detention has been many years.[182] No empirical evidence exists that this type of expert opinion is reliable or likely to be accurate. Like predictions of dangerousness, these medication predictions are clinically derived impressions about what might happen in the future. These opinions also are likely to be biased as a result of the partisan roles that these experts tend to play in these advocacy proceedings.

In addition, a release may be denied based on an expert's prediction that the living situations of the acquittees might be too stressful or harmful as a result of their not having adequate sources of income, housing, and/or care and treatment in the community. This is another catch-22 since these difficulties tend to arise because, as detailed in chapter 6, the necessary community services are generally unavailable or their status of being an insanity acquittee makes them ineligible to receive needed assistance. Moreover, even if the acquittees are able to present their own "expert" mental health testimony that rebuts any or all of the government's contentions, the jury or judge has the discretion to give more weight to the government's expert(s) in order to protect the community. As a practical matter, the burden is on the acquittees to prove the absence of dangerousness[183] because their continued dangerousness is presumed.

John Hinckley is a high-profile example of how the system can operate to prevent relatively objective release decisions from being made. He has remained confined over thirty years after his insanity acquittal, even though he has not acted dangerously since. In that case, his desire to have normal relationships with women has been used as psychiatric evidence of a continuing obsession—originally with Jodie Foster—that was the basis for his initial commitment in 1982. Clearly, Hinckley's situation is unique because he attacked a sitting president of the United States and maimed people in the presidential party. Nevertheless, his situation also demonstrates how governments, if they choose to do so—which they are predisposed to doing most of the time—can marshal evidence of dangerousness, with the help of state-retained psychiatrists and psychologists, from the most ambiguous or questionable circumstances. Considerable public pressure normally exists to extend confinements and other restrictions against insanity acquittees, who are perceived as being both "crazy" and dangerous. In this environment, most juries and judges—and almost all prosecutors—tend to be much less concerned with the rights of acquittees than they are with protecting the community.

Sexually and Other Mentally Disordered Offenders

The situation is no better, and in a number of ways probably worse, for offenders with sexual or other mental disorders who are quasi-civilly confined when their prison terms expire. "Currently, no other population is more despised, more vilified, more subject to media misrepresentation and more likely to be denied basic human rights."[184] Typically, their initial commitments depend on the state establishing that they have a behavioral condition or disposition to continue to commit serious crimes in the future. The key determinant is proof of a linkage between a so-called mental aberration—which broadly includes repeated antisocial behaviors or any other diagnosed mental disorders or conditions—and a loose prediction of dangerousness based on that aberration. What is considered a mental aberration encompasses a broad range of behaviors that our society deems inappropriate, with repeated sexual violence, including serial killings or rapes, on one end of the spectrum and viewing child pornography (pedophilia) or having sexual relations with mature and willing adolescents (hebephilia) on the other end.

It is important to remember that until the early 1970s, both the American Psychiatric Association and the American Psychological Association made sexual attraction to persons of the opposite sex (homosexuality) a mental disorder.[185] Historically, the inclusions and descriptions of sexual "mental" disorders in the *DSM* have been influenced by politically or morality-based decision-making, as opposed to empirical data that is supposed to support the inclusion of mental disorders in the *DSM*. Even today many Americans still believe that "pedophilia . . . is a homosexual problem"[186] and that homosexuals can be cured.

Once persons with treatment-resistant sexual and other mental conditions are committed, it is extremely difficult—if not practically impossible—for them to secure release. A vast majority of these respondents are sentenced to indefinite confinement or the threat of confinement for many years, or the rest of their lives, based on their presumed dangerousness. What constitutes evidence of future dangerousness for the purpose of sexually violent predator commitment schemes and mentally disordered offender statutes is behavior that the respondent allegedly cannot control, which, depending on the statute involved, might lead to future sexual violence or other dangerous behaviors.[187]

While the public, due to media saturation, tends to associate the behaviors of these sexually and mentally disordered respondents with extreme violence, including murders and brutal sexual assaults and rapes of women and children, many—and perhaps most—offenders with these disorders are guilty of lesser nonviolent crimes, such as viewing, collecting, or selling pornography; stealing; unarmed robbery; physical assaults without a dangerous weapon; consensual sex with a mature minor; nonviolent date rape; masturbating in public; or "sexting" naked images of themselves or others.[188] Yet, all of these so-called dangerous behaviors are typically lumped together, indiscriminately, as offenses that can form the basis for extended incarceration and/or a lifetime of state-imposed restrictions when such behaviors are linked to a diagnosis of a mental disorder, condition, or aberration. Many nonviolent crimes are considered violent due to a more general tendency to portray sexual crimes as violence without making critical distinctions amongst those felonies. Under the greatly expanded federal definition, in 2010 nearly 14 million people—mostly women—were victims of sexual violence.[189]

Not surprisingly, nonviolent sexual offenses or behaviors continue to be used to justify post-imprisonment commitments and other intrusive interventions based on sexual dangerousness. Several appellate court decisions illustrate how readily courts are willing to equate nonviolent sexual offenses or behaviors with dangerousness and how arbitrary those decisions can be. The U.S. Court of Appeals for the Sixth Circuit, for example, upheld a lower court that had sentenced a man who had pled guilty to distributing child pornography, to more than seven years in prison, plus a lifetime of strict government supervision.[190] The defendant was deemed to be a permanent danger to the community because he had refused to complete a psychosexual exam after the "plethysmograph" machine he was being "tested" with had malfunctioned. This controversial device, the reliability and relevancy of which is highly disputed and supported by little or no persuasive empirical evidence,[191] measures blood flow in penises. So-called experts, relying on these blood flow measurements, attempt to assess whether an offender has become aroused when viewing "inappropriate" sexual images, and, if he does become aroused, typically opine that the man is sexually dangerous.

Similarly, the Ninth Circuit affirmed a decision to sentence a defendant to ten years in prison plus a lifetime of supervised conditional release because he had pled guilty to possessing child pornography and had been convicted of *attempting* to sexually assault a child.[192] That decision was remanded, but only to ensure that the compelled treatment and penile plethysmograph testing that the lower court had ordered were based on medical findings, rather than the whims of the prosecutor and the courts.

A Massachusetts intermediate appeals court reversed a lower court, which had denied the state's petition to quasi-civilly commit an offender who had been found guilty of multiple counts of "open and gross lewdness" for having exposed himself to females and having masturbated in public.[193] That court ruled the requisite sexual dangerousness did not have to be based on proof that the respondent was likely to cause physical harm to others. It was sufficient that the respondent was a deemed "menace" to other people because his actions caused them mental or emotional distress.[194]

Finally, the North Dakota Supreme Court also affirmed a decision to recommit a respondent as a sexually dangerous predator of older teenage boys. Proof of his continuing dangerousness was based on his having had an affair with a consenting adult inmate—who had the youthful appearance of an adolescent—his failure to complete his sex offender treatment, and his disobeying treatment rules.[195]

One of the key elements the government is supposed to prove in these sexually or mentally disordered offender commitments is that the respondents are dangerous because they lack control over their behaviors due to their mental conditions and are thus likely to be recidivists. Oftentimes this alleged lack of control is established by psychological tests that predict higher recidivism rates for individuals who possess characteristics that have been found in specified groups of people to increase the risk of these criminal behaviors.[196] This is comparable in method and degree of accuracy to how insurance adjusters try to measure insurance risks.[197] Instead of "cooking" the results to minimize the payment of insurance claims, federal and state governments often "cook" the results to justify indefinitely confining offenders who have sexual and other mental disorders.

The main deficiency with this approach—in addition to the obvious practical problems related to its fair and equitable implementation—is that while it may be theoretically possible to achieve a reasonably high degree of accuracy in predicting the number of violent acts within large groups of people who share similar characteristics, such a degree of accuracy cannot be achieved reliably for specific individuals, particularly if they are respondents in quasi-civil commitment proceedings subject to varying legal standards and procedures.[198] Presently, even using highly structured actuarial methods—which are not commonly used anyway and rarely in courtrooms—only a very few individuals, if any, can be identified as such with a degree of accuracy that consistently exceeds being correct more often than being incorrect.[199] Also, the base rates that are relied on to develop the actuarial tables that are used for predicting the recidivism rates of these sexual offenders tend to be flawed to begin with.[200]

Making matters worse is the fact that "SVP laws do not define all the terms they invoke and do not specify the time period that recidivism estimates should cover."[201] Thus, even if these actuarial tables were relatively accurate in theory and the base rates were properly calculated, unless those actuarial estimates are calibrated using the specific legal standard of dangerousness being applied in that courtroom "many commitment candidates might be wrongly classified as predatory, whereas many others might be wrongly classified as nonpredatory."[202] Moreover, as a practical matter, it is reasonable to assume—in the absence of any persuasive evidence to the contrary—that most of these miscalculations involve false positives rather than false negatives. This is because governments and the legal system have a strong bias toward establishing predatory and other violent or illegal behaviors, rather than establishing the absence of such behaviors.[203] This bias turns out to be particularly inappropriate because the available empirical evidence indicates that these structured tools are not well-suited to prove dangerousness, but may be used more reliably to rebut accusations of dangerousness.[204]

As with dangerousness more generally, there is a misleading perception, which in turn can too easily become a de facto legal presumption, that sexual offenders with mental disorders have high recidivism rates. Thus, incarcerating them en masse indefinitely seems increasingly less arbitrary and capricious. Yet actual recidivism rates, even for convicted pedophiles, are far more ambiguous or unknown over the long term. In the leading study to date, after five years the recidivism rate for 400 convicted pedophiles who received community treatment was measured at less than 8 percent.[205] Similarly, in a New Jersey study the recidivism rates "up to 7 years later" for subsequent sexual offenses was 14 percent.[206] Ultimately, it is the disturbing nature of a minority of these crimes and the antisocial, repugnant behaviors that are involved more generally—rather than the strong likelihood that specific individuals will commit violent sexual crimes or repeat them—which in too many instances seem to justify prolonged incarceration and other extreme interventions. This is little more than a new-age variation of the logical fallacy known as guilt by association.

Studies show that experts tend to presume that if a respondent "looks like . . . a class of offenders who pose high risk . . . the judged probability must be high [that their risk is high as well],"[207] even if the true base rate is relatively low. In addition, studies indicate that as these offenders grow older, their rates tend to decrease because of changes that occur as these offenders age. Nevertheless, "SVP legislation tends to be applied to older sex offenders . . . who have achieved a lengthy criminal record and does not recognize important maturational changes that may mitigate the risk for recidivism."[208] Thus, while there appears to be a small core of very dangerous sex offenders, most are far less dangerous than society is willing or likely to recognize.

Given these popular misconceptions and misperceptions, the public is likely to consider every offender with a sexual or other mental disorder as highly dangerous merely because of the sexual predator, sexually dangerous, or mentally disordered offender labels that they are given and how those offenders are portrayed in the media. "[S]ex offender policies are often passed hastily and are not based on scientific evidence but on emotional reactions to high-profile, violent, disturbing cases."[209] Also, "[c]ommon misperceptions may interfere with offenders' treatment and reintegration into society as well as influence legislatures to pass laws that are misguided and inefficient."[210]

FUTURE DANGEROUSNESS ASSESSMENTS IN PRETRIAL MATTERS

Before defendants go to trial in criminal cases, there are two types of decisions judges make that involve assessments or impressions of future dangerousness. The first is determining whether pretrial detention of a defendant is justified; the other is whether juveniles and other children should be tried as adults. With pretrial detentions, the dangerousness assessment is likely to be made by the judge rather quickly, more intuitively than not, although in the federal system the law states that it is supposed to be based on a risk-assessment model in which the judge considers various factors related to flight risk and potential harm to the community.[211] With decisions as to whether a juvenile should be transferred to adult court, however, the likelihood is greater that one or both parties may submit expert psychiatric or psychological evidence related to dangerousness.

Pretrial Detention

Preventive detention in its most abused form is associated with undemocratic regimes that use it as a means of imprisoning persons for lengthy periods of time without a trial based on mere accusations of wrongdoing. In recent years, the United States has employed a variation on this type of detention to indefinitely incarcerate enemy combatants, foreign nationals, and even American citizens if they are secretly accused of being terrorists or aiding terrorists.[212] Federal and state jurisdictions embrace a less intrusive form of pretrial incarceration—with diminished due process protections—in order to "temporarily" detain persons charged with serious crimes because they are deemed to be dangerous,[213] or a flight risk before they can be tried. Nevertheless, even this type of preventive detention can have serious due process flaws that produce significant inequities for persons with mental disabilities deemed to be dangerous.

Federal statistics reveal that unnecessary pretrial incarcerations are not uncommon. Many are longer than they should be, and the decision whether to detain defendants is strongly affected by the economic circumstances of the individual involved, by stigma, and, most of all, by perceptions about the potential danger to the community that detainees might pose if they are allowed to go free.[214] This latter perception can be particularly problematic for defendants who have mental disabilities, which many of them do.[215] According to the commissioner of the New York Department of Correction, "City data show that mentally ill defendants . . . stay in jail twice as long as inmates who don't have mental health issues."[216] Due to sanism and pretexuality[217] most judges, like other people in society, tend to assume that defendants with mental disabilities are more dangerous than other defendants. The need for mental health care and treatment, which is widespread for these defendants, often provides a convenient justification for preventive detention where other justifications might be lacking.

According to a major study, 11 percent of "all defendants had received psychiatric treatment at some time during the two years prior to the initial [court] appearance."[218] Thus, even if defendants with mental disabilities are charged with nonviolent felonies or serious misdemeanors, courts may divert them into involuntary mental health treatment programs indefinitely in lieu of their being tried, convicted, and sentenced.[219] Moreover, courts may deny defendants with mental disabilities their release while they await trial, citing their need for mental health treatment as the basis for detaining them as potential threats to the community.[220]

Arguably those individuals, who later are convicted and sent to jail or prison, incur minimal deprivations of their liberty and other freedoms as a result of their pretrial incarcerations, but it is still a deprivation even though the time they have served is likely to be subtracted from their sentences, and it places them in a disadvantage in trying to prepare for their trials. Defendants who are arrested and eventually freed without being sentenced, however, frequently incur substantial deprivations of their freedoms without meaningful due process. For this second group, their pretrial detentions span the time from which the defendants are first arrested until they are released on bail, freed because the charges against them have been dismissed, or tried and then freed. These pretrial incarcerations may be as short as a few days, or often as long as eighteen months or more. For defendants who are confined pretrial so that they may receive mental health treatments, their lengths of confinement correspond more closely with the time that is deemed necessary to "treat" them—which may be many months—than the time that is required to hold a trial.[221] For them, pretrial detention is equivalent to de facto involuntary commitment without the normal heightened civil due process guarantees.

A primary reason why pretrial detentions have been permitted and are so widespread has to do with an understandable desire of those making policy decisions to protect their communities from potential harm by individuals who have been charged with committing serious crimes and to ensure those individuals do not flee the jurisdiction. Unfortunately, this desire tends to persist even when the available evidence suggests that for many or most of those who are detained there is a minimal or relatively low likelihood that they will do anything to violate the conditions of their release that pertain to committing new crimes.[222] Also, bureaucratic inefficiency undermines pretrial detention.[223] Thus, defendants frequently remain incarcerated much longer than is necessary because federal and state governments lack the resources and incentives to ensure that pretrial detention hearings and the subsequent trials will be speedy.

Pretrial detention is not something that rarely occurs or that is reserved for the most dangerous offenders. Extrapolating from federal Bureau of Justice Statistics regarding both federal and state correctional systems, each year there are approximately 1.5 million arrests, or more, in which pretrial detention may apply.[224] Almost all of these arrests result in at least short-term incarcerations until an initial bail hearing is held. More importantly, 45 percent of both state[225] and federal[226] defendants are incarcerated throughout the entire pretrial period because either their bail is denied, or they cannot provide the necessary financial guarantees to obtain bail, which is particularly likely to occur for defendants with serious mental disabilities. State court data shows that 50 percent of all defendants spend more than three months waiting for their cases to be adjudicated, and 14 percent are detained for more than a year.[227] The situation in the federal courts is even worse, where the *average* time until adjudication occurs exceeds a year.[228]

Most criminal defendants incur pretrial detention based on their broadly perceived threat to the community. Those who are not viewed as dangerous, or the relatively few that have the necessary financial resources and have committed nonviolent crimes, are likely to be released on bail. Most of the rest are detained indefinitely until their cases are resolved or heard. Unlike most dangerousness proceedings, but similar to many death penalty determinations, these assessments of dangerousness usually are made without the involvement of mental health experts. Generally judges—based on administrative reports filled with hearsay evidence and/or imprecise, subjective, and even arbitrary impressions about a defendant's dangerousness made in time frames measured in a very few minutes or less—determine whether bail is to be granted and, if so, how much money must be placed at risk. When defendants have significant mental disabilities, which tend to be associated with dangerousness, the potential for bias and pretexuality is greater. Moreover, the trials of defendants with mental disabilities may be delayed indefinitely while they receive care and treatment for their mental impairments.[229]

Juvenile Transfer Proceedings to Adult Court

One of the more startling, unfair, and counterproductive changes in sentencing policies has involved juveniles, who commit what are viewed as serious adult criminal offenses. Through much of the 1970s, juvenile and other child offenders were considered "delinquents" who could and should be rehabilitated. In the early 1980s, however, the pendulum swung away from rehabilitation toward the need to protect the public at almost any cost, as concerns heightened about perceived increases in violent crimes among teenagers and children even younger than that. The clinically and morally compelling principle that children are less responsible for their actions than adults[230] was replaced with the clinically and morally bankrupt presumption and tautology that children who are able to commit criminal offenses that adults commit are—by virtue of their actions—as criminally responsible as adults would be.[231]

Under this tortured legal reasoning, the more serious the crime, the more criminally responsible the child must be, and the less likely that the child will respond to rehabilitation. Ironically, if these "kid" offenders have serious mental disabilities, which many of them do,[232] they tend to be viewed as much more dangerous, and even less deserving of the care and treatment they need to be rehabilitated. For instance, the Idaho Supreme Court ruled that it was proper for a trial court to impose a life sentence on a teenager who pled guilty to murdering his mother. This was done despite the fact that at the time of the crime the defendant was only sixteen, in a psychotic state, and taking medications for major depression and anxiety disorder.[233]

Since the U.S. Supreme Court's 1966 decision in *Kent v. United States*,[234] our nation has deemed it constitutionally permissible to transfer juvenile offenders to be tried as adults, but only if certain extenuating circumstances existed. Originally, the key factor was a conclusion that the child could not be rehabilitated. Beginning in the 1980s, out of exaggerated concerns about violent crime by juveniles, the emphasis began to shift toward increasing the protections for communities from the perceived threats posed by juvenile violence and crime. Today, the most important factor in juvenile transfer decisions is the "potential risk of dangerousness," followed by the child's "level of sophistication—maturity."[235] Amenability to treatment is clearly third, if it is considered at all. Moreover, amenability to treatment in these juvenile proceedings is now viewed in the context of dangerousness, not vice versa.[236] As one researcher has observed, "current risk of violence . . . can change the likelihood of rehabilitation and dictate when and how a rehabilitation plan can be implemented."[237] Conversely, "estimates of future risk of harm necessarily include a judgment about the likelihood that rehabilitation will reduce the risk."[238]

Increasingly, courts rely on experts to make predictions about the dangerousness of juveniles based on the same controversial and highly questionable scales and measures that have been applied to adults. What makes these predictions more attenuated and even less reliable is that generally these assessment tools have never been validated for children of any age. A number of courts making these juvenile transfer determinations rely on experts who use the Psychopathy Checklist–Revised, which purports—based on very sketchy empirical evidence—to be able to identify dangerous psychopaths. It is believed—with inadequate empirical support—that as a group "psychopathic offenders commit disproportionate amounts of serious violent crime." This checklist is supposed to be "the strongest predictor of risk for violence and treatment response in adults,"[239] which, even if true, is faint praise indeed because almost all of the other predictors are so weak. Furthermore, deciding what characteristics should be used to categorize someone as being a psychopath is a subjective process with little or no scientific basis. Psychopathy is not a disease or medical condition; it is a socially determined construct that is heavily influence by politics and morality. Such a diagnosis also creates a hard-to-rebut presumption that the child with such a diagnosis is and always will be dangerous.

For a number of reasons, though, including in particular the well-recognized developmental differences between children and adults, even some of the experts who use the controversial Psychopathy Checklist on adults question whether it should be applied to adolescents and younger children. Based on a review of the existing literature, researchers have concluded that these juvenile psychopathy measures are so much in their "infancy" that using them "in the clinical/forensic setting may be considered unethical at this stage."[240] Also, "certain characteristics that have been empirically linked to psychopathy in adults may be no more than transient features of adolescent development in youths."[241] If accurate, this means that many or perhaps most of these juveniles probably would be amenable to treatment and rehabilitation as they age into adulthood.

A 2000 study by the federal Bureau of Justice Assistance (BJA) found that there were about 5,400 youths in adult prisons and 9,100 in local jails.[242] Furthermore, of the forty-four jurisdictions that send youths to adult prisons and jails, only eighteen have special units to house them separately.[243] Slightly more than half of those states mix adult and juvenile offenders together. Typically, juveniles who are sentenced as adults must serve their time with experienced criminals, even though as children they "face serious physical and emotional harm from older inmates and are more likely to commit suicide."[244] As compared to adolescents in juvenile detention facilities, those in jails and prisons are "five times more likely to be sexually assaulted, twice as likely to be beaten by staff, and fifty percent more likely to be attacked with a weapon."[245] Not surprisingly, studies also show that when juveniles are eventually released from adult prisons, they are more likely to commit new crimes than if they had been confined in the juvenile detention system.[246] The lack of rehabilitation in adult jails and prisons and having to associate and survive among adult criminals tend to make these juvenile offenders as a group more—not less—dangerous, and those with mental disabilities more impaired.

FUTURE DANGEROUSNESS AS A KEY FACTOR IN DEATH PENALTY CASES

Future Dangerousness

Courts often—and arguably almost always—rely on future dangerousness to justify the death penalty,[247] and this reliance can be either de facto or de jure. Governments, and in turn defense lawyers, often employ psychiatrists, psychologists, and other forensic mental health "experts" to help prove their cases either for or against execution. Such assessments by state-retained experts have proven to be unreliable, generally failing to meet even the lowest legal standard of proof—a preponderance of the evidence—much less the most rigorous beyond a reasonable doubt standard that our Constitution demands for criminal convictions, but not afterward for sentencing. In death penalty cases, the critical factor is what the jury believes, which has turned this type of sentencing into an evidentiary free-for-all that is worse when inherently faulty predictions of or assumptions about dangerousness are relied upon to execute persons with mental disabilities.[248] This is particularly disturbing because as studies substantiate, "[t]here is no question that the death penalty is disproportionately imposed in cases involving defendants with mental disabilities."[249]

In order to be executed in the majority of jurisdictions that continue to permit it, a defendant must be found guilty of a capital crime and then found to be "deserving" of the death penalty. Legally, whether a particular defendant deserves to die depends on a weighing of "aggravating" versus "mitigating" factors. The most common and decisive of the aggravating factors is whether the defendant is perceived to be a future danger to the community.[250] This does not mean that in every death penalty case the defendant's future dangerousness will be formally assessed in determining whether execution is appropriate. In many instances, no formal dangerousness assessment is involved. Nevertheless, studies indicate that most of the time jurors are directly affected in their death penalty decisions by their subjective perceptions of whether defendants might pose a future danger to society if they are not executed,[251] including their having a mental disability. As a practical matter, in order to show that defendants really do not pose a significant danger to society, many defense attorneys want juries to be informed that defendants, if they are not executed, will remain in prison permanently, or at least for a very, very long time.[252]

Not infrequently, prosecutors present formal evidence of future dangerousness as an "aggravating" factor to support a defendant being executed. In these cases, often the defense and the state retain forensic mental health experts. Yet it is up to the trier of fact—a jury with instructions from the judge—to decide the ultimate issue of future dangerousness based on often-contradictory expert testimony. Jurors are asked to assess a defendant's relative degree of dangerousness, and also to weigh dangerousness and other "aggravating" factors against "mitigating" circumstances, such as mental disabilities, abuse as a child, or prospects for rehabilitation. With regard to mental conditions and disorders, however, any mitigating benefits of reduced culpability more often than not are substantially outweighed by the ever-present bias that defendants with those mental disabilities should be viewed as being inherently more dangerous. In fact, sometimes defense counsel do not even present mitigating mental status evidence because it can be a "double-edged" sword if the prosecution uses dangerousness as an aggravator or the jury simply presumes the defendant is likely to be dangerous due to his or her mental impairment. The U.S. Supreme Court made this point when it specified that due to this double-edged effect, oftentimes mitigating mental retardation evidence should not be presented by defense counsel because to do so would constitute ineffective representation.[253]

The fairness of this sentencing process has been made even more tenuous by the Supreme Court's decision in *Kansas v. Marsh*,[254] which cedes broad discretion to jurisdictions wishing to facilitate the imposition of the death penalty. In that case, the Court upheld a state statute that requires execution if a jury unanimously finds the existence of a statutorily designated aggravating factor beyond a reasonable doubt, unless that factor is clearly outweighed by mitigating circumstances. Under such a scheme, if a jury believes that both aggravating and mitigating circumstances are present and they appear to be equal, then the death sentence is mandatory. Also, if the mitigating circumstances are given little or no weight, the most insubstantial aggravating circumstance, including a highly dubious dangerousness finding or belief associated with a defendant who has a mental disability, will be enough to compel and justify that defendant's execution.[255]

As with other types of dangerousness assessments, the reliability of even the most qualified expert opinions—generally these experts support the position held by the party that is paying them to testify—is at best questionable in death penalty cases, and arguably without any objective foundation in most such cases.[256] The Texas Defender Service found that in that state the prosecution experts that predict defendants' future dangerousness in death penalty cases were "wrong" 95 percent of the time, according to the criteria established in that study.[257] This startling percentage is particularly significant because from 1976 to 2003, Texas executed more than a third of all defendants put to death in the United States.[258]

Three psychologists independently replicated this survey methodology in a 2008 study using "federal prison disciplinary records of federal capital inmates."[259] Similarly, they found that "only a minority of capital offenders perpetrate serious violence in prison, and that it is *not* possible to reliably identify at trial which of these defendants are more likely than not to commit these acts."[260] Stated differently, "[g]overnment assertions of 'future dangerousness' as a nonstatutory aggravating factor were not predictive of prison misconduct."[261] This second study revealed that predictions of serious violence in the federal system were "wrong" 90 percent of the time.[262]

These two studies examined the disciplinary records of 300 inmates (155 and 145, respectively) who had been sentenced to death based on their future dangerousness, to determine whether subsequent to their sentencing they had engaged in any serious violent behaviors. By necessity, both studies examined the inmates in the prison environment, not in community settings. Nevertheless, the significance of this distinction is minimized greatly—and probably outweighed—by two countervailing factors. First, in a prison setting serious acts of violence are much more likely to be reported by the guards and other prison authorities than in society more generally because inmates' actions are under much closer scrutiny. Second, and more important, capital defendants who do not receive the death penalty are very likely to spend the rest of their lives in a maximum security prison anyway. Thus, the much more apt comparison is dangerousness within a secure environment, not dangerousness in the community.

Even conceding that there are certain methodological weaknesses in these studies, the overall results are still compelling. In both studies, the percentages of death row inmates who were found to have committed dangerous acts during the course of their incarcerations were remarkably low, 5 percent and 10 percent, respectively. These results are consistent with, and should be viewed in the context of, other studies indicating that mental health professionals tend to significantly overpredict dangerous behaviors when the decision to incarcerate or release respondents is at issue.[263]

Predictions of dangerousness always have been questionable when they are used to support the death penalty, but the evidentiary problems may be expanding again as courts are beginning to admit, and are being urged to admit, "computer-generated visual representations of the brain's structure or of its function"[264] as evidence of dangerousness. This use of "neuroimaging," based on various types of brain scans, presumes that there is some meaningful correlation between perceived damage and irregularities in certain parts of the brain and violent and other types of behaviors, including the inability to control one's actions. The actual correlations appear to be very low, even as applied to large groups of people, much less particular individuals.

Currently, "it is clear that some forms of pathological aggression, such as impulsive aggression . . . have an underlying neurobiology that we are only beginning to understand."[265] However, it is still uncertain—and may never be knowable with any convincing degree of precision—what specific areas of the brain are responsible for in terms of specific behaviors, whether those areas have multiple and overlapping functions, how much damage or irregularity is significant, how it should be measured, and whether any, a few, or many key brain functions differ significantly from one individual to another[266] or by gender or age. Ultimately, "[b]rain images . . . capture a brain state at only one moment in time and say nothing about its function before or after. . . . Also, "a 'high' level of activity in one person may be normal in another."[267]

All of these practical limitations negate the legal value of trying to identify areas of the brain in specific individuals that are damaged or irregular. Unfortunately, many of these brain experts have learned almost nothing from psychiatrists and psychologists, who mistakenly assumed that they could reliably predict dangerous behaviors in humans. Many of these neuroscientists believe that they have special abilities to predict behaviors in individuals, even though the science and empirical studies on this subject do not support such beliefs. Nevertheless, if courts should become convinced that as a profession, neuroscience generally accepts the relevance of those unsupported beliefs, then evidence based on neuro-imaging could be deemed admissible to prove dangerousness in the same flawed ways that psychiatric diagnoses have been accepted to prove dangerousness. As with other types of risk-assessment methods,[268] this information may be useful if it is used to exclude persons as being dangerous, but has very little potential utility in identifying individuals who are at a high risk of offending.

The unfairness to defendants with mental disabilities that arises from the fact that expert opinions about future dangerousness are unreliable becomes magnified when the death penalty is involved. First, in order to be eligible to be executed, a defendant must be found guilty beyond a reasonable doubt of committing a capital crime. Nevertheless, when a jury decides whether to apply the death penalty, after weighing aggravating and mitigating circumstances, all standards of proof—much less the highest standard—disappear from consideration. As a result, the key aggravating factor in most, if not virtually all, capital cases—that the defendant will continue to be a danger to the community—is not subject to any legal standard of proof. As a practical matter, whatever the jury collectively believes, for whatever the reason, is determinative.

Second, as explained earlier, when determining actual dangerousness, lay jurors are interpreting complicated and often misleading technical information as applied to somewhat arbitrary and often confusing legal standards. Even though social science has shown it to be highly unreliable, expert testimony predicting dangerousness is admissible under the rationale that it is up to the jury to give proper weight to the experts' opinions. By this legal sleight of hand, conflicting opinions about dangerousness, none of which may be reliable, can form the entire basis for a jury to vote to have a person executed. Moreover, in a majority of death penalty cases, the jurors are left to make life and death decisions based on their vague impressions or beliefs about a defendant's future dangerousness without any expert guidance.[269]

In either situation, whether "aided" by expert opinion or not, jurors are fundamentally unprepared to make dangerousness assessments or considerations and are likely to be substantially influenced in their decision-making by various biases they have about people with mental disabilities.

There is a strong tendency in our society to believe persons with mental disabilities are inherently dangerous. This is made worse by a societal imperative that the only way to reduce the risk of violent crime is to adopt the strongest measures possible to punish offenders, even if their actual culpability should have been reduced due to their mental disabilities. In such an environment, the critical life and death decisions that jurors ultimately make about future dangerousness, as applied to capital defendants with mental disabilities, are highly unreliable.

Finally, as a result of a 1999 U.S. Supreme Court decision,[270] if capital defendants introduce the argument that they should receive a life sentence without the possibility of parole, the prosecution must be given the opportunity to present aggravating circumstances, including evidence that the defendant is a future danger to the community due to a mental disability. As a result, defense counsels are faced with a dilemma: they can either take the risky step of giving the prosecution the opportunity during sentencing to present evidence of a defendant's future dangerousness due to a mental disability as an aggravating circumstance; or forego their opportunity to inform the jury that even if a capital defendant does not receive the death penalty, there is a very high likelihood that the person will be sentenced to life in prison without parole. Unfortunately, without the best information, most jurors are predisposed to assuming that defendants who are not executed will receive a much lighter sentence than what they actually receive.[271]

Mental Disability Bias in Death Penalty Cases

Despite the U.S. Supreme Court's 2002 decision in *Atkins v. Virginia*,[272] which holds that persons with mental retardation (now more correctly referred to as intellectual disabilities) may not be executed, all other capital defendants with mental impairments remain eligible for the death penalty. Moreover, in *Atkins* the justices gave considerable discretion to the states and the federal government to decide what constitutes mental retardation and how, procedurally, that determination should be made.[273] Not surprisingly, many of the states that still have the death penalty are doing everything possible to limit the scope of the *Atkins* ruling. Georgia, using such broad discretion, is unique in requiring persons with mental retardation to prove beyond a reasonable doubt that they have this condition and that it occurred before they turned eighteen.[274] Due to these and other legal restrictions that many jurisdictions impose, "it is extremely likely that some people with mental retardation will continue to be sentenced to death, and executed."[275] Also, Texas was allowed to execute a man with an I.Q. of 61 because the Texas Court of Appeals agreed that the "state [could] simply refus[e] to accept [the defendant] as retarded enough to be exempted from execution."[276]

In addition, a relatively large group of persons with attributes similar to mental retardation—low intelligence and problems functioning in society—continues to be eligible for execution. These defendants do not have mental retardation as narrowly defined by the states or federal government, or they cannot prove their conditions began before they turned eighteen, or their conditions, while strongly similar to mental retardation, are classified differently, such as dementia, organic brain damage, or fetal alcohol spectrum disorders.[277] Beyond mental retardation, the *Atkins* precedent does not protect defendants with severe mental disabilities that seriously affect reasoning, decision-making, cognitive awareness, and/or social functioning.

Anecdotal evidence and court decisions continue to suggest that mental disability plays a much more significant role in contributing to death penalty verdicts than in preventing them. There have been numerous legal decisions[278] and media reports in which persons with severe mental impairments have been executed or scheduled for execution. Until the U.S. Supreme Court ruled that it was unconstitutional to do so many persons with mental retardation were being executed, despite their cognitive and functional impairments.[279]

Department of Justice statistics and various studies reveal that a substantial percentage of persons with legally significant mental conditions are found in state and federal jails and prisons.[280] Defendants with mental illnesses, below normal intelligence, and other cognitive deficiencies, who are not protected by the *Atkins* decision, are particularly vulnerable to being executed. First, many, if not most, persons with serious mental disabilities are more likely to confess or be convinced to confess to capital crimes. At least some of the time, those confessions are entirely false.[281] Moreover, such confessions also may be inaccurate, misleading, or overly damning due to a cognitively-impaired defendant's misperceptions, delusions, compulsions, flawed reasoning, and poor decision-making. Also, many interrogators deliberately use a suspect's mental impairments to facilitate a confession, often employing methods of deception that are taught to police interrogators[282] and embraced by the legal system.[283]

Second, most jurisdictions have narrowed, or all but repealed, the statutes that used to allow defendants through counsel to pursue diminished culpability defenses—not guilty by reason of insanity or diminished capacity[284]—so that it is now even more difficult, if not close to impossible, for defendants to successfully argue, even if they were in the midst of a psychotic episode, that they lacked the necessary mental state to be convicted of a capital crime.

Third, as was mentioned earlier, even during sentencing, mental impairments are much more likely to be used as an aggravating factor or consideration explicitly or implicitly justifying the death penalty due to perceived dangerousness, than as a mitigating factor that would reduce their culpability.[285] The chilling effect of the double-edged nature of this evidence often results in the defense choosing not to present an argument of mitigation based on mental disability, even where such an impairment can be substantiated. Furthermore, risk assessments are even less reliable and have less predicative validity when they are applied to persons with intellectual disabilities.[286]

Fourth, most capital defendants lack the means to hire their own mental health experts to help their lawyers prepare mental status defenses and mitigation strategies, and to testify at trial.[287] At best, indigent defendants with mental impairments—and most are indigent—are entitled to very limited funds to hire their own experts; at worst they are not entitled to court-appointed experts, who have no special allegiance to the client's defense. Also, these defendants have no enforceable expectation that the expert they receive will be reasonably effective or competent.[288] At the same time, many publicly paid or pro bono lawyers provide compromised representation—as compared to privately retained counsel—due to overwhelming caseloads, insufficient resources, and/or lack of death penalty experience.

For all of these reasons and others, in 2006 the American Bar Association, the American Psychiatric Association, the American Psychological Association, and the National Alliance of the Mentally Ill jointly recommended that defendants with certain severe mental disorders—in addition to mental retardation—should not be executed.[289] Nevertheless, not a single jurisdiction has passed legislation to require such an exemption. As the *New York Times* observed, the "death penalty system fails to take adequate account of severe mental illness, whether at trial, at sentencing or in postconviction proceedings."[290] This lack of concern for persons with mental disabilities extends throughout our legal system.

6

DANGEROUSNESS AND THE UNCONSCIONABLE FAILURE TO PROVIDE HUMANE CARE AND TREATMENT TO PERSONS WITH SERIOUS MENTAL DISABILITIES

Humans are composed of more than flesh and bone. . . . [M]ental health, just as much as physical health, is a mainstay of life. (John F. Kennedy)[1]

Orr would be crazy to fly more missions and sane if he didn't, but if he was sane he had to fly them. If he flew them he was crazy and didn't have to; but if he didn't want to he was sane and had to. (Joseph Heller, *Catch-22*)[2]

Throughout its history, the United States has rarely, if ever, been adequately committed to providing care, treatment, and rehabilitation for persons with serious mental disabilities in need. In recent decades, we have not even made a good faith effort. In addition, our society has consistently failed to provide funding and resources that are necessary to provide humane care in the community to persons with legally significant mental disabilities, and too often have abused and neglected them when they have been forced into government custody. This is particularly true for children and older Americans with mental disabilities and persons with developmental disabilities who increasingly have been dumped into various types of nursing and civil detention facilities. Even worse, much—and arguably most—of the care and treatment of inmates and other detainees in our criminal and juvenile justice systems fails to meet even the disturbingly low constitutional threshold that the U.S. Supreme Court has pegged as "the minimal civilized measure of life's necessities."[3]

Today, all of these failures, omissions, and deliberate indifferences have been transformed into powerful and too often convenient legal justifications for involuntarily confining or otherwise coercively treating and intrusively managing the lives of persons diagnosed with or identified as having mental disabilities who have no adequate voluntary community alternatives. This type of catch-22 also is used to extend terms of confinement and other intrusive government restrictions when respondents with mental impairments fail to improve, become worse, or are predicted to become worse if they were to be released, given more liberties, or deprived of fewer rights. If all of this were not bad enough, our nation is now confronted with a large and expanding cohort of combat veterans with mental disorders and mental injuries,[4] many of whom—unless our public policies change—will likely find themselves in comparably desperate situations as other Americans with serious mental disabilities who are deemed to be or adjudicated as dangerous.[5]

INADEQUATE AND INHUMANE CIVIL MENTAL HEALTH CARE AND TREATMENT

The Civil Mental Health System for Adults

Today, instead of spending years in large custodial facilities, involuntary adult civil mental patients are more likely to spend days or weeks or sometimes months in smaller facilities and receive enough treatment, typically in the form of powerful, excessively dosed antipsychotic medications, to stabilize them so that they may be released as no longer legally dangerous.[6] Increasingly, courts also mandate intrusive restrictions to govern the lives of "outpatients" in order to ensure safety for the foreseeable future for the community and family members. Typically, though, because there are few mandated entitlements and no constitutional right to treatment, there is no guarantee that these so-called patients will receive humane and adequate care beyond the current overreliance on the

compelled administration of powerful antipsychotic drugs, with their serious and unpleasant side effects. This cycle of temporary hospitalization,
temporary stabilization, and intrusive restrictions is often repeated many
times over for each respondent.

Shorter and repeated hospital stays also are more commonplace for the
more fortunate people with substance abuse problems who are involuntarily committed rather than imprisoned.[7] Most of these illegal drug users
end up in prison, however. In addition, persons who are involuntarily
committed because they have intellectual or developmental disabilities
are more likely to be placed in community settings of varying quality. Yet
there also remains a relatively large core group of individuals with intellectual and developmental disabilities who spend all or most of their lives
in smaller institutions and/or nursing care facilities[8] receiving care, treatment, and habilitation that is inadequate, overly dependent on powerful
medications, and in many instances inhumane.[9]

In recent years, some of the most publicized rehabilitation and treatment deficiencies have involved patients who revolve in and out of involuntary or coercive outpatient and inpatient commitment situations onto
the streets, boarding homes, flop houses, and other substandard housing
alternatives.[10] There are relatively few consensual treatment and rehabilitation settings that most people with serious mental disabilities can afford
without federal and state subsidies. What government assistance exists is
hard to come by, becoming more scarce and generally inadequate even
when it is available.[11] Also, many individuals who might be eligible for
services are unwilling to participate in public programs because they are
afraid, or decide for other reasons that they do not want to be pressured
into taking antipsychotic medications that frequently have serious, unpleasant side effects, including uncontrollable twitching and tremors, loss
of affect, and worst of all, death.[12] Often, those who do not choose to take
those antipsychotic medications are eventually involuntarily committed
or threatened with commitment in order to compel them to take the drugs
that they have rejected. For many and arguably most of them, however,
once the coercion is lifted the cycle soon begins anew because there are
too few adequate voluntary programs in the community to fill the overwhelming need. This problem is getting worse as federal, state, and local
programs are cut to manage our deficits.[13]

Rehabilitation and treatment alternatives are not readily available in
the community, particularly since federal, state, and local governments

have been cutting back on their mental health services.[14] A number of states have special Medicaid waiver programs that provide some assistance to certain individuals, but these programs are quite limited and are at risk—along with public mental health and habilitation services more generally—due to the effects of our fragile economy on state and federal budgets.[15] Typically, many basic social services are unavailable as well, which substantially increases the possibility that persons with serious mental disorders, conditions, or aberrations will have relapses, which often are equated with repeat antisocial behaviors and offenses that must be coercively controlled. Even the U.S. Supreme Court in upholding the depopulation of the California prison system in 2011 observed that the "release of seriously mentally ill inmates [would be] likely to create special dangers because of their recidivism rates,"[16] and thus they should continue to be confined. As a result, they have been left to "languish . . . without access to necessary care . . . in crowded, unsafe, and unsanitary conditions,"[17] hoping that deinstitutionalization of other offenders may eventually ameliorate the unconstitutional conditions for those who remain.

The lack of adequate consensual mental health care and treatment has produced a revolving-door syndrome for involuntary civil patients who are forcibly committed to psychiatric hospitals, drug and alcohol treatment centers, or other detention facilities, repeatedly, for relatively short periods of time until they are stabilized. Yet once they are no longer in government custody, they have access to insufficient treatment and other support services in the community. For similar reasons, many children are incarcerated in juvenile detention centers each year, even though they have not been charged with any crimes, because they are awaiting mental health and related services in the community, which are in such short supply.[18] Our society's primary solution for the lack of adequate care and treatment for these troubled juveniles is to dump them into prison-like facilities where their troubles intensify and multiply.

What has remained constant over many decades is that the worst problems encountered by civilly institutionalized persons or persons threatened with such institutionalization are due to the absence of sufficient public funds and resources to support their treatment, rehabilitation, and living needs in the community. This was true when "patients" were warehoused in institutions in the 1950s and 1960s, deinstitutionalized in the 1970s and early 1980s, and now when patients are dumped into unwelcoming communities[19] or smaller facilities. The main difference is that in more recent years these individuals often end up incarcerated in our criminal or juvenile justice systems, which have become the primary governmental mechanisms for confining and controlling adults with mental disabilities when they are deemed dangerous, antisocial, and/or not worth helping.[20]

Special Populations: Children and Nursing Home Residents

The care, treatment, and rehabilitation inadequacies of our civil mental health systems have been—and continue to be—even worse for children and older Americans with mental impairments, who are at higher risk for nonconsensual institutionalizations and overmedication. In addition, many young and middle-aged adults with mental, intellectual, and developmental disabilities are being "dumped" into nursing homes and similar facilities inappropriately because there are no other places for them to go. In large part these additional risks for abuse and neglect are due to the fact that members of these populations tend to be substantially more dependent on others to make decisions about their care. While, legally, none of the coercive admissions that members of these populations face are considered to be involuntary commitments per se, generally those who are admitted to these facilities do not or cannot provide informed consent for their residential care and treatment. Many of them are institutionalized and coercively administered antipsychotic and other powerful behavior-stabilizing medications based on the presumption and belief that otherwise they might bring harm to themselves or others, but with the understanding that overmedication will make them easier to manage and help to fill empty beds.

Children and Adolescents

The Joint Commission on Mental Health of Children concluded in 1969 that "there is not a single community in this country which provides an acceptable standard of services for its mentally ill children." Mental health and juvenile justice experts have opined that this lack of proper care has remained entrenched ever since[21] and appears to be growing worse because essential services are being cut and eliminated. The "poor quality and intrusiveness" of mental health care, treatment, and habilitation for "troubled and troubling youth" who have been dumped into residential facilities and foster care has been especially disturbing. "Children and adolescents who are admitted to psychiatric facilities are often wards of the state"; other youth "come from families that are often reluctant volunteers who . . . placed their children [in institutions] because less intrusive alternatives are unavailable, unaffordable, or simply not offered."[22]

Tragically, "[t]he lack of adequate, appropriate and accessible mental health services for youth and families [remains] a national crisis."[23] This also is true for the growing number of children of military personnel in combat who "tend to have [even] higher rates of mental health problems than those [children] in the general population . . . especially during a parent's deployment."[24] Furthermore, children with developmental and intellectual disabilities, who reside in various types of custodial care facilities—like their adult counterparts—find themselves without appropriate habilitation and other necessary services.[25]

A disproportionate prevalence of mental disorders and conditions generally exists for "children and youth in the child welfare [system]."[26] As many as "[f]ifty percent [of all child welfare recipients] . . . have mental health problems. In particular, youth in residential treatment centers . . . have extremely high rates of mental and behavioral health disorders as compared to the general population."[27] For most of them, mental health care, treatment, and habilitation are inadequate or nonexistent. Because these already scarce social services are being cut, it is likely that even more kids with mental disabilities will be confined in inappropriate institutional settings—including even adult prisons—where mental health care, treatment, and habilitation are inadequate, nonexistent, inappropriate, and/or overly intrusive.

In addition, foster children—whether or not they end up in institutional settings—are at much higher risk for mental disorders and being overmedicated using powerful antipsychotic drugs. Studies indicate that youth in foster homes are at least three times more likely to receive Medicaid-funded psychotropic medications than are youth who receive Medicaid due to their family's low income.[28] This policy of administering powerful psychiatric drugs to youth in foster care is rampant even though there is no "substantive evidence as to its effectiveness and safety."[29] Foster children—whether or not they have a diagnosed mental disorder—"are being prescribed cocktails of powerful antipsychosis drugs just as frequently as some of the most mentally disabled youngsters on Medicaid . . .,"[30] who also are being overmedicated.

Many youth with mental disabilities, particularly those in foster care, end up institutionalized in the juvenile justice or correctional systems, where their mental conditions and problems typically intensify, worsen, or develop. In the absence of minimally adequate mental health services for youth and families, "[t]he number of adolescents with undiagnosed mental health disorders committed to the juvenile justice system has exploded. Estimates are that between 50% and 75% of the youth who are committed to juvenile justice have diagnosable mental health problems."[31]

Nursing Homes and Other Adult Care Facilities

Similar patterns of coercive dumping and excessive use of antipsychotic medications exist for adults with mental and developmental disabilities who have been institutionalized in nursing homes and other adult care centers that typically are not prepared to deal with people who have serious mental disorders. The Centers for Medicare and Medicaid reported that in 2008 "nearly 125,000 young and middle-aged adults [ages 22 to 64] with serious mental illness lived in U.S. nursing homes . . . [which] was a 41 percent increase from 2002."[32] Those numbers have continued to rise. In addition, there are many older nursing home patients who have mental impairments. Whether younger or older, these nursing home patients do not receive the mental health care, treatment, habilitation, and other supports they need to live in their communities.

Also, there is a pressing—yet perverse—economic incentive to fill nursing home beds because generally older people are "healthier than the generation before them and are more independent and more likely to stay in their homes."[33] In addition, the federal government helps states pay for the care of nursing home patients with mental disorders as long as the occupancy rate of those patients in a particular facility does not exceed 50 percent. The federal government and the states, however, typically will not pay to allow these patients to receive community-based mental health services.

The primary expressed concern with respect to such patient dumping is not the welfare of the nursing home residents who have untreated or undertreated mental disorders, but rather the presumed danger that these individuals may pose to other residents.[34] The typical response is not to provide these residents with mental health care in the community or even to place them into psychiatric facilities. Instead, the most cost-effective way for nursing homes to deal with this perceived danger is to heavily medicate those residents who become disruptive or are thought likely to become disruptive.

Inappropriately medicating residents in nursing homes and similar facilities using psychoactive drugs is widespread and "has troubled professionals in geriatrics for years."[35] Unfortunately, the Omnibus Budget Reconciliation Act of 1987, which was supposed to reform such abuses by encouraging comprehensive mental health screening and the "use of nonpharmacological treatments,"[36] has not worked. According to the inspector general of the federal Department of Health and Human Services, a federal audit found that over half of the antipsychotic medications of nursing home patients covered under Medicare were inappropriate and nearly "one in seven . . . nursing home residents . . . are given powerful atypical antipsychotic drugs even though the medicines increase the risks of death and are not approved for such treatments."[37] Furthermore, "83 percent of [those] antipsychotic prescriptions . . . were for uses not approved by federal drug regulators." The Centers for Medicare and Medicaid Services opined that this was due in part to "drug makers' paying kickbacks to nursing homes to increase prescriptions for the medicines."[38] In Florida, where many older persons reside, the overmedication problem has been comprehensively documented. A major study found that "71 percent of Medicaid residents in Florida nursing homes were receiving psychoactive medication . . . even though most were not taking such drugs in the months before they moved and didn't have psychiatric diagnoses. . . . But only 12 percent were getting nondrug treatments like behavioral therapy."[39]

The reasons why these medication abuses continue may be varied and complex,[40] but certainly not justified. To begin with, the 1987 Reconciliation Act had a major loophole, which has allowed states to exempt from screening nursing home residents who are transferred from hospitals. According to the federal data, less than 50 percent of the nursing home "residents with major illnesses receive the mandated assessment." Making matters worse, nursing home staffing is "stretched thin and inadequately trained in mental health care." In addition, access to psychiatrists, psychologists, and other mental health professionals is inadequate. In order to respond to perceived mental health–related harmful behaviors, drugs are "used as restraints."[41]

As a result of these and other substantial abuses of persons with mental impairments in nursing homes and other adult care facilities, there has been significant litigation in recent years to compel states to place these residents in more appropriate, more humane, and less restrictive and more integrated community settings. The state of Illinois, for example, agreed to "offer approximately 4,500 mentally ill nursing home residents the choice to move out of two dozen large facilities . . . into smaller [community-based] settings that experts say are more appropriate and less expensive."[42] Attorneys representing the plaintiffs observed that this was "the beginning of transforming a system that has been focused on institutionalizing people for decades into one that actually delivers what people want and need."[43]

Similarly, the U.S. Department of Justice ordered the state of North Carolina to find community-based placements for approximately "5,800 people with mental illness [who] live at 288 adult-care [centers] . . .," which violates the Americans with Disabilities Act.[44] As one advocate noted, "[i]t's an embarrassment that the state has released more than 7,500 individuals directly from psychiatric hospitals to adult-care homes in the past decade."[45] Also, New York state agreed to place in community-based housing "[h]undreds of mentally ill people who have been confined to nursing homes, sometimes in prisonlike conditions."[46] According to the plaintiffs, "psychiatric centers and nursing homes had developed 'turnaround agreements, which essentially were written agreements to transfer patients back and forth'"[47] between these residential facilities.

Unfortunately, these lawsuits represent only the tip of the iceberg when measured against the continuing abuses of persons with mental disabilities in nursing homes and other adult care facilities nationwide. For instance, New York's entire system of care for over a million people "with developmental disabilities, mental illnesses and other conditions that put them at risk" is being revamped because it has led to so many instances of "abuse and neglect."[48] Furthermore, Virginia reached an agreement with the Justice Department in which that state would move as many as 5,000 persons with developmental disabilities from large state institutions into "their own homes, their family's homes or group homes as part of a 10-year, 2.1 billion settlement."[49] Yet there are few adequate community-based housing alternatives for them and other people with serious mental disabilities now,[50] and nationally funds for such alternatives are being cut.

THE CRIMINAL JUSTICE SYSTEM

Introduction

Sometime in the late 1970s, our nation began rejecting and turning its back on the policy of trying to provide humane care, treatment, and rehabilitation to prisoners and quasi-civil detainees. Instead we created highly secure, punitive, and inhumane environments to keep inmates behind bars for as long as an increasingly flexible Constitution would permit.[51] The largely incorrect notion that most human beings who commit antisocial and criminal acts cannot change their behaviors—even when they are young—has become a persistent and now well-entrenched American conviction. This view has contributed to overly harsh punishments and injustices in a number of different ways throughout our correctional systems.

The implementation of such a cynical and unforgiving philosophy increasingly is being recognized as "a disastrous failure."[52] Unfortunately, this view also has defined the laws and policies governing inmates and ex-inmates with mental disabilities. Yet the negative impact for them has been enhanced because of the widespread belief that they are inherently dangerous and the fact that they are particularly vulnerable to abuse and neglect. Generally, inmates and ex-inmates with mental disabilities have been deprived of even minimally adequate mental health and related services that they need to live humanely. This has been true whether they reside in jails, prisons, detention facilities, or secure "treatment" facilities, or are eventually released into the streets, dilapidated housing, or other inadequate community facilities. When measured against the aspirations of therapeutic jurisprudence,[53] this is the "perfect storm" of counterproductive and destructive policies and practices.

Dangerousness—broadly conceived—is the conceptual linchpin used to justify policies in which people with mental disabilities have been incarcerated, intrusively restrained, abused, deprived of other rights, and even executed without meaningful due process. Dangerousness also justifies incarcerating those inmates indefinitely and depriving them of humane treatment and rehabilitation. Most people with mental disabilities who are sent to America's secure detention and treatment facilities due to their perceived or adjudicated dangerousness are confined for a very long time in substandard conditions without adequate care, treatment, and rehabilitation.[54] For persons with serious mental disabilities, jails, prisons, secure treatment facilities, and other forms of coerced detention and care in the criminal justice system are far worse than any civilized society should tolerate or condone. Moreover, those who are released become subject to harsh and intrusive "conditions" governing how they may live their lives on the outside. New laws and policies often extend the state's control over these former inmates indefinitely, sometimes permanently, and place onerous restrictions on their civil rights and liberties that even most ex-prisoners convicted of violent crimes do not have to endure.

Inside our prisons and jails are deplorable conditions and institutional abuses that affect all prisoners, but particularly inmates with mental disabilities,[55] who are likely to be more vulnerable and thus victims of overcrowded, unsanitary conditions. This includes the spread of communicable diseases, homosexual rapes, a culture of sodomy, assaults, and not infrequently even mayhem and murder.[56] Increasingly, disruptive or threatening prisoners, many of whom have mental disabilities, are subject to extreme isolation. "[P]rolonged solitary confinement, sometimes for months or even years, has become . . . routine . . . inflicting . . . inhumane suffering on tens of thousands of prisoners."[57] This is especially painful for prisoners with serious mental disabilities.

Most inmates with mental disabilities are confined in horrible conditions with few avenues for securing their basic human rights. They are subject to being abused and neglected by corrections personnel, and traumatized, injured, or even killed by fellow inmates.[58] Even the U.S. Supreme Court has recognized that "[l]iving in crowded, unsafe, and unsanitary conditions can cause prisoners with latent mental illnesses to worsen and develop overt symptoms."[59] A vast majority of these vulnerable inmates are deprived of adequate care, treatment, and rehabilitation. They also face repeated and escalating punishments—including segregation, extreme isolation, and extended prison time—for violating rules that due to their mental impairments they are unable or less able to follow or obey.[60]

Collectively these various indignities, mistreatments, and physical and psychological assaults are likely to make inmates' existing mental conditions worse and create new mental impairments as well. Many inmates with mental disabilities are administered powerful antipsychotic drugs with harmful and even dangerous side effects in order to manage their behaviors[61] or restore their competency to stand trial.[62] Many of the prison officials who make decisions about or administer these medications are unqualified or poorly trained to do so, which results in "many prisoners receiving . . . inappropriate kinds or amounts of psychotropic medication that further impairs their ability to function."[63] Overmedication appears to be a common practice, particularly where there is overcrowding,[64] which is almost everywhere.

In the American criminal justice system the assumption generally is embraced that prisoners and pretrial detainees cannot be successfully treated and rehabilitated. At best this is only partially true and only if one views treatment and rehabilitation narrowly like cures for a disease.[65] Sadly, this predisposition against treatment and rehabilitation justifies a punitive and counterproductive mind-set that prevents affirmative steps from being taken to help prisoners improve, to minimize brutality, or to eliminate or ameliorate the conditions that tend to significantly increase recidivism rates when those who are incarcerated are finally released.[66] Too often correction systems create or ignore conditions that make these inmates worse, which, when combined with inadequate funding, help ensure that these treatment and rehabilitation failures are self-fulfilling prophecies.

These harmful policies fall most heavily on prisoners with mental disabilities who have the greatest treatment needs and the least income potential. Moreover, these inequities are likely to be intensified with the aging of the prison and jail populations. Nationwide the number of inmates fifty-five or older has increased "282 percent . . . between 1995 and 2010."[67] As a result, "officials in crowded, understaffed correctional facilities [are] scrambling to care for . . . inmates who can no longer feed, dress or clean themselves and who . . . can no longer follow simple commands."[68]

The situation is similarly distressing for those who have been involuntarily committed to quasi-civil correctional facilities, often called secure detention centers. The most these inmates can expect are minimal standards of humane care, and too often even those minimums are not satis-

fied, or are substantially ignored. Protecting the public from the potentially dangerous behaviors of those who are confined is the overriding policy
consideration in almost all situations. Provision of humane care, treatment, and rehabilitation is mostly a secondary objective for quasi-civil
inmates with mental disabilities, and mostly an afterthought for those
found not guilty by reason of insanity or who are deemed to be offenders
with sexual or mental disorders.[69] In the absence of effective treatment
and rehabilitation, involuntary commitments for offenders with sexual
and mental disorders are likely to result in indefinite incarcerations that
may last many years or until they die.

The provision of mental health care and treatment is only a priority for
persons who are committed after they have been found incompetent to
stand trial, but that treatment tends to be limited to antipsychotic medications. These drugs often are administered without informed consent[70] to
help maximize the possibility that the inmates will become competent
enough that the government can try, sentence, and on occasion even
execute them. Restoration of competency also tends to undermine mental
status defenses since the jury will see the defendants in a stabilized mental state rather than how they were when they committed the crimes
charged.[71] Nevertheless, "because of critical shortages of state hospital
psychiatric beds and funding . . . [m]any of these [legally incompetent]
patients languish in jails and prison . . . during the prolonged wait for
treatment."[72]

The Antitherapeutic Consequences of Our Criminal Laws and Policies

In theory and good practice, the jurisprudence that allows significant
terms of incarceration and other extreme governmental interventions
against persons with mental disabilities, including even the death penalty,
should at least guarantee that those interventions are implemented in
ways that are humane, support rehabilitation, and minimize antitherapeutic consequences. The basic principles of "therapeutic jurisprudence" in
particular implore our judicial and correctional systems to maintain a
balance by providing fundamental due process protections to individuals
with mental disabilities, while meeting each of their needs for individualized care, treatment, and rehabilitation.[73] Now, as in the past, we have
done both inadequately and inhumanely.

The laws and policies used to incarcerate persons with serious mental disabilities only require that the most minimal constitutional due process and care standards be satisfied. Furthermore, these legislative and judicial shortcomings are made much worse because too often the governmental agencies and officials in charge of implementing these laws and policies fail to ensure that even these minimum standards are met. Such failings are due to a number of factors, especially inadequate funding, bureaucratic ignorance, and the lack of interest, commitment, and oversight needed to guarantee that these highly stigmatized individuals with mental disabilities, who are deemed to be dangerous, are treated fairly and humanely. Our Constitution has been marginalized in order to promote retribution and to create the largely false impression that we are improving security and ultimately saving money by targeting this particular population of Americans for incarceration and other deprivations of rights and freedoms. In the rush to embrace and exploit such popular ignorance, we often are punishing the wrong people, subjecting many of the "right" and "wrong" people to unconscionable forms of custodial care, and making our society less humane and less safe.

Mental health care and treatment deficiencies and abuses are widespread in our correction facilities, including jails, prisons, juvenile detention centers, and secure "treatment" centers. Withholding or ignoring rehabilitation and treatment to further punish offenders and to ensure that they are never released—or are re-incarcerated once they are conditionally released—remains a prominent implicit and even explicit characteristic of our modern corrections systems. Too often awful circumstances are tolerated or even embraced as additional deterrents to persons who would commit crimes. This punitive, antitherapeutic mind-set is reflected throughout the criminal and juvenile justice systems, where there are numerous examples that illustrate how convoluted and destructive these policies and practices have become.

Guilty But Mentally Ill

With the guilty but mentally ill verdict, the promise of rehabilitation and treatment is held out, usually without any or at best inadequate fulfillment, in order to enhance the possibility that defendants with severe mental disabilities will be fully punished for their crimes, regardless of their actual diminished culpability. Under this scheme, juries (or judges) are empowered to circumvent the fundamental notion of criminal responsibility by allowing determinations to be made that defendants with severe cognitive and other mental impairments are fully responsible for their criminal actions.[74] This alternative verdict was proposed based in part on the mistaken assumption that there were widespread abuses of the insanity defense, when reportedly relatively few defendants—less than 1 percent—used that plea even then.[75] Georgia extended the concept to specifically cover persons with mental retardation,[76] and that law still exists today even though several years ago the U.S. Supreme Court acknowledged in a different context that the culpability of persons with mental retardation is substantially less than for other people.[77]

The duplicity of these verdicts was revealed by the Illinois Supreme Court, which refused to allow a defendant to withdraw his guilty plea to burglary on grounds that his lawyer had been ineffective in failing to advise him to plead guilty but mentally ill instead. The state's high court explained that there was no benefit to the defendant in pursuing such an alternative plea agreement because it *would not have* altered the sentencing range that could have been imposed; guaranteed a higher level of treatment (or nontreatment) than any other inmate would have received; or ensured access to treatment that would have been unavailable otherwise.[78]

Moreover, actual broken promises with regard to the provision of care, treatment, and rehabilitation have not been viewed as significant legal impediments to using these statutory schemes anyway. State supreme courts have consistently upheld the constitutionality of guilty but mentally ill verdicts without treatment, pointing to the scarcity of resources available to all prisoners.[79] Incredibly, courts have ruled that because our correctional systems mistreat all prisoners, the deprivation of promised care and treatment for a particular segment of prisoners with mental disabilities is not constitutionally objectionable, even though it is widely acknowledged that these inmates are far more at risk and vulnerable for mistreatment and abuse than inmates generally.[80]

One state's high court even affirmed a life sentence for a defendant with schizophrenia, who was found guilty but mentally ill of first-degree manslaughter. The judges concluded that an enhanced sentence was justified based on the defendant's mental condition where he had pled guilty to a lesser charge than what he might otherwise have received had he gone to trial.[81] Also, in two even more perplexing decisions, the U.S.

Court of Appeals for the Tenth Circuit joined the New Mexico Supreme Court in declaring that state's legislature had not violated the U.S. Constitution or state law when it prohibited state judges from using their discretion to place guilty but mentally ill murder defendants in secure mental hospitals, rather than prisons. "Imposing the same sentence the defendant would have received if she had been found guilty, and preventing her from being sentenced to a treatment facility"[82] was considered to be a legitimate legislative determination.

Such convoluted policies and legal reasoning have culminated in legislatures and high courts in a number of jurisdictions—including Kentucky, Indiana, and South Carolina—deciding that it is appropriate to execute a person found guilty but mentally ill of a capital offense, even though an essential theoretical and practical component of this special verdict is to provide care and treatment to offenders with mental impairments.[83] The only plausible reason for finding someone guilty but mentally ill of a capital crime is to obscure the issue of insanity or diminished criminal responsibility from the jury to increase the possibility that the defendant will be executed. Despite the cynical logic underlying guilty but mentally ill death penalty verdicts, the U.S. Supreme Court decided not to review this death penalty issue when given the opportunity to do so in 1987,[84] and has not done so since.

Moreover, the states that have these dubious laws continue to implement them in ways that allow them to obtain convictions in increasingly questionable circumstances. The Georgia Supreme Court, for example, affirmed logically inconsistent verdicts in which a jury found a defendant not guilty by reason of insanity on a charge of murder with malice, yet that same jury was allowed to find him guilty but mentally ill of felony murder for the same criminal actions.[85] Not only did the state's high court conclude that the government was justified in prosecuting the defendant on these two separate charges for the same homicide, but it was convinced that the defendant's diminished mental state in each of the two crimes charged could be distinguished, legally, if not reasonably.

With regard to felony murder, the defendant had told the state's psychologist that as a convicted felon, he realized that in purchasing the firearm that he had used in the killing, he was violating the law. Using this flawed reasoning, the court found that while he was insane in forming the intent to commit murder, he was deemed to have "known" that as a felon he was prohibited from purchasing a firearm.[86] Consequently, he was convicted of knowingly purchasing a firearm that he had used to commit the homicide while he was insane. This second crime was deemed first-degree felony murder, because due process—as opposed to logic and common sense—allowed his proven insanity to be totally ignored in convicting him of a capital crime.

Significantly, the American Bar Association, the American Psychiatric Association, and the American Psychological Association have been firmly against such verdicts since the early 1980s.[87] The notion that defendants who are found guilty but mentally ill receive adequate mental health care and treatment is little more than a legal fiction that clearly favors state and federal governments over individuals with mental disabilities who are encumbered by these verdicts.

Forced Medication, But Lack of Other Treatments, When Facing Execution

Another substantial injustice occurs in cases of persons being restored to competency after being found incompetent either to stand trial for a capital offense or to be executed. These defendants and prisoners with severe mental disabilities—who in almost all other circumstances within the criminal justice system likely would be deprived of adequate mental health treatment and rehabilitative services—may be compelled to take intrusive, unpleasant, and potentially dangerous drugs[88] against their wills and/or without their consent, where the implicit purpose of that treatment is to facilitate their being tried for capital crimes or actually being executed. While the U.S. Supreme Court has never ruled on the constitutionality of this latter practice, jurisdictions that still permit the death penalty have policies in place to enable such treatment-facilitated executions to take place. By and large, courts have supported compelled treatment in order to restore the competency of capital defendants, as long as the trappings of due process accompany this inhumane judicial decision-making.[89]

Essentially, there are three accepted "rationales" that states may use to forcibly medicate incompetent defendants, including death row inmates. First is the direct approach, in which governments and courts are supposed to determine whether such treatment is in the best medical interests of the prisoner and supports a compelling state interest in ensuring that defendants are tried, sentenced, or executed for their alleged offenses.

This weighing of interests, as the Supreme Court explained in *Sell v. United States*—a 2003 non–death penalty case—is often quite complicated and has made it difficult for governments to meet their burden of proof that forcibly medicating a defendant is justified.[90] Still, the Supreme Court in an earlier ruling had employed another legal fiction against the interests of persons with mental disabilities to conclude that in certain circumstances even the involuntary administration of medication that facilitates the death penalty may serve those inmates' "best medical interest."[91]

Most psychiatrists and psychologists, however, at least in their public expressions, view their potential roles in such a "treatment" process as "angels of death" or social engineers and thus refuse to participate. Nevertheless, because there are enough mental health professionals who do participate—and few effective professional sanctions in place to prevent it—these executions typically are allowed to go forward with no or only small delays. In fact, after an initial hesitancy following the Supreme Court's warning that the legal justification process may be burdensome, state and federal officials have become increasingly practiced and aggressive in developing schemes and rationales that result in such "best interest" findings in many criminal incompetency cases, including those involving the death penalty.[92]

In addition, the Supreme Court in *Sell* endorsed two other broad rationales that justify treating defendants involuntarily for fictitious humanitarian purposes, so that in the process these inmates may become competent to be tried, sentenced, and occasionally executed. Under the majority's reasoning, states may forcibly medicate an incompetent inmate, if the stated purpose is to protect the inmate or others from what is deemed his or her "dangerous" behaviors, or the inmate is deemed incompetent and a legally appointed substitute decision-maker consents to such "treatment" as being in the patient's best medical interest.[93] Ultimately, the fact that coerced mental health treatment also may restore the inmate's competency to be tried, sentenced, and/or executed is obscured by the government's duty to protect the health and welfare of citizens in its custody—a duty which is rarely carried out or is carried out inadequately. Under these two rationales, even the fundamental life and death aspect of a decision to compel treatment with antipsychotic drugs in a capital case is given little or no legal recognition. Furthermore, with regard to determining whether inmates may be forcibly treated because they are dangerous, such outcomes are going to be based on the same types of flawed predictions of future events and behaviors that are used in other dangerousness proceedings.

In capital cases, once these prisoners become legally competent and if they already have been convicted, they are likely to be placed in extreme isolation waiting to be executed. The mental health care and related services that they receive is likely to be substandard or worse.[94] A U.S. Court of Appeals concluded that mental health care for death row prisoners in Mississippi was "grossly inadequate" and posed a serious risk of harm to their health.[95] These inmates would scream at night, fling feces, and create other disturbances that were viewed as being "enough to weaken even the strongest individual," and seriously jeopardize their mental well-being.[96] Such inhumane conditions inflame a widespread condition known as "death row syndrome,"[97] in which the mental health of inmates waiting to be executed deteriorates over time, particularly when they are kept in extreme isolation. Some psychiatrists believe that this syndrome is unique and severe enough that it should be listed as a separate mental disorder.[98]

Inadequate and Inhumane Mental Health Care and Treatment for Offenders

Unless there are widespread changes in public policies, any proposed plans to provide prisoners with minimally adequate rehabilitation and mental health and related treatments have little opportunity to succeed. As a practical matter, there is no entitlement to rehabilitation, treatment, and habilitation in most circumstances—except for instances in which the most blatant constitutional violations occur[99]—and minimal public support for providing needed services, unless the defendant has been convicted of a nonviolent, nonstigmatizing crime. Even most people addicted to illegal drugs do not receive treatment, or if they do receive "something more" than involuntary custodial care, that something is likely to fall well short of what is needed to give them a realistic opportunity to overcome their addictions.[100] Since the 1980s, there has been a strong preference to address drug use with extended incarceration instead of treatment.[101]

What has happened for a number of years now is that judges typically sentence defendants with mental disabilities to longer terms in prison and jail because courts view these offenders as being more dangerous, and dangerousness has become the dominant aggravating factor that justifies enhanced sentencing, including the death penalty. The Federal Sentencing Guidelines, which recommend longer sentences for "violent mentally ill offenders,"[102] triggered this phenomenon; then other state criminal statutes followed suit. Moreover, this pattern of enhancing the sentences of persons with mental disabilities appears to have actually increased after the U.S. Supreme Court ruled in 2005 that these federal guidelines were only advisory.[103] Instead of applying their judicial discretion to adjust for mental impairments as mitigating factors, many more federal judges have been using these impairments as justifications for imposing longer sentences, typically when courts believe that these defendants are either "dangerous or in need of treatment."[104] An Illinois federal court, for instance, ruled that a bank fraud defendant's alleged diminished responsibility should be viewed as an aggravating factor because his reduced mental capacity made his recidivism more likely.[105]

Unfortunately, existing programs to divert nonviolent defendants with mental disorders into special courts is of diminished value, or even counterproductive, in promoting the legal interests of many or even most of the offenders involved. While promising to provide meaningful rehabilitation and treatment,[106] these demonstration projects typically do not have the resources to comprehensively address the care and treatment needs of even a substantial minority of the nonviolent offenders in a given jurisdiction who would be eligible for this special attention. Nor do the participating judges have the authority to provide the same types of services to so-called violent offenders, many of whom could benefit from these programs without creating any significant additional risk to the community.[107]

Also, the definition of what offense is to be considered "violent," like dangerousness itself, is viewed over-inclusively in order to satisfy exaggerated community concerns for safety. More importantly, though, the underlying purpose of these courts generally has shifted away from what it was originally intended to accomplish—diverting nonviolent defendants with mental disorders into the community for treatment without punishment—to ensuring that these defendants are under strict government control until they are deemed rehabilitated, no matter how long that might take.[108] Should they fail to satisfy the strict conditions that most of these courts impose, they can be incarcerated indefinitely for periods that would exceed their sentences had they been tried and convicted.

The vast majority of defendants and inmates with mental disabilities receive little or no rehabilitation, care, or treatment services while they are confined,[109] and the situation does not improve much if they are released. According to the National Alliance on Mental Illness community-based mental health services for people with serious mental illnesses nationwide deserves a grade of D for "dismal."[110] Undoubtedly this lack of services has an even greater negative impact on former offenders with serious mental impairments, including in particular adolescents who have been sentenced as adults to jails and prisons. Reportedly, 70 percent of them have or will develop mental disorders.[111]

Unfortunately, improving care and treatment within the criminal justice system has not been a priority. For many policymakers the inhumane status quo seems to be viewed as a desirable outcome. Our laws and policies have created an environment in which social programs to treat mental impairments of potentially dangerous offenders have been largely replaced with imprisonment;[112] in turn, jails and prisons rarely provide effective rehabilitation and treatment once the offenders are inside. The overall conditions of confinement for prisoners with mental disabilities are so bad that Human Rights Watch has frequently cited the United States for widespread human rights abuses in this regard.[113] As a result, factors that typically make mental disabilities worse or cause mental impairments are far more likely to be present in our prisons and jails than opportunities for rehabilitation, care, and treatment. Moreover, nearly 60 percent of all inmates sustain at least one traumatic brain injury while imprisoned. These serious injuries "can alter behavior, emotion and impulse control, can keep prisoners behind bars . . . and increases the odds they will end up [in prison] again."[114]

Because our prison systems are overcrowded and underfunded, "most inmates [have] scant opportunities for work, training, education, treatment or counseling."[115] The second-largest American prison system— after the Federal Bureau of Prisons—is California's, which used to be the "nation's premier system . . . work[ing] to educate and rehabilitate its inmates."[116] Now it has "the worst overcrowding in the country." The California Rehabilitation Center, which was "[b]uilt to hold 1,800 inmates . . . bulges with more than 4,700 and is under nearly constant lockdown to prevent fights." Some buildings "are so antiquated that the electricity is shut off during rainstorms so the prisoners aren't electrocuted." In addition, the "once-vaunted drug rehab program has a three-month-long waiting list."[117]

The situation is "even worse throughout the rest of California's 32 other prisons . . .,"[118] and most of our nation's jails.[119] Instead of rehabilitation and education many, if not most, prison and jail inmates are subjected to cruel and horrific abuses. This includes homosexual rapes and other sexual attacks and being rented out to other prisoners as sex slaves.[120] Those who are confined in super-maximum security facilities are "locked alone or with a cellmate in small sometimes windowless cells from which they [are] released for only a few hours each week for solitary recreation or showers."[121] As bad as things are for prisoners generally, the Secretary of the California Department of Corrections and Rehabilitation acknowledged that the "most serious problem is providing enough appropriate space for seriously mentally ill inmates."[122]

In 2009, a federal appeals court decided that this chronic overcrowding and lack of medical care, especially for inmates with mental disorders, was so demonstrably unconstitutional that despite strong public opposition many of these prisoners would have to be released.[123] The U.S. Supreme Court affirmed the federal court, which had directed the entire California prison system to depopulate.[124] The justices, however, presumed without any factual support that prisoners who had serious mental impairments were not good candidates for release since they "[would be] likely to create special dangers because of their recidivism rates."[125]

Compounding these tragic prison-related problems, the legal system leaves most inmates who are being abused or neglected, particularly those with serious mental disabilities, with no viable avenues for relief. Very few lawyers are available to help them and that situation is growing worse as economic conditions deteriorate nationwide.[126] Also, even with an attorney, typically the legal requirements that have to be met in order to obtain redress—particularly under the federal Prison Litigation Reform Act[127]—present huge obstacles. For an overwhelming majority of these inmates with mental disabilities, opportunities to meaningfully redress legitimate grievances regarding their care and treatment or mistreatment are close to nonexistent.

The U.S. Court of Appeals for the Seventh Circuit, for example, upheld summary judgment for prison officials in a suit by an inmate who had been subjected to unconscionable conditions. Despite the fact that he had been diagnosed with schizophrenia and had attempted suicide many times, he had been locked in a hot, constantly illuminated cell without windows or air conditioning for all but four hours per week, and deprived of any mechanical or electronic possessions to help him deal with the voices in his head.[128] Both the lower and appeals courts acknowledged that prison officials probably should have known that such conditions of confinement would make the inmate's mental illness symptoms much worse and cause him grave psychological harm and extreme physical discomfort. Nevertheless, the evidence did not prove that the defendants actually knew or were deliberately indifferent. Also, because the inmate had been deemed dangerous, this mitigated prison officials' responsibility to ensure that he received humane care.[129]

The Failure to Provide Adequate Care as a Justification for Custodial Care and Confinement

One of the legal justifications for keeping inmates confined, after they have been involuntarily committed civilly or quasi-civilly, is the concern—often in the form of a prediction—that once they are in the community, these inmates will not receive the care, rehabilitation, and treatment deemed necessary to improve their mental disabilities and ameliorate or control dangerous behaviors. Furthermore, the assumption is ever present[130] that people with serious mental conditions are more likely to be dangerous and, as a result, should not be released. By not providing adequate care, rehabilitation, and treatment to persons who are involuntarily committed and by limiting the availability of needed services when they are released, federal and state governments—whether by neglect and/or some unstated policies—substantially increase the likelihood that those inmates will remain in custody or be confined again. State and federal governments are allowed to keep inmates confined, based on experts' predictions that it is likely the inmates will not comply—or will not be able to comply—with their treatment regimens if they were to be released.[131] This can happen whether or not noncompliance is due in large part or entirely to the absence of community-based services for those individuals.

The promise of humane care, rehabilitation, and treatment for those who are involuntarily committed or otherwise confined may be breached in several different ways, depending on whether the promise is made in the mental health or corrections systems. States and communities generally have no legal obligation to provide placements, care, treatments, and other support services that would mitigate a civil respondent's dangerousness. This holds true before and after these individuals are subjected to involuntary civil inpatient or outpatient commitment or other intrusive restrictions on their fundamental rights, freedoms, or liberties. What makes this reality especially unfair is that the absence of suitable placements and treatment in the community may be used as evidence to demonstrate that these civil or quasi-civil patients are likely to be dangerous if they were to be released[132] or placed in less restrictive settings.

Moreover, once these respondents are involuntarily civilly committed, typically much less evidence is required to justify their continued commitment. This is particularly true if the person is petitioning for release—as opposed to receiving a required periodic review. Respondents seeking their release typically bear the burden of demonstrating that they no longer meet the inpatient or outpatient commitment or other related criteria. Both initially and with most periodic reviews, the government is supposed to prove, by clear and convincing evidence, that respondents have a mental disorder and as a result are dangerous.[133] That burden is illusive, given our society's predisposition toward believing persons with mental disabilities are inherently dangerous, and the unreliable evidence—or subjective opinions masquerading as evidence—that is deemed admissible and persuasive in these types of proceedings.

This basic unfairness becomes even worse in the criminal justice system. Quasi-civil commitments are justified by the promise of adequate rehabilitation and treatment as an important *quid pro quo* for incarceration. Yet most of the time that promise is not kept.[134] The fiscal incentives against providing seemingly expensive treatments, rehabilitation, and habilitation services are even stronger than in our civil mental health systems. In addition, because inmates must show improvements in their mental disorders in order to secure their release,[135] the failure to provide treatment, habilitation, and rehabilitation helps achieve an implicit and sometimes explicit objective of most federal and state governments, which is to keep these quasi-civil inmates incarcerated for as long as legally possible.

Despite numerous opportunities to do so, the U.S. Supreme Court has never ruled that there is a constitutional right to treatment for persons who are involuntarily committed either civilly or quasi-civilly. Even in our civil mental health systems, the most that is constitutionally required

is a limited right of *nondangerous* persons to receive treatment or habilitation that is minimally necessary to maximize their freedom from bodily
harm and unnecessary restraints.[136] In addition, for nondangerous civil
inpatients who "have the potential to live outside an institution either with
or without the assistance of friends and relatives," they "must receive the
minimal community resources they need to be deinstitutionalized, including treatment and habilitation."[137] This tenuous possibility of receiving
necessary services if one is nondangerous bears little resemblance to an
actual constitutional right to treatment for involuntary patients.[138] Furthermore, with regard to involuntary quasi-civil commitments related to
criminal matters, typically a judicial finding of dangerousness—where
dangerousness is proven by the commission of any crime, violent or
not—is enough, without anything more, to justify incarceration initially
and thereafter. All that is required is that those quasi-civil respondents
have some mental disorder, condition, or aberration, which may have
been precipitated or aggravated by their incarceration and had nothing to
do with why they were committed in the first place.[139]

In 1997, while upholding the Kansas sexually violent predator law, a
majority of the Supreme Court explained this very limited right to treatment in particularly confusing terms for persons who are quasi-civilly
committed in the corrections system. That right is even less than what
traditional civil involuntary patients are entitled to. In that case, the justices upheld post-imprisonment sexual offender commitments, in large
part because of the promise of treatment. Yet they refused to decide
whether meaningful treatment had been provided to the inmates who
were being confined in that case, even though the record clearly demonstrated that, depending on the inmate, treatment was either deficient or
virtually nonexistent.[140] Four years later, the Supreme Court grudgingly
conceded that if a state statute actually specifies that adequate treatment
is *guaranteed*, then and only then does "due process [require] that the
conditions and duration of confinement bear some reasonable relation to
the purpose for which they [the inmates] are committed."[141] In other
words, something resembling treatment may or may not be required.

Moreover, even if such a vague and incomplete treatment promise
exists, state and federal courts are left with considerable discretion in
determining whether the actual care and treatment being provided is
minimally adequate. Many, if not a majority of courts, do not even believe that offenders with mental disabilities, particularly those with so-

called sexual disorders, are entitled to any more consideration when it comes to conditions of confinement and treatment than regular prisoners. As one California federal district court judge opined in criticizing the majority of judges on the Ninth Circuit, "modern penology views men and women being sent to prison as *punishment* rather than to be punished. The punishment consists in the separation from friends and family and being subjected to regimentation to maintain institutional discipline."[142] Thus, "it is difficult to see how one can distinguish between punitive and non-punitive treatment in evaluating the treatment of SVPs."[143]

Also, if inmates are deemed untreatable, as many offenders with sexual or other mental disorders are thought to be, then the Supreme Court has ruled that these individuals may be confined anyway, unless they can prove that they are no longer dangerous.[144] Proving a negative is extremely difficult to do, particularly since there is a presumption in our society, which the Supreme Court appears to share,[145] that these individuals are inherently dangerous to begin with.

Not surprisingly, treatment staffs experience role confusion. Should they "make an honest attempt to treat these individuals . . . thus enhancing their chances of release?"[146] Or should they "help ensure that their charges continue to remain committed . . .?"[147] What happens most of the time is that the staff "set impossibly high standards for release and then . . . maintain that individuals will be released as soon as they complete treatment,"[148] which may be a very long time, or never.

Also, by employing such hard-to-meet standards, staff members substantially reduce the potential for personal liability, public criticism, and/ or poor job performance ratings. These work-related incentives all strongly support a system in which confinement and other forms of custodial care represent the status quo. Accordingly, an editorial in the *British Medical Journal* warned doctors about "becoming agents of social control" when they support punishment over treatment.[149]

The same warning should be given to American doctors and other treatment providers with regard to persons with mental disabilities who are deemed to be dangerous. In one highly publicized case, for example, a Marine Corps private accused of leaking documents that were embarrassing to the United States was placed in solitary confinement and prohibited from wearing any clothing after a military psychiatrist concluded that the soldier might injure himself. The basis for this prediction was a "sarcastic quip" the soldier had made to his jailers.[150] A couple of weeks later, even though the psychiatrist reexamined the inmate and found him to have a "low risk" of self-harm, the military continued to keep the soldier nude in extreme isolation.[151]

Unfortunately, even if one accepts these widespread due process deprivations as being necessary, there is little reason to believe that those who are forcibly enrolled in these social control programs receive meaningful treatments.[152] According to a *New York Times* study, this approach to rehabilitation is a "troubled, politically fraught science. . . . Not only is relapse prevention of questionable value, but so are the . . . methods of predicting risk of reoffending."[153] Some corrections officials and politicians have expressed concerns about the lack of adequate rehabilitation and treatment in these programs, but most of them do so because they are afraid if minimum standards are not met, offenders with sexual and other mental disorders are more likely to obtain their release on due process grounds.

Comprehensively researched news stories focusing on two of the nation's largest sexually violent predator programs support the view that for public officials the most pressing treatment concerns have little to do with rehabilitation, and much more to do with ensuring that the affected inmates remain in custody. In California, two reporters on the *Sacramento Bee* reviewed court records of inmates who had been incarcerated under what had been touted as the toughest sexual predator law in the United States. The reporters opined that "rapists and child molesters . . . [who] failed to start or complete treatment" were being released because mental health professionals, judges, jurors, and even district attorneys were being fooled into believing that they were no longer dangerous.[154] On the other hand, inmates who accepted the proscribed treatments were much more likely to be held for a very long time until they were deemed cured— which rarely happened.[155]

Similarly, it was reported that inmates who had been civilly committed to Florida's sexual offender "treatment" center were being released due to "a loophole in the law [which] allows the men to refuse therapy." A comparison was made between respondents who had been released prematurely and inmates who accepted treatment and thus would be confined indefinitely until they could prove "they no longer pose a threat to the community."[156] In both California and Florida the public seemed to favor just enough treatment to avoid obvious due process problems that might lead to inmates being released.

In states that make no such promises, however, the failure to provide treatment creates no serious constitutional problems, and little incentive to do so merely because it would be humane.[157] Thus, a number of high-risk sex offenders see actual or chemical castration as the only available means for avoiding permanent incarceration.[158] A number of states already allow the "use of drugs to castrate sex offenders, including California, Florida, and Texas, where surgical castration is also an option."[159] Even if these inmates are castrated, however, there is no strong likelihood, much less a guarantee, that they will be released.

DETENTION AND OTHER CUSTODIAL CONFINEMENT FOR JUVENILES WITH MENTAL DISABILITIES

As compared to adults in our jails and prisons, mental health care and treatment are little better—and in many instances worse[160]—for minors in the juvenile justice system and even worse for adolescents if they are tried and convicted as adults. Kids who are in need of mental health services which they cannot access in the community are particularly at risk. "[O]ften due to a lack of psychiatric care in the community and inadequate insurance funding . . . youth with mental health disorders are being committed to the juvenile justice system, a system that was never designed to provide psychiatric care."[161] Nevertheless, "the juvenile justice system has become the avenue of last resort for youth with mental health disorders."[162] Unfortunately, that system "is ill-equipped to be the nation's primary provider of child and adolescent mental health care."[163] As a result, "entrance into the adult penal system is the typical trajectory for these youth."[164]

With many more juvenile offenders being tried as adults[165] and juvenile justice having become far more penal,[166] efforts to provide at-risk youth with meaningful opportunities for treatment and rehabilitative services have been met with stiff resistance. This is not to say that rehabilitation, treatment, and other services are never available, but that at least for so-called violent youthful offenders, punishment without hope of rehabilitation is viewed as an intractable reality more than an inhumane and counterproductive response that could and should be improved substantially with adequate prevention, intervention, and follow-up.[167] Maryland's entire system for treating juvenile offenders, for instance, has been

condemned as a "disgrace."[168] Independent monitors found: "overcrowding, understaffing . . . health safety issues . . . child abuse . . . and
continued assaults."[169] Similarly, a task force appointed by New York's
governor found that state's youth prisons, which, for the most part, are
populated by adolescents who committed offenses equivalent to adult
misdemeanors, were in "extreme crisis."[170] These New York detention
facilities have grossly inadequate mental health and related treatment
programs, even though more than half of these youthful offenders have a
diagnosis of mental problems and one-third have developmental disabilities.[171]

Providing youthful offenders with rehabilitation, treatment, and humane care is viewed as a waste of limited resources,[172] even if those
youthful offenders have severe mental impairments. Instead of receiving
rehabilitation, care, and treatment, most juvenile offenders are placed in
environments that teach and reinforce criminal behaviors and deprive
young offenders of the education and related skills that they need to hold
a job once they are released.[173]

A primary reason that many of the most vulnerable kids are being
confined in the first place is the absence of mental health and other
related services to protect them from the effects of abuse and neglect.[174]
Also, because adequate care is often unavailable and parents, guardians,
and states and localities are unable to "handle" these kids in homes and
foster care without those community services, institutionalization has become the default solution.[175] Many children with mental disabilities are
subjected to extended involuntary civil commitment; many others come
in contact with the police and are funneled into the juvenile detention
system or our adult jails and prisons. Foster kids who are recovering from
abuse and neglect often are treated like dangerous offenders. In Florida,
they are often shackled and handcuffed when they appear in court for
their disposition hearings, and then physical restraints are used when they
are institutionalized in psychiatric centers should they be viewed as a
threat to run away.[176]

Too often mental health services for children living at home are inadequate. Many parents or guardians actually give up custody of those children, so that they will qualify for Medicaid benefits at public expense.[177]
Unfortunately, this strategy also results in those children becoming wards
of the state. Federal officials have described the state institutions where
many of these children are placed as being "deplorable."[178] A House of

Representatives report found that in 2004 at least 15,000 kids in need of mental health services were "warehoused" in juvenile detention facilities because there was no other place for them to go.[179] Yet that sobering figure significantly understated the actual numbers because only those facilities that responded to the study were counted and a quarter of them—presumably many of the worst ones—did not reply. To make matters worse, the report found that the suicide rate for these juvenile detainees was four times greater than it was for other juveniles.[180]

The Bazelon Center for Mental Health Law has identified five factors that contribute to inappropriate incarceration of youth with mental disabilities in detention centers.[181] First, mental health services, which are limited to begin with, are only available to children during the daytime when school is in session. Thus, if these troubled kids "act out" in serious ways outside of school, they are not likely to be able to find the mental health services they need. Instead, they may be arrested and processed by police departments, which are open twenty-four hours a day.

Second, schools rarely provide mental health services and other supports to students who have behavior problems. "Education" officials are much more likely to adopt "zero tolerance" policies and overreact to any perceived danger (even as minor as a child bringing a plastic gun or prescription medication to school) by either expelling the child or directly involving the police.[182] Not surprisingly, children with special needs are much more likely to become criminalized at an early age. As an editorial in the *New York Times* opined, these kids "are allowed to fall behind. When they act out, they are often suspended or expelled, which makes them more likely to commit crimes and land in jails."[183]

Third, the social institutions, particularly the schools, which are supposed to be serving children and their families, have a "bias toward law enforcement solutions."[184] Instead of intervening to help solve behavioral problems, the schools tend to "pass the buck" by calling the police or telling the "parents to call the police."[185]

Fourth, there is a "lack of coordination" amongst the key social systems—child welfare, education, mental health, and juvenile justice—so that "a child can end up with several mental health diagnoses" as each agency refers the parents to another agency "for services that don't exist."[186] Thus, the meager services that do exist are often wasted or lost within poorly functioning bureaucracies.

Lastly, there is insufficient private or public insurance to pay for mental health care and related medical and social services, especially for those who are indigent.[187] Without insurance, many parents, guardians, and other custodians lack the financial resources, or are reluctant to spend what limited resources they do have, to provide essential mental health–related services for their children.

Instead, many children go without needed mental health care and treatment until something bad happens that gets the attention of governments; then many of them are arrested or otherwise detained in situations where they receive custodial care, but little in the way of effective mental health care and treatment.[188] Often these kids are given powerful antipsychotic drugs, which are prescribed "too cavalierly" for reasons of administrative convenience without properly taking into account the potential safety hazards, including suicides, fatal reactions, and harmful side effects.[189]

SOLDIERS AND VETERANS: AN EXPANDING COHORT OF POTENTIALLY "DANGEROUS" PERSONS

Well over two million American soldiers have served in Iraq and Afghanistan. A startling percentage of them have been or will be diagnosed with serious mental conditions, traumatic brain injuries, and substance abuse problems related to the events and conditions of combat. Studies indicate that as of 2008 "more than 300,000 [of these warriors had] endured mental health difficulties," including "deep depression, and alarming numbers [had] tried to or succeeded in committing suicide."[190] Tragically, such suicides have been on the rise for soldiers with traumatic brain injuries as well as for those with mental illnesses.[191]

Young veterans aged twenty to twenty-four are "two to four times as likely to commit suicide as non-veterans the same age,"[192] and suicide in that age cohort is much higher to begin with. In 2012, the number of troop-related suicides reached its zenith. More soldiers died at their own hands than in combat.[193] Today's soldiers and veterans are considerably more likely than ever before to have post-traumatic stress disorder (PTSD) and/or substance abuse diagnoses.[194] In addition, there are growing public concerns that returning soldiers are "exhibit[ing] an exceptionally high rate of criminal behavior,"[195] including the commission of violent and sexual crimes[196] that tend to be associated with persons with mental disabilities more generally, as well as risky, "thrill-seeking" behaviors, such as dangerous driving, which reportedly has led to their having "a 75 percent higher risk rate of fatal motor vehicle accidents than . . . civilians."[197]

According to a major study based on Veterans Administration (VA) data from 2002 through 2008, 36.9 percent of Iraq and Afghanistan war veterans had mental health diagnoses.[198] That staggering percentage included 21.8 percent with post-traumatic stress disorder (PTSD) and 17.4 percent with depression.[199] Many of these soldiers also abused alcohol, which "[s]everal studies have shown [has made them] . . . less likely to seek and receive appropriate diagnosis and treatment."[200] In addition, for the first time the U.S. military has a significant percentage (estimated to be around 10–15 percent) of deployed woman soldiers who are exposed to many of the same traumatic combat conditions, plus too many of them also experience severe sexual harassment and/or sexual assaults,[201] which can aggravate or trigger mental disorders. Furthermore, the children of soldiers are more likely to experience serious mental health problems.[202]

Unlike in past wars, soldiers today must cope with multiple tours of duty. With each additional tour, mental health and other adjustment problems tend to increase substantially.[203] Apparently this has created an ethical dilemma for VA mental health providers, who must decide whether to breach confidentiality to inform "active-duty commanders of a veteran's [mental] problems."[204] In addition, even more serious confidentiality and privacy concerns may present themselves if the proposed use of brain scans and blood tests to identify trauma-induced mental disorders or susceptibility to such disorders becomes widespread.

The *Navy Times* reported that two 2009 studies conducted at Duke and Yale, respectively, indicate that it is already possible to measure chemical changes in people with such disorders.[205] These measurements could be used to try to identify soldiers who have been mentally traumatized and attempt to predict which soldiers—or applicants to be soldiers—are particularly susceptible to having brain dysfunctions when they experience such traumas.[206] These chemical changes also could be used, along with existing diagnostic methods, to attempt to predict which returning soldiers or veterans are more likely to be dangerous in their home communities.

Unfortunately, what happens to soldiers in combat is not the only significant cause of their psychological problems. Soldiers' mental disorders may be aggravated or new ones set in motion by the social realities that often greet them at home,[207] including mental health and other problems experienced by their spouses and children. Ex-soldiers do not necessarily have a place of honor in our society, particularly if they have mental disorders. Their psychological wounds may be discounted or disbelieved by the military and exaggerated by their potential employers; their spouses and loved ones may leave them; and they may be treated like most other people in our society who have serious mental disabilities, badly.

What each of these soldiers or ex-soldiers will have, however, is sophisticated training that has taught them to kill their enemies without qualms or hesitation, which many of them will have practiced multiple times, often in actual warfare. As one would expect, studies indicate that soldiers who kill other people in combat are far more likely to be diagnosed with PTSD or other serious mental disorders.[208] Therefore, as a group, based on our ever-expanding dangerousness standards, these combat veterans with mental disabilities may be deemed dangerous to others or themselves at rates that are considerably higher than those of the general population, even though a vast majority of them will never act violently.

Reports about the large "number of servicemen implicated in violent crimes has raised alarm" amongst the public already.[209] In 2008, the *New York Times* had identified 121 cases in which soldiers returning from Iraq or Afghanistan were "charged with homicide." Also, "charges of domestic violence, rape and sexual assault have risen sharply [amongst these soldiers]."[210] Similarly, a Colorado newspaper's intensive six-month investigation of soldiers who had returned from Iraq revealed that they were involved in crimes and other criminal behaviors at rates that were much higher than for other local residents.[211] These behaviors included "a string of killings and other offenses that the ex-soldiers attribute[d] to lax discipline and episodes of indiscriminate killing during their grueling deployment."[212] A law professor, who himself is a veteran, has observed that: "if statistics hold, attorneys will see many more veterans in the criminal court system in coming years,"[213] including a high percentage with mental disorders.

They also will be subject to involuntary civil commitments as being dangerous to themselves. Soldier suicides are viewed as an epidemic. "[T]he Pentagon and Congress are moving to establish policies intended to separate at-risk service members from their personal weapons."[214] The difficulty is that there are no reliable means for accurately determining which soldiers will commit suicide or otherwise act dangerously to themselves or others. In addition, there are realistic concerns that most or at least "some veterans avoid mental health care because they fear their firearms will be confiscated,"[215] that other rights and freedoms will be taken away, and that they will be stigmatized.

Americans undoubtedly have sympathy for what has happened to these military men and women in combat, but that concern has not been translated into effective prevention programs and adequate care and treatment. Given the nation's fiscal problems, it is unlikely to happen soon. Instead, if these ex-soldiers should "go crazy" and act out in ways that we deem dangerous, they may well be disposed of as damaged goods that cannot be fixed, which is what we have done to other people with mental disabilities, especially our children and young adults.

Early on the possibility was held out that the military and Congress would adequately fund programs to try to minimize the psychological damage of combat, and help our soldiers readjust to civilian life when they sustain combat-related mental disorders. In 2008, a guest editorial in the *Journal of Rehabilitation Research and Development* by a psychologist employed by the Department of Veterans Affair embraced this perspective: "this country is responding well to the growing needs for treatment and rehabilitation of returning war veterans."[216] He attributed this enlightened response to the Walter Reed Army Institute of Research, the Department of Defense, and the VA, "which saw the early warning signs . . . [and] began preparation for the psychological and physical war injuries that are now know as the signature wounds of [today's wars] . . . PTSD and traumatic brain injury."[217]

Since then, there have been a few signs that the military was moving forward incrementally with programs to help returning soldiers with mental disabilities. Of particular interest appeared to be the treatment of "symptoms of combat stress and post-traumatic stress disorder for wounded warriors."[218] One such program voluntarily enrolled a small cohort of soldiers in intensive eight-hour-a-day outpatient therapy to address "multiple disciplines and interests" of the soldiers. That included "[e]ye movement desensitization and reprocessing . . . to activate both sides of the brain" in order to purge traumatic memories.[219] Another program hoped to provide future soldiers, before they deployed, with "intensive training in emotional resiliency . . . to improve performance in combat and head off the mental health problems . . . that plague . . . troops returning from Afghanistan and Iraq."[220] Other researchers funded by the federal government, however, were suggesting that post-traumatic stress disorder among returning veterans had been overblown. They suggested that "the picture emerging [was] one of remarkable psychological resilience" of our military, even though prevalence rates were between 10 percent and 20 percent.[221]

Also, "[s]tate criminal courts devoted to U.S. war veterans emerg[ed] across the country," including in New York, Oklahoma, and California. These courts have tried to address "a common thread of post-traumatic stress disorder (PTSD), substance abuse, head injuries and mental illness underlying the veterans' crimes."[222] As with other special mental health and drug courts, however, these judicial diversion programs have been few and far between and typically only attempt to serve the needs of veteran offenders who have committed nonviolent crimes and are not viewed as being a threat to the community.

This preselection process continues to create a curious dichotomy in which veterans who are deemed to be at the greatest risk to themselves and society receive relatively little or no rehabilitation, care, and treatment. Moreover, even though these programs are only available to nonviolent defendants, there is a "blending of legal coercion and intensive treatment . . . in which . . . offenders are placed on probation on condition of participation in treatment,"[223] oftentimes for many years or even the rest of their lives. If they fail to meet those intrusive and restrictive conditions, they can be—and often are—incarcerated for periods of time that exceed the sentences they would have received had they been found guilty of the crimes for which they were charged.

An even gloomier picture emerges, however, from soldiers and ex-soldiers, who have long complained of conspicuous neglect once they are no longer able to fight. The entire military health-care system has been under extreme stress, leaving many soldiers and veterans with poor care. "[T]he much-publicized scandal in 2007 at Walter Reed Army Medical Center . . . has proved to be only the tip of a large and ugly iceberg."[224] Due to impending budget cuts, maintaining the funding for those military programs that currently exist is questionable, and expansion, other than for high visibility inadequacies, unlikely.

Such care and treatment deficiencies are much worse for soldiers and veterans with mental disorders. In the military, "mental problems . . . are still widely stigmatized or ignored—and given lowball ratings from official disability assessment boards"[225]—so much so that in 2008 "two veterans groups sued the VA, citing long delays for processing applications and other problems in treatment of veterans at risk for suicide."[226] Those claims were summarily dismissed as being "clearly outside the court's jurisdiction" because "Congress . . . has entrusted decisions regarding veterans' medical care to the discretion of the VA Secretary."[227]

Three years later, a panel of the Ninth Circuit Court of Appeals found that the Department of Veterans Affairs had engaged in "'unchecked incompetence' and unconscionable delays in caring for veterans with mental health problems."[228] Even worse, "[i]nstead of working with the plaintiffs to address the court's concerns, the VA is appealing the ruling," hoping to have it overturned.[229] In the meantime, the VA has asked "hundreds of thousands of veterans experiencing excessive delays . . . on their disability claims . . . [t]o be patient . . . [since] the department is . . . hop[ing to] . . . break the backlog by 2015."[230]

The military culture has been and continues to be particularly insensitive in dealing with mental disabilities. The armed forces have consistently refused to make soldiers who have combat-related mental injuries eligible to receive the Purple Heart. According to the Defense Department, the Purple Heart "has never been awarded for mental disorders or psychological conditions resulting from witnessing or experiencing traumatic combat events."[231] Not surprisingly, soldiers with mental health needs continue to feel so stigmatized that many—and probably most—of them are reluctant to participate in treatment programs.[232] Instead, they try to hide their mental anguish, often turning to alcohol, drugs, and increasingly suicide.

Military doctors and the VA also often overlook, ignore, or try to minimize mental disorders, including serious combat-related concussions, which cause traumatic brain injuries, and post-traumatic stress disorder (PTSD), so benefits do not have to be paid.[233] In 2008, a year after the VA had finally agreed to create a special appeals process for ex-soldiers applying for veterans' disability benefits in response to widespread charges that the military was "manipulating disability ratings to save money . . . officials [had] yet to examine a single case."[234] On the other hand, "at least 31,000 service members" were deliberately misdiagnosed with mental disorders.[235] In those cases, military clinicians were encouraged or directed to make faulty psychiatric diagnoses so that commanders could discharge soldiers they viewed as having maladaptive behaviors.[236]

CONCLUSION

Due to omissions, neglect, deliberate indifference, and unenlightened self-interest, the overall funding and staffing for programs and resources in the United States to prevent violence from occurring, to care for and treat children and adults with severe mental disabilities, and to rehabilitate and care for children and adults who have been the victims of violence, have been grossly inadequate. In many instances, such programs have been virtually nonexistent. Instead, we have established clever schemes—often based on legal fictions—to incarcerate, forcibly treat, supervise, monitor, and restrict at-risk adults and children with mental disabilities when they act out or behave in ways that are deemed dangerous. In the process, we use vague promises of humane custodial care and treatment—which we never intend to keep—and our unwillingness to fund adequate consensual care and treatment in the community as excuses that justify such coercive and inhumane interventions.

As a society, we continue to believe—without substantial evidence—that individuals who have serious mental disabilities are much more likely to be dangerous than other people, and unlikely to improve. In addition, the meager national resources that we do devote to consensual mental health services and violence prevention are being reduced due to our current fiscal deficits. At the same time, hundreds of thousands of combat-impaired soldiers have returned home with serious mental impairments and are in dire need of specialized services. Most of these former soldiers, if they also are deemed dangerous, will be subject to the same draconian measures that are imposed on other people with mental disabilities, creating a potential cascade of new inequities and injustices in our legal system.

7

DEEMED DANGEROUS DUE TO A MENTAL DISABILITY

An Extremely Suspect Classification

[I]ndividuals with disabilities are a discrete and insular minority who have been faced with restrictions and limitations, subjected to a history of purposeful unequal treatment, and relegated to a position of political powerlessness in our society, based on characteristics that are beyond the control of such individuals and resulting from stereotypic assumptions. (U.S. Congress 1990, 42 U.S.C. §12101(a)(7))[1]

OVERVIEW

The Declaration of Independence and the U.S. Constitution—in particular the Bill of Rights—established in perpetuity the principle that all human beings are created equal and from that equality all individual rights emanate. Unfortunately, due to competing national priorities and community concerns, we do not always embrace what we proclaim to the rest of the world that we hold so dear. Much like the society that evolved in George Orwell's *Animal Farm*, everyone is equal in our legal system, but certain groups of people are more or less equal than others.

The most egregious present day example of how our legal system treats a particular group of Americans differently to their detriment is persons with mental disabilities, who are viewed as being dangerous. In recent times, no group of Americans has been subjected to as awful a "history of purposeful unequal treatment, and relegated to a [worse] position of political powerlessness in our society" than those who have been subjected to extreme deprivations of their legal rights after they have been diagnosed with, or officially labeled as having, a mental disorder, condition, or aberration and are deemed to be dangerous to others, the community, or themselves.[2] Except for Native Americans who were killed and thrown off their lands and Africans who were captured, held, and then brutalized as American slaves, no other group has suffered and endured as much mistreatment, bias, and stigmatization as persons with serious mental disabilities. Even Japanese-American citizens, who were dragged from their homes and put in relocation camps during World War II, had their citizenship restored after the war had ended.

Widespread incarceration, mistreatment, and other extreme deprivations of rights, freedoms, and liberties of persons with mental disabilities has been a constant refrain in American history, with one short interlude when substantial progress was being made to "deinstitutionalize" persons with mental disabilities from large, state, civil institutions during the 1970s,[3] but without the essential funding that was necessary to make it work reasonably well. Reinstitutionalization of this population—from the streets and dilapidated housing where many of them were "dumped"—into various types of detention facilities already had begun before the deinsitutionalization movement had peaked.

Today, large numbers of Americans are being indefinitely incarcerated in jails, prisons, and secure detention facilities—or intrusively constrained, medicated, and restricted in other ways—based on unreliable predictions or pretextual impressions that they are likely to be dangerous due to their mental impairments. In addition, except for the often excessive compelled administration of powerful antipsychotic drugs with significant—and occasionally deadly—side effects, consensual mental health care, treatment, rehabilitation, habilitation, and other essential social services are mostly unavailable for these individuals, and where available, often inadequate and/or ineffective.[4]

As a result, most of these individuals are subjected to cruel and inhumane conditions in secure "treatment" facilities that are worse in many ways—and even more expensive—than the jails and prisons where so many other people with serious mental disabilities reside. Furthermore, even if these "quasi-civil" and "civil" inmates and patients were to be released, it is increasingly likely that they will be isolated and placed under permanent or lengthy government supervision, restrictions, and controls—often for the rest of their lives—under circumstances that make it extremely difficult for them to be rehabilitated and reintegrated into our society.[5]

What makes such circumstances especially unconscionable is that these unfair, punitive, and inhumane government sanctions and restrictions against persons with mental disabilities are occurring today, while the *worst offenses* against all of the other systematically abused groups of Americans occurred in the more distant past. Moreover, it is apparent that the controlling majority in our society believe that what is being done now to people with mental disorders, conditions, or aberrations deemed to be dangerous is to be encouraged or ignored, rather than condemned and discontinued as the travesties of justice they are. In fact, there is a growing movement to involuntarily commit or otherwise coerce more persons with mental disorders for lengthier stays in civil mental health facilities and outpatient programs, which would capture—under the disguise of humane care and treatment—so-called dangerous people with mental disabilities who the criminal justice system has not otherwise been allowed to detain and hold.[6]

Amidst the public hysteria often generated by this extreme form of sanism, one would hope that our laws would be as objective and fair as possible. And where they were not, that our courts would act as the final arbiters of justice in upholding reason and fairness over ignorance, fear mongering, hate, and misplaced retribution. Instead, our legislatures and courts often add layers of subjectivity, pretexual judgments, and due process mystifications to these dangerousness proceedings,[7] which tend to strongly skew and distort the results in favor of the state and federal governments over the rights, freedoms, and liberties of the respondents and defendants who have mental disabilities. Once these individuals are officially "accused" of or otherwise labeled as being potentially dangerous, they are substantially hampered by our laws and courtroom rules and procedures. State and federal governments are allowed to present highly questionable expert testimony or make inflammatory or impressionistic statements about these individuals' presumed dangerousness. Such misleading and flawed evidence constitutes the primary basis for depriving them of their liberty and other fundamental rights and freedoms, including, on occasion, their right to live.

These invidious, government-sponsored, and judicially enabled depri-vations of liberty, freedoms, and rights provide a unique and ironic con-stitutional milieu for what has been termed a "suspect classification" under our Constitution. Instead of enhancing judicial scrutiny where the rights of people with mental disabilities deemed to be dangerous are at extreme risk, our legal system has systematically reduced the applicable judicial protections for this particular group of vulnerable Americans under the paternalistic guise of pretending to help them.

DUE PROCESS AND EQUAL PROTECTION

While American law as it is interpreted and implemented in our legal system has serious—and at times—overwhelming flaws, the pinnacle of its beauty, power, and resilience resides in our Constitution, particularly the Bill of Rights and other related amendments. They were intended to create protections for all Americans against unwarranted or excessive intrusions by the states or the federal government. Arguably the two most important, and certainly the most encompassing, constitutional provisions in this regard are the due process guarantees of the Fifth Amendment, and Section 1 of the Fourteenth Amendment, which was ratified after the Civil War to entitle all our citizens, but particularly former slaves, to equal protection and enforcement of our laws by the states.

The Fifth Amendment mandates in absolute terms that "no person . . . [shall] be deprived of life, liberty, or property, without due process of law."

The Fourteenth Amendment supplemented that historic human rights proclamation with three interrelated prohibitions that pertain to states specifically.

> No State shall make or enforce any law which shall abridge the privi-leges or immunities of citizens of the United States, nor shall any State deprive any person of life, liberty, or property without due process of law; nor deny to any person within its jurisdiction the equal protection of the laws.

Our fundamental constitutional rights to due process and equal protection are the most powerful legal antidotes for what Alexis de Tocqueville, and similarly John Stuart Mill and others, viewed as the ever-present threat that democratic governments, acting on behalf of the people, could—in various ways—facilitate and support tyrannies of the majority. The targets for such tyrannies have been our most vulnerable and insular minorities, which have included Native Americans; slaves; racial, ethnic, and religious groups; women; and persons with mental disabilities. In response to this human inclination to view people in "us or them" terms, the Supreme Court established special rules when "legal restrictions" are applied that "curtail the civil rights" of individuals who are considered to be a part of a "suspect classification."[8] In essence, three levels of judicial scrutiny have evolved.

The strictest scrutiny is reserved for prior restraints on fundamental constitutional rights in which the curtailments are implemented before a due process hearing can be convened. In theory, this type of governmental action is supposed to be limited to true emergencies, although with regard to the War on Terrorism and other more recent national security–related threats, the definition of emergency has been expanding significantly, apparently to even include the 2009 inauguration ceremonies of President Barack Obama.[9] Under current practices, the identified emergency-like conditions may endure indefinitely without an imminent threat before due process is required, even where it would be well within the means of government to provide a meaningful due process hearing. Similarly, other expanded definitions of emergency or exigent circumstances have been used to justify "civil" or "quasi-civil" inpatient or outpatient commitments of many more persons thought to be dangerous due to mental disabilities without a criminal due process hearing—or sometimes without any type of meaningful hearing at all.

Strict scrutiny is reserved for governmental restrictions that affect insular minorities that traditionally have been subjected to invidious discrimination and other intolerable abuses. To date, this extra layer of judicial protection has been limited to racial, ethnic, and religious groups. Normally, there is a presumption that governmental actions that serve a legitimate state interest are constitutional. When those laws, regulations, and other government-imposed restrictions curtail the constitutional rights of members of a suspect classification, however, the government must show that it has a compelling reason for taking those actions, and that the means being used are the least restrictive necessary to satisfy the stated governmental interest(s) involved. This strict scrutiny effectively reverses the presumption of legality by placing the burden on the government to justify actions that restrict the constitutional rights of the protected class of individuals.

In addition, there is what is referred to in the law as an intermediate level of scrutiny that falls somewhere between a presumption of constitutionality and a requirement that governments have a compelling justification for their actions. It is a lesser layer of judicial protection than what is applied when there is prior restraint or a suspect classification. This intermediate scrutiny has been used for government actions that impinge upon the fundamental rights of women, who are viewed as a quasi-suspect class.[10]

At the same time, in a parallel constitutional presumption of governmental sovereignty, discriminatory actions by the states or their agents are entitled to full or partial immunity from liability, unless the state has exempted itself from such immunity, or Congress has enacted legislation that specifically abrogates such immunity in order to enforce laws that are unambiguously intended to protect the constitutional rights of our citizens.[11] This presumption effectively insulates government officials from responsibility for most discriminatory, abusive, or neglectful actions that they may take, including those against persons who are thought to have mental disabilities and are perceived to be dangerous as a result. In either situation—whether heightened scrutiny of some kind pertains and/or the state's immunity can be abrogated to allow individual remedies against improper governmental actions—largely depends on establishing a history of abuse, invidious discrimination, and mistreatment against the group that is seeking protection from governmental actions, or financial relief against the offending state and state officials who are shielded by sovereign immunity.[12]

Generally, people with mental disorders, conditions, or aberrations have not fared well when the courts have calculated the amount of abuse, invidious discrimination, and mistreatment that they have sustained historically. In part, this is because people with mental disabilities continue to be the subjects of great stigma and antipathy in our society,[13] while those previously protected groups have become substantially more mainstream. Of even greater import, though, from a legal reasoning perspective, the categories of individuals with mental disabilities that the Supreme Court has formally evaluated for special judicial treatment in the past have only involved persons with mental retardation, which today are referred to as intellectual disabilities. Despite awful abuses against many of them, people with intellectual disabilities—like people with mental disabilities more generally—were not viewed collectively as being an insular minority or the victims of the same level of abuse and mistreatment as Native Americans, slaves, or Japanese Americans sent to relocation camps, for example. Nevertheless, in recent years, much has changed, not only with regard to how our society and legal system view and treat persons with mental disabilities deemed to be dangerous, but also with regard to how the Supreme Court now views persons with mental retardation as a special category.

PERSONS WITH MENTAL DISABILITIES AS A SUSPECT CLASSIFICATION

Persons with Mental Retardation

Twice the U.S. Supreme Court has ruled that unlike members of racial, ethnic, and religious groups, certain persons with mental disabilities are not a suspect classification—or even entitled to an intermediate level of scrutiny, like women—under the Equal Protection Clause of the Constitution. Both times the plaintiffs involved were people with mental retardation (intellectual disabilities), either living in the community or arguably able to live in the community with supportive services. The first decision in 1985 focused on plaintiffs with mental retardation who were being denied the opportunity to reside in a group home,[14] while the second decision eight years later concerned plaintiffs with mental retardation who were being committed to secure facilities purportedly for humane custodial care, protection, and habilitation.[15] Neither proposed suspect class was equated with those individuals with mental retardation who, as late as the mid-1970s, were being confined indefinitely—and usually permanently—in human warehouses where crimes against humanity were common and little or no treatment, habilitation, or humane care were provided.[16]

In the first decision, *City of Cleburne v. Cleburne Living Center*,[17] the Supreme Court concluded that collectively persons with mental retardation were deserving of no heightened level of scrutiny after the justices reviewed the circumstances surrounding a local zoning ordinance, which strictly limited the opportunity of members of this class of people to live in a small group home in a residential neighborhood. Despite all of the past abuses and inhumane conditions visited upon institutionalized people with mental retardation—many of whom were finally being moved into group homes and other smaller facilities as part of the deinstitutionalization movement—the Court's majority found that these prior inhumane circumstances did not apply to the entire class of individuals with mental retardation seeking to reside in group housing nationwide. That particular class of plaintiffs, taken as a whole, was not viewed as being part of a suspect classification, although ultimately that class was able to prevail in its lawsuit under the federal Fair Housing Amendments Act,[18] a circumstance that may have actually blunted the impact of the class members' constitutional equal protection arguments.

Eight years later in *Heller v. Doe*[19] a different Supreme Court majority concluded that persons with mental retardation were not entitled to heightened scrutiny when they challenged a state law that had allowed them to be involuntarily civilly committed under standards, procedures, and protections that were less rigorous in safeguarding their due process rights and liberty interests than the involuntary commitment standards, procedures, and protections that were applicable to persons with mental illnesses. Thus, the Court determined that the government's stated interests in treating the two groups differently were legitimate and rational enough to sustain this double standard since no heightened scrutiny was constitutionally required. In particular, the justices focused on the presumably beneficial involvement of parents and guardians as substitute decision-makers in the third-party consent process that was used to commit adults with mental retardation, which made these vulnerable respondents appear to be less in need of due process protections than most adults with mental illnesses who were being involuntarily committed by state governments.[20]

In 2002, however, a new Supreme Court majority made a historic ruling, which indirectly challenged and called into question much of the prior reasoning that people with mental retardation should not be viewed as a suspect class. In *Atkins v. Virginia*,[21] the Court determined that defendants with mental retardation—and only mental retardation—are protected by the Eighth Amendment's ban against cruel and unusual punishment in death penalty cases. As a result, they could not be executed, even though thirteen years earlier the justices had found in *Penry v. Lynaugh*[22] that no such protection existed. The *Atkins* decision had two major intertwined rationales, which requires treating people with mental retardation differently than any other category of adult capital defendants, with or without mental disabilities.

First, people with mental retardation, due to their intellectual deficits, are particularly vulnerable to abuse, mistreatment, and discrimination in the legal system. They confess to crimes they did not commit, are significantly less able to help their lawyers than "normal" clients, and appear to be fully culpable when in fact their ability to mask the true extent of their impairments often disguises their true culpability. Also, the Court noted that defense counsel often are severely limited in effectively presenting mitigating evidence of mental retardation in death penalty cases due to the fact that their condition can be used to prove the existence of an aggravating circumstance based on dangerousness.[23] This should have been sufficient to support the majority's ruling.

Unfortunately, it was not. A second—and arguably even more decisive rationale—was needed to justify the Court's overruling existing precedent. Law professor James Ellis convinced the Court, particularly Justice O'Connor, who cast the deciding vote that since 1989—when the Justices had decided that people with mental retardation could be executed—a new national consensus had evolved.[24] This shift in attitudes made the execution of persons with mental retardation morally offensive, which, under the Eighth Amendment as interpreted, provided the necessary constitutional linchpin for overruling the prior decision. Remarkably, it had been Professor Ellis himself who, more than anyone else, was responsible for changing the consensus by implementing a strategy to convince enough state legislatures to ban such executions.[25]

As brilliant, resourceful, and necessary as Ellis' legal strategy proved to be,[26] it also reinforced and expanded a legal precedent that someday could have negative repercussions for persons with mental disabilities. Ellis led the Supreme Court to conclude that the meaning of a fundamental right—in this case the Eighth Amendment's prohibition against cruel and unusual punishment—should be determined by the current will of a majority of Americans. The necessary popular support was measured by legislative actions in those states that had changed their laws regarding the execution of persons with mental retardation since the justices had last addressed this issue. In *Atkins*, the Court reasoned that a numerical majority of Americans was not needed as long as the legislative trend toward outlawing such executions was clearly established. That clarity was present because many states already had banned the death penalty. Thus, when that number was added to those states that had changed their laws to ban the execution of persons with mental retardation, this meant that there was now a majority of states that would not permit the execution of persons with mental retardation.[27]

Certainly a strong argument was made that this second line of reasoning was justified because obvious and particularly harmful and irrevocable injustices would be prevented. Yet this particular rationale also has potential negative implications generally, and arguably more so for people with mental disabilities, whose lack of popularity has made them especially vulnerable to abuse and injustice by majority acclimation. Fundamental constitutional rights become even more vital when they are not supported by a majority of our citizens, which is another compelling reason why persons with mental disabilities who are deemed to be dangerous need the special protections afforded to suspect classes.

Persons Who Are Deemed Dangerous Due to Their Mental Disabilities

It is in the context of the *Cleburne*, *Heller*, and *Atkins* decisions that the constitutional justifications—and arguably the constitutional necessity—for recognizing a suspect classification that encompasses persons with mental disabilities who are deemed to be dangerous (or harmful)—and thus subject to indefinite confinement, execution, and other forms of intrusive state controls in inhumane conditions—should be assessed. This particular class of persons with mental disabilities is clearly distinguishable from the plaintiffs with mental retardation in *Cleburne* and *Heller*, who were viewed with considerably more sympathy and understanding by the courts and the American public, and, as a class, were subject to less abuse, mistreatment, and discrimination. Furthermore, the *Atkins* opinion illustrates how critical public perceptions—or conversely, misconceptions—can be in determining how much, or how little, the Constitution as interpreted, our courts, and the rest of our legal system offer in the way of protections to a particular group of people. Under our Constitution, a population that is afforded demonstrably fewer legal protections than any other group because the public fears and devalues them should be considered a suspect class. Unfortunately, often the opposite is true because extreme, negative public perceptions—in this circumstance fueled by sanism and exaggerated fear—tend to distort the legal process as well.

Much of the reason why persons with disabilities generally, and those with mental disabilities in particular, have not been viewed as being a suspect classification has to do with the wide variety and types of conditions, disorders, and behaviors that exist, and the fact that not everyone who has a mental disability or mental impairment is similarly vulnerable or subjected to the same degree of abuse and mistreatment. Typically these classes have been defined too broadly or imprecisely to state categorically that everyone—or even most—of their members are part of a vulnerable and insular minority that has been subjected to an intolerable level of discrimination, abuse, and mistreatment. Typically, people with mental disabilities who are able to live in the community by themselves or with the assistance of others are considerably better off than those who are in our civil and criminal institutions or under other forms of government coercion and custody. An exception are those people with more serious mental disabilities who find themselves on the streets or in dilapidated housing of our major cities or suburbs without the basic resources to survive humanely, and thus are at high risk of being institutionalized and/or having other fundamental rights curtailed.

Generally courts have presumed—often incorrectly—that most people with intellectual disabilities (mental retardation) who are the subjects of involuntary commitment have someone making decisions in their best interests, including the decision that they should be cared for in a custodial or other coercive setting. The laws of most states view this type of third-party nonconsensual commitment as being voluntary, and thus typically distinguish it from involuntary civil inpatient or outpatient commitments in terms of the rigorousness of the standards and due process protections that should be provided to the person being detained or otherwise constrained.[28]

The U.S. Supreme Court has never specifically ruled that no subcategories of persons with mental disabilities should be considered a suspect class, only that persons with mental retardation in the circumstances that existed in those 1985 and 1993 cases were not. In the 1980s, for example, if it had continued to be the practice in the United States to involuntarily sterilize women with so-called mental deficiencies en masse, as had been done throughout much of the twentieth century, it would have been difficult to argue persuasively that these women did not have the historical characteristics necessary to be viewed as members of a suspect class. Also, several things have changed in recent years, which strongly supports the view that today people with mental disabilities whom the legal system, through our governments, deems as being dangerous are a highly—and arguably the most—suspect class of Americans.

First, as a result of *Atkins*, the Supreme Court and most of the rest of the judiciary should understand that people with mental retardation are a more insular and vulnerable minority than what the justices had opined in 1985 and 1993. Second, how the legal system treats persons with mental disabilities who are deemed dangerous has deteriorated to such an extent in recent years that this particular class of people has emerged as the most insular and vulnerable minority of all Americans. Moreover, the situation is becoming worse. Members of this suspect class are being subjected— often indiscriminately through new evidentiary rules and procedures—to myriad rights deprivations, including involuntary commitments in secure facilities indefinitely or other rights deprivations in the community without humane care and treatment. In addition, our nation has executed—or placed on death row in inhumane isolation to await execution—a disproportionate number of people in this suspect class.[29]

Since the U.S. Supreme Court first embraced the legal construct of a suspect classification in 1944, there is no group of American citizens or residents in our society which has been or continues to be subjected to more stigma, fear, misconceptions, legal injustices, physical and mental abuses, and inhumane treatment than people who are deemed by the states or federal government to be dangerous due to their mental disabilities. Yet instead of being given the benefit of stricter scrutiny by our courts, these individuals are part of a very different suspect classification. Special attention for them results in their receiving reduced judicial scrutiny, fewer rights and protections, and more punitive and constitutionally restrictive legal dispositions than others for comparable antisocial behaviors; or, much worse, the mere legal perception that such behaviors might occur in the future.

In our society, people who have been diagnosed with mental disorders, conditions, or aberrations and appear to be dangerous toward others, the community, or themselves are subjected to special rules of evidence and testimony and legal fictions that favor governments. This substantially increases the likelihood that members of this class will be found to satisfy the overbroad and vague dangerous-based criteria that are used to justify involuntary commitments, harsh and intrusive release conditions, executions, pretrial detention, trying juveniles as adults, and other rights deprivations. Furthermore, these individuals rarely receive the care and treatment that is supposed to be provided to them as a *quid pro quo* for their due process protections being reduced. Instead they are likely to be subjected to cruel and inhumane custodial care. Also, where criminal charges are involved, their dispositions often last longer and have more restrictions than if they had been found guilty of the crimes for which they were charged and they had no mental disabilities. [30]

Unlike in the 1960s and 1970s, when most in the legal community viewed severe mental disabilities as conditions that should reduce a person's punishment, today those conditions generally are equated with dangerousness, a status that is used to justify longer periods of confinement and other highly intrusive social controls. Lack of cognitive awareness and/or the ability to control one's behavior, which should reduce moral culpability, rarely lead to reduced periods of punishment. Instead, such mental impairments are much more apt to be viewed as persuasive reasons for the legal system to be less fair and more punitive and restrictive in order to protect society from unknowable and incalculable future dangers.

Our society has become even less tolerant and more apt to mistreat persons with mental disabilities perceived to be dangerous than ever before. It is the fear of the unknown—based on something that may, but most probably will not happen in the immediate future—which has pushed us to undermine our most hallowed constitutional principles. In the process, we have used our legal system to preventively restrict and restrain, discriminate against, and abuse people with mental impairments, whom we fear the most.

CONCLUSION

Persons diagnosed with mental disorders, conditions, or aberrations—or officially labeled as such—who are deemed by state or federal governments to be dangerous (or harmful), make up an insular minority, which should be recognized as a suspect classification under our Constitution. They have endured a long and unrelenting history of stigma, invidious discrimination, abuse, and mistreatment from members of our society and the legal system itself. One would be hard pressed to identify any group of Americans that continues to be treated worse. As a result, they fit within the traditional definition of a suspect class as much—if not more so—than any other population in our society, including those groups who already have been identified as suspect classes.

By establishing a constitutional imperative to strictly scrutinize the civil and criminal laws that impinge upon the fundamental rights of this particular class of individuals with mental disabilities, our judiciary would be pushed to correct many long-standing miscarriages of justice. At the same time, such a judicial imperative would provide our nation with a much-needed incentive to comprehensively address the legal rights and unmet needs of this vulnerable and stigmatized population far more rationally and humanely than we do now.

8

A NEW SYSTEM OF STATE AND FEDERAL LAWS AND PUBLIC HEALTH APPROACHES FOR PERSONS WITH MENTAL DISABILITIES DEEMED TO BE DANGEROUS

Initial Recommendations

Affirming what should be readily apparent—that persons with mental disabilities who are deemed dangerous are a suspect classification—would not by itself eliminate the neglect, abuse, and mistreatment that this steadily increasing population has been subjected to through our legal system. At the same time, recognizing and judicially addressing this suspect class is an essential first step. Ultimately, however, there also should be new state and federal laws to govern when, how, and to what extent the fundamental rights of persons with mental disabilities who are deemed to be dangerous may be restricted in our society.[1] Collectively, our existing laws are inhumane, unjust, unnecessarily coercive, and irrational. Accordingly, these initial recommendations—based on the findings and analyses in this book—identify what key components of our civil, quasi-civil, and criminal laws should be changed and what they should be replaced with.

In addition to reforming our laws, we should also fundamentally change our public health focus from coercive, legally enforced, or threatened mental disability care and treatment to publicly financed alternatives

that are holistic and consensual. This public health initiative would include substantially more funding and programs for prevention, voluntary
care, and treatment, as well as public education to address the attitudes of
Americans toward people with mental disabilities and about violence.

A NEW SUSPECT CLASSIFICATION

- Federal and state courts, led by the U.S. Supreme Court, should recognize that individuals, including minors, who satisfy three narrowly
  tailored criteria constitute a constitutionally protected suspect classification:

    a. a professional diagnosis, official determination, or official
       record exists or is being made that identifies them as having a
       mental disorder, condition, or aberration;

    b. a legal determination or official government allegation (or con-
       tention) has been made or is being made that due to this mental
       disorder, condition, or aberration they are and will continue to
       be a danger to others, the community, or themselves, or in the
       future are likely to harm others, the community, or themselves;
       and

    c. as a result of satisfying the first two criteria, their fundamental
       rights, liberties, and/or freedoms have been, or legally may be,
       subjected to substantial restrictions or intrusions.

Commentary

While it could be reasonably argued that a broader population of persons
with mental disabilities should be included as a constitutionally suspect
classification, this book has focused specifically on that subgroup of persons with mental disorders, conditions, or aberrations who have endured
and continue to endure the most discrimination, the most abuse, and the
most mistreatment because they have been deemed legally dangerous. In
addition, anyone who satisfies these three criteria can be easily and accurately identified as a member of this proposed constitutionally protected
suspect classification.

DANGEROUSNESS LAWS, STANDARDS, EVIDENCE, AND TESTIMONY SHOULD BE STRICTLY LIMITED

- Except as set out elsewhere in these recommendations:

  a. all laws, legal standards, or procedures that deprive American citizens or residents of their fundamental rights, freedoms, or liberties based on predictions of dangerousness or harm to others, the community, or oneself—when those laws, standards, or procedures are applied to individuals because they have a mental disorder, condition, or aberration—should be repealed or amended and narrowly tailored as reflected in (b) below;

  b. no evidence or testimony based on predictions of an individual's dangerousness or harm to others, the community, or oneself should be admitted in any court or used by juries or judges in making civil or criminal legal determinations, unless there is persuasive empirical and other objective evidence that the type of dangerousness prediction which is being proffered as evidence or testimony or being used as criteria to satisfy an applicable legal standard or procedure, is more likely than not to contribute to a relevant, accurate, and reliable legal determination, given the governing standards and burdens of proof in that particular case.

Commentary

While it is conceivable that in the foreseeable future social science will have progressed sufficiently to allow experts to make reasonably reliable, valid, and consistently accurate predictions of dangerousness with regard to a few specified legal standards applied to a few discrete groups of respondents or defendants in an adversarial courtroom environment, there is little if any empirical and other persuasive objective evidence that this has been achieved now with regard to any of our dangerousness standards. Thus, admitting evidence and testimony or creating legal standards or procedures in our legal system today based on predictions of dangerousness or of harmfulness—except in limited circumstances to rebut or refute accusations of dangerousness—is unjust, unfair, and counterproductive.

The burden should fall on state, federal, and local governments—which are relying on predictions of dangerousness or harmfulness to deprive persons with mental disorders, conditions, or aberrations of their fundamental rights, freedoms, or liberties—to demonstrate that such evidence or testimony and legal standards or procedures when used in a courtroom environment are reasonably relevant, reliable, valid, and accurate in each specific type of case in which dangerousness or harmfulness is to be determined. Moreover, courts should establish procedures that ensure that when such specialized knowledge or subjective impressions about future dangerousness or harmfulness are utilized in the courtroom they are presented in ways that are logical, reasonably objective, fair, and do not unnecessarily stigmatize and prejudice those individuals with mental disabilities whose rights, freedoms, or liberties are at issue.

In determining whether any such specialized knowledge or subjective impressions based on predictions of dangerousness or harmfulness should be admissible, it is essential to recognize that the burden and standard of proof, as well as the substantive and procedural standards being applied, are critical empirical and practical considerations. They fundamentally change how we should view the admissibility of such evidence, testimony, or subjective impressions of dangerousness in our courtrooms.

In addition, subjective impressions about future dangerousness or harmfulness made by juries and/or judges, particularly in death penalty and preventive detention cases, should be discouraged and curtailed. They are inherently prejudicial and discriminatory. What the defendant has actually done should be the criteria for determining immediate dangerousness, not what he or she may do in the unknowable future.

Furthermore, with few if any exceptions, expert mental status evidence and testimony as applied in our courtrooms today are logically, empirically, statistically, and/or scientifically deficient when they are used to prove an individual's future dangerousness or harmfulness. Merely because mental health professionals generally accept mental status evidence or testimony about dangerousness or harmfulness for use in clinical situations does not mean that such evidence or testimony is reliable in making courtroom determinations based on vague and over-inclusive legal definitions of dangerousness or harmfulness. To be reliable, these different legal definitions should be validated in the specific context of the legal procedures and standards—including different burdens and standards of proof—that are applied, which also differ depending on the jurisdiction and legal circumstances involved. This is no easy task and may not even be practically possible, but that substantial obstacle certainly does not justify using such flawed evidence and testimony anyway.

Establishing the legal appropriateness to justify admitting such questionable dangerousness or harmfulness evidence and testimony will and should be a formidable challenge for federal and state governments. Governments should have the burden of persuasion as the parties seeking to restrict or limit fundamental rights, freedoms, or liberties based on dangerousness evidence or testimony. On the other hand, that same type of mental status evidence is more likely to be minimally adequate—and thus the challenge considerably less formidable—when it is being used to rebut the government's position. Logically the burden of persuasion threshold should be less—or much less—in rebutting such evidence than in establishing it because the standard of proof is and should be less or much less. Empirical evidence demonstrates that while structured risk assessments are unreliable in identifying high-risk individuals, such assessments may be useful in identifying low-risk individuals.[2] Thus, before any such evidence should be deemed admissible, it is important to demonstrate first that the "type of prediction being proffered as evidence or testimony is more likely than not to contribute to a relevant, accurate and reliable legal determination, *given the governing standards and burdens in that particular case.*"

GENERALLY NONCONSENSUAL DEPRIVATIONS OF FUNDAMENTAL RIGHTS, LIBERTIES, AND FREEDOMS BASED ON DANGEROUSNESS TO OTHERS SHOULD BE HANDLED AS CRIMINAL MATTERS

- Except pursuant to a "legally recognized emergency" described in these recommendations, nonconsensual civil or quasi-civil deprivations of the fundamental rights, liberties, and freedoms of persons with mental disorders, conditions, or aberrations based on dangerousness or harmfulness to others should be prohibited. Such deprivations should be treated as criminal dispositions subject to our criminal laws with full criminal due process protections, unless the subjects of such deprivations, as described in the recommendations below, reach an agreement—either themselves or through an appointed substitute decision-maker defined below—to receive contractually specified care, treatment, and rehabilitation in a humane environment as a quid pro quo for diminishing their due process rights.

- If a governing authority and the respondent agree to an adjudicated consensual civil intervention option and the respondent fulfills that agreement or the government reneges on that agreement without just cause—such as nonperformance by the respondent—all related criminal (and/or juvenile justice) charges or dispositions should be extinguished.

- Criminal offenders with mental disabilities who do not reach an agreement with the government for their care and treatment should receive humane mental health care and treatment as described in the recommendations below.

Commentary

The due process distinctions between what is termed civil and criminal in our legal system should have much more to do with the actual rights, liberties, and freedoms that are at risk and the stigma that is involved in each particular situation than dubious semantic rationalizations and distinctions about what does or does not constitute punishment. Where the overall impact of the stigma and the deprivations of rights, liberties, and freedoms are reasonably equivalent to—or even greater than—a criminal disposition, the accompanying due process protections should be reasonably equivalent as well. It is the nature and degree of the stigma and of the deprivations of rights, liberties, and freedoms involved—and not some arbitrary or dubious civil versus criminal label—which should be legally significant.

In the United States, persons with mental disorders, conditions, or aberrations who are adjudicated as being dangerous to others frequently—and arguably most of the time—experience equal or greater deprivations of rights, freedoms, and liberties, and considerably more stigma, than if they were tried and convicted as criminals without taking their mental disorders, conditions, or aberrations into account. Thus, they should be entitled to full criminal due process, unless they consent (or have their duly-authorized representative consent) to receive an enforceable promise of adequate care, treatment, and rehabilitation in a humane environment as a *quid pro quo* for agreeing to dilute their due process guarantees. Given the poor record of federal, state, and local governments in providing adequate care, treatment, and rehabilitation to persons with mental disabilities in their custody, however, there should be mechanisms, as described in the recommendations below, to ensure that such care, treatment, and rehabilitation is consensual and provided for as intended.

Short-term emergency civil interventions may be pursued and mandated for persons with mental disorders, conditions, or aberrations who are deemed to be dangerous to others, but only while a "legally recognized emergency" as described below continues to exist. Also, contractually agreed-upon care and treatment, as described in these recommendations, should be pursued in lieu of a criminal prosecution whenever that option is appropriate. In addition, once a respondent fulfills his or her civil agreement, or the governing authority fails to live up to that agreement, any pending criminal or juvenile justice charges should be extinguished.

As with most of the recommendations below, the provisions governing dangerousness or harmfulness to others are intended to apply to anyone who is subject to such coercive governmental interventions, which should include minors as well as adults. What has happened is that many children have been treated like, or more like, adults with respect to punishments and rights deprivations, but often receive less—and sometimes far less—substantive and procedural due process protections. These recommendations support the principle that children, especially those with mental disabilities, should receive at least as much in terms of due process protections as adults.

LEGALLY RECOGNIZED EMERGENCY INTERVENTIONS: SERIOUS AND IMMINENT BODILY HARM

- A legally recognized emergency intervention without a court order should be based on persuasive evidence—more likely than not—that respondents, due to a mental disorder that was recently diagnosed by a qualified mental health expert: (a) caused serious bodily harm or attempted to cause serious bodily harm to others or themselves, or (b) currently have delusions, overwhelming compulsions, or other types of gross distortions of reality that would result in their imminent death or serious and imminent bodily harm to themselves. This ex parte intervention should last no more than [forty-eight hours] from the time the individual is first taken into custody.

- A legally recognized emergency intervention that extends beyond [forty-eight hours] should require a judicial determination in a due process hearing in which the respondent has competent legal representation. The government should have the burden of proving by clear and convincing evidence that the respondent has a mental disorder and due to that disorder, the respondent:

    a. caused death or serious bodily harm or attempted to cause death or serious bodily harm to others or him- or herself; or

    b. has a delusion, overwhelming compulsion, or other type of gross distortion of reality which prevents him or her from avoiding imminent death or imminent and serious bodily harm.

- A court-ordered legally recognized emergency intervention should never last longer than [seven days] from when the respondent was first detained, unless another legal proceeding consistent with these recommendations has been initiated and is concluded in a timely manner.

- Courts should lose jurisdiction over a respondent if the specified time-limits are exceeded or the respondent does not have competent legal representation, except in the rare circumstance that the respondent was responsible for the delays or has properly waived legal representation. Once the court loses jurisdiction, the respondent should be released, unless and until a new proceeding consistent with these recommendations is initiated.

- All emergency interventions, including commitments or other deprivations of fundamental rights, freedoms, or liberties, should be in the least restrictive setting possible based on the court-documented emergency circumstances in that particular case.

- These recommendations regarding emergency interventions should apply equally to adults, juveniles, and children.

Commentary

Emergency interventions, as applied to persons with mental disorders, conditions, or aberrations who are deemed dangerous, should be limited to situations in which respondents, due to a properly diagnosed mental disorder, have caused, attempted to cause, or more likely than not will cause death or serious and imminent harm to others or themselves. An emergency intervention that is not based on a court-adjudication should last no longer than forty-eight hours. The overriding objective should be to substantially reduce the number of instances in which these emergency circumstances arise in the first place, rather than trying to use coercive measures to respond to such emergency situations after conditions are allowed to deteriorate.

As established elsewhere in these recommendations, individuals should not be subject to these emergency interventions if they consent and continue to consent—either themselves or through a properly appointed substitute decision-maker—to receive agreed- upon, publicly funded social services, which would resolve the emergency. As noted elsewhere, consensual civil interventions should be strongly favored over emergency interventions.

Emergency interventions should be time-limited—[forty-eight hours] without a court-adjudication and [seven days] with. Also, because government incentives for not meeting deadlines are often substantial and past experience demonstrates that frequently deadlines are not met, these recommendations state that courts should lose jurisdiction when such deadlines pass, unless the respondents or their lawyers were responsible for the delays.

In addition, although the critical importance of competent and effective legal representation in such proceedings is well-documented, generally our nation's record in providing such representation has been poor. Therefore, it is recommended that competent legal representation should be made mandatory, unless it is properly waived, by depriving courts of jurisdiction if respondents are not competently represented. Both the duty and responsibility for ensuring that respondents receive appropriate counsel ultimately lie with the presiding judge. Judges should be the gatekeepers who ensure that these respondents with mental disabilities receive a fair trial, especially competent and effective legal representation.

EXTENDED AND INDEFINITE, CIVIL, INVOLUNTARY, HARM TO SELF INTERVENTIONS SHOULD BE DISPOSITIONS OF LAST RESORT

- Extended involuntary thirty-day dangerousness to self interventions should be strictly limited to those circumstances in which respondents have a continuing mental disorder and due to that disorder they have:
-
  a. acted in ways that more likely than not would lead to their imminent death or serious and imminent bodily harm; or

  b. delusions, compulsions, or other gross distortions of reality which, more likely than not, would result in their death or serious and imminent bodily harm.

- Extended dangerousness to self determinations should require court adjudications using a clear and convincing evidence standard of proof, but in which the respondents enjoy other criminal due process protections, including the right to competent legal representation and to call and cross-examine witnesses.

- A dangerousness to self proceeding should be barred if respondents are receiving—or would consent to receive—contractually specified, court-approved, publicly paid-for care, treatment, and other essential social services consistent with these recommendations.

- Proof that respondents are at risk of self-harm should not include dangerousness evidence and testimony that these recommendations would bar.

- Respondents who are adjudicated as dangerous to themselves under the thirty-day standard should be released promptly if:

  a. they agree to accept contractually specified, court-approved,

  b. they prove by a preponderance of the evidence that they are not dangerous as defined under these extended intervention recommendations;

  c. thirty days have passed since the original intervention proceeding and no other intervention proceeding authorized by these recommendations has been initiated; or

> d. the court loses jurisdiction as specified below.

- The government should only be allowed to file a petition for an extraordinary indefinite involuntary intervention if the respondent already is under a thirty-day intervention, which will expire within three days, and there is probable cause to believe that the respondent is incompetent to make his or her own care and treatment decisions and will require care and treatment for more than thirty additional days.

- A court should be allowed to order an indefinite involuntary intervention if it finds by clear and convincing evidence in a due process hearing that:

  > a. the respondent is incompetent to make the necessary care and treatment decisions and a duly authorized substitute decision-maker testifies or respondent's counsel informs the court that an indefinite intervention would be in that individual's best interest, given the respondent's medical condition and the absence of any reasonable community alternatives;

  > b. the respondent continues to meet the thirty-day dangerousness to self criteria;

  > c. the respondent's mental disorder is either permanent in nature or highly resistant to significant improvement; and

  > d. an individual plan has been prepared, which specifies what care, treatment, and other services will be provided, what the goals and objectives of the plan will be, and, assuming the respondent's condition does not appear to be permanent, when and in what circumstances he or she will be eligible for release or to be moved to a less restrictive setting, and what that setting will likely be.

- If a patient's substitute decision-maker revokes consent to a court-ordered indefinite intervention or the patient becomes competent again and revokes such consent, the patient should be released or promptly given an emergency hearing. Also, the respondent's legal counsel may petition a court *ex parte* for release any time counsel has reasonable grounds to believe a release is warranted. A due process hearing should be granted if there is probable cause to believe that the respondent no longer meets the indefinite intervention criteria or has become competent to make his or her own care and treatment decisions.

- Courts should lose jurisdiction over a respondent with regard to any type of extended intervention if:

  a. the specified time-limits are wrongfully exceeded;

  b. the respondent does not have competent legal representation (except where counsel dies, is incapacitated, or resigns, and proper steps are taken to promptly appoint new counsel or counsel is competently waived); or

  c. after being properly notified, the government continues to fail to provide the respondent with adequate care and treatment based on the individual treatment plan. (Lack of funds should never be an acceptable justification for failing to provide the respondent with necessary care and treatment.)

- When a court loses jurisdiction, the respondent should be promptly released from any extended interventions, unless a substitute decision-maker has been appointed, petitions the court for a new hearing, and certifies that the respondent continues to be incompetent and no less-restrictive, safe alternatives to an extended commitment have been identified.

- These provisions should apply equally to adults, juveniles, and children.

Commentary

Extended, non-emergency deprivations of fundamental rights based on dangerousness to oneself are distinguishable from similarly severe deprivations based on dangerousness to others. For persons with mental disorders, conditions, or aberrations, who are deemed dangerous to themselves, the government's primary role is to treat, care for, and protect them in the least-restrictive humane setting. At the same time, where fundamental and other important rights, freedoms, and liberties are at risk, strict due process should be observed that includes mandatory time-limits, the right to competent counsel, and the right to adequate care and treatment in a humane environment. Where these essential safeguards are not provided for, the courts should lose jurisdiction, which means the subjects should be promptly released, unless emergency involuntary intervention proceedings are filed as soon as practically possible.

Because of the fundamental and other important rights, freedoms, or liberties involved, extended dangerousness to self interventions should be strictly limited to those relatively few individuals who present an immediate and compelling danger to themselves, which is more likely than not to extend beyond the terms of a legally recognized emergency. Under these recommendations this type of involuntary extended intervention is deemed unnecessary if the respondent or the respondent's court-appointed substitute decision-maker consents to care and treatment under a contractual agreement with the government—which is the preferred option under these recommendations—or if a short-term emergency intervention would suffice.

Also, involuntary interventions with a specified maximum time limit of thirty days should be preferred over indefinite interventions. The use of indefinite interventions using a substitute decision-maker should be viewed as an extraordinary circumstance and strictly limited to those rare situations in which the respondent is incompetent to make his or her own care and treatment decisions, has no other reasonable care and treatment options, and his or her mental disorder, condition, or aberration is permanent or highly resistant to remediation. Without initiating a new proceeding or instituting an indefinite intervention, the maximum length of time a non-emergency civil dangerousness to self intervention may last would be until the respondent or his or her counsel—under a preponderance of the evidence standard—demonstrates that the respondent is no longer dangerous to self or thirty days have passed, whichever occurs first.

Proof of initial civil dangerousness to self should be based on actual dangerous actions, activities, omissions, or distortions of reality and not the type of future dangerousness evidence that is prohibited under these recommendations. Evidence based on dangerousness predictions should only be allowed for the limited purpose of demonstrating that there is clear and convincing proof that the respondent needs coerced care and treatment that would exceed the maximum time permitted for an emergency intervention, and thus justify a thirty-day or indefinite intervention.

A STRONG PREFERENCE FOR CONTRACTUALLY AGREED-UPON CARE AND TREATMENT

- Except in "legally recognized emergencies" before a court has become involved or if a person has been sentenced after being convicted of a crime, contractually agreed-upon, consensual care and treatment should be presumed to be preferable for persons with mental disorders, conditions, or aberrations over options that involve more restrictive deprivations of the individual's fundamental rights, liberties, or freedoms.

- If there is reasonable cause to believe that a respondent, who is in the process of contracting for care and treatment, lacks some or all of the abilities needed to make an informed decision about care and treatment due to mental or cognitive impairments, both the respondent's counsel and the governmental authority involved should have a separate duty to request that a court determine whether the respondent's competency to make care and treatment decisions should be adjudicated. The court also may make a competency determination on its own initiative. Any contractual arrangements made by an incompetent respondent without an appropriately appointed substitute decision-maker should be voidable at the option of the respondent or respondent's lawyer.

- The failure to provide, or to allocate the resources to provide, contractually agreed-upon care and treatment should result in the government involved being subject to contempt proceedings and prohibited—unless such care and treatment is promptly provided—from taking any further actions that deprive that respondent of his or her fundamental rights, liberties, or freedoms. The only exceptions should be legally recognized emergencies as described in these recommendations, or if the respondent is properly charged with committing a crime after the contractual agreement was reached.

- These provisions should apply equally to adults, juveniles, and children.

Commentary

The main reason that mental disability law principles involving both the entitlement to treatment and the least-restrictive setting have gone unfulfilled so often in the past is that state and federal governments have not been committed to those principles and have been excused in various legal ways from providing the financial and administrative resources required to properly implement them. These recommendations would create a legally enforceable contractual obligation on state and federal governments to provide agreed-upon care and treatment to avoid using involuntary or coercive interventions. The failure to provide such care and treatment would result in those governments being subject to contempt proceedings and not being allowed to deprive those individuals, who are owed such care and treatment, of their fundamental rights based on their dangerousness to self or others, except in legally recognized emergency situations or if crimes are subsequently committed. In order to properly agree to such a contract—unless a contract already existed before the government initiated intervention proceedings—respondents should be represented by counsel and provide consent consistent with these recommendations. Both the respondent's counsel and the government have a duty to notify the court if they have a good reason to believe the respondent may not be competent to make care and treatment decisions and a substitute decision-maker has not already been appointed.

SUBSTITUTED CONSENT FOR PERSONS ADJUDICATED AS INCOMPETENT TO MAKE CARE AND TREATMENT DECISIONS

- Either a respondent's lawyer adhering to the Model Rules of Professional Responsibility or—should the lawyer prefer or the court order for cause—an independent court-appointed, substitute decision-maker should provide "substituted consent" for any subsequent contractually agreed-upon care and treatment plan or individualized offender plan on behalf of:

    a. adults who have been adjudicated mentally incompetent to make care and treatment decisions or;

    b. minors who have no available, legally authorized parents or guardians to act as substitute decision-makers.

- Substituted consent should reflect the values and preferences of the individual involved, as set out in any legally recognized advanced directives or other preferences that the individual has made while a competent adult or mature minor, which can be proven clearly and convincingly.

- If the respondent's preferences have not been established clearly and convincingly, the substitute decision-maker should make care and treatment decision(s) based on the individual's best interests in consultation with the respondent's lawyer (assuming the lawyer is not the substitute decision-maker). What constitutes the individual's best interests should be informed by that person's known values and preferences. The traditional least-restrictive setting is presumed to be the appropriate disposition, unless the court finds based on clear and convincing evidence that a more restrictive disposition is required to protect the individual's health and safety or to implement the respondent's known personal preferences.

Commentary

Under these recommendations, providing competent legal representation for respondents is a high priority in all situations and mandatory in certain specified situations. Where the respondent involved has been adjudicated incompetent to make care and treatment decisions, a substitute mechanism should be in place consistent with the Model Rules of Professional Responsibility of lawyers to ensure that the respondent's interests are protected with regard to any subsequent contractually agreed-upon care and treatment decisions and individual offender plans.

Respondent's counsel—where the client is an adult, mature minor, or a minor without a duly authorized parent or guardian—should be given the first opportunity to decide whether it would be in his or her client's legal and other related interests for that lawyer to serve as the substitute decision-maker. Second, the court should appoint an independent substitute decision-maker for the respondent or reaffirm an existing substitute decision-maker, if either the respondent's lawyer so requests or the court determines for cause that the lawyer would be an inappropriate substitute decision-maker. If the court makes such an appointment, the substitute decision-maker should consult with the respondent's lawyer before making final care and treatment decisions. Parents or duly authorized guardians for minors should be allowed to make care and treatment decisions on behalf of their children who are not mature minors.

In providing substituted consent, the substitute decision-maker should consider the respondent's wishes if they are known or can be proven clearly and convincingly. If those wishes are unknown or unclear, the least restrictive alternative should govern, unless a court rules that a more restrictive—or arguably more restrictive—disposition is required to protect that individual's best interests, which should be defined in terms of the respondent's health and safety and known personal preferences. Both competent adults and mature minors should have the right to express their preferences and have those preferences followed.

GUN CONTROL FOR PERSONS WITH MENTAL DISABILITIES

- The constitutional right of persons with mental disabilities to own or possess guns should only be restricted in the following narrowly tailored circumstances:

    a. the respondent is currently under an involuntary intervention order or has entered into a care and treatment agreement with a government authority that specifies he or she may not own or possess firearms or munitions while the contract is in effect; or

    b. a court has found that based on clear and convincing evidence the respondent is either mentally incompetent to use a gun safely, or has a mental disorder and within the past year used a gun unsafely.

- After one year, if there is probable cause to believe the respondent is able to use guns safely, he or she should be allowed to challenge the continuation of that gun restriction in a new hearing.

COMMENTARY

While there are many good and even compelling reasons to limit gun ownership and possession in this country, the constitutional right to bear arms should be applied to persons with mental disabilities in the same way as it is applied to anyone else. The burden should be on the government to demonstrate that a respondent, due to a mental disability, is currently unable to use a gun safely, unless he or she has consented not to use guns as part of a contractual care and treatment agreement or currently is under an involuntary commitment/intervention order. Otherwise, a court should be required to find, using a clear and convincing standard of proof, that the respondent either is mentally incompetent to use guns safely or, in the past year, used a gun unsafely due to a mental disorder. After a year or more, however, the respondent should be allowed to challenge such a court order if there is probable cause to believe that he or she is now able to use a gun safely.

Given what social science has demonstrated about developmental immaturity, it is reasonable to give governments more leeway in how they restrict guns by minors, including minors with mental disabilities.

HUMANE CARE AND TREATMENT FOR PRETRIAL DETAINEES AND OFFENDERS WITH MENTAL DISABILITIES, INCLUDING INDIVIDUAL TREATMENT PLANS

- Pretrial detainees and convicted offenders with mental disorders, conditions, or aberrations, who as a result of their conditions would benefit from special care, treatment, and/or rehabilitation outside the regular jail or prison environment, should be transferred to separate units, centers, or facilities. They should receive a level of care, treatment, and/or rehabilitation, which would allow them to reasonably benefit as specified in an individual offender plan.

- Pretrial detainees and convicted offenders should have a private right of action—after exhausting reasonable and prompt administrative remedies—to compel the governing authority to provide what has been specified in an individual treatment plan and/or to demonstrate that their plan does not provide them with a level of care, treatment, and/or rehabilitation, which would constitute a reasonable benefit.

- Pretrial detainees and convicted offenders with mental disorders, conditions, or aberrations who have not been adjudicated incompetent may choose to accept or reject such care, treatment, and/or rehabilitation, but their incompetency should be formally adjudicated if the government, the respondent's lawyer, or the court has good cause to request an incompetency hearing.

- Consistent with these recommendations, an independent substitute decision-maker should be appointed with the authority to provide substituted consent for the care, treatment, and/or rehabilitation of a pretrial detainee or convicted offender who has been adjudicated incompetent to make care and treatment decisions.

- For the purposes of these recommendations, anyone with a mental disorder, condition, or aberration who is being held in a jail, prison, or detention facility operated by a private entity is considered to be in the custody of the government that is paying that entity for the services being provided.

Commentary

To ensure that pretrial detainees and convicted offenders with mental disabilities receive humane care and treatment while in government custody—particularly given the poor care and treatment such individuals typically have received in the past—the government that has custody of such individuals (or is paying private entities to care for those individuals) should be given enforceable incentives for ensuring that adequate care and treatment is being provided to all such individuals. Adequate mechanisms should be in place to ensure that individual planning is carried out that will meet the specified needs of each detainee or offender. The key factor—as has been shown to be true with regard to special education, vocational rehabilitation, and the provision of other services for persons with disabilities—is mandating the creation of individual plans, which will allow the detainee or offender to receive a meaningful benefit. In addition, such care and treatment should be provided outside the normal jail or prison milieus, since placements in correctional facilities generally result in inmates with mental disabilities becoming worse and/or being abused or mistreated.

Currently, detainees and convicted offenders with mental disabilities do not have effective avenues to challenge and redress legitimate grievances when their care and treatment needs are not met. These recommendations would create a private right of action that would take effect once reasonable administrative remedies have been exhausted or if the respondent's administrative remedies were not provided promptly, whether or not the individual is in government custody or the custody of a private entity funded by the government. The federally funded Protection and Advocacy Systems in each state could play a meaningful role in helping to ensure that these prisoners receive adequate legal representation.

Ensuring that these detainees and convicted offenders with mental disabilities are competent to make the necessary care and treatment decisions is a threshold concern, but there should always be an initial presumption that the individual is competent, unless a court adjudication has been made to the contrary. At the same time, these recommendations allow the person's lawyer or the government to request an incompetency adjudication or for the court to order such an adjudication on its own.

As detailed in other recommendations, if the detainee or convicted offender is found to be incompetent, a substitute decision-maker should be appointed to provide "substituted consent." Once again, if the respondent has clearly expressed his or her care and treatment preferences, those expressions should be used to make care and treatment decisions. If no clear expression exists, then a modified best-interest standard should apply in which the final decision would be made from the respondent's point of view.

MENTAL HEALTH CARE AND TREATMENT FOR DEFENDANTS FOUND NOT GUILTY BY REASON OF INSANITY OR INCOMPETENT TO STAND TRIAL, INCLUDING INDIVIDUAL TREATMENT PLANS

- Defendants who successfully plead not guilty by reason of insanity (NGBRI) or are found incompetent to stand trial should be placed in time-limited government custody so that they may receive planned, individualized care and treatment in humane settings, which will allow them to progress to less restrictive settings with a realistic goal of being released from custody once their individual care and treatment plans have been achieved.

- Insanity acquittees and incompetent defendants should not be incarcerated in secure detention facilities to receive their planned individual care and treatment if either: (a) the crime(s) they committed or were charged with are misdemeanors; or (b) a court-approved consensual civil intervention is agreed upon instead of incarceration. If insanity acquittees or incompetent defendants who have been found NGBRI of or charged with first-time nonviolent felonies cannot agree with governmental authorities on a court-approved consensual civil intervention, in appropriate situations courts should be allowed to order conditional supervised release for planned, individual care and treatment in the least-restrictive humane residential setting.

- While they are in government custody, insanity acquittees and incompetent defendants should receive court-approved, planned mental health care and treatment in the least-restrictive humane setting as set out in individual treatment plans. Unless it is part of a court-approved consensual intervention or the government demonstrates a compelling medical reason to do so, planned care and treatment should not interfere with: (a) an inmate's right to refuse unwanted mental health care and treatment; or (b) other legal rights and interests established in these recommendations.

- While in government custody, insanity acquittees and incompetent defendants should be represented by competent legal counsel and have a due process right, with or through counsel, to: (a) challenge their individual treatment plans, the crimes they are charged with, or violations of their legal rights; and (b) obtain their release if planned care and treatment is not provided to them without just cause or they are wrongfully denied legal counsel.

- Insanity acquittees who are tried for nonviolent, first-time felonies should be released from government custody if they demonstrate by a preponderance of the evidence that they: (a) no longer meet the legal definition of insanity; (b) have been wrongfully deprived of legal counsel; or (c) have been wrongfully deprived of planned care and treatment and, as a result, their legal, mental health, or medical interests have been seriously jeopardized. However, upon being released, these acquittees should be subject to civil interventions consistent with these recommendations.

- Insanity acquittees who are tried for violent felonies or who have been convicted or found not guilty by reason of insanity of prior felonies should only be released from government custody if, by a preponderance of the evidence, they demonstrate that they no longer meet the legal definition of insanity and in the past year, they have not acted or threatened to act in a way that would cause serious harm to another person. Acquittees also should be released from custody if they are improperly denied competent legal counsel or the officials in charge of the acquittee's care, after being properly notified, continue to fail to provide the acquitee with required care and treatment.

- Defendants found incompetent to stand trial should be released from government custody and given a speedy trial once their competency is restored. Defendants also should be released if their competency has not been restored after a year unless the government can demonstrate with clear and convincing evidence that the defendants did not reasonably participate in their individual treatment plans. In addition, defendants should be released if they can prove by a preponderance of the evidence that they did not commit the crime(s) charged or they have been wrongfully deprived of legal representation. Defendants who are released may be subject to civil interventions consistent with these recommendations.

Commentary

Two significant variations of the general rule that persons with mental disabilities who are deemed to be dangerous to others should only be subject to criminal punishments with full criminal due process protections are persons who plead not guilty by reason of insanity or who are found incompetent to stand trial. Most of these acquittees or defendants should be placed in government detention initially in order to provide them with promised mental health care and treatment in the least-restrictive humane setting. This care and treatment should provide them with a reasonable opportunity to be released from government custody by restoring their sanity or competency. Certain defendants, however, should be conditionally released initially, if they committed or were charged with a misdemeanor, or may be released at the court's discretion, if they committed a nonviolent first-time felony. Also, any defendant may be released pursuant to an agreement with the government to accept a court-approved civil intervention consistent with these recommendations.

Defendants have both medical and legal best interests, which often are consistent, but sometimes they conflict and need to be balanced against each other. When such a conflict arises due process becomes critical. The key participants in this balancing process are the defendants with or through legal counsel, the facility-affiliated mental health staffs, and, whenever there are unresolved disagreements involving important individual rights or interests—particularly related to care, treatment, legal representation, and release—the courts. Wrongful denial of legal representation that seriously harms or threatens to harm the medical or legal interests of a defendant or inmate that are guaranteed in these recommendations constitutes a serious due process violation. Such a violation should be remedied by releasing the defendant or inmate from quasi-criminal custody and thus making that individual only subject to civil interventions.

Under these recommendations the primary purpose of government custody shifts from incarcerating so-called dangerous offenders for as long as they are perceived to be dangerous, which cannot be accurately measured, to providing necessary mental health care and treatment while it is both medically and legally necessary to do so. If the medical and legal justifications for custody are no longer compelling or applicable, release from criminal custody should be ordered. Throughout this period of government custody, the affected inmates should have competent legal representation and reasonable and meaningful opportunities to challenge the mental health care and treatment that is being proposed for them or actually provided to them, as well as to enforce any other legal rights under these recommendations.

OFFENDERS WITH SEXUAL AND OTHER MENTAL DISORDERS

- Offenders with sexual and other mental disorders, including those who are labeled "sexually violent predators" or "sexually dangerous persons," should be subject to criminal punishments with full criminal due process protections, except—as defined in these recommendations—in a "legally recognized emergency" or if a consensual civil intervention is agreed upon instead.

- If a governing authority and an offender with a sexual or other mental disorder agree to an adjudicated consensual civil intervention and that respondent fulfills the agreement or the government wrongfully fails to fulfill that agreement, all related criminal (and/or juvenile justice) charges should be extinguished.

- Sexual offender registration laws should be repealed or, if continued, they should be narrowly tailored so that they only cover adult sexual offenders who:

    a. within the past [five] years have been adjudicated as "civilly dangerous" consistent with these recommendations; or

    b. within the past [five] years were convicted of a sexual crime that is reasonably identified as being a violent crime under the applicable federal or state definition.

- Sexual offender registries should be used to accurately inform authorities and victims of violent sexual crimes, but in the absence of additional due process protections described below, should not be released to the public or be the basis for depriving individuals listed on such registries of their civil rights and entitlements.

- Before any governmental agency or body may limit or revoke any rights or entitlements, including the right to privacy, based on an individual being listed as a registered sexual offender, it should have the burden of proving by clear and convincing evidence that the individual meets the aforementioned sexual offender registration criteria. In addition, if these offenders appear on a sexual offender registration list, they should not lose their eligibility for income, housing, or medical assistance simply because they are on such a list.

- No one should lose their civil rights or governmental entitlements or have them restricted because they choose to associate with or are related to a person who is placed on a sexual offender registration list.

- Anyone placed on a sexual offender registration list should have a due process right to promptly prove by a preponderance of the evidence that they currently do not meet the sexual offender registration criteria.

- Any revisions to sexual offender registration laws consistent with these recommendations, including their repeal, should be retroactive, and those who no longer meet these revised standards should be promptly purged from these registries.

- These provisions should apply equally to adults, juveniles, and children.

Commentary

Convicted offenders with sexual and other mental disorders should be treated as criminals or juvenile offenders with full due process protections, except if the government pursues a civil emergency intervention instead or the offender enters a contractual agreement with the government to receive specified care and treatment. Subjecting offenders with sexual and other mental disorders to indeterminate, punitive, involuntary, quasi-civil interventions based on mental disorders, conditions, or aberrations that have been linked to unreliable and inaccurate predictions of dangerousness is demonstrably unfair and unjust. This is particularly true with regard to "sexually violent predator," "sexually dangerous person," or "mentally disordered offender" laws that apply to convicts after they have served their criminal sentences.

In addition, sexual offender registration laws are ill-conceived, frequently inaccurate, overinclusive, unjust, and too often counter-productive and poorly implemented. If such laws continue to exist, they should more precisely and accurately identify sexually violent individuals based on adjudications of sexual violence consistent with these recommendations. Also, these registration laws should be time-limited dispositions. Five years from the last sexual offender registration adjudication is the recommended maximum amount of time that should be allowed to pass before a new adjudication is required. After five years, if there is no new adjudication consistent with these recommendations, the individual's name should be promptly removed from all sexual offender registries.

Because of the serious and often profound implications in terms of rights and extreme stigma associated with having to register and being listed as a sexual offender, substantive and procedural due process protections should accompany the decision whether to place someone on such a list, and what freedoms, rights, liberties, and entitlements they may lose as a result of being on such a list. First, stricter standards and procedures should be used to govern who may be placed on such lists initially. Second, anyone who is placed on such a list should have a fair opportunity to challenge the accuracy and sufficiency of that placement decision or determination. Third, eligibility or entitlement to necessary social services, including income, mental health care and housing, should not be based on whether an individual is on such a list. Also, eligibility or entitlement to essential social services should not be limited or denied to someone because they choose to live with or otherwise associate with a person who is on such a registration list.

THE DEATH PENALTY AND PERSONS WITH SEVERE MENTAL DISABILITIES

- In states that continue to apply the death penalty, persons with severe mental disabilities should be barred from such punishments consistent with the 2006 joint recommendations of the American Bar Association (ABA), the American Psychiatric Association, the American Psychological Association, and the National Alliance of the Mentally Ill.[3] The following recommendations would cover defendants or inmates awaiting execution who:

    a. "[A]t the time of the offense . . . had significant limitations in both their intellectual functioning and adaptive behavior, as expressed in conceptual, social, and practical adaptive skills, resulting from mental retardation, dementia, or a traumatic brain injury";

    b. "[A]t the time of the offense . . . had a severe mental disorder or disability that significantly impaired their capacity (i) to appreciate the nature, consequences or wrongfulness of their conduct,

(ii) to exercise rational judgment in relation to conduct, or (iii) to conform their conduct to the requirements of law. A disorder manifested primarily by repeated criminal conduct or attributable to the acute effects of voluntary use of alcohol or other drugs does not, standing alone, constitute a mental disorder or disability for the purposes of this provision";

c. "[A]fter sentencing the prisoner has a mental disorder or disability that significantly impairs his or her capacity (i) to make a rational decision to forgo or terminate post-conviction proceedings available to challenge the validity of the conviction; (ii) to understand or communicate pertinent information, or otherwise assist counsel, in relation to specific claims bearing on the validity of the conviction or sentence that cannot be fairly resolved without the prisoner's participation; or (iii) to understand the nature and purpose of the punishment, or to appreciate the reason for its imposition in the prisoner's own case."[4]

- "If a court finds at any time that a prisoner under sentence of death has a mental disorder or disability that significantly impairs his or her capacity to understand or communicate pertinent information, or otherwise to assist counsel, in connection with post-conviction proceedings, and that the prisoner's participation is necessary for a fair resolution of specific claims bearing on the validity of the conviction or death sentence, the court should suspend the proceedings. If the court finds that there is no significant likelihood of restoring the prisoner's capacity to participate in post-conviction proceedings in the foreseeable future, it should reduce the prisoner's sentence to the sentence imposed in capital cases when execution is not an option."[5]

- "If, after challenges to the validity of the conviction and death sentence have been exhausted and execution has been scheduled, a court finds that a prisoner has a mental disorder or disability that significantly impairs his or her capacity to understand the nature and purpose of the punishment, or to appreciate the reason for its imposition in the prisoner's own case, the sentence of death should be reduced to the sentence imposed in capital cases when execution is not an option."[6]

Commentary

The rationale for adopting these substantive and procedural death penalty standards are fully articulated in the "Report" prepared by the multidisciplinary Task Force on Mental Disability and the Death Penalty—convened by the ABA's Section of Individual Rights and Responsibilities and chaired by Ronald J. Tabak—which prepared those recommendations. That report can be found in volume 30, issue 5 of the ABA's *Mental & Physical Disability Law Reporter*. Members of that task force included the author of this book and the following distinguished individuals: Dr. Michael Abramsky; Dr. Xavier F. Amador; Michael Allen, Esq. (Bazelon Center on Mental Health Law); Donna Beavers, American Psychological Association; Professor John H. Blume; Professor Richard J. Bonnie; Colleen Quinn Brady, Esq.; Richard Burr, Esq.; Dr. Joel Dvoskin; Dr. James R. Eisenberg; Professor I. Michael Greenberger; Dr. Kirk S. Heilbrun; Ronald Honberg, Esq. (National Alliance of the Mentally Ill); Ralph Ibson; Dr. Matthew B. Johnson; Professor Dorean M. Koenig; Dr. Diane T. Marsh; Hazel Moran; Professor Jennifer Radden; Professor Laura Lee Rovner; Robyn S. Shapiro, Esq.; and Professor Christopher Slobogin. Doctors Paul S. Appelbaum, Howard V. Zonana, and Jeffrey Metzner also contributed significantly to the report.

JUVENILES AND CHILDREN WITH MENTAL DISABILITIES WHO ARE PERCEIVED TO BE DANGEROUS

- Juveniles and children with mental disorders, conditions, or aberrations who are perceived to be dangerous should be entitled to no less in terms of substantive and procedural due process protections than adults.

- While parents and guardians should have a rebuttable preference to be selected to provide substituted consent for care and treatment of their children, under these recommendations the same rigorous due process standards and protections should apply to intrusive decisions no matter who is providing substituted consent.

Commentary

Juveniles and children, including those with mental disabilities, should receive no less in terms of substantive and procedural due process than adults, and in many situations they deserve additional protections. Policies that allow juveniles and children to be punished as adults and/or to have their due process rights diminished more than adults should be viewed with great skepticism, particularly if they have mental disabilities. While certainly it can be argued that juveniles and children should receive more in terms of protection and procedural and substantive due process, it is hard to understand why providing less should be permitted.

Also, while it should be expected that parents and properly appointed guardians are appropriate substitute decision-makers for their children— unless there is specific evidence indicating that they are not appropriate— the same substantive and procedural due process protections should be provided to these children as for adults when courts review and approve intrusive care and treatment decisions. Protecting juveniles and children with mental disabilities from bad care and treatment decisions, abuse, and neglect should take priority over the possibility that on occasion parents and guardians could have their traditional prerogatives diminished unnecessarily.

CREATE A LIMITED ENTITLEMENT TO CONSENSUAL MENTAL DISABILITY CARE AND TREATMENT

- Federal, state, and local governments should provide sufficient funding, programs, and administrative structures to ensure that every minor and adult with a serious mental disorder, condition, or aberration has access to consensual mental health, habilitation, rehabilitation, housing, and income maintenance services and assistance in the community as part of an individual care and treatment plan. Any mental impairment should be considered serious if concerns about that individual's mental health have been documented by law enforcement, a public agency, or public or private school officials, which could result in that individual being subjected to criminal, involuntary, or other coercive government interventions or restrictions.

- Every eligible adult or emancipated minor, unless they have been adjudicated as incompetent, should be allowed to consent to and receive services that are part of an individual care and treatment plan. If an individual is unable or not allowed to consent due to actual or perceived mental incompetency, a court should decide whether a substitute decision-maker should be appointed to provide consent on that person's behalf consistent with any living will or other written instructions or documents that have been prepared while that person was legally competent to do so.

- Any non-emancipated minor or incompetent adult should be allowed to consent to an individual care and treatment plan through a legally authorized guardian, or a parent in the case of a minor.

- Courts should presume that anyone who has an individual care and treatment plan should not be subjected to involuntary governmental intervention proceedings, unless there is probable cause to believe that they have committed a crime or are in need of an emergency intervention consistent with these recommendations.

Commentary

Involuntary and coercive mental health care and treatment for persons with mental impairments has been a public health failure and has led to myriad different types of abuses, mistreatment, and rights violations. While many people believe that consensual care and related services should be available to anyone who has a medically diagnosed mental impairment, this probably is not yet a politically viable policy in this country, particularly as the federal, state, and local governments are cutting back on services. What should be viable—given the nation's concerns, beliefs, and perceptions about persons with mental disabilities who might act dangerously if left untreated—is a targeted approach that provides consensual and holistic mental disability care and related services to individuals who have been identified by school officials, law enforcement, and public agencies as being at heightened risk of acting in ways that could lead to their being subjected to criminal, involuntary, or other coercive government interventions. This preventive approach will save money in the long run, better target care and treatment to those most in need, and substantially curtail more costly and less effective coercive interventions consistent with these recommendations.

PUBLIC EDUCATION TO REDUCE STIGMA, SANISM, VIOLENCE, AND IMAGES OF VIOLENCE

- The federal government in cooperation with states, localities, and private donors should provide annual funding and an administrative structure for initiating and maintaining a national public education campaign, through our schools and media, in order to substantially reduce and change public perceptions about:

  a. Stigma and sanism against persons with mental disabilities; and

  b. Violence and the images of violence in our society, particularly images that associate violence with persons who have mental disabilities.

Commentary

The five primary factors that have contributed to invidious discrimination, violations of rights, mistreatment, and other abuses experienced by persons with mental disabilities who are deemed to be dangerous are our existing laws, the lack of proper care and treatment, stigma, sanism, and our exaggerated fears about violence associated with those who have mental disabilities. The first two factors have been addressed with recommendations that call for a reformation of our laws and our public mental health care and treatment policies. In order to address stigma, sanism, and violence, however, there should be a concerted national effort to change our attitudes and public perceptions. This should begin in our public and private schools and extend to our major media outlets. Without the same types of attitudinal changes that have helped to address racism, religious intolerance, and sexual and gender discrimination in this country, it will be difficult to make substantial progress in changing our laws and public health policies that negatively affect persons with mental disabilities.

NOTES

INTRODUCTION

1. Richard T. Ford, "Moving beyond Civil Rights," *New York Times*, Oct. 27, 2011; See also Richard T. Ford, *Rights Gone Wrong: How Law Corrupts the Struggle for Equality* (New York: Farrar, Straus, and Giroux, 2011).

2. See Samuel J. Brakel and Ronald S. Rock, *The Mentally Disabled and the Law* 2d ed. (Chicago: University of Chicago Press, 1971), xv.

3. Lawrence M. Krauss, "Op-Ed: Deafness at Doomsday," *New York Times*, Jan. 16, 2013.

4. See e.g., Thomas Insel, "Transforming Diagnosis," The National Institute of Mental Health, Apr. 29, 2013,www.nimh.nih.gov; P. Belluck & B. Carey, "Psychiatrist's Guide Is Out of Touch with Science, Experts Say," *New York Times*, May 6, 2013. See also, Allen Francis, *An Insider's Revolt Against Out-of-Control Psychiatric Diagnosis, DSM-5, Big Pharma, and the Medicalization of Ordinary Life* (New York: William Morrow, 2013); Gary Greenberg, *The Book of Woe: DSM and the Unmaking of Psychiatry* (New York: Blue Rider Press, 2013).

5. Richard Bonnie, "Political Abuse of Psychiatry in the Soviet Union and in China: Complexities and Controversies," *J. Am. Acad. Psychiatry Law* 30 (2002): 136–44; Jim Birley, "Political Abuse of Psychiatry in the Soviet Union and China: A Rough Guide for Bystanders," *J. Am. Acad. Psychiatry Law* 30 (2002): 145–47; Sidney Bloch and Peter Reddaway, *Russia's Political Hospitals: The Abuse of Psychiatry in the Soviet Union* (1977).

6. Michael L. Perlin, "International Human Rights and Comparative Mental Disability Law: The Role of Institutional Psychiatry in the Suppression of Political Dissent," *Israel L. Rev.* 39 (2006): 69; See also Andrew Jacobs, "Chinese

Paper Says Whistleblowers Are Sent to Mental Wards," *International Herald-Tribune*, Dec. 8, 2008.

7. Barbara A. Weiner, "Mental Disability and the Criminal Law," in *The Mentally Disabled and the Law*, ed. Samuel J. Brakel, John Parry, and Barbara A. Weiner 3d ed. (Chicago: American Bar Foundation, 1985), 707–9.

8. See Gregory B. Leong, "Diminished Capacity and Insanity in Washington State: The Battle Shifts to American Admissibility," *Am. J. of Acad. Psychiatry & L.* 28 (2000): 77.

9. See Developments in the Law—The Law of Mental Illness, "Booker, the Federal Sentencing Guidelines, and Violent Mentally Ill Offenders," *Harv. L. Rev.* 121 (Feb. 2008): 1133.

10. Weiner.

11. See National Institute of Mental Health and Mental Health Law Project, "Civil Commitment," in *Legal Issues in State Mental Health Care: Proposals for Change, Ment. Dis. L. Rep.* 2 (1977): 75–159.

12. *Graham v. Florida*, 560 U.S. (2010).

13. Karen H. Seal, et al., "Trends and Risk Factors for Mental Health Diagnoses among Iraq and Afghanistan Veterans Using Department of Veterans Affairs Health Care, 2002–2008," *Am. J. of Pub. H.* 99, no. 9 (2009): 1651–58.

14. Christopher Hawthorne, "Bringing Baghdad into the Courtroom: Should Combat Trauma in Veterans Be Part of the Criminal Justice Equation," *Criminal Justice* 24, no. 2 (Summer 2009): 5; James Dao, "As Military Suicides Rise, Focus Is on Private Weapons," *New York Times*, Oct. 7, 2012; Ernesto Londono, "More U.S. Troops Lost to Suicide Than Combat in 2012," *Washington Post*, Jan. 15, 2012.

15. See Lizette Alvarez and Dan Frosch, "A Focus on Violence by Returning G.I.'s," *New York Times*, Jan. 2, 2009 (citing Seal).

16. See Lynne Marek, "Courts for Veterans Spreading across U.S.," *National Law Journal*, Dec. 22, 2008; Joseph P. Morrissey, et al., "New Models of Collaboration between Criminal Justice and Mental Health Systems," *A. J. of Psychiatry* 166, no. 11 (Nov. 2009): 1211–14.

17. John La Fond and Mary Durham, *Back to the Asylum: The Future of Mental Health Law and Policy in the United States* (1992). See also K. A. Findley, "Innocents at Risk: Adversary Imbalance, Forensic Science, and the Search for Truth," *Seton Hall L. Rev.* 38 (2008): 893, 928.

18. Ibid.

19. See, for example, *United States v. Beatty*, 2011 WL 1515216 (6th Cir. Apr. 22, 2011) (refusing to unconditionally release an insanity acquittee from civil commitment not clearly erroneous even though his antisocial personality disorder and continued drug use were not the conditions for which he was originally committed after being found not guilty by reason of insanity); In re G.L.D.,

795 N.W.2d 346 (N.D. Sup. Ct. 2011) ("A choice between two permissible views of the weight of the evidence is not clearly erroneous," where lower court decided to believe the state's expert over the court-appointed expert that a sex offender should continue to be confined as a sexually dangerous individual).

20. *Cavazos v. Smith*, 565 U.S. (2011) (*per curiam*).

21. See Michael L. Perlin and Keri K. Gould, "Roshomon and the Criminal Law: Mental Disability and the Federal Sentencing Guidelines," *Am. J. Crim. L.* 22 (1995): 431, 442–43; Michael L. Perlin, "'Baby, Look Inside Your Mirror': The Legal Profession's Willful and Sanist Blindness to Lawyers with Mental Disabilities," *U. of Pitt. L. Rev.* 69 (Spring 2008): 589.

22. See John Monahan, "Structured Risk Assessment of Violence," in *Textbook of Violence Assessment and Management*, eds. R. Simon and K. Tardiff (Washington, D.C.: American Psychiatric Pub., 2008); Vernon Quinsey, et al., *Violent Offenders: Appraising and Managing Risk* 2d ed. (Washington, D.C.: American Psychological Association, 2006).

23. In *Brown v. Plata*, 565 U.S. (2011), the U.S. Supreme Court concluded that the conditions for California inmates with mental disabilities were "incompatible with the concept of human dignity and [have] no place in a civilized society." Yet, in affirming an order to depopulate California's prisons, the Court warned that "release of seriously mentally ill inmates [would be] likely to create special dangers because of their recidivism rates." Thus, most of these mentally ill inmates will remain in these unconstitutional conditions with only the slim hope that depopulation eventually improves the situation for them.

24. See *Barefoot v. Estelle*, 463 U.S. 880 (1983).

I. PERSONS WITH MENTAL DISABILITIES AND THE AMERICAN LEGAL SYSTEM

1. Patricia Wald, "Basic Personal and Civil Rights," in *The Mentally Retarded Citizen and the Law*, ed. Michael Kindred, et al. (New York: Free Press, 1976), 5.

2. See Samuel J. Brakel and Ronald S. Rock, *The Mentally Disabled and the Law*, 2d ed. (Chicago: University of Chicago Press, 1971), 1–14; American Bar Foundation, "Hospitalization and Treatment of Mental Cases," unpublished memorandum (Feb. 1955); William D. Andrews, "Developments in the Law: Civil Commitment of the Mentally Ill," *Harvard L. Rev.* 87, no. 6 (1974): 1193–1201; Albert Deutch, *The Mentally Ill in America: A History of Their Care and Treatment from Colonial Times* (New York: Columbia University Press, 1949); D. J. Rothman, *The Discovery of the Asylum: Social Order and Disorder in the New Republic* (Boston: Little, Brown, 1971).

3. See Barbara A. Weiner, "Rights of Institutionalized Persons," and John Parry, "Decision-making Rights over Persons and Property," in *The Mentally Disabled and the Law*, ed. Samuel Jan Brakel, John Parry, and Barbara A. Weiner 3rd ed. (Chicago: American Bar Foundation, 1985), 251–325, 435–506; John Q. La Fond and Mary L. Durham, *Back to the Asylum: The Future of Mental Health Law and Policy in the United States* (New York: Oxford University Press, 1992), 5–15.

4. See Brakel and Rock, *Mentally Disabled*, xv–xviii, 8–13.

5. La Fond and Durham, *Back to the Asylum*, 15–20.

6. Michael Gerson, "The Eugenics Temptation," *Washington Post*, Oct. 24, 2007.

7. See Miss. Code Ann. §99-13-1 (definition of "feeble-minded").

8. Parry, "Decision-making Rights," 435.

9. Ibid.

10. Harold Maio, "U.S. Supreme Court Cases Contained Error," http://www.news-press.com/fdcp/?unique=131764132109 (Oct. 3, 2011). See, e.g., *Brown v. Plata*, 131 S. Ct. 1910 (2011), where as recently as 2011, the Supreme Court referred to the "mentally ill" categorically ("programs for the mentally ill may be cancelled altogether during lockdowns").

11. See Weiner, "Rights of Institutionalized Persons," 251–325; Parry, *Decision-making Rights*, 435–506.

12. Samuel J. Brakel, "Historical Trends," in *The Mentally Disabled and the Law*, ed. Samuel J. Brakel, John Parry, and Barbara A. Weiner 3rd ed. (Chicago: University of Chicago Press, 1985), 15–16.

13. Ibid., 16.

14. Brakel and Rock, *Mentally Disabled*, xv.

15. Hal Kennedy, "Introduction," from *A Guide to Willowbrook State School Resources at Other Institutions*, http://www.library.csi.cuny.edu/archives/WillowbrookRG.htm, last modified October 2005.

16. See, e.g., National Institute of Mental Health and Mental Health Law Project, *Legal Issues in State Mental Health Care: Proposals for Change* (1976); Bruce D. Sales, et al., *Disabled Persons and the Law: State Legislative Issues* (New York: Plenum Press, 1982).

17. Samuel J. Brakel, "Involuntary Institutionalizaton," in *The Mentally Disabled and the Law*, ed. Brakel, Parry, and Weiner (Chicago: University of Chicago Press, 1985), 21.

18. Ibid., 21–22.

19. See A. N. Sofari and L. C. Kaldjian, "Eugenic Sterilization and a Qualified Nazi Analogy: The United States and Germany, 1930–1945," *Annals Internal Med.* 132 (2000): 312–19.

20. See Weiner, "Institutionalized Persons," 251–97.

21. See Andrews, "Developments in the Law."

22. John Parry, "Incompetency, Guardianship, and Restoration," in *The Mentally Disabled and the Law*, ed. Brakel, Parry, and Weiner (Chicago: University of Chicago Press, 1985), 371–75.

23. Parry, "Decision-making Rights," 438–41, 447–61.

24. Sandra G. Boorman, "'Lobotomist Serves as a Warning,'" *Washington Post*, Jan. 15, 2008.

25. Benedict Carey, "Surgery for Mental Ills Offers Hope and Risk," *New York Times*, Nov. 27, 2009.

26. Ibid.

27. Duff Wilson, "F.D.A. Panel Is Split on Electroshock Risks," *New York Times*, Jan. 29, 2011. See also Royal College of Psychiatrists, "Electroconvulsive Therapy," www.rcpsych.ac.uk/menthealthinoforall/treatments/ect.aspx?, last visited Mar. 26, 2011.

28. Anna Stolley Persky, "A Question of Education," *ABA Journal*, Jan. 2103, www.abajournal.com, last modified Jan. 1, 2013. See also Ed Pilkington, "Shock Tactics: Treatment or Torture?" *Guardian*, www.guardian.co.uk/society/2011/mar/12/electric-shock--school-mathew-israel/print, last modified Mar. 12, 2011.

29. Disabilities Rights International, "JRC Banned from Shocking New Admissions," http://www.disabilityrightsintl.org/2011/11/07/an-end-to-electric-shock-punishments-at-jrc/, last modified Nov. 7, 2011.

30. Samuel Jan Brakel, "Family Laws," in *The Mentally Disabled and the Law*, ed. Samuel Jan Brakel, John Parry, and Barbara A. Weiner (Chicago: Chicago University Press, 1985), 522–23.

31. Ibid., 522.

32. Ibid., 523.

33. 274 U.S. 200 (1927).

34. Ibid., 207.

35. Brakel, "Family Laws," 523.

36. Kim Severson, "Thousands Sterilized, A State Weighs Restitution," *New York Times*, Dec. 9, 2011.

37. Ibid. See also, Kim Severson, "Payments for Victims of Eugenics Are Shelved," *New York Times,* June 20, 2012.

38. Brakel, "Family Laws," 523.

39. Ibid., 528.

40. John Krupa, "Doctor Gets Reprimand," *Arkansas Democrat-Gazette*, Aug. 8, 2008.

41. Dan Slater, "The Judge Says: Don't Get Pregnant: A Lapsed Law Now Sees New Life," *Wall Street Journal*, Sept. 29, 2008.

42. Morton Birnbaum, "The Right to Treatment," 46 A.B.A. J. 499 (1960).

43. Ibid.

44. Ibid., 503.

45. 373 F.2d 451 (D.C. Cir. 1966).

46. 364 F.2d 657, 660 (D.C. Cir. 1966).

47. 364 U.S. 479 (1960).

48. 334 F. Supp. 1341 (M.D. Ala. 1971).

49. Stanford University, "*Wyatt v. Stickney*," http://www.stanford.edu/group/
psychlawseminar/Wyatt.htm, last accessed Jan. 15, 2013.

50. Ibid.

51. Ibid.

52. Ibid.

53. Ibid.

54. 349 F. Supp. 1078 (E.D. Wis. 1972), vacated and remanded, 414 U.S.
473, on remand, 379 F. Supp. 1376 (E.D. Wis. 1974), vacated and remanded,
421 U.S. 957 (1975), reinstated, 413 F. Supp. 1318 (E.D. Wis. 1976).

55. Brakel, "Involuntary Institutionalization," 35–36.

56. *Lessard v. Schmidt*, 349 F. Supp. 1078 (E.D. Wis. 1972), vacated and
remanded, 414 U.S. 473, on remand, 379 F. Supp. 1376 (E.D. Wis. 1974),
vacated and remanded, 421 U.S. 957 (1975), reinstated, 413 F. Supp. 1318 (E.D.
Wis. 1976).

57. For example, Judge David Bazelon, Dr. Morton Birnbaum, Charles Halpern, James Ellis, Bruce Ennis, David Ferleger, Paul Friedman, Joel Klein, Judge
Frank Johnson, Jerome Shestack, Dr. Allan Stone, and Thomas Zander.

58. Kennedy, "Introduction."

59. *Unforgotten*: *25 Years after Willowbrook*, http://www.amazon.com/
Unforgotten-Twenty-Five-Years-After-Willowbrook/dp/B00375LBK8.

60. Based on the minutes and reports of the ABA's Commission on the Mentally Disabled from 1973 to 1975. The author became the director of the commission in 1980 and editor of the commission's *Mental Disability Law Reporter* in
1979. He also worked as a law clerk for Bruce Ennis at the American Civil
Liberties Union in 1976 and Mr. Ennis was chair of the Commission on the
Mentally Disabled from 1983 to 1985 and a member from 1979 to 1982 while
the author was its director.

61. Ruth O'Brien, *Crippled Justice: The History of Modern Disability Policy
in the Workplace* (Chicago: University of Chicago Press, 2001), 63–87. See also
reports to the ABA's House of Delegates from the Commission on the Mentally
Disabled from 1973 to 1975 and the report in 1972 urging the ABA to create the
commission.

62. Kennedy, "Introduction."

63. Erving Goffman, *Stigma: Notes on the Management of Spoiled Identity*
(Englewood Cliffs, NJ: Prentice-Hall, 1963).

64. Thomas S. Szasz, *The Myth of Mental Illness: Foundations of a Theory of Personal Conduct* (New York: Harper and Row, 1974).

65. 344 F. Supp. 387, 396 (M.D. 1972).

66. *Donaldson v. O'Connor*, 493 F.2d 507 (1974).

67. Ibid.

68. Based on conversations the author had with Mr. Ennis when he was a member and then chair of the ABA's Commission on the Mentally Disabled (1979–1985) and the author was its director.

69. See Chief Justice Burger's concurring opinion in *O'Connor v. Donaldson*, 422 U.S. 563 (1975).

70. 422 U.S. 563 (1975).

71. Ibid., 573.

72. Ibid.

73. John Parry, "Involuntary Civil Commitment in the 90's: A Constitutional Perspective," *Mental and Physical Disability Law Reporter* 18, no. 3 (1994): 320.

74. Chris Koyangi, "Learning from History: Deinstitutionalization of People with Mental Illness As Precursor to Long-Term Care Reform," Kaiser Commission on Medicaid and the Uninsured (Aug. 2007), 6, 12–13.

75. Ibid., 11–12.

76. See U.S. General Accounting Office, "Returning the Mentally Disabled to the Community: Government Needs to Do More" (Washington, D.C.: U.S. General Accounting Office, 1977); Task Force Panel Reports Submitted to the President's Commission on Mental Health 4 (1978), 427; E. Bassuk and S. Gerson, "Deinstitutionalization and Mental Health Services," *Scientific American* 238, no. 2 (1978): 46–53; L. L. Bachrach, "Commentary," *Hospital & Community Psychiatry* 34 (1983): 105.

77. U.S. General Accounting Office, "Returning"; Bachrach, "Commentary."

78. See National Institute of Mental Health and Mental Health Law Project, "Legal Issues in State Mental Health Care: Proposals for Change: Civil Commitment (1976), 2; *Mental Disability Law Reporter* (1977), 77, 94–96.

79. See J. Stromberg and A. Stone, "A Model State Law on Civil Commitment of the Mentally Ill," *Harv. J. on Legis.* 20 (1983): 275.

80. See, e.g., R. Lamb, "Deinstitutionalization and the Homeless Mentally Ill," *Hospital & Community Psychiatry* 35 (1984): 899; Kevin M. Gilmartin, "The Correctional Officer Stockholm Syndrome: Management Implications: The Effects of Psychiatric Deinstitutionalization on Community Policing," *Police Chief Magazine* (Dec. 1986); P. S. Appelbaum, "The New Preventive Detention: Psychiatry's Problematic Responsibility for the Control of Violence," *Am. J. Psychiatry* 145 (1988): 779; E. Fuller Torrey, *Out of the Shadows: Confronting*

America's Mental Illness Crisis (New York: John Wiley, 1996); Dan Hurley, "Imminent Danger," *Psychology Today* (July 1994).

81. See Parry, "Involuntary Civil Commitment in the 90's."

82. *Addington v. Texas*, 441 U.S. 418 (1979).

83. A. Dershowitz, "The Law of Dangerousness: Some Fictions about Predictions," *J. Legal Educ.* 23 (1970): 24; B. Rubin, "Predictions of Dangerousness in Mentally Ill Criminals," *Archives Gen. Psychiat.* 27 (1970): 397; D. B. Wexler and S. E. Scoville, "Special Project: The Administration of Psychiatric Justice: Theory and Practice in Arizona," *Ariz. L. Rev.* 13 (1971): 96; Andrews, "Developments in the Law," 1240–1245.

84. Andrews, "Developments in the Law," 1240–1245.

85. Bruce J. Ennis and Thomas R. Litwack, "Psychiatry and the Presumption of Expertise: Flipping Coins in the Courtroom," *California Law Review* 62, no. 3 (May 1974): 693–752.

86. John Monahan, *The Clinical Prediction of Violent Behavior* (Washington, D.C.: Government Printing Office, 1981) (DHHS Publication Number ADM 81-921).

87. Ibid.

88. 463 U.S. 880 (1983).

89. Ibid.

90. In an e-mail to the author from Ronald J. Tabak (Sept. 30, 2011).

91. *Daubert v Merrell Dow Pharmaceuticals, Inc.*, 509 U.S. 579 (1993).

92. See extended discussion of dangerousness in chapter 3.

93. Brown v. *Plata*, 131 S. Ct. 1910, 1962 (2011).

94. Brakel and Rock, *Mentally Disabled*, 376.

95. M'Naughten's Case, 10 Clark & Fin. 200, 8 Eng. Rep. 718 (1843).

96. Frank T. Lindman and Donald M. McIntyre, *The Mentally Disabled and the Law* (Chicago: University of Chicago Press, 1961), 331.

97. Ibid.

98. Ibid.

99. Brakel and Rock, *Mentally Disabled*, 377.

100. See Szasz, *Myth of Mental Illness*.

101. Ibid.

102. John Parry and Eric Y. Drogin, *Mental Disability Law, Evidence and Testimony* (Washington, D.C.: American Bar Association Publishing, 2007), 209.

103. Ibid., 209–210.

104. Ibid., citing *State v. Thompson*, Wright's Ohio Rep. 617 (1834).

105. Barbara A. Weiner, "Mental Disability and the Criminal Law," in *The Mentally Disabled and the Law*, ed. Samuel J Brakel, John Parry, and Barbara A. Weiner (Chicago: American Bar Foundation, 1985), 711–12.

106. Ibid., 711.

107. Model Penal Code Sec. 4.01.

108. Ibid.

109. Ibid.

110. Weiner, "Mental Disability," 712.

111. See A. L. Halpern, "Reconsideration of the Insanity Defense and Related Issues in the Aftermath of the Hinckley Trial," *Psychiatric Quarterly* 54 (Winter 1982): 260; R. Slovenko, "Commentary: Should Mental Health Professions Honor Bazelon or Burger?" *Mich. Soc. of Psychoanalytic Psychology News* 16 (Feb. 2006).

112. Weiner, "Mental Disability," 714.

113. Ibid.

114. Brakel and Rock, *Mentally Disabled*, 380–381.

115. See R. C. Petrella, E. P. Benedek, S. C. Bank, and I. K. Packer, "Examining the Application of the Guilty But Mentally Ill Verdict in Michigan," *Hosp. and Comm. Psych.* 36 (March 1985): 254–259; C. A. Palmer and M. Hazelrigg, "The Guilty But Mentally Ill Verdict: A Review and Conceptual Analysis of Intent and Impact," *J. Amer. Acad. Psych. Law* 28, no. 1 (2000): 47–54; J. D. Melville and D. Naimark, "Punishing the Insane: The Verdict of Guilty But Mentally Ill," *J. Am. Acad. Psych. Law* 30 (2002): 553–555.

116. See Petrella, Benedek, Bank, and Packer, "Examining"; Palmer and Hazelrigg, "Guilty"; Melville and Naimark, "Punishing the Insane."

117. John T. Woolley and Gerhard Peters, "President Ronald Reagan's Radio Address to the Nation on Crime and Criminal Justice," Santa Barbara, CA, The American Presidency Project [online]: University of California (hosted), Gerhard Peters (database) (Sept. 11, 1982), http://www.presidency.ucsb.edu/ws/?pid=42952.

118. Martin Weil and Judith Valente, "Sanity Evidence Was Lacking, Juror Says," *Washington Post*, June 22, 1982, A1.

119. See V. P. Hans and D. Slater, "John Hinckley, Jr., and the Insanity Defense: The Public's Verdict," *Public Opinion Quarterly* 47, no. 2 (1983): 202–212; See also L. Caplan, "The Insanity Defense, Post-Hinckley," *New York Times*, Jan. 17, 2011.

120. Weiner, "Mental Disability," 714.

121. *Finger v. Nevada*, 27 P.3d 66 (Nev. 2001).

122. Nev. A.B. No. 193 (2007), *Ment. and Phys. Dis. L. Rep.* 31 (2007): 665.

123. B. Weiner, "Mental Disability," 717.

124. Lisa Callahan et al., "Insanity Defense Reform in the United States—Post Hinckley," *Ment. & Phys. Dis. L. Rep.* 11 (1987): 54.

125. Ibid.

126. Ibid. See, e.g., 18 U.S.C. §17.

127. *Leland v. Oregon*, 343 U.S. 790 (1952). See also Christopher Hawthorne, "Bringing Baghdad into the Courtroom: Should Combat Trauma in Veterans Be Part of the Criminal Justice Equation?" *Criminal Justice* 24, no. 2 (Summer 2009).

128. Hawthorne, "Bringing Baghdad into the Courtroom," 7.

129. 126 S. Ct. 2709 (2006).

130. Parry and Drogin, *Mental Disability Law*, 205.

131. Nevada vacillated but eventually embraced the guilty but mentally ill verdict.

132. See "Subcommittee on Criminal Justice: Background Paper," New Freedom Commission on Mental Health (June 2004); Council of State Governments, *The Criminal Justice/Mental Health Consensus Project*, "Introduction" (New York: Council of State Governments, Eastern Regional Conference, 2002); H. Ascher-Svanum et al., "Involvement in the U.S. Criminal Justice System and Cost Implications for Persons Treated for Schizophrenia," *BMC Psychiatry* 10 (2010): 11; Jacques Baillargeon et al., "Psychiatric Disorders and Repeat Incarcerations: The Revolving Prison Door," *Am. J. of Psychiatry* 166, no. 1 (2009): 103.

133. New Freedom Commission, "Subcommittee on Criminal Justice"; Council on State Governments, "Introduction."

134. See New Freedom Commission, "Subcommittee on Criminal Justice"; Council on State Governments, "Introduction"; Ascher-Svanum et al., "Involvement," 11; Baillargeon et al., "Psychiatric Disorders," 103.

135. Lamb, "Deinstitutionalization," 899. See also R. J. Isaac and V. C. Armat, *Madness in the Streets* (New York: Free Press, 1990).

136. Ronald Reagan's radio address to the nation on crime and criminal justice.

137. See A. L. Halpern, "Reconsideration," 114; R. J. Simon and D. E. Aronson, *The Insanity Defense: A Critical Assessment of Law and Policy in the Post-Hinckley Era* (New York: Praeger, 1988), 1–2; S. Taylor, "The Hinckley Riddle," *New York Times*, June 24, 1982.

138. Charles M. Blow, "Drug Bust," *New York Times*, June 10, 2011.

139. New Freedom Commission on Mental Health, "Subcommittee on Criminal Justice," 5.

140. *Brown v. Plata*, 131 S. Ct. 1910, 1962 (2011).

141. New Freedom Commission on Mental Health, "Subcommittee on Criminal Justice," 5. See also H. J. Steadman et al., "A Specialized Crisis Response Site as a Core Element of Police-Based Diversion Programs," *Psychiatric Services* 52, no. 2 (2001): 219–222.

142. Council of State Governments, "Introduction," 7.

143. Ascher-Svanum et al., "Involvement"; Baillargeon et al., "Psychiatric Disorders."

144. New Freedom Commission on Mental Health, "Subcommittee on Criminal Justice," 3.

145. Bureau of Justice Statistics Report, "Mental Health and Treatment of Inmates and Probationers," July 1999.

146. Baillargeon et al., "Psychiatric Disorders," 113.

147. Jeffrey L. Metzner et al., "Treatment in Jails and Prisons," in *Treatment of Offenders with Mental Disorders*, ed. Robert M. Wettstein (New York: Guilford Press, 1998), 211.

148. Linda Teplin, "The Prevalence of Severe Mental Disorder among Male Urban Jail Detainees: Comparison with the Epidemiologic Catchment Area Program," *American J. of Pub. Health* 80, no. 6 (June 1990): 663–669.

149. Council of State Governments, "Chapter IV: Incarceration and Reentry" (2002), 152. See also *Brown v. Plata*, 131 S. Ct. 1910 (2011).

150. Council of State Governments, "Incarceration," 152.

151. Ibid.

152. See *Atkins v. Virginia*, 536 U.S. 304 (2002).

153. D. J. James and L. E. Glaze, "Mental Health Problems of Prison and Jail Inmates," Bureau of Justice Statistics Special Report (Sept. 2006).

154. Ibid.

155. Ibid., 4.

156. Ibid., 4.

157. Council of State Governments, "Introduction," 7.

158. K. Coucouvanis et al., "Current Populations and Longitudinal Trends of State Residential Settings (1950–2003)," in *Residential Services for Persons with Developmental Disabilities: Status and Trends through 2002*, ed. R. W. Prouty, Gary Smith, and K. C. Lakin (University of Minnesota, Research and Training Center on Community Living, Institute on Community Integration, 2003), 14 (table 1.8).

159. Human Rights Watch Report, "Ill-Equipped: U.S. Prisons and Offenders with Mental Illness" (2003): 5–7, www.hrw.org/reports/2003/usa1003/3.htm.

160. NAMI Press Release, "Department of Justice Study: Mental Illness of Prison Inmates Worse Than Past Estimates," Sept. 6, 2006.

161. *Community Servs., Inc. v. Heidelberg Twp.*, 2006 WL 2080384 (M.D. Pa. July 25, 2006).

162. Id.

163. Meris Bergquist, "No Exit for Patients Confined at the Vermont State Hospital," *Vermont Bar. J.* 32 (Summer 2006): 34.

164. Council of State Governments, 26.

165. Tom Jackman, "Fairfax Police Knew That Man Shot by Officer Is Mentally Ill," *Washington Post*, Feb. 11, 2010; Eugene O'Donnel, "Cops and the Mentally Ill: How Police Can Better Handle Emotionally Disturbed Citizens,"

Newsweek, July 31, 2008, http://www.newsweek.com/id/149630; M. J. Stephey, "De-Criminalizing Mental Illness," *Time*, Aug. 16, 2007, http://www.time.com/time/health/article/0,8599,1651002,00.html.

166. See J. H. Blume, S. P. Garvey, and S. L. Johnson, "Future Dangerousness in Capital Cases: Always 'At Issue.'" *Cornell L. Rev.* 86 (2001): 404–408.

167. Council of State Governments, "Incarceration," 154.

168. Ibid., 159.

169. See U.S. House Committee on the Judiciary, "The Impact of the Mentally Ill on the Criminal Justice System" (Sept. 21, 2001).

170. Mich. Comp. Laws §780.501–509 (repealed 1968).

171. Parry and Drogin, *Mental Disability Law*, 260.

172. Ibid.

173. *Kansas v. Hendricks*, 521 U.S. 346 (1997); *Seling v. Young*, 531 U.S. 250 (2001).

174. American Bar Association, *Criminal Justice Mental Health Standards* (Washington, D.C.: American Bar Association, 1989), 7–8.1.

175. 521 U.S. 346 (1997).

176. Ibid.

177. *Seling v. Young*, 531 U.S. 250 (2001).

178. Ibid.

179. *Kansas v. Crane*, 534 U.S. 407 (2002).

180. John Parry, *Criminal Mental Health and Disability Law, Evidence and Testimony* (Chicago: American Bar Association Publishing, 2009), 176; N.M. Stat. Ann. §§31-20-5:2 and MD S.B. No. 280 (2010), *Ment. & Phy. Dis. L. Rep.* 34 (2010): 663.

181. The Adam Walsh Act, 73 Fed Reg. 70278 (2008), *Ment. & Phys. Dis. L. Rep* 33:175.

182. See *Clark v. Arizona*, 126 S. Ct. 2709 (2006).

183. *U.S. v. Comstock*, 130 S. Ct. 1949 (2010).

184. See Megan A. Janicki, "Better Seen Than Herded: Residency Restrictions and Global Positioning System Tracking Law for Sex Offenders," *Boston Univ. Public. Interest. L. J.* 16 (Spring 2007): 85; Emily Horowitz, "Growing Media and Legal Attention to Sex Offenders: More Safety or More Injustice?" *J. Inst. Just. Int'l Stud.* 164 (2007): 143.

185. See discussion in chapter 5.

186. Horowitz, "Growing Media," 187.

187. Ibid.

188. Monica Davey, "Case Shows Limits of Sex Offender Alert Programs," *New York Times*, Sept. 2, 2009.

189. Ibid.

190. See Chris L. Jenkins, "Va Family Still Suffers Effects of Guilty Plea to a False Charge," *Washington Post*, Nov. 26, 2011; Editorial, "Righting a Wrongful Conviction in Virginia," *Washington Post*, Dec. 5, 2011.

191. 463 U.S. 880 (1983).

192. Ibid.

193. 18 U.S.C. §4243.

194. 504 U.S. 71 (1992).

195. Ibid., 88.

196. *Atkins v. Virginia*. See also, *Clark v. Arizona*.

197. *Clark v. Arizona*.

198. 406 U.S. 715 (1972).

199. Ibid., 738.

200. 494 U.S. 210 (1990).

201. Ibid.

202. Ibid.

203. 539 U.S. 166 (2003).

204. Ibid.

205. Ibid.

206. 498 U.S. 38 (1990) (per curiam).

207. Ibid.

208. *Louisiana v. Perry*, 610 So.2d 746 (La. 1992).

209. *Singleton v. Norris*, 319 F.3d 1018 (8th Cir. 2003).

210. American Medical Association, *American Medical News* 50, no. 29 (Aug. 6, 2007).

211. *Tibbals v. Carter*, No. 11-218; *Ryan v. Gonzales*, No. 10-930 (U.S. Sup. Ct., Oct. 9, 2012). See also Adam Liptak, "Supreme Court Considers Indefinite Stays of Execution," *New York Times*, Oct. 9, 2012.

212. Parry and Drogin, *Mental Disability Law*, 2–3.

213. David B. Wexler and Bruce J. Winick, "Therapeutic Jurisprudence and Criminal Justice Mental Health Issues," *Ment. & Phys. Dis. L. Rep.* 16 (1992): 225.

214. Parry and Drogin, *Mental Disability Law*, 2.

215. Wald, "Basic Personal and Civil Rights," 5.

216. Joseph P. Morrissey et al., "New Models of Collaboration between Criminal Justice and Mental Health Systems," *Am J. of Psychiatry* 166, no. 11 (2009): 1211.

217. See "Editorial: The Misuse of Life without Parole," *New York Times*, Sept. 12, 2011; "Editorial: Falling Crime, Teeming Prisons," *New York Times*, Oct. 29, 2011; Albert R. Hunt, "A Country of Inmates," Bloomberg News, Nov. 11, 2011.

218. John Pfaff, "Reform School," *Slate*, Feb. 19, 2009, http:www.slate.com/id/2211585.

2. SANISM AND AMERICA'S EXAGGERATED FEAR OF VIOLENCE

1. Substance Abuse and Mental Health Services Administration (SAMH-SA), "Violence and Mental Illness: The Facts" (SAMHSA, 2010).

2. E. Fuller Torrey, *The Insanity Offense: How America's Failure to Treat the Seriously Mentally Ill Endangers Its Citizens* (New York: W. W. Norton, 2008), 140.

3. SAMHSA, "Violence."

4. H. Stuart, "Violence and Mental Illness: An Overview," *World Psychiatry* 2, no. 2 (June 2003): 121.

5. SAMHSA, "Violence."

6. Ken Pope, "Resources for Therapists Who Are Threatened, Attacked or Stalked by Patients," accessed June 18, 2013, kspope.com/stalking.php, citing Ken Pope and Melba Vasquez, *Ethics in Psychotherapy and Counseling: A Practical Guide*, 4th ed. (Hoboken, NJ: Wiley, 2011).

7. Ibid.

8. Ibid.

9. *American Heritage Dictionary*, http://www.answers.com/topic/counter-transference.

10. David Glenn, "Our Hidden Prejudices on Trial; If Bias Is Unconscious, Should People Be Held Legally Responsible for It?" *Chronicle of Higher Education* (Apr. 15, 2008).

11. Xiaojing Xu et al., "Do You Feel My Pain? Racial Group Membership Modulates Empathic Neural Responses," *Journal of Neuroscience* 29, no. 26 (July 1, 2009): 8525–8529, last accessed Mar. 18, 2013, www.jneurosci.org/content/29/26/8525.full.

12. See Stephen P. Hinshaw, *The Mark of Shame: Stigma of Mental Illness and an Agenda for Change* (New York: Oxford University Press, 2007).

13. Claire Henderson and Graham Thornicroft, "Stigma and Discrimination in Mental Illness: Time to Change," *Lancet* 373, no. 9679 (June 6, 2009): 1928–1930.

14. John Parry and Eric Y. Drogin, *Mental Disability Law, Evidence and Testimony* (Washington, D.C.: American Bar Association Publishing, 2007), 5, citing Michael L. Perlin and Keri K. Gould, "Roshomon and the Criminal Law: Mental Disability and the Federal Sentencing Guidelines," *Am. J. Crim. L.* 22 (1995): 431, 442–43.

15. Parry and Drogin, *Mental Disability Law*, 5.

16. Michael L. Perlin, "'Baby, Look inside Your Mirror': The Legal Profession's Willful and Sanist Blindness to Lawyers with Mental Disabilities," *U. of Pitt. L. Rev.* 69 (Spring 2008): 589.

17. Michael L. Perlin, "Representing Defendants in Incompetency and Insanity Cases: Some Therapeutic Jurisprudence Dilemmas," New York Law School Legal Studies Research Paper No. 07/08-23, Apr. 15, 2008.

18. Ibid.

19. Ibid.

20. See Benedict Carey, "Psychiatry Manual Drafters Back Down on Diagnoses," *New York Times*, May 8, 2012; Sally Satel, "Prescriptions for Psychiatric Trouble: The Proposed New Edition of Diagnostic and Statistical Manual of Mental Disorders Could Place Large Swaths of the Population under the Umbrella of Pathology," *New York Times*, Feb. 19, 2010.

21. Perlin, "Representing Defendants," citing Perlin and Gould, "Roshomon," 443.

22. James N. Butcher et al., "Potential Bias in MMPI-2 Assessments Using the Fake Bad Scale (FBS)," *Psychol. Injury and Law* 1, no. 3 (Dec. 2007): 191, DOI 10.1007/s12207-007-9002-Z.

23. Melinda Beck, "Is Sex Addiction a Sickness, Or Excuse to Behave Badly?" *Wall Street Journal*, Sept. 30, 2008.

24. John La Fond and Mary Durham, *Back to the Asylum: The Future of Mental Health Law and Policy in the United States* (New York: Oxford University Press, 1992).

25. *Addington v. Texas*, 441 U.S. 418 (1979).

26. *Vitek v. Jones*, 445 U.S. 480 (1980).

27. Barbara A. Weiner, "Mental Disability and the Criminal Law," in *The Mentally Disabled and the Law*, ed. Samuel J. Brakel, John Parry, and Barbara A. Weiner, 3d ed. (Chicago: American Bar Foundation, 1985), 713.

28. Torrey, *Insanity Offense*, 132, 140–160; Treatment Advocacy Center, "Violent Behavior: One of the Consequences of Failing to Treat Individuals with Severe Mental Illness," accessed Feb. 13, 2010, www.treatmentadvocacycenter.org.

29. Bureau of Justice Statistics, National Crime Victimization Survey and the FBI's Uniform Crime Reports, "Violent Crime," http:bjs.ojp.usdoj.gov/index.cfm?ty=tp&tid=31 (Apr. 7, 2011); Charles Lane, "Triumph over Crime: Reaping the Benefits of Falling Rates," *Washington Post*, Dec. 27, 2011.

30. Bureau of Justice Statistics, "Crime against People with Disabilities," 2008 (NCJ 231328), http://bjs.ojp.usdoj.gov, accessed Dec. 10, 2010.

31. SAMHSA, "Violence."

32. Louis P. Masur, *Rites of Execution: Capital Punishment and the Transformation of American Culture, 1776–1865* (New York: Oxford University Press, 1989), 4.

33. Bureau of Justice Statistics, "Since 1994 Violent Crime Rates Have Declined, Reaching the Lowest Level Ever in 2005," www.ojp.usdoj.gov/bjs/glance/viort.htm (Aug. 15, 2009); Holly Watt, "Violent Crime Fell in 2007 from Previous Year," *Washington Post,* Sept. 16, 2008.

34. Torrey, *Insanity Offense*, "The Consequences of Unconstrained Civil Liberties: Violent and Homicidal," 140–160.

35. Position Statement, "Violence in America: A Community Mental Health Response," Oct. 8, 2004, http://www.nmha.org/prevention/previol.html.

36. L. R. BeVier, "Controlling Communications That Teach or Demonstrate Violence: 'The Movie Made Them Do It,'" *J. of Law, Medicine & Ethics* 32 (Spring 2004): 47.

37. Ibid.

38. See American Psychiatric Association, "Psychiatric Effects of Media Violence: APA Position Statement on Violence" (Oct. 2004), www.psych.org/public_info/media_violence.cfm; National Mental Health Association Position Statement, "Violence in America: A Community Mental Health Response" (Oct. 2004), www.nmha.org/prevention/previol.html, Senate Committee on the Judiciary, "Children, Violence, and the Media: A Report for Parents and Policy Makers" (Sept. 1999).

39. Ibid.

40. See B. Bushman and J. Whitaker, "Like a Magnet: Cartharsis Beliefs Attract Angry People to Violent Video Games," *Psychological Science* 21 (June 2010): 790–92; A. Markman, "What You Don't Know Can Hurt You: Violence, Catharsis, and Video Games," *Psychology Today*, July 19, 2010, http://www.psychologytoday.com; S. Bhattacharya, "Violent Song Lyrics Increase Aggression," *New Scientist*, May 4, 2003, www.newscientist.com/article/dn3695-violent-song-lyrics-increase-aggression.html; B. J. Bushman, R. F. Baumeister, and A. D. Stack, "Catharsis, Aggression, and Persuasive Influence: Self-Fulfilling or Self-Defeating Prophecies?" *J. of Personality and Social Psychology* 76, no. 3 (1999): 367–76.

41. BeVier, "Controlling Communications," citing J. G. Johnson et al., "Television Viewing and Aggressive Behavior during Adolescence and Adulthood," *Science* 295 (2002): 2468, 2470.

42. B. J. Bushman and C. A. Anderson, "Media Violence and the American Public," *American Psychologist* 56, nos. 6, 7 (June/July 2001): 477, 480.

43. David Finkelhor et al., "Children's Exposure to Violence: A Comprehensive National Survey," *Office of Juvenile Justice and Delinquency Prevention Bulletin*, Oct. 2009.

44. American Psychiatric Association, "Violence and Mental Illness," Oct. 11, 2005, www.psych.org/public_info/VIOLEN~1.cfm; Jeffrey Swanson et al., "The Socio-Environmental Context of Violent Behavior in Persons Treated for Severe Mental Illness," *A. J. of Public Health* 92, no. 9 (Sept. 2002): 1523–31.

45. Robert N. Parker and Kathleen Auerhahn, "Alcohol, Drugs, and Violence," *Annual. Rev. Sociol.* 24, (1998): 291–311.

46. J. Bryant, D. Zillman, and A. A. Raney, "Violence and the Enjoyment of Media Sports," in *Mediasport*, ed Lawrence A. Wenner (New York: Routledge, 1998).

47. American Psychiatric Association, Position Statement.

48. American Psychological Association, "Violence on Television—What Do Children Learn? What Can Parents Do?" Oct. 15, 2004, 1999, StudyMode.com. Retrieved 7/31/13 from http://www.studymode.com/essays/violence-on-television-what-do-children-1205645.html.

49. National Mental Health Association.

50. Majority staff, Senate Committee on the Judiciary, "Children, Violence, and the Media: A Report for Parents and Policy Makers," Sept. 14, 1999, www.indiana.edu/~cspc/ressenate.htm.

51. American Psychiatric Association, Position Statement.

52. J. H. Walma van der Molen, "Violence and Suffering in Television News: Toward a Broader Conception of Harmful Television Content for Children," *Pediatrics* 133, no. 6 (June 2004): 1771, 1772.

53. J. Timmer, "Incrementalism and Policymaking on Television Violence," *Communication. L. & Policy* 9 (Summer 2004): 351.

54. Bushman and Anderson, "Media Violence," 482.

55. Ibid., 485.

56. James Poniewozik, "Serial Killing: How TV Dramas, Good and Bad, Have Become Addicted to Blood," *Time*, Mar. 11, 2013, 50.

57. Bushman and Anderson, "Media Violence," 485.

58. Timmer, "Incrementalism," 352–53.

59. Ibid., 353.

60. Ibid.

61. Tom Feran, "V-Chips Grow Stale in TV-Content Battles," *Cleveland Plain Dealer*, Apr. 19, 2005.

62. Timmer, "Incrementalism," 354.

63. See Timothy Egan, "Sex and the Supremes," *New York Times* (July 7, 2011) discussing Justice Breyer's dissent in *Brown v. Entertainment Merchants Assoc.* 564 U.S. (2011).

64. BeVier, "Controlling Communications," 47.

65. Frank Palumbo, American Academy of Pediatrics, "Testimony: The Social Impact of Music Violence," Senate Subcommittee on Oversight of Government Management, Restructuring, and the District of Columbia, Nov. 6, 1997.

66. Ibid.

67. American Academy of Pediatrics, "Media Violence," *Pediatrics* 108, no. 5 (Nov. 2009): 1222.

68. B. Staples, "How Hip-Hop Music Lost Its Way and Betrayed Its Fans," *New York Times*, May 12, 2005.

69. See T. M. Adams and D. B. Fuller, "The Words Have Changed but the Ideology Remains the Same: Misogynistic Lyrics in Rap," *Journal of Black Studies*, 36, no. 6 (July 2006): 938-957.

70. BeVier, "Controlling Communications," 47.

71. See D. Grossman and L. Frankowski, *The Two Space War* (Riverdale, NY: Baen Books, 2004).

72. Alex Pham, "Marathon Sessions Take Over Players: Is That Sick?" *Los Angeles Times*, June 22, 2007.

73. Jim Meyers, "Did VA Tech Murderer Learn from Video Games?" *Newsmax.com*, April 18, 2007.

74. Ibid.

75. BeVier, "Controlling Communications," 54.

76. *Brown v. Entertainment Merchants Assn.*

77. Robert H. Boyle, *Sport: Mirror of American Life* (Boston: Little, Brown, 1963).

78. Charles Harary, "Aggressive Play or Criminal Assault? An In-Depth Look at Sports Violence and Criminal Liability," *Colum. J. Law & Arts* 25 (2001–2002): 197.

79. Bryant, Zillman, and Raney, "Violence and the Enjoyment of Media Sports."

80. Harary, "Aggressive Play."

81. See also C. Samson, "No Time Like the Present: Why Recent Events Should Spur Contress to Enact a Sports Violence Act," *Ariz. St. L. J.* 37 (2005): 949; K. Fritz, "Going to the Bullpen: Using Uncle Sam to Strike Out Professional Sports Violence," *Cardozo Arts & Ent. L. J.* 20 (2002): 189; D. R. Kanron, "Winning Isn't Everything, It's the Only Thing. Violence in Professional Sports: The Need for Federal Regulation and Criminal Sanction," *Ind. L. Rev.* 25 (1991–1992): 147.

82. Peter Grier, "For Sports News, See Business, Crime Pages," *Christian Science Monitor*, Mar. 12, 2004.

83. Maryann Hudson, "From Box Scores to the Police Blotter," *LA Times*, Dec. 27, 1995.

84. Ibid.

85. Daniel B. Wood, "NFL Arrests: Violence and the Culture of Star Athletes," *Christian Science Monitor*, Feb. 7, 2000.

86. Douglas O. Linder, "Famous Trials," University of Missouri–Kansas City School of Law, http://www.law.umkc.edu/faculty/projects/ftrials/Simpson/simpson.htm

87. Steve Friess, "O. J. Simpson Convicted of Robbery and Kidnapping," *New York Times*, Oct. 4, 2008.

88. Paul Newell, "Rae Carruth Sentenced," *Associated Press*, Jan. 23, 2001.

89. CNN-Sports Illustrated, "Lewis Murder Charges Dropped," June 5, 2000, CNNSI.com.

90. Larry O'Dell, "23 Months for Michael Vick Dogfighting Conviction," *Associated Press*, Dec. 10, 2007, www.wausaudailyherald.com.

91. "Vick Recipient of Block Courage Award," ESPN.com, Dec. 23, 2009; Sean Leahy, "Tony Dungy Defends Courage Award Given to Eagles' Michael Vick," *USA Today*, Dec. 24, 2009.

92. See William Rhoden, "No More Free Passes for Roethlisberger," *New York Times*, Apr. 14, 2010.

93. Tina Gianoulis, "Mike Tyson," *St. James Encyclopedia of Popular Culture* (1999).

94. "Rape Case against Bryant Dismissed," NBCSports.comnewsservices, Sept. 2, 2004.

95. "Bertuzzi Receives Conditional Discharge, Probation," CBCSports.ca, Dec. 24, 2004.

96. Rod Aydelotte, *Associated Press*, June 15, 2005.

97. Pete Thamel, "Lacrosse Player Charged with Murder of Another," *New York Times*, May 3, 2010.

98. Joe Nocera, "It's Not Just Penn State," *New York Times*, Dec. 3, 2011.

99. Associated Press, "Roundup: Beaten Fan in Coma," *New York Times*, Apr. 3, 2011.

100. "Previous Examples of Fan Violence," http://sportsillustrated.cnn.com/baseball/news/2002/09/19/fan_violence.

101. Ibid.

102. Liz Robbins, "Union and Pacers to Fight Suspensions," *New York Times*, Nov. 23, 2004.

103. Ibid.

104. Tim Dahlberg, "Violence Plagues Youth Sports: Overbearing Parents Creating Dangerous Situations on the Field," *Associated Press*, March 24, 2004, http://net/gremlins_common/main_insert/violence.htm.

105. Ibid.

106. Ibid.

107. Mike Wise, "An Ugly Tradition That Should Be Sacked," *Washington Post*, Mar. 4, 2012. See also Judy Battitsa, "Coach Who Preached Violence Rewarded It for Years," *New York Times*, Mar. 4, 2012; Mark Maske, "Probe to Target Redskins over Hits," *Washington Post*, Mar. 4, 2012.

108. Wise, "Ugly Tradition."

109. Anahad O'Connor, "Trying to Reduce Head Injuries, Youth Football Limits Practices," *New York Times*, June 13, 2012; R. S. Moser and P. S. Chatz, "Enduring Effects of Concussions on Youth Athletes," *Archives of Clinical Neuropsychology* 17, no. 1 (Jan. 2002): 91–100.

110. Viv Bernstein, "Nascar's Call for Aggressiveness Is Met by A Crash," *New York Times*, Mar. 8, 2010.

111. "Dan Wheldon Dies in Huge Crash at IndyCar Finale," *Associated Press*, Oct. 15, 2011.

112. Ken Belson, "'Perfect Storm' of Events Led to Wheldon's Death, IndyCar Report Says," *New York Times*, Dec. 15, 2011.

113. "Posey's Injury Stirs Debate on Baseball Collisions," *Associated Press*, May 27, 2011.

114. See B. W. Benson et al., "A Prospective Study of Concussions among National Hockey League Players during Regular Season Games: The NHL-NHLPA Concussion Program," *Canadian Med. Assoc. J.*, Apr. 18, 2011, DOI:10.1503/cmaj.092190; D. C. Viano, I. R. Casson, and E. J. Pellman, "Concussion in Professional Football: Biomechanics of the Struck Player—Part 14," *Neurosurgery* 61, no. 2 (2007): 313–27; D. C. Viano et al., "Concussion in Professional Football: Comparison with Boxing Head Impacts—Part 10," *Neurosurgery* 57, no. 6 (2005): 1154–72.

115. H. Fendrich, "Some Players Still Willing to Hide Concussions," *Associated Press*, Dec. 26, 2011. See also, "More Ex-Players Sue League, Citing Concussion Damage," *Associated Press*, Dec. 23, 2011.

116. M. Halstead and K. D. Walter, clinical report: "Sport-Related Concussion in Children and Adolescents," *American Academy of Pediatrics*, Aug. 2010, http://pediatrics.aappublications.org/content/126/3/597; "Concussion Experts: For Kids—No Sports, No Schoolwork, No Text Messages," *Science Daily*, June 8, 2009.

117. Halstead and Walter, "Sport-Related Concussion."

118. D. A. Kreager, "Unnecessary Roughness? School Sports, Peer Networks, and Male Adolescent Violence," *Amer. Sociological Rev.* 72 (2007): 705.

119. Ibid.

120. See *The Early Show, CBS News*, "Violence Becoming Norm for Women's Sports?" Nov. 10, 2009, http://www.cbsnews.com/2100-500202_162-5603333.html.

121. Walma van der Molen, "Violence and Suffering," 1771.

122. P. Klite, R. A. Bardwell, and J. Salzman. "Local TV News: Getting Away with Murder," *Harvard International Journal of Press/Politics* 2 (1997): 102–12.

123. Bryant, Zillman, and Raney, "Violence and the Enjoyment of Media Sports," 252.

124. Walma van der Molen, "Violence and Suffering," 1772.

125. Ibid.

126. Bushman and Anderson, "Media Violence."

127. Walma van der Molen, "Violence and Suffering, 1772.

128. Ibid.

129. Ibid.

130. Lizette Alvarez, "A Florida Law Gets Scrutiny after a Teenager's Killing," *New York Times*, Mar. 20, 2012; Fla. S.B.436 (2005).

131. E. J. Dionne, "Windows into the Right," *Washington Post*, Mar. 26, 2012.

132. *Taylor v. Taintor*, 83 U.S. 366 (1872).

133. Associated Press, "Acquittal in Killing of Intruder" *Washington Post*, Sept. 28, 2008.

134. See Linda A. Teplin, "Police Discretion and Mentally Ill Persons, *National Institute of Justice Journal* (July 2000): 8–15; Editorial, "Police and the Mentally Ill," *St. Petersberg Times*, Mar. 17, 2003; Elizabeth Ferander and Susan Sward, "The Use of Force/ Police Need Greater Understanding of the Mentally Ill, Advocates Say," *S.F. Chronicle*, Dec. 5, 2006.

135. Associated Press, "Colo. Police Pepper-Spray 8-Year-Old Boy," *Washington Post*, Apr. 7, 2011.

136. Editorial, "Walter Cronkite," *New York Times*, July 20, 2009.

137. Walma van der Molen, "Violence and Suffering."

138. See, e.g., Tim Padgett, "Florida Epidemic: Teachers Sleeping with Students," *Time*, May 30, 2009, www.time.com; Alex Tresniowski, "Mary Kay Letourneau and Vili Fualaau: One Year Later," *People*, May 5, 2006; Julie Hislop, *Female Sex Offenders: What Therapists, Law Enforcement and Child Protective Services Need to Know* (Ravendale, WA: Issues Press, 2001).

139. See *United States v. Polouizzi*, 697 F. Supp. 2d 381 (E.D.N.Y. 2010); Erica Goode, "Life Sentence for Possession of Child Pornography Spurs Debate over Severity," *New York Times*, Nov. 4, 2011.

140. See Heather Cucolo and Michael Perlin, "Preventing Sex-Offender Recidivism through Therapeutic Jurisprudence Approaches and Specified Community Integration," New York Law School (presented in part to the Academy of Criminal Justice Sciences annual conference, New York City, Mar. 2012).

141. See Frederick Kunkle, "Caught in a Neighborhood Web," *Washington Post*, May 13, 2006.

142. Monica Davey, "Case Shows Limits of Sex Offender Alert Programs," *New York Times*, Sept. 2, 2009.

143. See Center for Sexual Offender Management, "Community Notification and Education" (Apr. 2001), www.csom.org/pubs/notedu.pdf; Hugh Kirkegaared and Wayne Nortley, "The Sex Offender as a Scapegoat," emory.edu/college.

144. See Cucolo and Perlin, "Preventing Sex-Offender Recidivism"; Megan A. Janicki, "Better Seen Than Herded: Residency Restrictions and Global Positioning System Tracking Law for Sex Offenders," *B.U. Pub. Interest. L. J.* 16 (Spring 2007): 285; Emily Horowitz, "Growing Media and Legal Attention to Sex Offenders: More Safety or More Injustice?"*J. Inst. Just. Int'l Stud.* 164 (2007): 143.

3. SANIST WORDS AND LANGUAGE

1. Peter J. Smith, "New Legal Fictions," *Georgetown L. J.* 95 (June 2007): 1435.

2. Steven Pinker, *The Stuff of Thought* (New York: Viking, 2007), 127.

3. Ibid., 3.

4. Ibid., 431.

5. Ibid., 26.

6. Joseph LeDoux, "Manipulating Memory," *Scientist* 23, no. 3 (Mar. 2009): 40.

7. See Leon Festinger, *A Theory of Cognitive Dissonance* (Stanford, CA: Stanford University Press, 1957).

8. See chapter 1.

9. See chapter 4.

10. Pinker, *Stuff of Thought*, 217.

11. Festinger, *Theory*.

12. See chapter 4.

13. See chapter 5.

14. Pinker, *Stuff of Thought*, 18.

15. Ibid., 19.

16. Ibid., 24.

17. Ibid., 26.

18. Ibid., 29.

19. Ibid.

20. Ibid., 196.

21. Ibid., 214.

22. See *Kumho Tire v. Carmichael*, 536 U.S. 137 (1999).

23. John Monahan and Eric Silver, "Judicial Decision Thresholds for Violence Risk Management," *International Journal of Forensic Mental Health* 2, no. 1 (2003): 1.

24. John Monahan, editorial, "Statistical Literacy: A Prerequisite for Evidence-Based Medicine," *Psychological Science in the Public Interest* 8, no. 2 (2008): i.

25. *Roper v. Simmons*, 543 U.S. 551 (2005); *J.D.B. v. North Carolina*, 131 S. Ct. 2394 (2011).

26. See *United States v. Portman*, 599 F.3d 633 (7th Cir. 2010). The appeals court opined that the federal district court had erred in "suggest[ing] that because reduced mental capacity would make recidivism more likely, an increased sentence would be necessary."

27. See chapter 1, "The Insanity Defense Post-Hinckley"; *Clark v. Arizona*, 548 U.S. 735 (2006); Lisa Callahan et al., "Insanity Defense Reform in the United States—Post-Hinckley," *Ment. & Phys. Dis. L. Rep.* 11 (1987): 54.

28. See chapter 1, "'Quasi-Civil' Commitment of Disordered Criminals and Those Charged with Crimes."

29. See chapter 4. See also *Brown v. Plata*, 563 U.S. (2011).

30. See chapter 2.

31. Pinker, *Stuff of Thought*, 167.

32. Ibid.

33. Pamela Mason, "Psychiatrist at Mitchell Hearing Worth His $500,000 Fee, U.S. Attorney Says," *Salt Lake City Tribune*, Dec. 21, 2009.

34. Pinker, *Stuff of Thought*, 258.

35. Ibid.

36. *Robinson v. California*, 370 U.S. 550 (1962).

37. *Powell v. Texas*, 392 U.S. 514 (1968).

38. *Kansas v. Hendricks*, 521 U.S. 346 (1997). See also A. Tsesis, "Due Process in Civil Commitments," *Wash & Lee L. Rev.* 68 (2011): 253.

39. See editorial, "The Misuse of Life without Parole," *New York Times*, Sept. 12, 2011.

40. T. N. Wanchek and R. J. Bonnie, "Use of Longer Periods of Temporary Detention to Reduce Mental Health Civil Commitments," *Psychiatric Services* (July 1, 2012), doi:10.1176/appi.ps.201100359.

41. See Morton Birnbaum, "The Right to Treatment," *American Bar Association Journal* 46 (1960): 499.

42. Ibid.

43. *O'Connor v. Donaldson*, 422 U.S. 564 (1975).

44. See *Kansas v. Hendricks*, 521 U.S. 346 (1997); *Kansas v. Crane*, 534 U.S. 407 (2002).

45. See §7–7.6.

46. See *Kansas v. Hendricks*, 521 U.S. 346 (1997); *Kansas v. Crane*, 534 U.S. 407 (2002).

47. *Jones v. United States*, 463 U.S. 354 (1983).

48. See chapter 5.

49. *Kansas v. Crane*, 534 U.S. 407 (2002).

50. Ibid.

51. See John Parry, *Criminal Mental Health and Disability Law, Evidence and Testimony* (Chicago: American Bar Association Publishing, 2009), 205–206, 233–237; John Parry, *Civil Mental Disability Law, Evidence and Testimony* (Chicago: American Bar Association Publishing, 2010), 455–464.

52. Justice Alito dissenting in *Brown v. Plata*, 131 S. Ct. 1919 (2011).

53. See Parry, *Criminal Mental Health*, 234–236; Parry, *Civil Mental Disability*, 458–461.

54. See, e.g., Prison Litigation Reform Act, 18 U.S.C. §3626; Civil Rights Act §1983; *Blum v. Yaretsky*, 457 U.S. 991 (1982) (plaintiffs must show that defendants acted under state law to recover); Antiterrorism and Effective Death Penalty Act (AEDPA), 28 U.S.C. §2244(b)(3) (provides numerous limitations on inmates trying to pursue claims against the federal government); Federal Arbitration Act 9 U.S.C §1 et seq (plaintiffs must arbitrate certain claims before maintaining a private right of action).

55. See, e.g., *Barnes v. Gorman*, 536 U.S. 181 (2002) (Americans with Disabilities Act Title II that applies to public facilities does not permit punitive damages); also many state statutes limit damages involving medical malpractice.

56. See Parry, *Criminal Mental Health*, 233–234; Parry, *Civil Mental Disability*, 456–458.

57. See, e.g., Prison Litigation Reform Act, 18 U.S.C. §3626; Civil Rights Act §1983; Americans with Disabilities Act Title II.

58. See Parry, *Civil Mental Disability*, 65; Michael L. Perlin, "'I Might Need a Good Lawyer, Could be Your Funeral, My Trial': Global Clinical Legal Education and the Right to Counsel in Civil Commitment Cases," *Washington University Journal of Law and Policy* 28, no. 1 (2008): 241.

59. *Deshaney v. Winnebago County Department of Social Services*, 489 U.S. 189 (1989).

60. Pinker, *Stuff of Thought*, 135.

61. Samuel J. Brakel, "Involuntary Institutionalization," in *The Mentally Disabled and the Law*, ed. Samuel J. Brakel, John Parry, and Barbara Weiner (Chicago: American Bar Foundation, 1985): 22–23.

62. Pinker, *Stuff of Thought*, 439.

4. PREDICTIONS OF DANGEROUSNESS IN THE COURTROOM

1. E. Fuller Torrey, *The Insanity Offense: How America's Failure to Treat the Seriously Mentally Ill Endangers Its Citizens* (New York: W. W. Norton, 2008), 7.

2. Steven Pinker, *The Stuff of Thought* (New York: Viking, 2007), 196.

3. Leonard Mlodinow, "Mining Truth from Data Babel: Nate Silver's 'Signal and the Noise' Examines Predictions," *New York Times*, Oct. 23, 2012.

4. Lawrence H. Summers, "Promoting the Rebound," *Washington Post* (Mar. 26, 2012).

5. See, e.g., A. R. Teo, S. R. Holley, M. Leary, and D. E. McNiel, "The Relationship between Level of Training and Accuracy of Violence Risk Assessment," *Psychiatric Services* 63 (Nov. 2012): 1089–94, doi:10.1176/appi.ps.20120019. (Increased risk assessment accuracy for psychiatrists using structured tools in predicting whether patients with severe mental illnesses, often schizophrenia, subsequently became physically aggressive toward staff by engaging in behaviors such as hitting, kicking, or biting.)

6. W. M. Brooks, "The Tail Wags the Dog: The Persuasive and Inappropriate Influence by the Psychiatric Profession on the Civil Commitment Process," *N. Dakota L. Rev.* 86 (2010): 259, 269. See also Seena Fazel, Jay P. Singh, Helen Doll, and Martin Grann, "Use of Risk Assessment Instruments to Predict Risk of Violence and Antisocial Behaviour in 73 Samples Involving 24,827 People: Systematic and Meta-Analysis," *British Medical Journal* 345 (July 24, 2012): doi: http://dx.doi.org/10.1136/bmj.e4692 (Published July 24, 2012) .; B. A. Arrigo, "Paternalism, Civil Commitment and Illness Politics: Assessing the Current Debate and Outlining Future Direction," *J.L. & Health* 7 (1992–1993): 131, 144; C. W. Lidz et al., "The Accuracy of Predictions of Violence to Others," *JAMA* 269 (1993): 1007, 1008.

7. Gary B. Melton et al., *Psychological Evaluations for the Courts* 3d ed. (New York: Guilford Press, 2007), §10.05 at 326; Brooks, "Tail Wags the Dog," 270.

8. See B. Ennis and T. Litwack, "Psychiatry and the Presumption of Expertise: Flipping Coins in the Courtroom, *Calif. L. Rev.* 62 (1974): 639; A. Stone, "The *Tarasoff* Decisions: Suing Psychotherapists to Safeguard Society," *Harvard. L. Rev.* 90 (1976): 358.

9. Brooks, "Tail Wags the Dog," 274–75; see also P. S. Appelbaum, "Civil Commitment from a Systems Perspective," *Law and Hum. Behav.* 16 (1992): 61, 65; E. P. Mulvey and C. W. Lidz, "Back to Basics: A Critical Analysis of Dangerousness Research in a New Environment," *Law and Hum. Behav.* 9 (1985): 209, 214; R. L. Goldstein, "Hiring the Hired Gun: Lawyers and Their Psychiatric Experts," *Legal Stud. Forum* 11 (1987): 41.

10. See M. A. Norko, "Commentary: Dangerousness—A Failed Paradigm for Clinical Practice and Service Delivery," *J. Am. Acad. Psychiatry and Law* 28 (2000): 282, 286.

11. See John Monahan, "Structured Risk Assessment of Violence," in *Textbook of Violence Assessment and Management*, ed. R. Simon and K. Tardiff (Washington, D.C.: American Psychiatric Publications, 2008); Vernon Quinsey et al., *Violent Offenders: Appraising and Managing Risk*, 2d ed. (Washington, D.C.: American Psychological Association, 2006), 197; Brooks, "Tail Wags the Dog."

12. See Monahan, "Structured Risk Assessment."

13. Ibid.

14. See T. Fortney et al., "Sexual Offender Treatment," *Sexual Offender Treatment* 2, no 1 (2007), www.sexual-offender-treatment.org/55.html, accessed Feb. 11, 2010; Robert A. Prentky, Eric Janus, Howard Barbaree, Barabara K. Schwartz, and Martin P. Kafka, "Sexually Violent Predators in the Courtroom: Science on Trial," William Mitchell College of Law, Legal Studies Research Paper Series, Working Paper No. 50 (Oct. 2006); Richard Wollert, "Low Base Rates Limit Expert Certainty When Current Actuarials Are Used to Identify Sexually Violent Predators: An Application of Bayes's Theorem," *Psychology, Pub. Policy & Law* 12, no. 1 (2006): 56–85; Eric S. Janus and Robert A. Prentky, "Forensic Use of Actuarial Risk Assessment with Sex Offenders: Accuracy, Admissibility and Accountability," *Amer. Crim. Law Rev.* 40 (2003): 1443.

15. See A. Tsesis, "Due Process in Commitments," *Wash & Lee L. Rev.* 68 (2011): 253.

16. John Monahan, editorial, "Statistical Literary: A Prerequisite for Evidence-Based Medicine," *Psychological Science in the Public Interest* 8, no. 2 (2008): i.

17. John Monahan, "Clinical and Actuarial Predictions of Violence," in *Modern Scientific Evidence: The Law and Science of Expert Testimony*, ed. David L. Faigman et al. (St. Paul, MN: West Group, 2005–2006; ed. updated Dec. 2008), §10:18; See also SAMHSA, "Violence and Mental Illness: The Facts," www.samhsa.gov (June 9, 2010); Eric B. Elbogen and Sally C. Johnson, "The Intricate Link between Violence and Mental Disorder: Results from the National Epidemiologic Survey on Alcohol and Related Conditions," *Arch. of Gen. Psychiatry* 66, no. 2 (2009): 152–61; H. Stuart, "Violence and Mental Illness: An Overview," *World Psychiatry* 2, no. 2 (June 2003): 121–24.

18. Larry J. Siever, "Neurobiology of Aggression and Violence," *Am J. of Psychiatry* 165 (2008): 429.

19. Ewen Callaway, "Murderer with 'Aggression Genes' Gets Sentence Cut," *New Scientist* 22 (Nov. 2009): 27, http://www.newscientist.com/article/dn18098-

murderer-with-aggression-genes-gets-sentence-cut.html?full=true&print=true, accessed Mar. 20, 2013.

20. Siever, "Neurobiology."

21. See Charles W. Lidz et al., "Violence and Mental Illness: A New Analytic Approach," *Law and Hum. Behav.* 31 (Feb. 2007): 23.

22. Ibid.

23. Ibid.

24. Tsesis, "Due Process."

25. Fazel, Singh, Doll, and Grann, "Use of Risk Assessment Instruments."

26. See Judge Weinstein in *United States v. Fatico*, 458 F. Supp. 388, 403 (E.D.N.Y. 1978), aff'd, 603 F.2d 1053 (2d Cir. 1979); L. B. Sand and D. L. Rose, "Proof beyond All Possible Doubt: Is There a Need for a Higher Burden of Proof When the Sentence May Be Death?" *Chi-Kent L. Rev.* 78, no. 3 (2003): 1359, 1363; E. Stoffelmayr and S. S. Diamond, "The Conflict between Precision and Flexibility in Explaining 'Beyond a Reasonable Doubt'" *Psychol. Pub. Pol'y & L.* 6 (Sept. 2000): 769, 774.

27. John Monahan and Eric Silver, "Judicial Decision Thresholds for Violence, Risk Management," *Int. J. of Forensic M.H.*, 2, no. 1 (2003): 1.

28. See T. R. Litwack, "Assessments of Dangerousness: Legal, Research and Clinical Developments," *Administration and Policy in Mental Health* 21 (1994): 361–77; J. Monahan, "Mental Disorders and Violent Behavior: Perceptions and Evidence," *American Psychologist* 47 (1992): 511–52; Michael L. Perlin, *Mental Disability Law: Civil and Criminal* (Charlottesville, VA: Michie, 1989), 120–26.

29. Eric Lillquist, "Recasting Reasonable Doubt: Decision Theory and the Virtues of Variability," *U.C. Davis L. Rev.* 36 (2002): 85, 112.

30. Tsesis, "Due Process," 294, citing Enrique Baca-Garcia et al., "Diagnostic Stability of Psychiatric Disorders in Clinical Practice," *Brit. J. Psychiatry* 190 (2007): 210 (an indictment of current psychiatric diagnostic practices).

31. Melinda Beck, "Confusing Medical Ailments with Mental Illness," *Wall Street Journal*, Aug. 9, 2011; See also Barbara Schildkrout, *Unmasking Psychological Symptoms* (Hoboken, NJ: Wiley and Sons, 2011).

32. See Jonathan M. Metzl, *The Protest Psychosis: How Schizophrenia Became a Black Disease* (Boston: Beacon Press, 2010); L. R. Snowden et al., "Disproportionate Use of Psychiatric Emergency Services by African Americans," *Psychiatric Services* 60 (2009): 1664, 1669.

33. S. M. Eack et al. , "Interviewer-Perceived Honesty As a Mediator of Racial Disparities in the Diagnosis of Schizophrenia," *Psychiatric Services* (Sept. 1, 2012): 875–80, doi: 10.1176/appi.ps.201100388); Tsesis, "Due Process," 295, citing R. D. Alarcon, "Culture, Cultural Factors and Psychiatric Diagnosis: Review and Projections," *World Psychiatry* 8 (2009): 131, 132.

34. See C. Slobogin, "Rethinking Legally Relevant Mental Disorder," *Ohio N. U. L. Rev.* 29 (2003): 487, 504; John Parry and Eric Y. Drogin, *Civil Law Handbook on Psychiatric and Psychological Evidence and Testimony* (Washington, D.C.: American Bar Association, 2001), 272; T. E. Petti, "Discussion: Diagnosis Is Relevant to Psychiatric Hospitalization," *J. Am. Acad. Child & Adolescent Psychiatry* 37 (1998): 1038–40.

35. See, e.g., Thomas Insel, "Transforming Diagnosis," *The National Institute of Mental Health*, Apr. 29, 2013, www.nimh.nih.gov; P. Belluck & B. Carey, "Psychiatrist's Guide Is Out of Touch with Science, Experts Say," *New York Times*, May 6, 2013. See also Allen Francis, *An Insider's Revolt Against Out-of-Control Psychiatric Diagnosis, DSM-5, Big Pharma, and the Medicalization of Ordinary Life* (William Morrow, 2013); Gary Greenberg, *The Book of Woe: DSM and the Unmaking of Psychiatry* (Blue Rider Press, 2013).

36. See Jonas Rappaport and Gustav Bychowski, *The Clinical Evaluation of Dangerousness of the Mentally Ill* (Springfield, IL: C. C. Thomas, 1967).

37. *Barefoot v. Estelle*, 463 U.S. 880, 899 (1983).

38. Monahan, *Predictions of Violence*, 300.

39. The new position statement of the APA, approved by its general assembly and board of trustees, acknowledges that "psychiatrists . . . cannot predict dangerousness with definitive accuracy" but permits them to use such predictions to decide "whether a patient is in need of intervention to prevent harm to others." See "Position Statement on Assessing the Risk for Violence," which was approved in July 2012.

40. American Psychiatric Association, Fact Sheet, "Violence and Mental Illness,"Jan. 1998.

41. S. Fazel et al., "Schizophrenia and Violence: Systematic Review and Meta-Analysis," *Public Library of Science and Medicine* 6, no. 8 (August 2009).

42. O. Nielssen et al., "Homicide of Strangers by People with Psychotic Illness," *Schizophrenia Bulletin* 37, no. 3 (2011).

43. J. Swanson et al., "The Socio-Environmental Context of Violent Behavior in Persons Treated for Severe Mental Illness." *American Journal of Public Health* 92, no. 9 (Sept. 2002). See also Elbogen and Johnson, "The Intricate Link."

44. Michael R. Rand et al., *Alcohol and Crime: Data from 2002 to 2008* (Washington, D.C.: Bureau of Justice Statistics, Sept. 3, 2010). See also Elbogen and Johnson, "The Intricate Link."

45. See Eric Goode, "Drugs and Crime: What Is the Connection?" in *Drugs in American Society* (Boston: McGraw-Hill, 2005); B. McCarthy and E. Lawrence, "Economic Crime: Theory," in *Encyclopedia of Crime and Justice* (New York: Macmillan Reference, USA, 2002).

46. Goode, "Drugs and Crime"; McCarthy and Lawrence, "Economic Crime."

47. R. N. Nash Parker and K. Auerhahn, "Alcohol, Drugs, and Violence," *Annual Rev. of Sociology* 24 (1998): 291–311.

48. Ibid., 294.

49. Stuart, "Violence," 121.

50. American Psychiatric Association, "Violence and Mental Illness."

51. Fazel et al., "Schizophrenia and Violence."

52. Kevin Douglas, Laura Guy, and Stephen Hart, "Psychosis as a Risk Factor for Violence to Others: A Meta-Analysis," *Psychological Bulletin* 135, no. 5 (2009): 679.

53. Stuart, "Violence," 121.

54. See Thomas R. E. Barnes, *Antipsychotic Drugs and Their Side-Effects* (San Diego, CA: Academic Press, 1993).

55. Wayne A. Ray et al., "Atypical Antipsychotic Drugs and the Risk of Sudden Cardiac Death," *N. England J. of Med.* 360, no. 3 (2009): 225–35.

56. Peter Allan, "Conflicts of Interest," *Psychiatric News* 42, no. 18 (Sept. 29, 2007); Gardiner Harris, "Top Psychiatrists Didn't Report Drug Makers' Pay, Files Show," *New York Times*, Oct. 4, 2008; Tara Parker-Pope, "Psychiatry Handbook [DSM Revision] Linked to Drug Industry," *New York Times*, May 7, 2008; Keven Freking, "Drug Companies to Reveal Payments to Academic Doctors and Others," *Associated Press*, Apr. 11, 2008; See also Peter Whoriskey, "Can Drug Research Still Be Trusted?" *Washington Post*, Nov. 25, 2012. ("Even the most respected of medical journals, [pharmaceutical] firms' influence over studies opens door to bias.")

57. Swanson et al., "The Socio-Environmental Context."

58. B. Jancin, "Blast-Related Traumatic Injuries Turning Up in Civilian Practice," *Internal Medicine News*, Apr. 25, 2011. See also T. Tanielian and L. H. Jacox, *Invisible Wounds of War: Psychological and Cognitive Injuries, Their Consequences, and Services to Assist Recovery* (Santa Monica, CA: Rand Corporation, 2008).

59. Joel Dvoskin and Kirk Heilbrun, "Risk Assessment and Release Decision-Making: Toward Resolving the Great Debate," *J. Am. Acad. Psychiatry & L.* 29 (2001): 6.

60. Ibid.

61. Gary B. Melton et al., *Psychological Evaluations*, 277–93.

62. American Psychiatric Association, "Position Statement."

63. Parry and Drogin, *Civil Law Handbook*, 11. See also A. Bauer et al., "Reflections on Dangerousness and Its Prediction—A Truly Tantalizing Task?" *Med Law.* 21, no. 3 (2002): 495–497; Dvoskin and Heilbrun, "Risk Assessment"; Gary Melton et al., *Psychological Evaluations*, 277–93.

64. See E. Beecher-Monas, "The Epistemology of Prediction: Future Danger-ousness Testimony and Intellectual Due Process," *Wash. & Lee L. Rev.* 60 (Spring 2003): 353, 362–63; A. Bauer et al., "Reflections"; Dvoskin and Heil-brun, "Risk Assessment"; Gary Melton et al., *Psychological Evaluations*, 277–93.

65. Michael S. Odeh, Robert A. Zeiss, and Mathew T. Huss, "Cues They Use: Clinicians' Endorsement of Risk Cues in Predictions of Dangerousness," *Behavior Science & The Law* 24, no. 2 (2006): 147–56.

66. Fazel, Singh, Doll, and Grann, "Use of Risk Assessment Instruments."

67. Monahan, "Structured Risk Assessment."

68. Ibid., 20.

69. Ibid., 21.

70. Ibid., 31.

71. A. Bauer et al., "Reflections."

72. Parry and Drogin, *Civil Law Handbook*, 12–13.

73. David Brown, "No Easy Task to Identify a Mass Killer," *Washington Post*, Jan. 4, 2013 (citing the MacArthur Violence Risk Assessment Study).

74. Parry and Drogin, *Civil Law Handbook*, 13 (citing Melton et al., *Psychological Evaluations*, 292).

75. Ibid., 13.

76. Parry and Drogin, *Civil Law Handbook*, 27.

77. Ibid.

78. See Lidz et al., "Violence and Mental Illness."

79. Ibid.

80. Douglas Mossman, "Commentary: Assessing the Risk of Violence—Are 'Accurate' Predictions Useful?" *J. Am. Acad. Psychiatry & Law* 28 (2000): 272.

81. Odeh, Zeiss, and Huss, "Cues They Use."

82. Ibid.

83. David Leonhardt, "Why Doctors So Often Get It Wrong," *New York Times*, Feb. 22, 2006.

84. *Clark v. Arizona*, 126 S.Ct. 2709 (2006).

85. See Bernard Diamond, "The Fallacy of the Impartial Expert," *Archives of Criminal Psychodynamics* 3, no. 221 (1959); Seymour Halleck and Nancy Halleck, *Law in the Practice of Psychiatry* (New York: Plenum Medical Book Co., 1980); Elise J. Katch, "The Misuse and Abuse of Psychological Experts in Court," *Colo. Law* 23 (1994): 2757.

86. See David E. Bernstein, "Expert Witnesses, Adversarial Bias, and the (Partial) Failure of the Daubert Revolution," *Iowa L. Rev.* 93 (2008): 451.

87. See Susan Stefan, "'Discredited' and 'Discreditable': The Search for Political Identity by People with Psychiatric Diagnoses," *William and Mary L. Rev.* 44, no. 3 (2003): 1341.

88. Stephen Bergman, "The Farce of the Dueling Psychiatrists," *Boston Globe*, July 13, 2009.

89. Benedict Carey, "Psychiatric Manual Drafters Back Down on Diagnoses," *New York Times*, May 8, 2012; J. C. McPartland, Brian Reichow, and F. R. Volkmar, "Sensitivity and Specificity of Proposed DSM-5 Diagnostic Criteria for Autism Spectrum Disorder," *J. of the American Acad. of Child & Adolescent Psychiatry* 51, no. 4 (Apr. 2012); Benedict Carey, "Grief Could Join List of Disorders," *New York Times*, Jan. 24, 2012; Allen Frances, "A Warning Sign on the Road to DSM-V: Beware of Its Unintended Consequences," *Psychiatric Times*, June 26, 2009; Robert L. Spitzer, "APA and DSM-V: Empty Promises," *Psychiatric Times*, July 2, 2009; Sally Satel, "Prescriptions for Psychiatric Trouble," *Wall Street Journal*, Feb. 19, 2010; Shari Roan, "Psychiatrist Rewriting the Mental Health Bible," *Los Angeles Times*, May 26, 2009; Courtney B. Worley, Marc D. Feldman, and James C. Hamilton, "Distinguishing Factitious Disorder from Malingering," *Psychiatric Times*, Nov. 5, 2009.

90. J. Shelder et al.,"Personality Disorders in DSM-5," *A. J. of Psychiatry* 167 (2010): 1026. See also Carey, "Grief Could Join List" (proposed "new diagnoses include 'binge eating disorder,' 'premenstrual dysphoric disorder,' and 'attenuated psychosis syndrome,'" and revisions would make "grieving . . . a disorder.").

91. Greg Miller and Constance Holden, "Proposed Revisions to Psychiatry's Canon Unveiled," *Science* 327 (Feb. 12, 2010): 5967; Allen Frances, "A Warning Sign on the Road to DSM-V: Beware of Its Unintended Consequences," *Psychiatric Times*, June 26, 2009; Robert L. Spitzer, "APA and DSM-V: Empty Promises," *Psychiatric Times*, July 2, 2009; Roger Collier, "DSM Revision Surrounded by Controversy" early release, *Canadian Medical Association Journal* (Nov. 17, 2009).

92. Allen Frances, "DSM-5 Field Trials Discredit the American Psychiatric Association," *Huffington Post*, Oct. 31, 2012, www.Huffingtonpost.com.

93. Ibid.

94. Ibid.

95. John Solomon, "FBI's Forensic Test Full of Holes," *Washington Post*, Nov. 18, 2007.

96. Lois Rogers, "The Expert as Judge and Jury," *London Sunday Times*, Nov. 18, 2007.

97. Keith Devlin, *Mathematical Association of America Newsletter* (July–Aug. 2007).

98. Joseph Sanders, "Expert Witness Ethics," *Fordham L. Rev.* 76, no. 1539 (Dec. 2007), quoting Samuel R. Gross, "Expert Evidence," *Wisc. L. Rev.* 1991: 1178.

99. "Trial Experts on Touchy Ground," *Louisville Courier-Journal*, Oct. 1, 2007.

100. Faith McLellan, "Mental Health and Justice: The Case of Andrea Yates," *Lancet* 368, no. 9551 (Dec. 2006): 1951–54.

101. See Kenneth S. Pope, "10 Fallacies in Psychological Assessment," http://kspope.com/fallacies/assessment.php, accessed Mar. 12, 2013.

102. See L. M. Schwartz and S. Woloshin, "How the FDA Forgot the Evidence: The Case of Donepezil 23 MG," *British Medical Journal* 344 (Mar. 22, 2012): e1086; Anthony G. Greenwald, "What (and Where) Is the Ethical Code concerning Researcher Conflict of Interest?" *Perspectives on Psychological Science* 4, no. 1 (Jan. 2009): 32–35, doi:10.1111/j.1745-6924.2009.01086.x.

103. See Whoriskey, "Can Drug Research Still Be Trusted?"; Keith Winston and Suzanne Sataline, "Health Journal Comes Clean; Correction Comes on Cancer Study Long under Cloud," *Wall Street Journal*, Apr. 3, 2008; Kevin Freking, "Drug Companies to Reveal Grant Practices," *Associated Press*, Apr. 11, 2008; Stephanie Saul, "Merck Wrote Drug Studies for Doctors," *New York Times*, Apr. 16, 2008.

104. Editorial, "An Unbiased Scientific Record Should Be Everyone's Agenda," *PLOS Med* 6, no. 2 (Feb. 23, 2009): e1000038, doi:10.1371/journal.pmed.1000038.

105. David H. Freedman, "Lies, Damned Lies, and Medical Science," *Atlantic*, Nov. 2010.

106. Sylvain Mathieu et al., "Comparison of Registered and Published Primary Outcomes in Randomized Controlled Trials," *J. of the Am. Med. Assoc.* 302, no. 9 (Sept. 2, 2000): 985; See also Whoriskey, "Can Drug Research Still Be Trusted?"

107. David B. Resnik, "Punishing Medical Experts for Unethical Testimony: A Step in the Right Direction or a Step Too Far?" *Journal of Philosophy, Science & Law* 4 (Dec. 7, 2004): 10, www.psljournal.com.

108. Paul M. Ridker and Jose Torres, "Reported Outcomes in Major Cardiovascular Clinical Trials Funded by For-Profit and Not-for-Profit Organizations: 2000–2005," *J. of Amer. Med. Assoc.* 295, no. 19 (2006): 2270; Winston and Sataline, "Health Journal." See also Ray Moynihan, "Doctors' Education: The Invisible Influence of Drug Company Sponsorship," *British Medical Journal* 336, no. 7641 (Feb. 23, 2010).

109. Allan Stone, "Conflicts of Interest," *Psychiatric News* 42, no. 18 (Sept. 29, 2007). See also Avery Johnson, Shirley Wang, and Jeanne Whalen, "AstraZeneca Drug's Effectiveness Questioned," *Wall Street Journal*, Feb. 28, 2009.

110. Gardiner Harris, "Academic Researchers' Conflicts of Interest Go Unreported," *New York Times*, Nov. 19, 2009.

111. Duff Wilson, "Drug Maker Said to Pay Ghostwriters for Journal Articles," *New York Times*, Dec. 13, 2008; news release, "Clinical Trials: Unfavorable Results Often Go Unpublished"; "Systematic Review of All the Existing Re-

search in This Area," Wiley-Blackwell, Publisher of the Cochrane Library from the UK Cochrane Center in Oxford, UK (Jan. 21, 2009); "Eli Lilly 'Ghostwrote' Articles to Market Zyprexa, Files Show,'" *Miami Herald*, June 13, 2009.

112. Resnik, "Punishing Medical Experts," 8.

113. Greenwald, "What (and Where) Is the Ethical Code"; Stone, "Conflicts of Interest."

114. Damon Adams, "Mississippi Board Approves Expert Witness Regulations," *American Medical News* 49, no. 23 (June 12, 2006).

115. Rich Daly, "Expert Medical Witnesses Get Heightened Scrutiny," *Psychiatric News* 42, no. 13 (July 6, 2007).

116. Ibid.

117. American Psychological Association, "Speciality Guidelines for Forensic Practice," http://www.apa.org/practice/guidelines/forensic-psychology.aspx, accessed Feb. 1, 2013.

118. Mark Hansen, "Three Strikes," *ABA Journal* (Nov. 2012): 58–59.

119. Resnik, "Punishing Medical Experts," 16.

120. Ibid., 19–20.

121. Adams, "Mississippi Board."

122. Joseph Sanders, "Expert Witness Ethics," *Fordham L. Rev.* 76, no. 1539 (Dec. 2007).

123. *Daubert v. Merrell Dow Pharmaceuticals*, 509 U.S. 579 (1993).

124. See Demosthenes Lorandos and Terence W. Campbell, *Benchbook in the Behavioral Sciences* (Durham, NC: Carolina Academic Press, 2005), 3–4, 14–17.

125. Brooks, "Tail Wags the Dog," 265.

126. Ibid., 285.

127. Monahan, "Structured Risk Assessment."

128. 293 F. 1013 (D.C. Cir. 1923).

129. Ibid., 1014.

130. John Parry and F. Philips Gilliam, *Handbook on Mental Disability Law* (Washington, D.C.: American Bar Association Publishing, 2003), 16, quoting from Federal Rule of Evidence 702.

131. 509 U.S. 579 (1993).

132. Parry and Gilliam, *Handbook*, 16.

133. Ibid., 17.

134. E. Beecher-Monas, "Epistemology," 360.

135. See Michael L. Perlin, "'Half-Wacked Prejudice Leaped Forth': Sanism, Pretexuality, and Why and How Mental Disability Law Developed As It Did," *J. of Contemp. L. Issues* 10 (1999): 3–36.

136. See Stone, "Conflicts of Interest"; Resnik, "Punishing Medical Experts"; Ridker and Torres, "Reported Outcomes"; Moynihan, "Doctors' Education"; Harris, "Academic Researchers' Conflicts of Interest"; Wilson, "Drug Maker."

137. Bernstein, "Expert Witnesses."

138. C. Guthrie, J. Rachlinski, and A. J. Wistrich, "Blinking on the Bench: How Judges Decide Cases," *Cornell Law Review* 93, no. 1 (2007):1-44.

139. Ibid.

140. Peter J. Smith, "New Legal Fictions," *Geo. L. J.* 95 (June 2007): 1435.

141. 463 U.S. 880 (1983).

142. Ibid.

143. Ibid., 900.

144. Ibid., 901.

145. Ibid.

146. *United States v. Sampson*, 335 F. Supp. 166, 219 (D. Mass. 2004).

147. E. Beecher-Monas, "Epistemology," 367–68.

148. See Greenwald, "What (and Where) Is the Ethical Code"; Resnik, "Punishing Medical Experts"; Adams, "Mississippi Board"; Daly, "Expert Medical Witnesses"; Sanders, "Expert Witness Ethics."

149. See John La Fond and Mary Durham, *Back to the Asylum: The Future of Mental Health Law and Policy in the United States* (New York: Oxford University Press, 1992); See, e.g., *In re Care and Treatment of Williams*, 2011 WL 1522363 (Kan. Sup. Ct., Apr. 22, 2011) (actuarial instrument scores that indicated less than 50 percent likelihood of recidivism could be used to support proof beyond a reasonable doubt); *In re G.L.D.*, 795 N.W. 2d 346 (N.D. Sup. Ct. 2011) (no error in believing state's expert over court-appointed independent expert and concluding that there was clear and convincing evidence supporting commitment).

150. Edward Stein, "The Admissibility of Expert Testimony about Cognitive Science Research on Eyewitness Identification," *Law, Probability and Risk* 2, no. 4 (2003): 295–303; Brett Trowbridge, "Admissibility of Expert Testimony concerning Eyewitness Evidence in Washington on Post Traumatic Stress Disorder and Related Trauma Syndromes: Avoiding the Battle of the Experts by Restoring the Use of Objective Psychological Testimony in the Courtroom," *Seattle U Law Review* 27 (2003): 453. See also editorial, "Tainted Witness," *New York Times*, Nov. 3, 2011; editorial, "What Did They Really See?" *New York Times*, Aug. 27, 2011; Stephen Hunt, "High Court Ruling to Allow Eyewitness Experts' Testimony; Overturns Guilty Verdict," *Salt Lake Tribune*, Dec. 19, 2009 (until this recent opinion, Utah was part of the majority of jurisdictions that made it very difficult for such testimony to be deemed admissible).

151. Christopher Slobogin, "The Supreme Court's Recent Criminal Mental Health Cases," *Criminal Justice* 22, no. 3 (Fall 2007): 8, 13.

152. *Sanborn v. Parker*, 629 F.3d 554 (6th Cir. 2010).

153. La Fond and Durham, *Back to the Asylum*. See also K. A. Findley, "Innocents at Risk: Adversary Imbalance, Forensic Science, and the Search for Truth," *Seton Hall L. Rev.* 38 (2008): 893, 928.

154. C. Slobogin, "Supreme Court's Recent Criminal Mental Health Cases."

155. See Torrey, *Insanity Offense*.

156. Edward J. Imwinkelried, "Impoverishing the Trier of Fact: Excluding the Proponent's Expert Testimony Due to the Opponent's Inability to Afford Rebuttal Evidence," *Conn. L. Rev.* 40 (Dec. 2007): 317. See also David Medine, "The Constitutional Right to Expert Assistance for Indigents in Civil Cases," *Hastings L. J.* 41 (1989–1990): 281.

157. Fazel, Singh, Doll, and Grann, "Use of Risk Assessment Instruments."

158. K. Bouton, "From Hitler to Mother Teresa: 6 Degrees of Empathy," *New York Times*, June 14, 2011.

5. ASSUMPTIONS BASED ON THE UNKNOWABLE

1. See Samuel J. Brakel, "Involuntary Institutionalization," in *The Mentally Disabled and the Law*, ed. Samuel Jan Brakel, John Parry, and Barbara A. Weiner 3d ed. (Chicago: American Bar Foundation, 1985), 22–31.

2. See chapter 1.

3. Dena Potter, "Mental Patients Isolated for Years Despite Laws," *Associated Press*, Dec. 24, 2008.

4. Based on the increasing number of such cases reported in the American Bar Association's *Mental & Physical Disability Law Reporter*, particularly in 2010 and 2011, which covered virtually every such case that can be found using WESTLAW.

5. Treatment Advocacy Center, "Restoring Reason to Treating Mental Illness," www.Treatmentadvocacycenter.org, accessed Dec. 3, 2010. See also John Parry, *Civil Mental Disability Law, Evidence and Testimony* (Chicago: American Bar Association, 2010), 489–93.

6. T. N. Wanchek and R. J. Bonnie, "Use of Longer Periods of Temporary Detention to Reduce Mental Health Civil Commitments," *Psychiatric Services*, July 1, 2012, doi:10.1176/appi.ps.201100359.

7. Bruce Winick, "Civil Commitment," in *Encyclopedia of Psychology & Law*, ed Brian L. Cutler (Thousand Oaks, CA: Sage Publications, 2008), www.brucewinick.com, last accessed Dec. 3, 2010. See also V. A. Hiday et al., "Outpatient Commitment for 'Revolving Door' Patients: Compliance and Treatment," *J. of Nervous and Mental Disease* 179, no. 2 (1991): 83–88.

8. See chapter 6.

9. See David A. Pollack, "Moving from Coercion to Collaboration in Mental Health Services," Substance Abuse and Mental Health Services Administration (2004); B. Link, D. M. Castille, and J. Stuber, "Stigma and Coercion in the Context of Outpatient Treatment of Persons with Mental Illnesses," *Social Science & Medicine* 67 (Apr. 30, 2008), www.elsevier.com/locate/socscimed; P. H. Rawal et al., "Regional Variation and Clinical Indicators of Antipsychotic Use in Residential Treatment: A Four-State Comparison," *J. of Behav. Health Services & Research* 31, no. 2 (Apr. 2004).

10. National Disability Rights Network 2007 Annual Report, http://www.ndrn.org/pub/AnnRept/2007%20PAIMI%20Report.pdf, accessed Nov. 15, 2010. (The federally created Protection and Advocacy for Individuals with Mental Illness program, which exists in every state and the District of Columbia, reported in 2007 that over 25 percent of the complaints that they handled involved overmedication and the failure to provide other more appropriate treatments.) See also R. L. Binder and D. E. McNiel, "Emergency Psychiatry: Contemporary Practices in Managing Acutely Violent Patients in 20 Psychiatric Emergency Rooms," *Psychiatric Services* 50 (Dec. 1999): 1553–54 ("One could argue that these practices involve risks of excessive coercion, overmedicating patients, and exacerbating underlying medical conditions.")

11. See Bazelon Center for Mental Health, "Fact Sheet: Children in Residential Centers," www.bazelon.org, accessed July 2, 2009; Robert L. Findling, "Dosing of Atypical Antipsychotics in Children and Adolescents," *Primary Care Companion J. Clin. Psychiatry* 5, supp. 6 (2003): 10; David Satcher, "Overview of Cultural Diversity and Mental Health Services," in *Mental Health: A Report by the Surgeon General* (Rockville, MD: Department of Health and Human Services, 1999); Laura Odesky, "Nursing Home Investigation Finds Errors by Druggists," *New York Times*, Jan. 29, 2012; Paula Span, "Overmedication in the Nursing Home," *New York Times*, Jan. 11, 2010; V. Molinari et al., "Provision of Psychopharmacological Services in Nursing Homes," *J. Gerontology: Psychological Science* 65 (Jan. 2010): 157; and Laurie Tarkan, "Doctors Say Medication Is Overused in Dementia," *New York Times*, June 24, 2008.

12. See "Failing to Treat Mental Illness," Treatment Advocacy Center, www.treatmentadvocacycenter.org, accessed Feb. 20, 2010; E. Fuller Torrey, *The Insanity Offense* (New York: W. W. Norton, 2008); T. Phi Le, "Mind over Murder," *Washington Lawyer*, Feb. 2012, 21–28.

13. See Le, "Mind over Murder," 24–26, 28; Ruth O'Brien, *Crippled Justice: The History of Modern Disability Policy in the Workplace* (Chicago: University of Chicago Press, 2001), 63–87; Bazelon Center on Mental Health Law, "Position Statement on Involuntary Commitment," www.bazelon.org, accessed Feb. 20, 2010.

14. Le, "Mind over Murder," 24.

15. Ibid., 28.

16. General Accounting Office, "Mental Health: Community-Based Care Increases for People with Serious Mental Illness," GA #01-224 (Fed. Document Clearinghouse, 2000). See also Le, "Mind over Murder."

17. Steven Gold, "Nursing Home Industry's Political Contributions and Congress' Failure to Enact the Community Choice Act," *Information Bulletin* no. 257 (Aug. 8, 2008).

18. See Council of State Governments, *Criminal Justice Mental Health Consensus Project* (June 2002).

19. Marc Lacey, Kevin Sack, and A. G. Sulzberger, "States' Budget Crises Cut Deeply into Financing for Mental Health Programs," *New York Times*, Jan. 20, 2011.

20. See Torrey, *Insanity Offense*.

21. See Le, "Mind over Murder," 21, 23–24.

22. Mark Fritz, "A Doctor's Fight: More Forced Care for the Mentally Ill; Torrey's Push for State Laws Sparks Growing Debate over Rights of Patients," *Wall Street Journal*, Feb. 1, 2006. See also Amy Lynn Sorrel, "Involuntary Outpatient Treatment for Mentally Ill Spurs New Debate; Advocates Say It's the Best Way to Protect Patients and the Public; Opponents Argue That It Violates Civil Liberties," *American Medical News* 49, no. 10 (March 6, 2006); Allison Pfeffer, note: "'Imminent Danger' And Inconsistency: The Need for National Reform of the 'Imminent Danger' Standard for Involuntary Civil Commitment in the Wake of the Virginia Tech Tragedy," *Cardozo L. Rev.* 30 (Sept. 2008): 277.

23. See Council of State Governments, *Criminal Justice*; H. Stuart, "Violence and Mental Illness: An Overview," *World Pschiatry* 2, no. 2 (June 2003): 121–24.

24. See John Monahan, "Structured Risk Assessment of Violence," in *Textbook of Violence Assessment and Management*, ed. R. Simon and K. Tardiff (Washington, D.C.: American Psychiatric Publications, 2008); Vernon Quinsey et al., *Violent Offenders: Appraising and Managing Risk* 2d ed. (Washington, D.C.: American Psychological Association, 2006), §10:17.

25. Christyne E. Ferris, "The Search for Due Process in Civil Commitment Hearings: How Procedural Realities Have Altered Substantive Standards," *Vanderbilt. L. Rev.* 61 (Apr. 2008): 959.

26. See chapter 6.

27. See Nassim N. Taleb, *The Black Swan: The Impact of the Highly Improbable* (New York: Random House, 2009).

28. See B. Ennis and T. Litwack, "Psychiatry and the Presumption of Expertise: Flipping Coins in the Courtroom," *Calif. L. Rev.* 62 (1974): 639; A. Stone, "The *Tarasoff* Decisions: Suing Psychotherapists to Safeguard Society," *Harv. L. Rev.* 90 (1976): 358.

29. Michael L. Perlin, "'I Might Need a Good Lawyer, Could Be Your Funeral, My Trial': Global Clinical Legal Education and the Right to Counsel in Civil Commitment Cases," *Washington University Journal of Law and Policy* 28, no. 1 (2008): 241.

30. Ibid.

31. *Goetz v. Crosson*, 967 F.2d 29 (1992); See also W. M. Brooks, "The Tail Wags the Dog: The Persuasive and Inappropriate Influence by the Psychiatric Profession on the Civil Commitment Process," *N. Dakota L. Rev.* 86 (2010): 259, 263–64.

32. Edward J. Imwinkelried, "Impoverishing the Trier of Fact: Excluding the Proponents Testimony Due to the Opponent's Inability to Afford Rebuttal Evidence," *Conn. L. Rev.* 40 (Dec. 2007): 317.

33. Ibid.

34. Brooks, "Tail Wags the Dog," 263–64.

35. See J. Waldman, "Should Dangerousness Indicate Inpatient Psychiatric Treatment," *CPA Bulletin de l'APC*, June 2003; Brooks, "Tail Wags the Dog," 284–87.

36. Ibid.

37. Editorial, "Good Neighbors," *New York Times*, Nov. 7, 2008.

38. J. Monahan, "Mandated Community Treatment: Applying Leverage to Achieve Adherence," *J. Am. Acad. Psychiatry Law* 36 (2008): 282–85; David Ignatius, "Helping the Mentally Ill: There Are Tools, If We're Willing to Use Them," *Washington Post*, Jan. 19, 2011; Le, "Mind over Murder," 28.

39. 527 U.S. 581 (1999).

40. See D. Ferleger, "The Constitutional Right to Community Services," *Georgia. St. U. L. Rev.* 26 (2010): 764.

41. See Parry, *Civil Mental Disability Law*, 467–75.

42. Brooks, "Tail Wags the Dog," 287–91.

43. Ibid., 267–69, 291–97; Parry, *Civil Mental Disability Law*.

44. Parry, *Civil Mental Disability Law*.

45. Ibid., 470.

46. See chapter 6.

47. *Parham v. J.R.*, 442 U.S. 584 (1979).

48. Parry, *Civil Mental Disability Law*, 493–94.

49. Ibid., 469–71; See also Melinda Beck, "Confusing Medical Ailments with Mental Illness," *Wall Street Journal*, Aug. 9, 2011; Carla K. Johnson, "Mentally Ill Violence in Nursing Homes?" *Associated Press*, Mar. 22, 2009.

50. Parry, *Civil Mental Disability Law*, 659. See also John Parry and Eric Y. Drogin, *Civil Law Handbook on Psychiatric and Psychological Evidence and Testimony* (Washington, D.C.: American Bar Association Publishing, 2001), 323.

51. *Clark v. Arizona*, 126 S. Ct. 2709 (2006).

52. Demosthenes Lorandos and Terence W. Campbell, *Benchbook in the Behavioral Sciences* (Durham, NC: Carolina Academic Press, 2005), 114; A. Tsesis, "Due Process in Commitments," *Wash & Lee L. Rev.* 68 (2011): 293–95; J. C. Wakefield, "False Positives in Psychiatric Diagnoses: Implications for Human Freedom," *Theoretical Med. & Bioethics* 31 (2010): 5, 9.

53. See *In re M.D.W.*, 45 P.3d 1046 (Or. Ct. App. 2002).

54. *O'Connor v. Donaldson*, 422 U.S. 564 (1975).

55. See Parry, *Civil Mental Disability Law*, 472–75.

56. See *U.S. v. Comstock*, 130 S. Ct. 1949 (2010).

57. See Parry, *Civil Mental Disability Law*, 472–75.

58. *Kansas v. Hendricks*, 521 U.S. 346, 357 (1997).

59. Ark. Code Ann. §§20-47-202(17),-207(c)(1)(C).

60. Utah Code §§62A-15-602(13),-631(3).

61. Va. Code Ann. §37.2-817(C).

62. Parry, *Civil Mental Disability Law*, 472–75.

63. Ibid., 473–75.

64. Ibid., 484–89.

65. See Ark. Code Ann. §§20-47-202(17),-207(c)(1)(C); Utah Code §§62A-15-602(13),-631(3); Va. Code Ann. §37.2-817(C).

66. Parry, *Civil Mental Disability Law*, 474–75.

67. Ibid., 474.

68. Ibid., 473–75.

69. Ariz. Rev. Stat. Ann. §36-501(33).

70. Alaska Stat. §47.30.915(7).

71. See Utah Code §§62A-15-602(13),-631(3); Va. Code Ann. §37.2-817(C).

72. See Parry, *Civil Mental Disability Law*, 472–73, 485–89.

73. Ibid., 482–83; *People v. Hoffman*, 489 N.E.2d 460, 465 (Ill. App. 1986)

74. See J. Monahan, editorial, "Statistical Literary: A Prerequisite for Evidence-Based Medicine," *Psychological Science in the Public Interest* 8, no. 2 (2008): i–ii.

75. S. P. Segal, "Civil Commitment Law, Mental Health Services, and US Homicide Rates," *Social Psychiatry and Psychiatric Epidemiology* 47, no. 9 (Nov. 10, 2011): 1449–58, doi: 10.1007/s00127-011-0450-0.

76. *Lidberg v. Steffen*, 514 N.W.2d 779 (Minn. 1994).

77. *Thomas v. State Department of Mental Health and Mental Retardation*, 620 So. 2d 18 (Ala. Civ. App. 1993).

78. J. Monahan and E. Silver, "Judicial Decision Thresholds for Violence Risk Management," *International Journal of Forensic Mental Health* 2, no. 1 (2003): 1.

79. *In re Victor*, 665 A.2d 8 (Pa. Super. Ct. 1995).

80. See, Parry, *Civil Mental Disability Law*, 482–84.

81. Ibid., 472.

82. *In re Gregory R.*, 590 N.W.2d 282 (Wis. App. 1999).

83. *In re Rovelstad*, 67 N.E.2d 720 (Ill. App. 1996).

84. Brooks, "Tail Wags the Dog," 264, 293. See, e.g., *Suzuki v. Yuen*, 617 F.2d 173, 176 (9th Cir. 1980); *State v. Krol*, 344 A.2d 289, 301 (N.J. 1975).

85. *In re Nyflot*, 340 N.W.2d 178 (N.D. 1983), cited with approval in *In re H.G.*, 632 N.W.2d 458 (N.D. 2001).

86. See *Commonwealth v. Grant*, 73 Mass. App. Ct. 471 (2009) (quasi-civil commitment of sexual offender); *Lynch v. Baxley*, 386 F. Supp. 378, 392 (D. Ala. 1974).

87. *Jones v. United States*, 463 U.S. 354 (1983).

88. Alan Dershowitz, "The Origins of Preventive Confinement in Anglo-American Law—Part I: The English Experience," 43 *U. Cin. L. Rev.* 1 (1974).

89. Brooks, "Tail Wags the Dog," 265.

90. J. K. Cornwell, "Understanding the Role of the Police and *Parens Patriae* Powers in Involuntary Civil Commitment before and after Hendricks," *Psychol. Pub. Policy & L.*, 4 (1998): 377, 378 n. 6.

91. Office of Applied Studies, SAMHSA, National Survey of Substance Abuse Treatment Services (N-SSATS), 2002, table 4.2a.

92. "Substance Abuse Treatment Admissions Referred by the Criminal Justice System: 2002," Drug and Alcohol Services Information Report, SAMHSA, July 30, 2004.

93. "Coerced Treatment among Youths: 1993–1998," Drug and Alcohol Services Information System, SAMHSA (Sept. 21, 2001).

94. Ibid.

95. T. Kaplan and D. Hakim, "New York Has Gun Deal, with Focus on Mental Ills," *New York Times*, Jan. 14, 2013.

96. B. Dennis and L. H. Sun, "Mental-Health Data Prove Elusive," *Washington Post*, Jan. 17, 2013.

97. "House OKs Gun Bill to Limit Buys by Mentally Ill," *Washington Times*, June 13, 2007.

98. 18 U.S.C. §922(g)(4).

99. Ibid.

100. Pub. L. No. 110–180 (Jan. 8, 2008), 122 Stat. 2559.

101. 18 U.S.C. §922(g)(3).

102. *United States v. Yancey*, 621 F.3d 681 (7th Cir. 2010), 35 *MPDLR* 29.

103. *United States v. Waters*, 23 F.3d 29 (2d Cir. 1994), 18 *MPDLR* 650.

104. *United States v. Chamberlain*, 159 F.3d 656 (1st Cir. 1998), 23 *MPDLR* 31.

105. *United States v. Midgett*, 198 F.3d 143 (4th Cir. 1999), 24 *MPDLR* 39.

106. *United States v. B.H.*, 466 F. Supp. 2d 1139 (N.D. Iowa 2006), 31 *MPDLR* 19.

107. Ind. Code §§35-47-14-1 & 14-2.

108. Cal. Welf. & Inst. Code §5150.

109. *California v. Keil*, 73 Cal. Rptr. 3d 600 (App. 2008).

110. Ibid., 603.

111. Kaplan and Hakim, "New York."

112. Ibid.

113. *Morris v. Blaker*, 821 P.2d 482 (Wash. 1992).

114. Wash. Rev. Code §9.41.047.

115. Fla. Stat. §790.065(2)(a)(4)(d); Iowa Code §724.31.

116. Me. Rev. Stat. Ann. tit. 15, §393.

117. Ariz. Rev. Stat. §13-925.

118. Va. Code Ann. §18.2-308.1:1.

119. W.Va. Code §61-7-7.

120. Michael Luo, "Some with Histories of Mental Illness Petition to Get Their Gun Rights Back," *New York Times*, July 2, 2011.

121. "Background Paper," Subcommittee on Criminal Justice, New Freedom Commission on Mental Health (June 2004), 3; D. J. James and L. E. Glaze, "Mental Health Problems of Prison and Jail Inmates," Bureau of Justice Statistics Special Report (Sept. 2006).

122. See M. I. Jeffery, "An Arctic Judge's Journey with FASD," *J. of Psych. & Law* 38, no. 4 (Winter 2010).

123. See, e.g., Ga. S.B. No. 39 (2011), *Ment & Phys. Dis. L. Rep.* 35 (2011): 570.

124. Joseph P. Morrissey et al., "New Models of Collaboration Between Criminal Justice and Mental Health Systems," *A. J. of Psychiatry* 166, no. 11 (Nov. 2009): 1211–14.

125. 18 U.S.C. § 4243.

126. See Morrissey, "New Models"; 18 U.S.C §4243.

127. See, e.g., *New Mexico v. Trujillo*, 2006 P.3d 125 (N.M. 2009).

128. *Born v. Thompson*, 117 P.3d 1098 (Wash. 2005) (clear and convincing evidence); *Massachusetts v. Hatch*, 783 N.E.2d 393 (Mass. 2003) (defendants may present evidence at a discretionary hearing that they did not commit the crimes alleged).

129. See, e.g., Colo. Rev. Stat. §16-8.5-111 (a court may choose to release a defendant found incompetent a second time for the same crime if the defendant agrees to obtain outpatient treatment); *Born v. Thompson*, 117 P.3d 1098 (Wash. 2005) (those charged with nonviolent misdemeanors).

130. Morrissey, "New Models."

131. See *New Mexico v. Trujillo*, 2006 P.3d 125 (N.M. 2009).

132. Nev. S.B. No. 380 (2007), *Ment. & Phys. Dis. L. Rep.* 31 (2007): 666.

133. *Jones v. United States*, 463 U.S. 354 (1983).

134. *Sastrom v. Psychiatric Sec. Rev. Bd.*, 938 A.2d 1233 (Conn. Ct. App. 2008).

135. *United States v. Beatty*, 2011 WL 1515216 (6th Cir. Apr. 22, 2011).

136. J. A. Ragazzo, "Forensic Mental Health Issues in Criminal Law: Statute and Case Summaries," California Protection & Advocacy, Inc., 2001; http://www.disabilityrightsca.org/pubs/507701.htm.

137. See Monica Davey, "Iowa's Residency Rules Drive Sex Offenders Underground," *New York Times*, Mar. 15, 2006.

138. MD S.B. 280 (2010), *Ment. & Phys. Dis. L. Rep.* 34 (2010): 663.

139. Ibid.

140. Norimitsu Onishi, "Suit Says New Law Violates Sex Offenders' Rights Online," *New York Times*, Nov. 18, 2012.

141. Ibid.

142. Ian Lovett, "Neighborhoods Seek to Banish Sex Offenders by Building Parks," *New York Times*, Mar. 9, 2013.

143. Onishi, "Suit Says."

144. Ibid.

145. In re Maedche, 788 N.W.2d 331 (N.D. Sup. Ct. 2010).

146. Cal. Penal Code 2960 *et seq.*

147. 18 U.S.C. §4246(a)(2000).

148. Ibid.

149. *U.S. v. Comstock*, 507 F. Supp. 2d 522 (4th Cir. 2009).

150. *U.S. v. Comstock*, 130 S.C. 1949 (2010).

151. Ibid. Note that the Supreme Court did not address the constitutionality of the federal law with respect to substantive and procedural due process arguments.

152. Editorial, "Wrong Turn on Sex Offenders," *New York Times*, Mar. 13, 2007.

153. Abby Goodnough and Monica Davey, "Effort to Track Sex Offenders Draws Resistance," *New York Times*, Feb. 9, 2009.

154. Washington State Institute for Public Policy, "Comparison of State Laws Authorizing Involuntary Commitment of Sexually Violent Predators, 2006 Update," Aug. 2007.

155. W. Lawrence Fitch, "Sexual Offender Commitment in the United States: Legislative and Policy Concerns," *Annals of the New York Academy of Sciences* 989 (2003): 489, 492.

156. Washington State Institute for Public Policy, "Comparison." In 2007, New Hampshire, RSA 135-E, and New York, chapter 7 of S.3318, enacted such laws. MD S.B. 280 (2010), *Ment. & Phys. Dis. L. Rep.* 34 (2010): 663. See also

Wendy Koch, "States Get Tougher with Sex Offenders," *USA Today*, May 24, 2006.

157. Mareva Brown and Sam Stanton, "Law Lets Sex Predators Avoid Treatment," *Sacremento Bee*, Feb. 16, 2006.

158. Jerry Markon, "Sex Offenders More Difficult to Monitor; Increased Arrests, Lack of Manpower, Electronics Cited," *Boston Globe*, Nov. 29, 2009.

159. Maggie Jones, "How Can You Distinguish Budding Pedophiles from Kids with Boundary Problems?" *New York Times*, July 18, 2007.

160. Jon Hurdle, "Court Asked to Allow Prosecution for 'Sexting,'" *Reuters*, Jan. 15, 2010; J. Hoffman, "A Girl's Nude Photo, and Altered Lives," *New York Times*, Mar. 28, 2011.

161. Jones, "How Can You Distinguish."

162. David Finkelhor, Richard Ormrod, and Mark Chaffin, "Juveniles Who Commit Sex Offenses against Minors," *Juvenile Justice Bulletin*, Dec. 2009.

163. *In re Interest of R.Y.*, 2008 WL 4380868 (Pa. Super. Ct. Sept. 29, 2008).

164. Ibid.

165. John Parry, "Sexually Violent Predators; Sexual Offenders," in *Mental and Physical Disability Law Digest*, section 2.03 (Washington, D.C.: American Bar Association, 2011): 1–2.

166. See chapter 6.

167. Robert A. Prentky, Eric Janus, Howard Barbaree, Barbara K. Schwartz, and Martin P. Kafka, "Sexually Violent Predators in the Courtroom: Science on Trial," William Mitchell College of Law, Legal Studies Research Paper Series, Working Paper No. 50 (Oct. 2006), 24–25, 29; Monica Davey and Abby Goodnough, "Doubts Rise as States Hold Sex Offenders after Prison, *New York Times*, Mar. 4, 2007.

168. Washington State Institute for Public Policy, "Comparison," 1, 5 (exhibit 3).

169. Davey and Goodnough, "Doubts" 168.

170. Ibid.

171. Adam Liptak, "Death Penalty in Some Cases of Child Sex Is Widening," *New York Times*, June 10, 2006.

172. *Kennedy v. Louisiana*, 554 U.S. 407 (2008).

173. Sara Kugler, *Associated Press*, June 25, 2008.

174. See Okla. Stat. Tit. 22 §1175.1 *et seq.*

175. Brenda C. Desmond and Paul J. Lenz, "Mental Health Courts: An Effective Way for Treating Offenders with Serious Mental Illness," *Ment. & Phys. Dis. L. Rep.* 34 (2010): 525, 528.

176. Ibid., 527.

177. Ibid., 526.

178. See *Born v. Thompson*, 117 P.3d 1098 (Wash. 2005); Ariz. Chap. 250, S.B. 1273, *Ment & Phys. Dis. L. Rep*. 19 (1995): 382; A.B. 2104 and 3130, S.B. 1391, amending Cal. Penal Code §§130 & 1370.1, 1600, 3000 and Cal. Welf. & Inst. Code §§4800, 4801, and adding Cal. Welf. & Inst. Code 6609 (1996), *Ment. & Phys. Dis. L. Rep*. 20 (1996): 887.

179. See, e.g., *New Mexico v. Trujillo*, 206 P.3d 125 (2009).

180. See, e.g., Nev. S.B. No. 380 (2007); Okla. Stat. tit. 22 §1175.1 *et seq*.

181. See *Connecticut v. Corr*, 867 A.2d 124 (Conn Ct. App. 2005); *Nagel v. Georgia*, 442 N.E.2d 446 (Ga. 1994).

182. See *Foucha v. Louisiana*, 504 U.S. 71 (1992) (some medical justification for continued commitment is enough); *Connecticut v. Corr*, 867 A.2d 124 (Conn. App. 2005) (failed to prove that he would continue to take his medication and receive other treatment if released).

183. See John Parry, *Criminal Mental Health and Disability Law, Evidence and Testimony* (Chicago: American Bar Association, 2009), 173; Candice M. Monson et al., "Stopping (or Slowing) the Revolving Door: Factors Related to NGRI Acquittees' Maintenance of a Conditional Release," *Law & Hum. Behav*. 25 (2001): 257.

184. See H. Cucolo and M. L. Perlin, "Preventing Sex-Offender Recidivism through Therapeutic Jurisprudence: Approaches and Specialized Community Integration," presented in part at the Academy of Criminal Justice Sciences annual conference, New York City, March 2012, http:/ssrn.com/sol3/papers.cfm?abstract=2116424. Citing A. Deming, "Sex Offender Civil Commitment Programs: Current Practices, Characteristics, and Resident Demographics," *J. Psychiatry & L*. 36 (2008): 439, 443.

185. See Ronald Bayer, *Homosexuality and American Psychiatry: The Politics of Diagnosis* (Princeton, NJ: Princeton University Press, 1987).

186. Chad Griffin, editorial: "Calling Out Hate Speech," *Washington Post*, Aug. 21, 2012.

187. Parry, "Sexually Violent Predators," 4–5.

188. See Cucolo and Perlin, "Preventing Sex-Offender Recidivism."

189. C. H. Sommers, "A False Portrait of U.S. Sexual Violence," *Washington Post*, Jan. 29, 2012.

190. *United States v. Kennedy*, 499 F.3d 547 (6th Cir. 2007).

191. American Psychiatric Association, *Diagnostic and Statistical Manual of Mental Disorders* (4th ed., text rev. 2000), 524 (paraphilias); R. A. Prentky, R. A. Knight, and A. F. S. Lee, "Risk Factors Associated with Recidivism among Extrafamilial Child Molesters." *Journal of Consulting and Clinical Psychology* 65, no. 1 (Feb. 1997): 141–49.

192. *United States v. Cope*, 506 F.3d 908 (9th Cir. 2007).

193. *Commonwealth v. Grant*, 73 Mass. App. Ct. 471 (2009).

194. Ibid.

195. *In re M.D.*, 757 N.W.2d 559 (N.D. 2008).

196. See Eric S. Janus and Robert A. Prentky, "Forensic Use of Actuarial Risk Assessment with Sex Offenders: Accuracy, Admissibility and Accountability," *Amer. Crim. Law Rev.* 40 (2003): 1443.

197. See Seena Fazel, Jay P. Singh, Helen Doll, and Martin Grann, "Use of Risk Assessment Instruments to Predict Risk of Violence and Antisocial Behaviour in 73 Samples Involving 24,827 People: Systematic and Meta-Analysis," *British Medical Journal* 345e (July 24, 2012): 4692.

198. See Janus and Prentky, "Forensic Use." See also Cucola and Perlin, "Preventing Sex-Offender Recidivism."

199. John Monahan, "Clinical and Actuarial Predictions of Violence," in *Modern Scientific Evidence: The Law and Science of Expert Testimony*, ed. David L. Faigman et al. (St. Paul, MN: West Group, 2005–2006 ed., updated Dec. 2008): §10.13.

200. Richard Wollert, "Low Base Rates Limit Expert Certainty When Current Actuarials Are Used to Identify Sexually Violent Predators: An Application of Bayes's Theorem," *Psychology, Pub. Policy & Law* 12, no. 1 (2006): 56–85.

201. Ibid. See also Prentky, Janus, Barbaree, Schwartz, and Kafka, "Sexually Violent Predators," 2.

202. Wollert, "Low Base Rates." See also Prentky, Janus, Barbaree, Schwartz, and Kafka, "Sexually Violent Predators," 14–24.

203. See Janus and Prentky, "Forensic Use." See also Cucola and Perlin, "Preventing Sex-Offender Recidivism."

204. Fazel, Singh, Doll, and Grann, "Use of Risk Assessment Instruments."

205. Joan Arehart-Treichel, "Psychiatrists, Criminal Justice Experts at Odds over Handling of Pedophiles," *Psychiatric News* 41, no. 10 (May 19, 2006).

206. K. M. Zgoba, and L. M. Simon, "Recidivism Rates of Sexual Offenders Up to 7 Years Later: Does Treatment Matter?" *Criminal Justice Rev.* 30, no. 2 (Sept. 2005): 155.

207. Prentky, Janus, Barbaree, Schwartz, and Kafka, "Sexually Violent Predators," 19.

208. Ibid.

209. T. Fortney et al., "Sexual Offender Treatment," *Sexual Offender Treatment* 2, no. 1 (2007), www.sexual-offender-treatment.org/55.html, accessed Feb. 11, 2010.

210. Ibid.

211. M. VanNostrand and Gena Keebler, "Pretrial Risk Assessment in Federal Court," (2009).

212. See Jane Mayer, "The Hard Cases," *New Yorker*, Feb. 23, 2009; P. Rosenzweig and J. Carafano, "Preventive Detention and Actionable Intelligence," Heritage Foundation, Sept. 16, 2004.

213. See *United States v. Salerno*, 481 U.S. 739 (1987).

214. Bureau of Justice Statistics, "Special Report: Federal Pretrial Release and Detention, 1996," Feb. 1999; Bureau of Justice Statistics, "Compendium of Federal Justice Statistics, 1998," May 2000; Bureau of Justice Statistics, "State Court Processing Statistics: Felony Defendants in Large Urban Counties, 2000," Dec. 2003. See also Russ Buettner, "Top Judge Says Bail in New York Isn't Safe or Fair," *New York Times*, Feb. 6, 2013 (only four states do not use public safety in making bail determinations).

215. See Council of State Governments, Criminal Justice Mental Health Consensus Project, "Pretrial Issues, Adjudication and Sentencing." See also, letter to the editor from Dora B. Schriro, commissioner, New York Department of Correction, "Bail and the Mentally Ill," *New York Times*, Feb. 8, 2013.

216. Schriro, "Bail and the Mentally Ill."

217. M. L. Perlin and K. K. Gould, "Rashomon and the Criminal Law: Mental Disability and the Federal Sentencing Guidelines," *American Journal of Criminal Law* 22 (1005): 431–60.

218. VanNostrand and Keebler, "Pretrial Risk Assessment."

219. See Council of State Governments, "Pretrial Issues."

220. Ibid.

221. Ibid.

222. See Buettner, "Top Judge."

223. See "Blueprint for Cost-Effective Pretrial Detention, Sentencing, and Corrections Systems," American Bar Association Criminal Justice Section (Aug. 2002), http://www.michbar.org/prisons/pdfs/MIBLUEPRINT.pdf.

224. BJS, Federal Pretrial Release, 2 (56,664 in 1996 for federal courts); BJS, Felony Defendants, 16 (projecting state courts monthly figure of 52,448 to be 629,375 per year for 37 percent of the population surveyed, which projects roughly to 1.7 million per year nationwide).

225. BJS, Felony Defendants, 16–17 (figure 10 and table 14).

226. BJS, Federal Pretrial Release, table 1 and appendix table 1A.

227. BJS, Felony Defendants, iv. See also Schriro, "Bail and the Mentally Ill."

228. BJS Compendium, 55 (table 4.3).

229. See Council of State Governments, "Policy Statement 11: Pretrial Release/Detention Hearing" ("It is particularly important . . . that mental illness itself not be used as a reason to detain a defendant.").

230. See Gary B. Melton et al., *Psychological Evaluations for the Courts*, 3d ed. (New York: Guilford Press, 1997), 418; Lisa A. Cintron, "Rehabilitating the

Juvenile Court System: Limiting Juvenile Transfers to Adult Criminal Court," *Northwestern U. L. Rev.* 90 (1996): 1254, 1258.

231. T. Guest, "The Evolution of Crime and Politics in America," *McGeorge L. Rev.* 33 (Summer 2002): 759, 762; See also Cintron, "Rehabilitating," 1258.

232. See chapter 6.

233. *Idaho v. Windom*, 2011 WL 891318 (Idaho Sup. Ct. Mar. 16, 2011).

234. 383 U.S. 541 (1966).

235. D. N. Brannen et al., "Transfer to Adult Court," *Psychology Pub. Policy & Law* 12 (Aug. 2006): 332.

236. Ibid.

237. Vanessa L. Kolbe, "A Cloudy Crystal Ball: Concerns Regarding the Use of Juvenile Psychopathy Scores in the Judicial Waiver Hearings," *Developments in Mental Health Law* 26, no. 1 (Jan. 2007): 1, 10.

238. Ibid.

239. Ibid., 1.

240. Carla Sharp and Sarah Kine, "The Assessment of Juvenile Pschopathy: Strengths and Weaknesses of Currently Used Questionnaire Measures," *Child & Adolescent Mental Health* 13, no. 2 (2008): 85–95.

241. Kolbe, "Cloudy Crystal Ball," 18.

242. James Austin, Kelly Dedel Johnson, and Maria Gregoriou, "Juveniles in Adult Prisons and Jails: A National Assessment," Bureau of Justice Assistance, Oct. 2000, x.

243. Ibid.

244. Ibid., 142.

245. Kolbe, "Cloudy Crystal Ball," 11.

246. Austin, Johnson, and Gregoriou, "Juveniles," 155.

247. J. H. Blume, S. P. Garvey, and S. L. Johnson, "Future Dangerousness in Capital Cases: Always 'At Issue,'" *Cornell L. Rev.* 86 (2001): 397, 404.

248. See, R. J. Tabak, "Capital Punishment," in *The State of Criminal Justice 2010*, ed. Myrna Raeder (Washington, D.C.: American Bar Association, 2011), 224–25.

249. Michael L. Perlin, *Mental Disability and the Death Penalty* (Lanham, MD: Rowman and Littlefield, 2013), 3.

250. Blume, Garvey, and Johnson, "Future Dangerousness." See also Christopher Slobogin, "Mental Illness and the Death Penalty," *Calif. Crim. L. Rev.* 1 (2000): 3

251. Blume, Garvey, and Johnson, "Future Dangerousness."

252. Ibid.

253. *Atkins v. Virginia*, 536 U.S. 304 (2002); See also American Bar Association, "Recommendation and Report on the Death Penalty and Persons with Men-

tal Disabilities" (adopted by ABA August 7–8, 2006), *Ment. & Phys. Dis. L. Rep.* 30 (2006): 668.

254. 126 S.Ct. 2516 (2006).

255. Ibid.

256. E. Beecher-Monas, "The Epistemology of Prediction: Future Dangerousness Testimony and Intellectual Due Process," *Wash. & Lee L. Rev.* 60 (Spring 2003): 353.

257. Texas Defender Service, "Deadly Speculation: Misleading Texas Capital Juries with False Predictions of Future Dangerousness," March 2004.

258. Ibid.

259. M. D. Cunningham, T. J. Reidy, and J. R. Sorensen, "Assertions of 'Future Dangerousness' at Federal Capital Sentencing: Rates and Correlates of Subsequent Prison Misconduct and Violence," *Law & Hum. Behav.* 32 (Feb. 2008): 46.

260. Ibid.

261. Ibid.

262. Ibid.

263. H. J. Steadman, "From Dangerousness to Risk Assessment of Community Violence: Taking Stock at the Turn of the Century," *J. Am. Acad. Psychiatry & Law* 28 (2000): 265–71.

264. Abram S. Barth, "A Double-Edged Sword: The Role of Neuroimaging in Federal Capital Sentencing," *Am. J. L. & Med.* 33 (2007): 501. See also O. C. Snead, "Neuroimaging and the 'Complexity' of Capital Punishment," *N.Y. U. L. Rev.* 82 (Nov. 2007): 1265.

265. Larry J. Siever, "Neurobiology of Aggression and Violence," *American Journal of Psychiatry* 165 (2008): 429.

266. See Barth, "Double-Edged Sword"; Snead, "Neuroimaging."

267. Benedict Carey, "Decoding the Brain's Cacophony," *New York Times*, Oct. 31, 2011 (summarizing Michael S. Gazzaniga, *Who's in Charge? Free Will and the Science of the Brain* [New York: HarperCollins, 2011]).

268. Fazel, Singh, Doll, and Grann, "Use of Risk-Assessment Instruments."

269. Ibid.

270. *Jones v. United States*, 527 U.S. 373 (1999).

271. Blume, Garvey, and Johnson, "Future Dangerousness."

272. 122 S. Ct. 2242 (2002).

273. 122 S. Ct. 2242 (2002).

274. *Stripling v. Georgia*, 2011 WL 2304667 (Ga. Sup. Ct. June 13, 2011); Ga OCGA §17-7-131(c)(3) and (j).

275. Ronald J. Tabak, "Foreward," in *The Future of America's Death Penalty: An Agenda for the Next Generation of Capital Punishment Research*, ed. Charles

S. Lanier, William J. Bowers, and James R. Acker (Durham, NC: Carolina Academic Press, 2009).

276. Editorial, "Mentally Retarded and on Death Row," *New York Times*, Aug. 3, 2012.

277. See W. J. Edwards and S. Greenspan, "Adaptive Behavior and Fetal Alcohol Spectrum Disorder," *J. of Psychiatry and Law* 38 (Winter 2010): 419–420, 443.

278. See death penalty cases involving persons with mental disabilities reported in the American Bar Association's *Mental and Physical Disability Law Reporter* (1990–2011).

279. Ibid.

280. Bureau of Justice Statistics report, *Mental Health and Treatment of Inmates and Probationers* (July 1999); President's New Freedom Commission on Mental Health, Subcommittee on Criminal Justice: Background Paper, June 2004, 1.

281. Major Peter Kageleiry, "Psychological Police Interrogation Methods: Pseudoscience in the Interrogation Room Obscures Justice in the Courtroom," *Military L. Rev.* 193 (Fall 2007): 1.

282. See Richard A. Leo, "The Third Degree and the Origins of Psychological Interrogation," in *Interrogations, Confessions, and Entrapment*, ed. G. Daniel Lassiter (New York: Kluwer Academic/Plenum Publishers, 2004), 58–60.

283. *Frazier v. Cupp*, 394 U.S. 731, 739 (1969*)*; *In re D.A.S.*, 391 A.2d 255 (D.C. App. 1978).

284. G. L. Blau and R. A. Pasework, "Statutory Changes and the Insanity Defense: Seeking the Perfect Insane Person," *Law & Psychology Rev.* 18 (1994): 69.

285. Blume, Garvey, and Johnson, "Future Dangerousness."

286. D. McMillan, R. P. Hastings, and J. Coldwell, "Clinical and Actuarial Prediction of Physical Violence in a Forensic Intellectual Disability Hospital: A Longitudinal Study," *J. of Applied Research in Intellectual Disabilities* 17, no. 4 (Dec. 2004)*:* 255–65.

287. See Edward J. Imwinkelried, "Impoverishing the Trier of Fact: Excluding the Proponent's Testimony Due to the Opponent's Inability to Afford Rebuttal Evidence," *Conn. L. Rev.* 40 (Dec. 2007): 317.

288. *Fairbank v. Ayers*, 632 F.3d 612 (9th Cir. 2011).

289. ABA Recommendation and Report on the Death Penalty and Persons with Mental Disabilities.

290. Editorial, "A Stay of Execution," *New York Times*, June 6, 2012.

6. DANGEROUSNESS AND THE UNCONSCIONABLE FAILURE TO PROVIDE HUMANE CARE AND TREATMENT TO PERSONS WITH SERIOUS MENTAL DISABILITIES

1. Developments in the Law—The Law of Mental Illness, "Introduction," *Harv. L. Rev.* 121 (Feb. 2008): 1114, quoting John F. Kennedy.

2. Joseph Heller, *Catch-22* (New York: Simon and Schuster, 1961).

3. *Wilson v. Seiter*, 501 U.S. 294, 298 (1991) (quoting *Rhodes v. Chapman*, 452 U.S. 337, 347 [1981]).

4. See A. Friel, T. White, and A. Hull, "Posttraumatic Stress Disorder and Criminal Responsibility," *J. of Forensic Psychiatry & Psychology* 19, no. 2 (2008): 64–85.

5. See Lizette Alvarez and Dan Frosch, "A Focus on Violence by Returning G.I.'s," *New York Times*, Jan. 2, 2009.

6. See Paul S. Appelbaum, "Thinking Carefully about Outpatient Commitment," *Psychiatric Services* 52, no. 3 (Mar. 2001): 347–48.

7. S. G. Kertesz et al., "Slowing the Revolving Door: Stabilization Programs Reduce Homelessness Persons' Substance Use after Detoxification," *J. of Subst. Abuse Treat.* 24, no. 3 (Apr. 2003): 197; Substance Abuse and Mental Health Services Administration, "Incarceration vs Treatment: Drug Courts Help Substance Abusing Offenders" part 1, *SAMHSA News 14*, no. 2 (Mar./Apr. 2006).

8. K. Coucouvanis et al., "Current Populations and Longitudinal Trends of State Residential Settings (1950–2003), University of Minnesota Research and Training Center on Community Living, 2004.

9. Anita Kumar, "Virginia to Transform Care of Developmentally Disabled," *Washington Post*, Jan. 27, 2012; D. Hakim, "U.S. Report Criticizes New York on Monitoring Care of Developmentally Disabled," *New York Times*, Jan. 10, 2012; D. Hakim, "In Treating Disabled, Potent Drugs and Few Rules," *New York Times*, Dec. 22, 2011; editorial, "Better Care for the Disabled," *New York Times*, Dec. 20, 2011.

10. See National Coalition of the Homeless, "Mental Illness and Homelessness," July 2009; S. Newman and H. Goldman, "Housing Policy for Persons with Severe Mental Illness," *Policy Studies Journal* 37, no. 2 (2009): 299–324. See also Bazelon Center for Mental Health Law, press release, "U.S. Justice Department Joins Advocates' *Lynn E. v. Lynch Suit* Citing Lack of Community Mental Health Services in New Hampshire," http://www.bazelon.org/News-Publications.aspx, accessed Mar. 28, 2012.

11. See Maia Szalavitz, "America's Failing Mental Health System: Families Struggle to Find Quality Care," *Times*, Dec. 20, 2012, http://health-land.time.com/2012/12/20/americas-failing-mental-health-system-families-

struggle-to-find-quality-care/; L. Aron, R. Honberg, K. Duckworth, et al., National Alliance on Mental Illness, "Grading the States 2009: A Report on America's Health Care System for Adults with Serious Mental Illness," March 2009, www.nami.org; P. Cunningham, K. McKenzie, and E. F. Fries, "The Struggle to Provide Community-Based Care to Low-Income People with Mental Illnesses," *Health Affairs* 25, no. 3, (May–June 2006): 694–95; National Institute of Mental Health, press release, "Mental Illness Exacts Heavy Toll, Beginning in Youth," June 6, 2005, www.nimh.nih.gov/science-news/2005.

12. Wayne A. Ray et al., "Atypical Antipsychotic Drugs and the Risk of Sudden Cardiac Death," *New England J. of Med.* 360, no. 3 (2009): 225–35.

13. See L. M. Szalavitz, K. Sack, and A. G. Sulzberger, "States' Budget Crises Cut Deeply into Financing for Mental Health Programs," *New York Times*, Jan. 20, 2011; D. Ignatius, "Helping the Mentally Ill: There Are Tools, If We Are Willing to Use Them," *Washington Post*, Jan. 19, 2011; editorial, "Housing and a Chance," *New York Times*, Jan. 22, 2011; A. Shin, "Suit Set on D.C.'s Care of Disabled," *Washington Post*, Dec. 23, 2010.

14. See Aron, Honberg, and Duckworth, "Grading the States"; Cunningham, McKenzie, and Fries, "Struggle."

15. Szalavitz, Sack, and Sulzberger, "States' Budget Crises"; Aaron Levin, "MH Services on Chopping Block as States Slash Spending," *Psychiatric News* 44, no. 5 (Mar. 6, 2009); Katie Zezima, "State Cuts Put Officers on Front Lines of Mental Care," *New York Times*, Dec. 5, 2010.

16. *Brown v. Plata*, 131 S. Ct. 1910, 1940 (2011).

17. Ibid.

18. United States House of Representatives, Committee on Government Reform—Minority Staff Special Investigations Division, "Incarceration of Youth Who Are Waiting for Community Mental Health Services in the United States," July 2004.

19. See National Coalition of the Homeless, "Mental Illness and Homelessness"; Newman and Goldman, "Housing Policy"; M. P. Acordino, D. F. Porter, and T. Morse, "Deinstitutionalization of Persons with Severe Mental Illness: Context and Consequences," *J. of Rehabilitation* 67, no. 2 (Apr.–June 2001).

20. See President's New Freedom Commission on Mental Health, Subcommittee on Criminal Justice, Background Paper, June 2004.

21. Gary B. Melton, Phillip M. Lyons, and William J. Spaulding, *No Place to Go: The Civil Commitment of Minors* (Lincoln: University of Nebraska Press, 1998), 1; S. Stagman and J. L. Cooper, "Children's Mental Health: What Policymakers Should Know," National Center for Children in Poverty, Apr. 2010, 1, http://nccp.org/publications/pub_929.html, accessed Dec. 7, 2011; International Society of Psychiatric-Mental Health Nurses, "Meeting the Mental Health Needs

of Youth in Juvenile Justice," Feb. 6, 2008, 1. See also Szalavitz, Sack, and Sulzberger, "States' Budget Crises."

22. Melton, Lyons, and Spaulding, *No Place to Go*, 4–5.

23. International Society of Psychiatric-Mental Health Nurses, "Meeting the Mental Health Needs," 1.

24. Ibid., 2.

25. Kumar, "Virginia"; Hakim, "U.S. Report Criticizes"; Hakim, "In Treating Disabled"; *New York Times* editorial, "Better Care."

26. National Center for Children in Poverty, "Children's Mental Health," 1.

27. Ibid.

28. J. M. Zito et al., "Psychotropic Medication Patterns among Youth in Foster Care," *Pediatrics* 121, no. 1 (Jan. 2008): 157–63.

29. Ibid.

30. Benedict Carey, "Drugs Used for Psychotics Go to Youths in Foster Care," *New York Times*, Nov. 22, 2011 (citing S. dos Reis et al., "Antipsychotic Treatment among Youth in Foster Care," *Pediatrics* 128, no. 6 (Dec. 2011): 1459–66.

31. Id. See L. A. Teplin et al., "Psychiatric Disorders in Juvenile Detention," *Archives of Gen. Psychiatry* 59 (2002): 1133–43.

32. *Associated Press*, "Mentally Ill Endanger Nursing Home Patients," Mar. 22, 2009.

33. Ibid.

34. Ibid.

35. Paula Span, "Overmedication in the Nursing Home," *New York Times*, Jan. 11, 2010, http://oldage.glogs.nytimes.com/2010/01/11/study-nursing-home-residents-overmedicated-undertreated/; See also L. Udesky, "Nursing Home Investigation Finds Errors by Druggists," *New York Times*, Jan. 29, 2012.

36. Span, "Overmedication"; Udesky, "Nursing Home Investigation."

37. Gardiner Harris, "Antipsychotic Drugs Called Hazardous for the Elderly," *New York Times*, May 9, 2011, citing Office of Evaluation and Inspection Services, "Medicare Atypical Antipsychotic Drug Claims for Elderly Nursing Home Residents," report (OEI-07-08-00150, May 4, 2011).

38. Ibid.

39. Span, "Overmedication," citing V. Molinari et al., "Provision of Psychopharmacological Services in Nursing Homes," *J Gerontol B Psychol Sci Soc Sci* 65B, no. 1 (2010): 57–60, doi: 10.1093/geronb/gbp080.

40. Ibid.

41. Ibid.

42. David Jackson and Gary Marx, "New Hope for Illinois' Mentally Ill Nursing-Home Residents," *Chicago Tribune*, Mar. 15, 2010.

43. Ibid.

44. Associated Press, *Winston-Salem Journal*, July 30, 2011.

45. Ibid.

46. Anemona Hartocollis, "In Deal, Hundreds of Mentally Ill People Will Leave Confinement of Nursing Home," *New York Times*, Sept. 13, 2011.

47. Ibid.

48. Danny Hakim, "Deal in Albany on Policing Abuse of Disabled," *New York Times*, June 17, 2012. See also Danny Hakim, "Cuomo Seeking New Agency to Police Care of Disabled," *New York Times*, May 6, 2012.

49. Kumar, "Virginia."

50. Laura Vozzella, "Left to Languish in Va. Hospitals," *Washington Post*, June 27, 2012.

51. See, D. A. Andrews and J. Bonta, "Rehabilitating Criminal Justice Policy and Practice," *Psychology, Public Policy & Law* 16, no. 1 (2010): 39–55; editorial, "The Misuse of Life without Parole," *New York Times*, Sept. 12, 2011; A. R. Hunt, "A Country of Inmates," *Bloomberg News*, Nov. 22, 2011, www.nytimes.com; editorial, "Falling Crime, Teeming Prisons," *New York Times*, Oct. 29, 2011.

52. Andrews and Bonta, "Rehabilitating"; Hunt, "Country of Inmates." See also editorial: "Treatment, Not Jail, for the Mentally Ill," *New York Times*, Jan. 31, 2013.

53. See D. B. Wexler, "Therapeutic Jurisprudence and Changing Conceptions of Legal Scholarship," *Behav. Sci & L.* 11 (1993): 17.

54. See J. Fellner, "A Corrections Quandry: Mental Illness and Prison Rules," *Harvard Civil Rights–Civil Liberties L.R.* 41 (2006): 392; *Brown v. Plata*, 131 S.Ct. 1910 (2011).

55. C. L. Blitz, N. Wolff, and J. Shi, "Physical Victimization in Prison: The Role of Mental Illness," *J. of L. and Psychiatry* 31, no. 5 (2009): 385–93.

56. See J. J. Gibbons and N. Katzenback, Vera Institute of Justice, "Confronting Confinement: A Report of the Commission on Safety and Abuse in America's Prisons, 2007, www.prisoncommission.org.; See also *Brown v. Plata*, 131 S.Ct. 1910 (2011); editorial, "Unsafe behind Bars," *New York Times*, May 28, 2012; editorial, "Sexual Abuse in Prisons," *Washington Post*, Apr. 29, 2012.

57. Editorial, "Cruel Isolation," *New York Times*, Aug. 1, 2011. See also "The Abuse of Solitary Confinement," *New York Times*, June 28, 2012.

58. Human Rights Watch, "Mental Illness, Human Rights, and US Prisons," statement for the record, Senate Judiciary Committee, Subcommittee on Human Rights and the Law, Sept. 22, 2009. See also editorial, "Cruel Isolation," *New York Times*, Aug. 1, 2011; editorial, "The Abuse of Solitary Confinement," *New York Times*, June 20, 2012.

59. *Brown v. Plata*, 131 S. Ct. 1910 (2011).

60. Fellner, "Corrections Quandry." See also editorial, "The Abuse of Solitary Confinement," *New York Times*, June 20, 2012; editorial, "Cruel Isolation," *New York Times*, Aug. 1, 2011.

61. See Jamie Floyd, "The Administration of Psychotropic Drugs to Prisoners: State of the Law and Beyond," *California Law Review* 78, no. 5 (Oct. 1990): 1243–85.

62. See Kathy Swedlow, "Forced Medication of Legally Incompetent Prisoners: A Primer," *Human Rights Magazine*, Winter 2002.

63. Fellner, "Corrections Quandry," 391.

64. Associated Press, "AP Exclusive: Calif. Prisons Spend Big On Anti-Psychotics for Inmates; Fear of Lawsuits Cited," *Wasthington Post*, May 1, 2013.

65. See N. Wolff, "Courts as Therapeutic Agents: Thinking Past the Novelty of Mental Health Courts," *J. Am Acad. Psychiatry Law* 30, no. 3 (Nov. 2002): 431, 432–33.

66. See M. A. Simons, "Departing Ways: Uniformity, Disparity and Cooperation in Federal Drug Sentences," *Villanova L. Rev.* 47 (2002): 921, 927–28; T. Guest, "The Evolution of Crime and Politics in America," *McGeorge L. Rev.* 33 (2002): 759, 767.

67. Editorial, "Dementia behind Bars," *New York Times*, Mar. 25, 2012.

68. Ibid.

69. See *Care and Treatment of Brasch v. Missouri*, 332 S.W.3d 115 (Mo. Sup. Ct. 2011) (lack of treatment is no bar to indeterminant confinement); *In Civil Commitment of Navratil*, 2011 Wo 2304169 (Minn. Ct. App. June 13, 2011) (lack of treatment made it "intrinsically probable" that the respondent continued to meet the sexually dangerous person criteria); See also H. Cucolo and M. L. Perlin, "Preventing Sex-Offender Recidivism through Therapeutic Jurisprudence: Approaches and Specialized Community Integration," presented in part at the Academy of Criminal Justice Sciences annual conference (New York City, Mar. 2012), http://papers.ssrn.com/sol3/papers.cfm?abstract_id=2116424; A. Deming, "Sex Offender Civil Commitment Programs: Current Practices, Characteristics, and Resident Demographics, *J. Psychiatry & L.* 36 (2008): 439, 443.

70. See *Sell v. United States*, 123 S. Ct. 2174 (2003).

71. Thai Phi Le, "Mind over Murder? Mental Health Cases Fuel Rights vs Safety Debate," *Washington Lawyer*, Feb. 2012, 28.

72. H. Worzel et al., "Crisis in the Treatment of Incompetence to Stand Trial: Harbinger of a Systemic Illness," *J. of Am. Acad. Psychiatry Law* 35, no. 3 (2007): 357.

73. Wexler, "Therapeutic Jurisprudence."

74. Barbara A Weiner, in *The Mentally Disabled and the Law*, ed. Samuel J. Brakel, John Parry, Barbara A. Weiner (Chicago: American Bar Foundation, 1985), 714, citing Mich. Comp. Laws. Ann. §768.36 (Supp. 1982).

75. Ibid., 708.

76. OCGA §§17-1-130.1, 131.

77. *Atkins v. Virginia*, 536 U.S. 304 (2002).

78. *Illinois v. Manning*, 883 N.E.2d 492 (Ill. Sup. Ct. 2008).

79. *People v. Kaeding*, 456, N.E.2d 11 (Ill. 1983); *State v. Neely*, 819 P.2d 249 (N.M. 1991).

80. See *Brown v. Plata*, 131 S.Ct. 1910 (2011).

81. *South Dakota, v. Pulfrey*, 548 N.W.2d 34 (S.D. 1996).

82. *Neely v. Newton*, 149 F.3d 1074 (10th Cir. 1998).

83. *Kentucky v. Ryan*, 1999 WL 680248 (Ky. Sup. Ct. Aug. 26, 1999); *Harris v. State*, 499 N.E.2d 723 (Ind. 1986), *cert denied*, 482 U.S. 909 (1987); *State v. Wilson*, 413 SE 2d 19 (S.C. 1992).

84. *Harris v. State*, 499 N.E.2d 723 (Ind. 1986), *cert denied*, 482 U.S. 909 (1987).

85. *Shepherd v. Georgia*, 626 S.E.2d 96 (Ga. 2006).

86. Ibid.

87. Samuel J. Brakel and Ronald S. Rock, *The Mentally Disabled and the Law* 2d ed. (Chicago: University of Chicago Press, 1971), 380–81.

88. See Wayne A. Ray et al., "Atypical Antipsychotic Drugs and the Risk of Sudden Cardiac Death," *N. England J. Med.*, 360 (2009): 225–35.

89. John Parry, *Criminal Mental Health and Disability Law, Evidence and Testimony* (Chicago: American Bar Association, 2009), 104–6; See also Melody McDonald, "Judge Rules Condemned Man Must Take Anti-Psychotic Drug," *Star-Telegram.com*, Apr. 11, 2006.

90. 123 S.Ct. 2174 (2003).

91. *Singleton v. Norris*, 124 S. Ct. 74 (2003).

92. See, e.g., Calif. S.B. No. 1794 (2004), which requires courts to order the involuntary administration of antipsychotic medications if the factors established by the U.S. Supreme Court exist, and *United States v. Bradley*, 417 F.3d 1107 (10th Cir. 2005), where the Tenth Circuit ruled that testimony that a clinical psychologist was guardedly optimistic that the medication to be administered involuntarily would help restore a defendant's competency was sufficient to show that it was medically appropriate.

93. See Calif. S.B. No. 1794; *U.S. v. Bradley*.

94. President's New Freedom Commission on Mental Health, Subcommittee on Criminal Justice: Background Paper, June 2004, 1–5.

95. *Gates v. Cook*, 376 F.3d 323 (5th Cir. 2004).

96. Ibid.

97. See H. I. Schwartz, "Death Row Syndrome and Demorilization: Psychiatric Means to Social Policy Ends," *J. Am. Acad. Psych. L.* 33, no. 2 (June 2005): 153.

98. Ibid.

99. See, e.g., *Brown v. Plata*, 131 S. Ct 1910; *Coleman v. Schwartznegger*, 2009 WL 2430820 (E.D. Cal. Aug. 4, 2009).

100. Joseph A. Califano, Jr., "Copping Out on Kids; Both Candidates Ignore the Most Vexing Threat to Converting Their Rhetoric Into Reality: Drug, Alcohol and Tobacco Abuse and Addiction," *Washington Post*, July 13, 2000 (citing the National Center on Addiction and Substance Abuse at Columbia University).

101. M. A. Simons, "Departing Ways: Uniformity and Cooperation in Federal Drug Sentences," *Villanova L. Rev.* 47 (2002): 921, 925.

102. Ibid.

103. *United States v. Booker*, 543 U.S. 220 (2005).

104. See Developments in the Law—The Law of Mental Illness.

105. *United States v. Portman*, 2007 WL 3231438 (N.D. Ill. Oct. 26, 2007), aff'd 599 F.3d 633 (7th Cir. 2010).

106. See Developments in the Law: The Law of Mental Illness, "Mental Health Courts and the Trend toward a Rehabilitative Justice System," 1168.

107. Ibid.

108. Joseph P. Morrissey et al., "New Models of Collaboration between Criminal Justice and Mental Health Systems," *A. J. of Psychiatry* 166, no. 11 (Nov. 2009): 1211–14.

109. Human Rights Watch, "Mental Illness, Human Rights, and U.S. Prisons," Senate Judiciary Committee Subcommittee on Human Rights and the Law, 2010; Human Rights Watch, "Ill-Equipped: US Prisons and Offenders with Mental Illness," Oct. 2003, www.hrw.org/en/reports/2003/10/21/ill-equipped-0.

110. NAMI, "Grading the States 2009." See also Szalavitz, Sack, and Sulzberger, "States' Budget Crises."

111. Eve Bender, "Youth Sentenced to Adult Prisons Have High Mental Illness Rates," *Psychiatric News* 43, no. 18 (2008).

112. S. J. Boretos, "The Role of Discrimination and Drug Policy in Excessive Incarceration in the United States," *U. D.C. L. Rev.* 6 (Fall 2001): 73, 87.

113. See, e.g., Human Rights Watch, "Mental Illness, Human Rights, and U.S. Prisons," Senate Judiciary Committee, Subcommittee on Human Rights and the Law, 2010; "United States: Human Rights Developments," *Human Rights Watch World Report*, 2001, http://www.hrw.org/wr2k1/usa/index.html, accessed May 25, 2006; Human Rights Watch, "Ill-Equipped: US Prisons and Offenders with Mental Illness."

114. Katherine Harmon, "Brain Injury Rate 7 Times Greater among U.S. Prisoners," *Scientific American*, Feb. 4, 2012, www.scientificamerican.com/article.cfm?id=traumatic-brain-injury-prison.

115. "United States: Human Rights Developments," *Human Rights Watch World Report*, 2001, 10, http://www.hrw.org/wr2k1/usa/index.html, accessed May 25, 2006.

116. John Pomfret, "California's Crisis in Prison Systems: A Threat to Public," *Washington Post*, June 11, 2006.

117. Ibid.

118. Ibid.

119. Human Rights Watch, "Mental Illness, Human Rights, and U.S. Prisons," Senate Judiciary Committee, Subcommittee on Human Rights and the Law, Sept. 22, 2009.

120. Ibid.

121. Ibid.

122. Malia Wollan, "Judges to Decide Whether Crowded California Prisons Are Unconstitutional," *New York Times*, Dec. 8, 2008.

123. Solomon Moore, "Court Orders California to Cut Prison Population," *New York Times*, Feb. 10, 2009.

124. *Brown v. Plata*, 563 U.S. (2011).

125. Ibid.

126. See, e.g., editorial, "Hard Times for the Right to Counsel," *New York Times*, Nov. 21, 2008.

127. 18 U.S.C. §3626.

128. *Scarver v. Litscher*, 2006 WL 120430 (7th Cir. Jan 18, 2006).

129. Ibid.

130. *Brown v. Plata*, 131 S. Ct. 1910 (2011).

131. See chapter 5.

132. *In re Victor*, 665 A.2d 8 (Pa. Super. Ct. 1995).

133. John Parry, *Civil Mental Disability Law, Evidence and Testimony* (Chicago: American Bar Association, 2010), 473–75, 486–87.

134. *In re Det. of Post*, 241 P.3d 1234 (Wash. Sup. Ct. 2010). See also Cucolo and Perlin, "Preventing Sex-Offender Recidivism."

135. See, e.g., *Care and Treatment of Brasch v. Missouri*, 332 S.W.3d 115 (Mo. 2011).

136. *Youngberg v. Romeo*, 457 U.S. 307 (1982).

137. John Parry, "Involuntary Civil Commitment in the 90's: A Constitutional Perspective," *Ment. & Phys. Dis. L. Rep.* 18 (1994): 320, 323–24.

138. See chapter 3.

139. See, e.g., *United States v. Beatty*, 2011 WL 1515216 (6th Cir. Apr. 22, 2011) (insanity acquittee continued to be held even though he no longer had the mental condition for which he was found insane).

140. *Kansas v. Hendricks*, 521 U.S. 346 (1997).

141. *Seling v. Young*, 531 U.S. 250 (2001).

142. *Cerniglia v. County of Sacramento*, 2008 WL 2488669 (E.D. Cal. June 17, 2008).

143. Ibid.

144. *Seling v. Young*, 531 U.S. 250 (2001).

145. *Brown v. Plata*, 131 S. Ct. 1919 (2011).

146. Robert A. Prentky, Eric Janus, Howard Barbaree, and Barbara K. Schwartz, "Sexually Violent Predators in the Courtroom: Science on Trial," William Mitchell College of Law Legal Studies Research Paper Series, Working Paper No. 50 (Oct. 2006), 25.

147. Ibid.

148. Ibid.

149. D. Grubin and A. Beech, "Chemical Castration for Sex Offenders: Doctors Should Avoid Becoming Agents of Social Control," *British Medical Journal*, Jan. 2010), 340.

150. S. Shane, "Obama Defends Detention Conditions for Soldier Accused of WikiLeaks Case," *New York Times*, Mar. 12, 2011.

151. Ibid.

152. Cucolo and Perlin, "Preventing Sex-Offender Recidivism."

153. Abby Goodnough and Monica Davey, "For Sex Offenders, a Dispute over Therapy Benefits," *New York Times*, Mar. 6, 2007.

154. Mareva Brown and Sam Stanton, "Release of Sex Convict Delayed: Elk Grove, Folsom Protesters Say Proposed Sites Are Too Risky," *Sacramento Bee*, May 20, 2006.

155. Ibid.

156. Jason Grotto, "Some of Florida's Worst Sex Offenders Aren't Getting Treatment," *Macon, Georgia Telegraph*, Feb. 8, 2005.

157. See *Care and Treatment of Brasch v. Missouri*, 332 S.W.3d 115 (Mo. Sup. Ct. 2011); *In re Det. of Post*, 241 P.3d 1234 (Wash. 2010). See also Cucolo and Perlin, "Preventing Sex-Offender Recidivism."

158. Candace Rondeaux, "Can Castration Be a Solution for Sex Offenders? Man Who Mutilated Himself in Jail Thinks So. . . ." *Washington Post*, July 5, 2006.

159. Ibid.

160. Bureau of Justice Statistics, "Sexual Victimization in Juvenile Facilities Reported by Youth, 2008–09," Jan. 2010, bjs.ojp.usdoj.gov.

161. International Society of Psychiatric-Mental Health Nurses, "Meeting the Mental Health Needs," 2.

162. Ibid.

163. Ibid.

164. Ibid.

165. See B. Langemo, "Serious Consequences for Serious Juvenile Offenders: Do Juveniles Belong in Adult Court?" *Ohio N.U. L. Rev.* 30 (2004): 141; editorial, "Fixing the Mistake with Young Offenders," *New York Times*, Apr. 3, 2011.

166. See J. A. Butts and A. V. Harrell, "Delinquents or Criminals? Policy Options for Young Offenders," Urban Institute, June 1998, www.urban.org/urlprint.cfm?ID=6390.

167. Ibid. See also "ACLU Fact Sheet on the Juvenile Justice System," American Civil Liberties Union, June 2004, www.archive.aclu.org/library/fctsht.html.

168. Editorial, "Disgrace Unchecked," *Washington Post*, May 30, 2006.

169. Ibid.

170. Nicholas Confessore, "New York Finds Extreme Crisis in Youth Prisons," *New York Times*, Dec. 14, 2009.

171. Ibid.

172. See Langemo, "Serious Consequences"; Butts and Harrell, "Delinquents"; "ACLU Fact Sheet."

173. Ibid.

174. United States House of Representatives, Committee on Government Reform—Minority Staff Special Investigations Division, "Incarceration of Youth Who Are Waiting for Community Mental Health Services in the United States," July 2004.

175. Ibid.

176. Carol Miller, "Restraining of Mentally Ill Foster Kids Questioned," *Miami Herald*, Aug. 25, 2008.

177. Robert Pear, "Mental Care Poor for Some Children in State Custody," *New York Times*, Sept. 1, 2003; Chris L. Jenkins, "Mental Illness Sends Many to Foster Care: Medical Costs Overwhelm Va. Parents," *Washington Post*, Nov. 29, 2004.

178. Pear, "Mental Care."

179. U.S. House of Representatives, "Incarceration of Youth Who Are Waiting for Community Mental Health Services."

180. Ibid.

181. Bazelon Center for Mental Health Law, "Out of Luck and behind Bars," *In Brief*, Fall 2004, 3.

182. Id. See also D. S. George, "Teenager Suspended from Fairfax School over Acne Drug," *Washington Post*, Mar. 10, 2011; M. A. Chandler, "Birth Control Pill Lands Fairfax Girl Two Week Suspension," *Washington Post*, Apr. 5, 2009.

183. Editorial, "Writing Off Disabled Children," *New York Times*, Aug. 9, 2008.

184. Bazelon Center, "Out of Luck," 3.

185. Ibid.

186. Ibid.

187. Ibid. See also News Release, National Institute of Mental Health, Dec. 14, 2009.

188. Bazelon Center, "Out of Luck."

189. See Gardiner Harris, "Use of Antipsychotics in Children Is Criticized," *New York Times*, Nov. 19, 2008.

190. Bob Herbert, "Help Is On the Way," *New York Times*, Nov. 23, 2008; See also David Zucchino, "Military Suicides Rise to an Average of One a Day," *Los Angeles Times*, June 11, 2012.

191. Lisa A Brenner et al., "Suicidality and Veterans with a History of Traumatic Brain Injury: Precipitating Events, Protective Factors, and Preventive Strategies," *Rehabilitation Psychology* 54, no. 4 (2008): 390–97. See also E. Bumiller, "Suicides among Active Soldiers Hit Record; Sex Crimes Jump 30 Percent," *New York Times*, Jan. 18, 2012.

192. Herbert, "Help."

193. Ernesto Londono, "More U.S. Troops Lost to Suicide Than Combat in 2012," *New York Times*, Jan. 15, 2013.

194. Karen H. Seal et al., "Trends and Risk Factors for Mental Health Diagnoses among Iraq and Afghanistan Veterans Using Department of Veteran Affairs Health Care—2002–2008," *A. J. of Pub. Health* 99, no. 9 (Sept. 2009): 1651–58.

195. R. Jeffrey Smith, "Crime Rate of Veterans in Colorado Unit Cited," *Washington Post*, July 28, 2009.

196. Bumiller, "Suicides"; Associated Press, "Army Studying Why Soldiers Commit Violent Crimes," July 16, 2009. See also J. Dao, "Reprehensible Behavior Is a Risk of Combat, Experts Say," *New York Times*, Jan. 13, 2012.

197. D. Brown, "Combat Veterans at High Risk of Deadly Crashes," *The Washington Post,* May 6, 2013.

198. Seal et al., "Trends."

199. Ibid.

200. Cynthia M. A. Geppert, "From War to Home: Psychiatric Emergencies of Returning Veterans," *Psychiatric Times*, Oct. 8, 2009.

201. Ibid.

202. International Society of Psychiatric-Mental Health Nurses, "Meeting the Mental Health Needs," 2.

203. Ibid.

204. H. Bernton, "Soldiers' Emotional Battle Scars Put Doctors in Dilemma," *Seattle Times*, July 26, 2009.

205. K. Kennedy, "Studies Find Breakthrough in PTSD Treatment; Brain Scans, Blood Tests May Help Predict Condition," *Navy Times*, Dec. 27, 2009.

206. Ibid.

207. L. Downes, "For Many Returning Veterans, Home Is Where the Trouble Is," *New York Times*, Jan. 3, 2011; K. Hawkins, "Plan Gives Aid to Soldiers, Vets Coping with Coming Home," *Redstone Rocket*, Feb. 25, 2009, www.army.mil/news; B. Wegner, "The Difficult Reintegration of Soldiers to Society and Family After Deployment," ESSAI: Vol. 9, Article 41 (2011). Available at: http://dc.cod.edu/essai/vol9/iss1/41.

208. S. Maguen et al., "The Impact of Reported Direct and Indirect Killing on Mental Health Symptoms in the Iraq War Veterans," *J. of Traumatic Stress* 23, no. 1 (2010): 86; S. Maguen et al., "The Impact of Killing in War on Mental Health Symptoms and Related Functioning," *J. of Traumatic Stress* 22, no. 5 (2009): 435.

209. Alvarez and Frosch, "Focus"; See also Dao, "Reprehensible Behavior."

210. Dao, "Reprehensible Behavior." See also Bumiller, "Suicides."

211. Smith, "Crime Rate."

212. Ibid.

213. Christopher Hawthorne, "Bringing Baghdad into the Courtroom: Should Combat Trauma in Veterans Be Part of the Criminal Justice Equation?" *Criminal Justice* 24, no. 2 (Summer 2009): 5, 6.

214. James Dao, "As Military Suicides Rise, Focus Is on Private Weapons," *New York Times*, Oct. 7, 2012.

215. Ibid.

216. Thomas M. Keane, "Guest Editorial: Posttraumatic Stress Disorder: Future Directions in Science and Practice," *J. Rehabilitation Research and Development* 45, no. 3 (2008): vii.

217. Ibid.

218. Press Release, U.S. Department of Defense, July 3, 2009.

219. Ibid.

220. Benedict Carey, "Mental Stress Training Is Planned for U.S. Soldiers," *New York Times*, Aug. 18, 2009.

221. A. D. Mancini, "A Postwar Picture of Resilience," *New York Times*, Feb. 5, 2012.

222. Lynne Marek, "Courts for Veterans Spreading across U.S.," *National Law Journal*, Dec. 22, 2008.

223. Morrissey et al., 1211–14.

224. Sydney J. Freedberg, Jr., "Curing a Disabled System," *National Journal*, July 19, 2008, 61.

225. Ibid., 65; Bryan Bender, "Veterans Forsake Studies of Stress: Stigma Impedes Search for Remedies," *Boston Globe*, Aug. 24, 2009.

226. Katyharine Eupherat, "Suicide Hot Line Got Calls from 22,000 Veterans," *Associated Press*, July 28, 2008.

227. Reuters, "Judge Dismisses Lawsuit over War Veteran Care," June 25, 2008.

228. Editorial, "More Excuses and Delays from the V.A.," *New York Times*, Aug. 21, 2011, citing *Veterans for Common Sense v. Shinseki*, No. 08-16728 (9th Cir. May 10, 2011).

229. Ibid.

230. R. J. Nicholson and T. G. Bowman, "Vets Deserve Better Than a Backlog," *New York Times*, Nov. 12, 2012.

231. Jeff Schogol, "Pentagon: No Purple Heart for PTSD," *Stars and Stripes*, Jan. 6, 2009, European edition.

232. Bryan Bender, "Veterans Forsake Studies of Stress: Stigma Impedes Search for Remedies," *Boston Globe*, Aug. 24, 2009.

233. Lizette Varez, "War Veterans' Concussions Often Overlooked; TBI, PTSD," *New York Times*, Aug. 26, 2008. See also Mancini, "Postwar Picture."

234. Kevin Maurer, "Veterans Still Waiting on Disability Appeals; One Year after Bill, Not a Single Case Has Been Heard," *Associated Press*, Dec. 11, 2008.

235. James Dao, "Branding a Soldier with 'Personality Disorder,'" *New York Times*, Feb. 24, 2012.

236. Ibid.

7. DEEMED DANGEROUS DUE TO A MENTAL DISABILITY

1. Americans with Disabilities Act of 1990, 42 U.S.C. §12101 (2000).

2. See chapter 1.

3. Ibid.

4. See chapter 6.

5. Ibid.

6. See E. Fuller Torrey, *The Insanity Defense* (New York: W. W. Norton: 2008); Treatment Advocacy Center, www.treatmentadvocacycenter.org.

7. See the many law review articles on this subject by law professor Michael Perlin, including "'Baby, Look inside Your Mirror': The Legal Profession's Willful and Sanist Blindness to Lawyers with Mental Disabilties," *U. of Pitt. L. Rev.* 69 (Spring 2008): 589; Michael L. Perlin and Keri K. Gould, "Roshomon

and the Criminal Law: Mental Disability and the Federal Sentencing Guidelines," *Am. J. Crim. L.* 22 (1995): 431, 442–43; Michael L. Perlin, "Representing
Defendants in Incompetency and Insanity Cases: Some Therapeutic Jurisprudence Dilemmas," NYLS Legal Studies Research Paper, Apr. 2008, doi:
10.2139/ssrn.1120891. See also John La Fond and Mary Durham, *Back to the
Asylum: The Future of Mental Health Law and Policy in the United States* (New
York: Oxford University Press, 1992).

   8. *Korematsu v. United States*, 323 U.S. 214 (1944).

   9. Sheryl Gay Stolberg, "Bush Declares State of Emergency for Inauguration," *The Caucus: The Politics and Government Blog of The Times*, Jan. 13,
2009, nytimes.com.

   10. See *Nevada Dep't. of Human Resources v. Hibbs*, 538 U.S. 721 (2003).

   11. See *Pennhurst Stat Sch. & Hosp. v. Halderman*, 465 U.S. 89 (1984);
Atascadero State Hospital v. Scanlon, 473 U.S. 234 (1985).

   12. See *United States v. Georgia*, 546 U.S. 151 (2006). With sovereign immunity, the key question in this regard is whether Congress has the power to breach
state immunity by enacting and having laws enforced that protect the rights of
Americans who are members of a class whose fundamental constitutional rights
are being or have been threatened by unconstitutional state actions.

   13. See chapters 2, 3.

   14. *City of Cleburne v. Cleburne Living Center*, 473 U.S. 432 (1985).

   15. *Heller v. Doe*, 509 U.S. 312 (1993).

   16. See chapter 1.

   17. 473 U.S. 432 (1985).

   18. Ibid.

   19. 509 U.S. 312 (1993).

   20. Ibid.

   21. 536 U.S. 304 (2002).

   22. *Penry v. Lynaugh*, 492 U.S. 302 (1989).

   23. Ibid.

   24. *Penry v. Lynaugh*, 492 U.S. 302 (1989).

   25. Conversations with Professor Ellis, particularly when he was on the ABA
Commission on Mental and Physical Disability Law from 2000 to 2003 and I
was its director.

   26. Professor Ellis was named the 2002 *National Law Journal*'s Lawyer of
the Year for his work on the *Atkins* case.

   27. 536 U.S. 304 (2002).

   28. John Parry, *Civil Mental Disability Law, Evidence and Testimony* (Chicago: American Bar Association, 2010), 469–71; David M. English, "The Authority of a Guardian to Commit an Adult Ward," *Ment. & Phys. Dis. L. Rep.* 20
(1996): 584–87.

29. Michael Perlin, *Mental Disability and the Death Penalty* (Lanham, MD: Rowman & Littlefield, 2013), 3.

30. See chapter 1.

8. A NEW SYSTEM OF STATE AND FEDERAL LAWS AND PUBLIC HEALTH APPROACHES FOR PERSONS WITH MENTAL DISABILITIES DEEMED TO BE DANGEROUS

1. See Samuel J. Brakel and Ronald S. Rock, *The Mentally Disabled and the Law* 2d ed. (Chicago: University of Chicago Press, 1971), xv.

2. See S. Fazel, J. P. Singh, H. Doll, and M. Grann, "Use of Risk Assessment Instruments to Predict Violence and Antisocial Behaviour in 73 Samples Involving 24,827 People: Systemic Review and Meta-Analysis," *British Medical Journal* 345 (July 24, 2012): 4692.

3. American Bar Association Task Force on Mental Disability and the Death Penalty, "Recommendation and Report on the Death Penalty and Persons with Mental Disabilities, *Ment. & Phys. Dis. L. Rep.* 30 (2006): 668.

4. Ibid.

5. Ibid.

6. Ibid.

BIBLIOGRAPHY

Accordino, M. P., D. F. Porter, and T. Morse. "Deinstitutionalization of Persons with Severe Mental Illness: Context and Consequences." *Journal of Rehabilitation* 67, no. 2 (April/June 2001).

Addington v Texas, 441 U.S. 418 (1979).

Alarcon, R. D. "Culture, Cultural Factors and Psychiatric Diagnosis: Review and Projections." *World Psychiatry* 8 (2009): 131.

American Academy of Pediatrics. "Media Violence." *Pediatrics* 108, no. 5 (November 2009): 1222.

American Bar Association. "Recommendation and Report on the Death Penalty and Persons with Mental Disabilities." *Mental and Physical Disability Law Reporter* 30, no. 5 (2006): 668.

American Bar Association Criminal Justice Section. "Blueprint for Cost-Effective Pretrial Detention, Sentencing, and Corrections Systems." August 2002.

———. *Criminal Justice Mental Health Standards*. Washington, D.C.: American Bar Association, 1989.

American Bar Foundation. "Hospitalization and Treatment of Mental Cases." Unpublished memorandum, February 1955.

American Law Institute. *Model Penal Code—Complete Statutory Text*. Philadelphia. 1962.

American Psychiatric Association. *Diagnostic and Statistical Manual of Mental Disorders*. 4th text rev. Washington, D.C.: American Psychiatric Association, 2000.

Anderson, C. A., and B. J. Bushman. "Media Violence and the American Public." *American Psychologist* 56, nos. 6, 7 (June/July 2001): 477.

Andrews, William D. "Developments in the Law: Civil Commitment of the Mentally Ill." *Harvard Law Review* 87, no. 6 (April 1974): 1190–1406.

Appelbaum, P. S. "Civil Commitment from a Systems Perspective." *Law and Human Behavior* 16 (1992): 61.

———. "The New Preventive Detention: Psychiatry's Problematic Responsibility for the Control of Violence." *American Journal of Psychiatry* 145 (1988): 779.

———. "Thinking Carefully about Outpatient Commitment." *Psychiatric Services* 52, no. 3 (2001): 347–348.

Armat, V. C., and R. J. Isaac. *Madness in the Streets*. New York: Free Press, 1990.

Aronson, D. E., and R. J. Simon. *The Insanity Defense: A Critical Assessment of Law and Policy in the Post-Hinkley Era*. New York: Praeger, 1988.

Arrigo, B. S. "Paternalism, Civil Commitment and Illness Politics: Assessing the Current Debate and Outlining Future Direction." *Journal of Law and Health* 7 (1992–1993): 131.

Aron, L., R. Honberg, and K. Duckworth. *Grading the States 2009: A Report on America's Health Care System for Adults with Serious Mental Illness.* National Alliance on Mental Illness, March 2009.

Atascadero State Hospital v. Scanlon, 473 U.S. 234, 1985.

Atkins v. Virginia, 536 U.S. 304 (2002).

Auerhahn, Kathleen, and Robert N. Parker. "Alcohol, Drugs, and Violence." *Annual Review of Sociology* 24 (1998): 291–311.

Austin, J., K. D. Johnson, and M. Gregoriou. "Juveniles in Adult Prisons and Jails: A National Assessment." Bureau of Justice Assistance. October 2000.

Baca-Garicia, E., et al. "Diagnostic Stability of Psychiatric Disorders in Clinical Practice." *British Journal of Psychiatry* 190 (2007): 210.

Bachrach, L. L. "Commentary." *Hospitals and Community Psychiatry* 34 (1983): 105.

Baillargeon, Jacques, et al. "Psychiatric Disorders and Repeat Incarcerations: The Revolving Prison Door." *American Journal of Psychiatry* 166, no. 1 (2009): 103.

Barefoot v. Estelle, 463 U.S. 880 (1983).

Barnes v. Gorman, 536 U.S. 181 (2002).

Barnes, Thomas R. E. *Antipsychotic Drugs and Their Side-Effects.* Neuroscience Perspectives Series. San Diego, CA: Academic Press, 1993.

Barth, Abram S. "A Double-Edged Sword: The Role of Neuroimaging in Federal Capital Sentencing." *American Journal of Law and Medicine* 33 (2007): 501.

Bassuk, E. L., and S. Gerson. "Deinstitutionalization and Mental Health Services." *Scientific American* 238, no. 2 (1978): 46–53.

Bauer, A., et al. "Reflections on Dangerousness and Its Predictions—A Truly Tantalizing Task." *Medicine and Law* 21, no. 3 (2002): 495.

Bayer, Ronald. *Homosexuality and American Psychiatry: The Politics of Diagnosis.* Princeton, NJ: Princeton University Press, 1987.

Beech, A., and D. Grubin. "Chemical Castration for Sex Offenders: Doctors Should Avoid Becoming Agents of Social Control." *British Medical Journal* 7744 (February 2010): 433–434.

Beecher-Monas, E. "The Epistemology of Prediction: Future Dangerousness Testimony and Intellectual Due Process." *Washington and Lee Law Review* 60 (Spring 2003): 353.

Bensen, B. W., W. H. Meeuwisse, J. Rizos, J. Kang, and C. J. Burke. "A Prospective Study of Concussions among National Hockey League Players during Regular Season Games: The NHL-NHLPA Concussion Program." *Canadian Medical Association Journal*, April 2011.

Bergquist, Meris. "No Exit for Patients Confined at the Vermont State Hospital." *Vermont Bar Journal* 32 (Summer 2006): 34.

Bernstein, David E. "Expert Witnesses, Adversarial Bias, and the (Partial) Failure of the Daubert Revolution." *Iowa Law Review* 93 (2008): 451.

BeVier, L. R. "Controlling Communications That Teach or Demonstrate Violence: 'The Movie Made Them Do It.'" *Journal of Law, Medicine and Ethics* 32 (Spring 2004): 47.

Bhattacharya, S. "Violent Song Lyrics Increase Aggression." *New Scientist*, May 2003.

Birley, Jim. "Political Abuse of Psychiatry in the Soviet Union and China: A Rough Guide for Bystanders." *Journal of American Academy of Psychiatry and Law* 30 (2002): 145–147.

Birnbaum, Morton. "The Right to Treatment." *American Bar Association Journal* 46 (1960): 499.

Blitz, C. L., N. Wolff, and J. Shi. "Physical Victimization in Prison: The Role of Mental Illness." *Journal of Law and Psychiatry* 31, no. 5 (2009): 385–393.

Bloch, Sidney, and Peter Reddaway. *Russia's Political Hospitals: The Abuse of Psychiatry in the Soviet Union.* London: Gollancz, 1977.

Blum v. Yaretsky, 457 U.S. 991 (1982).

Blume, J. H., S. P. Garvey, and S. L. Johnson. "Future Dangerousness in Capital Cases: Always 'At Issue.'" *Cornell Law Review* 86 (2001): 397.

Bonnie, R. J. "Political Abuse of Psychiatry in the Soviet Union and in China: Complexities and Controversies." *Journal of Academy of Psychiatry and Law* 30 (2002): 135–144.

Bonnie, R. J., and T. N. Wanchek. "Use of Longer Periods of Temporary Detention to Reduce Mental Health Civil Commitments." *Psychiatric Services*, July 2012.

Andrews, D. A., and J. Bonta. "Rehabilitating Criminal Justice Policy and Practice." *Psychology, Public Policy and Law* 16, no. 1 (2010): 39–55.

Boretos, S. L. "The Role of Discrimination and Drug Policy in Excessive Incarceration in the United States." *University of the District of Columbia Law Review* 6 (Fall 2001): 73.

Boyle, Robert H. *Sport: Mirror of American Life.* Boston: Little, Brown, 1963.

Brakel, Samuel J., John Parry, and Barbara A. Weiner. *The Mentally Disabled and the Law.* 3d. ed. Chicago: American Bar Foundation, 1985.

Brakel, Samuel J., and Ronald S. Rock. *The Mentally Disabled and the Law.* 2d. Chicago: University of Chicago Press, 1971.

Brannen, D. N., et al. "Transfer to Adult Court." *Psychology, Public Policy and Law* 12 (August 2006): 332.

Brenner, L. A., et al. "Suicidality and Veterans with a History of Traumatic Brain Injury: Participants, Events, Protective Factors, and Preventive Strategies." *Rehabilitation Psychology* 54, no. 4 (2008): 390–397.

Brooks, W. M. "The Tail Wags the Dog: The Persuasive and Inappropriate Influence by the Psychiatric Profession on the Civil Commitment Process." *N. Dakota L. Rev.* 86 (2010): 259.

Brown v. Plata, 131 S. Ct. 1910 (2011).

Bryant, J., D. Zillman, and A. A. Raney. "Violence and the Enjoyment of Media Sports." In *Mediasport*, edited by Lawrence A. Wenner. New York: Routledge, 1998.

Bureau of Justice Statistics. "Crime against People with Disabilities." U.S. Department of Justice, 2008.

———. *Mental Health and Treatment of Inmates and Probationers.* Washington, D.C.: U.S. Department of Justice, July 1999.

———. "Sexual Victimization in Juvenile Facilities Reported by Youth, 2008–09." January 2010.

Bushman, B. J., R. F. Baumeister, and A. D. Stack. "Catharsis, Aggression, and Persuasive Influence: Self-Fulfilling or Self-Defeating Prophecies?" *Journal of Personality and Social Psychology* 76, no. 3 (1999): 367–376.

Bushman, B., and J. Whitaker. "Like a Magnet: Catharsis Beliefs Attract Angry People to Violent Video Games." *Psychological Science* 21 (June 2010): 790–792.

Butcher, J. N., et al. "Potential Bias in MMPI-2 Assessments Using the Fake Bad Scale (FBS)." *Psychological Injury and Law* 1, no. 3 (December 2007): 191.

Butts, J. A., and A. V. Harrell. *Delinquents or Criminals? Policy Options for Young Offenders.* Urban Institute, June 2008.

Bychowski, Gustav, and Jonas Rappaport. *The Clinical Evaluation of Dangerousness of the Mentally Ill.* Springfield, IL: C. C. Thomas, 1967.

Callahan, L., C. Mayer, H. Steadman. "Insanity Defense Reform in the United States—Post-Hinckley." *Mental and Physical Disability Law Reporter 11*, no. 1 (1987): 54.

Carafano, J., and P. Rosenzweig. *Preventive Detention and Actionable Intelligence.* Heritage Foundation, September 16, 2004.

Centers for Disease Control and Prevention. "Effects on Violence of Laws and Policies Facilitating the Transfer of Youth from the Juvenile to Adult System: A Report on the Recommendations of the Task Force on Community Preventive Services." Morbidity Weekly Report Series, November 2007.

Cintron, Lisa A. "Rehabilitating the Juvenile Court System: Limiting Juvenile Transfers to Adult Criminal Court." *Northwestern University Law Review* 90 (1996): 1254.

City of Cleburne v. Cleburne Living Center, 473 U.S. 432 (1985).

Clark v. Arizona, 126 S. Ct. 2709 (2006).

Cornwell, J. K. "Understanding the Role of the Police and Parens Patriae Powers in Involuntary Civil Commitment before and after Hendricks." *Psychology, Public Policy and Law* 4 (1998): 377.

Coucouvanis K., et al. *Current Populations and Longitudinal Trends of State Residential Settings (1950–2003).* Research and Training Center on Community Living, University of Minnesota, 2004.

Council of State Governments. *Criminal Justice/Mental Health Consensus Project*. New York: Council of State Governments, Eastern Regional Conference, 2002.

Cucolo, Heather, and Michael Perlin. "Preventing Sex-Offender Recidivism through Therapeutic Jurisprudence Approaches and Specified Community Integration." *New York Law School*, November 4, 2011.

Cunningham, M. D., T. J. Reidy, and J. R. Sorensen. "Assertions of 'Future Dangerousness' at Federal Capital Sentencing: Rates and Correlates of Subsequent Prison Misconduct and Violence." *Law and Human Behavior* 32, no. 1 (2008): 46.

Cunningham, P., K. McKenzie, and E. F. Fries. "The Struggle to Provide Community-Based Care to Low-Income People with Serious Mental Illnesses." *Health Affairs* 25, no. 3 (May–June 2006): 694–695.

Daubert v. Merrell Dow Pharmaceuticals, 509 U.S. 579 (1993).

David Finkelhor, Richard Ormrod, and Mark Chaffin. "Juveniles Who Commit Sex Offenses against Minors." *Juvenile Justice Bulletin*, December 2009.

Deming, A. "Sex Offender Civil Commitment Programs: Current Practices, Characteristics, and Resident Demographics." *Journal of Psychiatry and Law* 36 (2008): 439.

Dershowitz, Alan. "The Law of Dangerousness: Some Fictions about Predictions." *Journal of Legal Education* 23 (1970): 24.

———. "The Origins of Preventive Confinement in Anglo-American Law—Part I: The English Experience." *University of Cincinnati Law Review* 43 (1974): 1.

Deshaney v. Winnebago County Department of Social Services, 489 U.S. 189 (1989)

Desmond, Brenda C., and Paul J. Lenz. "Mental Health Courts: An Effective Way for Treating Offenders with Serious Mental Illness." *Mental and Physical Disability Law Reporter* 34, no. 4 (July/August 2010): 525.

Deutch, Albert. *The Mentallly Ill in America: A History of Their Care and Treatment in Colonial Times*. New York: Columbia University Press. 1949.

Developments in the Law—The Law of Mental Illness. "Booker, the Federal Sentencing Guidelines, and Violent Mentally Ill Offenders." *Harvard Law Review* 121 (February 2008): 1133.

Diamond, Bernard. "The Fallacy of the Impartial Expert." *Archives of Criminal Psychodynamics* 3 (1959): 221.

Douglas, K., L. Guy, and S. Hart. "Psychosis As a Risk of Violence to Others: A Meta-Analysis." *Psychological Bulletin* 135, no. 5 (2009): 679.

Dvoskin, J., and K. Heilbrun. "Risk Assessment and Release Decision-Making: Toward Resolving the Great Debate." *American Academy of Psychiatry and the Law* 29 (2001): 6.

Eacketal, S. M. "Interviewer-Perceived Honesty as a Mediator of Racial Disparities in the Diagnosis of Schizophrenia." *Psychiatric Services* (September 2012): 875–880.

Edwards, W. J., and S. Greenspan. "Adaptive Behavior and Fetal Alcohol Spectrum Disorders." *Journal of Psychiatry and Law* 38 (2010): 419.

Elbogen, E. B., and S. C. Johnson. "The Intricate Link between Violence and Mental Disorder: Results from the Epidemiologic Survey of Alcohol and Related Conditions." *Archive of General Psychiatry* 66, no. 2 (2009): 152–161.

Ennis, B. J., and T. R. Litwack. "Psychiatry and the Presumption of Expertise: Flipping Coins in the Courtroom." *California Law Review* 62, no. 3 (1974).

Fazel, S., et al. "Schizophrenia and Violence: Systematic Review and Meta-Analysis." *Public Library of Science and Medicine* 6, no. 8 (August 2009).

Fazel, S., J. P. Sing, H. Doll, and M. Grann. "Use of Risk Assessment Instruments to Predict Risk of Violence and Antisocial Behaviour in 73 Samples Involving 24,827 People: Systematic and Meta-Analysis." *British Medical Journal* 345 (July 2012): 4692.

Fellner, J. "A Corrections Quandry: Mental Illness and Prison." *Harvard Civil Rights-Civil Liberties Law Review* 41 (2006): 392.

Ferleger, David. "The Constitutional Right to Community Services." *Georgia State University Law Review* 26 (2010): 764.

Ferris, C. E. "The Search for Due Process in Civil Commitment Hearings: How Procedural Realities Have Altered Substantive Standards." *Vanderbilit Law Journal* 61 (April 2008): 959.

Festinger, Leon. *A Theory of Cognitive Dissonance*. Stanford, CA: Stanford University Press, 1957.

Findley, K. A. "Innocents at Risk: Adversary Imbalance, Forensic Science, and the Search for Truth." *Seton Hall Law Review* 38 (2008): 893.

Finkelhor, D., et al. "Children's Exposure to Violence: A Comprehensive National Survey." *Office of Juvenile Justice and Delinquency Prevention Bulletin*, October 2009.

Fitch, W. L. "Sexual Offender Commitment in the United States: Legislative and Policy Concerns." *Annals of the New York Academy of Sciences* 989 (2003): 489.

Floyd, Jamie. "The Administration of Psychotropic Drugs to Prisoners: State of the Law and Beyond." *California Law Review* 78, no. 5 (October 1990): 1243–1285.

Ford, Richard T. *Rights Gone Wrong: How Law Corrupts the Struggle for Equality*. New York: Farrar, Straus and Giroux, 2011.

Fortney, T., et al. "Sexual Offender Treatment." *Sexual Offender Treatment* 2, no. 1 (2007).

Frances, Allen, *An Insider's Revolt Against Out-of-Control Psychiatric Diagnosis, DSM-5, Big Pharma, and the Medicalization of Ordinary Life*. New York: William Morrow, 2013.

Friel, A., T. White, and A. Hull. "Posttraumatic Stress Disorder and Criminal Responsibility." *Journal of Forensic Psychiatry and Psychology* 19, no. 2 (2008): 64–85.

Fritz, K. "Going to the Bullpen: Using Uncle Sam to Strike Out Professional Sports Violence." *Cardozo Arts and Entertainment Law Journal* 20 (2002): 189.

Gazzaniga, Michael S. *Who's in Charge? Free Will and the Science of the Brain*. New York: HarperCollins, 2011.

Gianoulis, Tina. *St. James Encyclopedia of Popular Culture*. 1999.

Gibbons, J. J., and N. Katzenbach. *Confronting Confinement: A Report of the Commission on Safety and Abuse in American Prisons*. New York: Vera Institute of Justice, 2007.

Goffman, Erving. *Stigma: Notes on the Management of Spoiled Identity*. Englewood Cliffs, NJ: Prentice-Hall, 1963.

Goldstein, R. L. "Hiring the Hired Gun: Lawyers and Their Psychiatric Experts." *Legal Studies Forum* 11 (1987): 41.

Goode, Eric. "Drugs and Crime: What Is the Connection?" In *Drugs in American Society*. Boston: McGraw-Hill, 2005.

Greenberg, Gary, *The Book of Woe: DSM and the Unmaking of Psychiatry*. New York: Blue Rider Press, 2013.

Greewald, Anthoney. "What (and Where) Is the Ethical Code Concerning Researcher Conflict of Interest?" *Perspectives on Psychological Science* 4, no. 1 (2009): 32–35.

Gross, Samuel R. "Expert Evidence." *Wisconsin Law Review* 1991 (1991): 1113.

Grossman, D., and L. Frankowski. *The Two Space War*. Riverdale, NY: Baen Books, 2004.

Guest, T. "The Evolution of Crime and Politics in America." *McGeorge Law Review* 33 (Summer 2002): 759.

Guthrie, C., J. Rachlinski, and A. J. Wistrich. "Blinking on the Bench: How Judges Decide Cases." *Cornell Law Review* 93, no. 1 (2007): 1–44.

Halleck, Seymour, and Nancy Halleck. *Law in the Practice of Psychiatry*. New York: Plenum Medical Book Co., 1980.

Halpern, A. L. "Reconsideration of the Insanity Defense and Related Issues in the Aftermath of the Hinckley Trial." *Psychiatric Quarterly* 54 (Winter 1982): 260.

Halstead, M. E., and K. D. Walter. "Clinical Report: Sport-Related Concussions in Children and Adolescents." *Pediatrics* 126, no. 3 (August 2010): 597–615. http://pediatrics.aapublications.org/content/126/3/597.

Hans, V. P., and D. Slater. "John Hinckley and the Insanity Defense: The Public's Verdict." *Public Opinion Quarterly* 47, no. 2 (1983): 202–212.

Harary, Charles. "Aggressive Play or Criminal Assault? An In Depth Look at Sports Violence and Criminal Liability." *Columbia Journal of Law and Arts* 25 (2001–2002): 197.

Hawthorne, Christopher. "Bringing Baghdad into the Courtroom: Should Combat Trauma in Veterans Be Part of the Criminal Justice Equation?" *Criminal Justice* 24, no. 2 (Summer 2009): 7.

Heller v. Doe, 509 U.S. 312 (1993).

Henderson, C., and G. Thornicroft. "Stigma and Discrimination in Mental Illness: Time to Change." *Lancet* 373, no. 9679 (June 2009): 1928–1930.

Hiday, V. A., et al. "Outpatient Commitment for 'Revolving Door' Patients: Compliance and Treatment." *Journal of Nervous and Mental Disease* 179, no. 2 (1991): 83–88.

Hinshaw, Stephen P. *The Mark of Shame: Stigma of Mental Illness and an Agenda for Change.* New York: Oxford University Press, 2007.

Hislop, Julie. *Female Sex Offenders: What Therapists, Law Enforcement and Child Protective Services Need to Know.* Ravendale, WA: Issues Press, 2001.

Horowitz, Emily. "Growing Media and Legal Attention to Sex Offenders: More Safety or More Injustice." *Journal of the Institute of Justice and International Studies* 164 (2007): 143.

Human Rights Watch. *Ill-Equipped: U.S. Prisons and Offenders with Mental Illness.* New York: Human Rights Watch, 2003.

Imwinkelried, Edward J. "Impoverishing the Trier of Fact: Excluding the Proponent's Expert Testimony Due to the Opponent's Inability to Afford Rebuttal Evidence." *Connecticut Law Review* 40, no. 2 (December 2007): 317.

International Society of Psychiatric–Mental Health Nurses. "Meeting the Mental Health Needs of Youth in Juvenile Justice." February 2008.

J. D. B. v. North Carolina, 131 S.Ct. 2394 (2011).

James, D. J., and L. E. Glaze. *Mental Health Problems of Prison and Jail Inmates.* Special report. Washington, D.C.: Bureau of Justice Statistics, September 2006.

Janicki, M. A. "Better Seen Then Herded: Residency Restrictions and Global Positioning System Tracking for Sex Offenders." *Boston University Public Interest Law Journal* 16 (Spring 2007): 285.

Janus, E. S., and R. A. Prentky. "Forensic Use of Actuarial Risk Assessment with Sex Offenders: Accuracy, Admissibility and Accountability." *American Criminal Law Review* 40 (2003): 1443.

Jeffery, M. I. "An Arctic Judge's Journey with FASD." *Journal of Psychiatry and Law* 38, no. 4 (Winter 2010).

Johnson, J. G., et al. "Television Viewing and Aggressive Behavior during Adolescence and Adulthood." *Science* 295 (2002): 2468.

Jones v. United States, 463 U.S. 354 (1983).

Kageleiry, Peter. "Psychological Police Interrogation Methods: Pseudoscience in the Interrogation Room Obscures Justice in the Courtroom." *Military Law Review* 193 (Fall 2007): 1.

Kansas v. Crane, 534 U.S. 407 (2002).

Kansas v. Hendricks, 521 U.S. 346 (1997).

Katch, Elise J. "The Misuse and Abuse of Psychological Experts in Court." *Colorado Law* 23 (1994): 2757.

Keane, Thomas M. "Guest Editorial. Posttraumatic Stress Disorder: Future Directions in Science and Practice." *Journal of Rehabilitation, Research and Development* 45, no. 3 (2008): vii.

Kennedy v. Louisiana, 554 U.S. 407 (2008).

Kennedy, H. "Introduction: From a Guide to Willowbrook State School Resources at Other Institutions." http://www.library.csi.cuny.edu/archives/WillowbrookRG.htm, October 2005 (accessed November 18, 2006).

Kent v. United States, 383 U.S. 541 (1966).

Kerteszetal, S. G. "Slowing the Revolving Door: Stabilization Programs Reduce Homelessness Persons' Substance Abuse after Detoxification." *Journal of Subtance Abuse Treatment* 24, no. 3 (April 2003): 197.

King, M. T. "Security, Scale, Form and Function: The Search for Truth and the Exclusion of Evidence in Adversarial and Inquisitional Justice Systems." *International Legal Perspectives* 12 (Spring 2002): 185.

Klite, P., R. A. Bardwell, and J. Salzman. "Local TV News: Getting Away with Murder." *Harvard International Journal of Press/Politics* 2 (1997): 102–112.

Kolbe, V. L. "A Cloudy Crystal Ball: Concerns regarding the Use of Juvenile Psychopathy Scores in the Judicial Waiver Hearings." *Developments in Mental Health Law* (Institute of Law, Psychiatry and Public Policy, University of Virginia) 26, no. 1 (January 2007): 1.

Korematsu v. United States, 323 U.S. 214 (1944).

Koyangi, Chris. *Learning from History: Deinstitutionalization of People with Mental Illness as Precursor to Long-Term Care Reform*. Washington, D.C.: Kaiser Commission on Medicaid and the Uninsured, August 2007.

Kreager, D. A. "Unnecessary Roughness? School Sports, Peer Networks, and Male Adolescent Violence." *American Sociological Review* 72 (2007): 705.

Kumho Tire v. Carmichael, 536 U.S. 137 (1999).

La Fond, John Q., and Mary L. Durham. *Back to the Asylum: The Future of Mental Health Law and Policy in the United States*. New York: Oxford University Press, 1992.

Lamb, R. "Deinstitutionalization and the Homeless Mentally Ill." *Hospitals and Community Psychiatry* 35 (1984): 899.

Lanier, C. S., et al. *The Future of America's Death Penalty: An Agenda for the Next Generation of Capital Punishment Research*. Durham, NC: Carolina Academic Press, 2009.

Le, T. Phi. "Mind over Murder." *Washington Lawyer* (February 2012): 21–28.

LeDoux, Joseph. "Manipulating Memory." *Scientist* 23, no. 3 (March 2009): 40.

Leo, Richard A. "The Third Degree and the Origins of Psychological Interrogation." In *Interrogations, Confessions, and Entrapment*, edited by G. Daniel Lassiter. New York: Kluwer Academic/Plenum Publishers, 2004.

Leong, Gregory B. "Diminished Capacity and Insanity in Washington State: The Battle Shifts to American Admissibility." *Journal of American Academy of Psychiatry and Law* 28 (2000): 77.

Lidz, C. W., E. P. Mulvey, and W. Gardner. "The Accuracy of Predictions of Violence to Others." *Journal of the American Medical Association* 269, no. 8 (1993): 1007.

Lidz, C. W., et al. "Violence and Mental Illness: A New Analytic Approach." *Law and Human Behavior* 31, no. 1 (February 2007): 23.

Lillquist, E. "Recasting Reasonable Doubt: Decision Theory and the Virtues of Variability." *University of California at Davis Law Review* 36, part 1 (2002): 85.

Lindman, Frank T., and Donald M. McIntyre. *The Mentally Disabled and the Law*. Chicago: University of Chicago Press, 1961.

Link, B., D. M. Castille, and J. Stuber. "Stigma and Coercion in the Context of Outpatient Treatment for People with Mental Illnesses." *Social Science and Medicine* 67 (2008).

Litwack, T. R. "Assessments of Dangerousness: Legal, Research and Clinical Developments." *Administration and Policy in Mental Health* 21 (1994): 361–377.

Longemo, B. "Serious Consequences for Serious Juvenile Offenders: Do Juveniles Belong in Adult Court?" *Ohio Northern University Law Review* 30, part 1 (2004): 141.

Lorandos, Demosthenes, and Terence W. Campbell. *Benchbook in the Behavioral Sciences*. Durham, NC: Carolina Academic Press, 2005.

Maguen, J., et al. "The Impact of Killing in War on Mental Health Symptoms and Related Functioning." *Journal of Traumatic Stress* 22, no. 5 (2009): 435.

Maguen, J., et al. "The Impact of Reported Direct and Indirect Killing on Mental Health Symptoms in the Iraq War Veterans." *Journal of Traumatic Stress* 23, no. 1 (2010): 86.

Maio, Harold. http://www.news-press.com/fdcp/?unique=131764132109. October 3, 2011.

Markman, A. "What You Don't Know Can Hurt You: Violence, Catharsis, and Video Games." *Psychology Today*, July 19, 2010.

Masur, Louis P. *Rites of Execution: Capital Punishment and the Transformation of American Culture, 1776–1865*. New York: Oxford University Press, 1989.

Mathieu, S., et al. "Comparison of Registered and Published Primary Outcomes in Randomized Controlled Trials." *Journal of the American Medical Association* 302, no. 9 (September 2000): 985.

McCarthy, B., and E. Lawrence. "Economic Crime: Theory." In *Encyclopedia of Crime and Justice*, edited by Joshua Dressler. New York: Macmillan Reference, USA, 2002.

McLellan, Faith. "Mental Health and Justice: The Case of Andrea Yates." *Lancet* 368 (December 2006): 1951–1954.

McMillan, D., R. P. Hastings, and J. Coldwell. "Clinical and Actuarial Prediction of Physical Violence in a Forensic Intellectual Disability Hospital: A Longitudinal Study." *Journal of Applied Research in Intellectual Disabilities* 17, no. 4 (December 2004): 255–265.

McPartland, J. C., B. Reichow, and F. R. Volkmar. "Sensitivity and Specificity of Proposed DSM-5 Diagnostic Criteria for Autism Spectrum Disorder." *Journal of the American Academy of Child and Adolescent Psychiatry* 51, no. 4 (April 2012).

Medine, D. "The Constitutional Right to Expert Assistance for Indigents in Civil Cases." *Hastings Law Journal* 41 (1989–1990): 281.

Melton, G. B., P. M. Lyons, and W. J. Spaulding. *No Place to Go: The Civil Commitment of Minors.* Lincoln: Unversity of Nebraska Press, 1998.

Melton, Gary B., et al. *Psychological Evaluations for the Courts.* 3d. ed. New York: Guilford Press, 2007.

Melville, J. D., and D. Melville. "Punishing the Insane: The Verdict of Guilty But Mental Ill." *Journal of American Academy of Psychiatry and Law* 30 (2002): 553–555.

Mental Health: Community-Based Care Increases for People with Serious Mental Illness. Washington, D.C.: General Accounting Office, Federal Document Clearinghouse, 2000.

Metzl, Jonathan M. *The Protest Psychosis: How Schizophrenia Became a Black Disease.* Boston: Beacon Press, 2010.

Metzner, Jeffrey, et al. "Treatment in Jails and Prisons." In *Treatment of Offenders with Mental Disorders,* edited by Robert M. Wettstein. New York: Guilford Press, 1998.

Miller, G., and C. Holden. "Proposed Revisions to Psychiatry's Canon Unveiled." *Science* 327 (February 2010): 5967.

Molen, J. H. Walma van der. "Violence and Suffering in Television News: Toward a Broader Conception of Harmful Television Content for Children." *Pediatrics* 133, no. 6 (June 2004): 1771.

Molinari, V., et al. "Provision of Psychopharmacological Services in Nursing Homes." *Journal of Gerontology. Series B, Psychological Sciences and Social Sciences* 65B, no. 1 (2010): 57–60.

Monahan, John. "Clinical and Actuarial Predictions of Violence." In *Modern Scientific Evidence: The Law and Science of Expert Testimony,* edited by David L. Faigman et al., Section10. St. Paul, MN: West Group, 2005–2006.

———. *The Clinical Predictions of Violent Behavior.* Department of Health and Human Services ADM 81-921, Washington, D.C.: Government Printing Office, 1981.

———. "Mandated Community Treatment: Applying Leverage to Achieve Adherence." *Journal of American Academy of Psychiatry and Law* 36 (2008): 282–285.

———. "Mental Disorders and Violent Behavior: Perceptions and Evidence." *American Psychologist* 47 (1992): 511–521.

———. "Statistical Literacy: A Prerequisite for Evidence-Based Medicine." *Psychological Science in the Public Interest* 8, no. 2 (2008): i.

———. "Structured Risk Assessment of Violence." In *Textbook of Violence Assessment and Management,* edited by R. Simon and K. Tardiff. Washington, D.C.: American Psychiatric Publications, 2008.

Monahan, J., and E. Silver. "Judicial Decision Thresholds for Violence, Risk Management." *International Journal of Forensic Mental Health* 2, no. 1 (2003): 1–6.

Monson, C. M., et al. "Stopping (or Slowing) the Revolving Door: Factors Related to NGRI Acquittees' Maintenance of a Conditional Release." *Law and Human Behavior* 25 (2001): 257.

Morrissey, J. P. "New Models of Collaboration between Criminal Justice and Mental Health Systems." *American Journal of Psychiatry* 166, no. 11 (2009): 1211.

Moser, R. S., and P. Schatz. "Enduring Effects of Concussions on Youth Athletes." *Archives of Clinical Neuropsychology* 17, no. 1 (January 2002): 91–100.

Mossman, D. "Commentary: Assessing the Risk of Violence—Are 'Accurate' Predictions Useful?" *Journal of American Academy of Psychiatry and Law* 28, no. 3 (2000): 272.

Moynihan, R. "Doctors' Education: The Invisible Influence of Drug Company Sponsorship." *British Medical Journal* 336, no. 7641 (February 2010).

Mulvey, E. P., and C. W. Lidz. "Back to Basics: A Critical Analysis of Dangerousness Research in a New Environment." *Law and Human Behavior* 9 (1985): 209.

Nash, R. N., et al. "Alcohol, Drugs, and Violence." *Annual Review of Sociology* 24 (1998): 291.

National Coalition for the Homeless. "Mental Illness and Homelessness." July 2009.
National Institute of Mental Health and Mental Health Law Project. "Legal Issues in State Mental Health Care: Proposals for Change." 1976.
National Mental Health Association Position Statement. "Violence in America: A Community Mental Health Response." October 8, 2004. http://www.nmha.org/prevention/previol.html.
Needell, M. H. "Are Medical Ethics Different from Legal Ethics?" *St. Thomas Law Review* 14 (Fall 2001): 31.
Nevada Department of Human Resources v. Hibbs, 538 U.S. 721 (2003).
Newman, S., and H. Goldman. "Housing Policy for Persons with Severe Mental Illness." *Policy Studies Journal* 37, no. 2 (May 2009): 299–324.
Nielssen, O., et al. "Homicide of Strangers by People with Psychotic Illness." *Schizophrenia Bulletin* 37, no. 3 (2011): 572–579.
Norko, M. A. "Commentary: Dangerousness—A Failed Paradigm for Clinical Practice and Service Delivery." *Journal of the American Academy of Psychiatry and Law* 28 (2000): 282.
O'Brien, Ruth. *Crippled Justice: The History of Modern Disability Policy in the Workplace.* Chicago: University of Chicago Press, 2001.
O'Connor v. Donaldson, 422 U.S. 563 (1975).
Odeh, M. S., R. A. Zeiss, and M. T. Huss. "Cues They Use: Clinicians' Endorsement of Risk Cues in Predictions of Dangerousness." *Behavior Science and the Law* 24, no. 2 (2006): 147–156.
Palmer, C. A., and M. Hazelrigg. "The Guilty But Mentally Ill Verdict: A Review and Conceptual Analysis of Intent and Impact." *Journal of American Academy of Psychiatry* 28, no. 1 (2000): 47–54.
Parham v. J.R., 442 U.S. 584 (1979).
Parry, John. *Criminal Mental Health and Disability Law, Evidence and Testimony.* Chicago: American Bar Association Publishing, 2009.
———. "Involuntary Civil Commitment in the 90's: A Constitutional Perspective." *Mental and Physical Disability Law Reporter* 18, no. 3, 1994: 320.
———, ed. *Mental and Physical Disability Law Reporter* (formerly *Mental Disability Law Reporter*). Washington, D.C.: American Bar Association, 1979–2011.
———. "Sexually Violent Predators; Sexual Offenders." In *Mental and Physical Disabilty Law Digest*, section 2.03. Washington, D.C.: American Bar Association, 2011.
Parry, John, and Eric Y. Drogin. *Mental Disability Law, Evidence and Testimony.* Washington, D.C.: American Bar Association Publishing, 2007.
Parry, John, and F. Philips Gilliam. *Handbook on Mental Disability Law.* Washington, D.C.: American Bar Association Publishing, 2003.
Blau, G. L., and R. A. Pasewark. "Statutory Changes and the Insanity Defense: Seeking the Perfect Insane Person." *Law and Psychology Review* 18 (1994): 69.
Pennhurst State School and Hospital v. Halderman, 465 U.S. 89 (1984).
Penry v. Lynaugh, 492 U.S. 302 (1989).
Perlin, M. L. "Baby, Look inside Your Mirror: The Legal Profession's Willful and Sanist Blindness to Lawyers with Mental Disabilities." *University of Pittsburgh Law Review* 69, no. 3 (2008): 589.
———. "'Half-Wacked Prejudice Leaped Forth': Sanism, Pretexuality, and Why and How Mental Disability Law Developed As It Did." *Journal of Contemporary Legal Issues* 10 (1999): 3–36.
———. "I Might Need a Good Lawyer, Could Be Your Funeral, My Trial: Global Clinical Legal Education and the Right to Counsel in Civil Commitment Cases." *Washington University Journal of Law and Policy* 28, no. 1 (2008): 241.
———. "International Human Rights and Comparative Mental Disability Law: The Role of International Psychiatry in the Suppression of Political Dissent." *Israel Law Review* 39 (2006): 69.
———. *Mental Disability and the Death Penalty: The Shame of the States.* Lanham, MD: Rowman and Littlefield, 2013.
———. *Mental Disability Law: Civil and Criminal.* Charlottesville, VA: Michie, 1989.

Perlin, Michael L., and Keri K. Gould. "Roshomon and the Criminal Law: Mental Disability and the Federal Sentencing Guidelines." *American Journal of Criminal Law* 22 (1995): 431.

Perry v. Louisiana, 498 U.S. 38 (1990).

Petti, T. E. "Discussion: Diagnosis Is Relevant to Psychiatric Hospitalization." *Journal of the American Academy of Child and Adolescent Medicine* 37 (1998): 1038–1040.

Pfeffer, A. "Note: 'Imminent Danger' and Inconsistency: The Need for National Reform of the 'Imminent Danger' Standard for Involuntary Civil Commitment in the Wake of the Virginia Tech Tragedy." *Cardozo Law Review* 30 (September 2008): 277.

Pinker, Steven. *The Stuff of Thought*. New York: Viking, 2007.

Pollack, David A. "Moving from Coercion to Collaboration in Mental Health Services." Substance Abuse and Mental Health Services Administration, 2004.

Pope, K. S. "Resources for Therapists Who Are Threatened, Attacked or Stalked by Patients." *Ken Pope Resources for Vulnerable Therapists*. http://kspope.com/stalking.php (accessed June 18, 2013).

Pope, K. S. "10 Fallacies in Psychological Assessment." http://kspope.com/fallacies/assessment.php (accessed March 12, 2013).

Powell v. Texas, 392 U.S. 514 (1968).

Prentky, R. A., E. Janus, H. Barbaree, B. K. Schwarz, and M. P. Kafka. "Sexually Violent Predators in the Courtroom: Science on Trial." Legal Studies Research Paper Series. William Michell College of Law, October 2006.

Prentky, R. A., R. A. Knight, and A. F. S. Lee. "Risk Factors Associated with Recidivism among Extrafamilial Child Molesters." *Journal of Consulting and Clinical Psychology* 65, no. 1 (February 1997): 141–149.

Petrella, R. C., E. P. Benedek, S. C. Bank, and I. K. Packer. "Examining the Application of the Guilty But Mentally Ill Verdict in Michigan." *Hospital and Community Psychiatry* 36 (March 1985): 254–259.

Rand, Michael R., et al. *Alcohol and Crime: Data from 2002 to 2008*. Washington, D.C.: U.S. Dept. of Justice, Bureau of Justice Statistics, September 2010.

Rawal, P. H., et al. "Regional Variation and Clinical Indicators of Antipsychotic Use in Residential Treatment: A Four-State Comparison." *Journal of Behavioral Health Services and Research* 31, no. 2 (April 2004).

Ray, W. A., et al. "Atypical Antipsychotic Drugs and the Risk of Sudden Cardiac Death." *New England Journal of Medicine* 360, no. 3 (2009): 225–235.

Reis, S. dos, et al. "Antipsychotic Treatment among Youth in Foster Care." *Pediatrics* 128, no. 6 (December 2011): 1459–1466.

Resnik, D. B. "Punishing Medical Experts for Unethical Testimony: A Step in the Right Direction or a Step Too Far?" *Journal of Philosophy, Science and Law* 4 (December 2007): 10.

Ridker, P. M., and J. Torres. "Reported Outcomes in Major Cardiovascular Clinical Trials Funded by For-Profit and Not-for-Profit Organizations: 2000–2005." *Journal of the American Medical Association* 295, no. 19 (2006): 2270.

Robinson v. California, 370 U.S. 550 (1962).

Roper v. Simmons, 543 U.S. 551 (2005).

Rothman, David J. *The Discovery of the Asylum: Social Order and Disorder in the New Republic*. Boston: Little, Brown, 1971.

Rubin, B. "Predictions of Dangerousness in Mentally Ill Criminals." *Archives of General Psychiatry* 27 (1970): 397.

Sales, Bruce, D. M. Powell, and R. Van Duizend. *Disabled Persons and the Law: State Legislative Issues*. New York: Plenum Press, 1982.

Samson, C. "No Time Like the Present: Why Recent Events Should Spur Congress to Enact a Sports Violence Act." *Arizona State Law Journal* 37 (2005): 949.

Sand, J. L. B., and D. L. Rose. "Proof beyond All Possible Doubt: Is There a Need for a Higher Burden of Proof When the Sentence May Be Death?" *Chicago-Kent Law Review* 78, no. 3 (2003): 1359.

Sanders, Joseph. "Expert Witness Ethics." *Fordham Law Review* 76 (2007): 1539.

Satcher, David. "Overview of Cultural Diversity and Mental Health Services." In *Mental Health: A Report of the Surgeon General*. Washington, D.C.: Office of Surgeon General, 1999.

Schildkrout, Barbara. *Unmasking Psychological Symptoms*. Hoboken, NJ: John Wiley and Sons. 2011.

Schwartz, H. I. "Death Row Syndrome and Demonization: Psychiatric Means to Social Policy Ends." *Journal of Academy of Psychiatry and Law* 33, no. 2 (June 2005): 153.

Schwartz, L. M., and S. Woloshin. "How the FDA Forgot the Evidence: The Case of Donepezil 23 MG." *British Medical Journal* 344 (2012): 1086.

Seal, K. H., et al. "Trends and Risk Factors for Mental Health Diagnoses among Iraq and Afghanistan Veterans Using Department of Veterans Affairs Health Care, 2002–2008." *American Journal of Public Health* 99, no. 9 (2009): 1651–1658.

Segal, S. P. "Civil Commitment Law, Mental Health Services, and US Homicide Rates." *Social Psychiatry, Psychiatry and Epidemiology* 47, no. 9 (2011): 1449–1458.

Seling v. Young, 531 U.S. 250 (2001).

Sell v. United States, 539 U.S 166 (2003).

Sharp, C., and S. Kine. "The Assessment of Juvenile Psychopathy: Strengths and Weaknesses of Currently Used Questionnaire Measures." *Child and Adolescent Mental Health* 13, no. 2 (2008): 85–95.

Shelder, J., et al. "Personality Disorders in DSM-5." *American Journal of Psychiatry* 167 (2010): 1026.

Siever, Larry J. "Neurobiology of Aggression and Violence." *American Journal of Psychiatry* 165 (2008): 429.

Simons, M. A. "Departing Ways: Uniformity, Disparity and Cooperation in Federal Drug Sentences." *Villanova Law Review* 47 (2002): 921.

Singleton v. Norris, 124 S. Ct. 74 (2003).

Slobogin, C. "Mental Illness and the Death Penalty." *California Criminal Law Review* 1 (2000): 3.

———. "Rethinking Legally Relevant Mental Disorder." *Ohio Northern University Law Review* 29 (2003): 487.

———. "The Supreme Court's Recent Criminal Mental Health Cases." *Criminal Justice* 22, no. 3 (Fall 2007): 8.

Slovenko, R. "Commentary: Should Mental Health Professions Honor Bazelon or Burger?" *Michigan Society of Psychoanlytic Psychology News*, February 2006.

Smith, Peter J. "New Legal Fictions." *Georgetown Law Journal* 95 (June 2007): 1435–1495.

Snead, O. C. "Neuroimaging and the 'Complexity' of Capital Punishment." *New York University Law Review* 82 (2007): 1265.

Snowden, L. R., et al. "Disproportionate Use of Psychiatric Emergency Services by African Americans." *Psychiaric Services* 60 (2009): 1664.

Sofair, A. N., and L. C. Kaldjian. "Eugenic Sterilization and a Qualified Nazi Analogy: The United States and Germany, 1930–1945." *Annals of Internal Medicine* 132, no. 4 (2000): 312–319.

Stagman, S, and J. L. Cooper. *Children's Mental Health: What Policymakers Should Know*. National Center for Children in Poverty, April 2010.

Steadman, H. J. "From Dangerousness to Risk Assessment of Community Violence: Taking Stock at the Turn of the Century." *Journal of the American Academy of Psychiatry and the Law* 28 (2000): 265–271.

Steadman, H. J., et al. "A Specialized Crisis Response Site as a Core Element of Police-Based Diversion Programs." *Psychiatric Services* 52, no. 2 (2001): 219–222.

Stefan, S. "'Discredited' and 'Discreditable': The Search for Political Identity by People with Psychiatric Diagnoses." *William and Mary Law Review* 44, no. 3 (2003): 1341.

Stein, E. "The Admissibility of Expert Testimony about Cognitive Science Research on Eyewitness Identification." *Law, Probability and Risk* 2, no. 4 (2003): 295–303.

Stoffelmayr, E., and S. S. Diamond. "The Conflict between Precision and Flexibility in Explaining 'Beyond a Reasonable Doubt.'" *Psychology, Public Policy & Law* 6 (September 2000): 769.

Stone, A. "The Tarasoff Decisions: Suing Psychotherapists to Safeguard Society." *Harvard Law Review* 90 (1976): 358.

Stromberg, C. D., and A. Stone. "A Model State Law on Civil Commitment of the Mentally Ill." *Harvard Journal on Legislation* 20 (1983): 275.

Stuart, H. "Violence and Mental Illness: An Overview." *World Psychiatry* 2, no. 2 (June 2003): 121.

Subcommittee on Criminal Justice: Background Paper. Washington, D.C.: New Freedom Commission on Mental Health, June 2004.

Substance Abuse and Mental Health Services Administration. Office of Applied Studies. "National Survey of Substance Abuse Treatment Services." 2002, table 4.2a.

Substance Abuse and Mental Health Services Administration. Drug and Alcohol Services Information Service. "Coerced Treatment among Youths: 1993–1998." September 21, 2001.

———. "Substance Abuse Treatment Admissions Referred by the Criminal Justice System: 2002." July 30, 2004.

Substance Abuse and Mental Health Services Administration. "Violence and Mental Illness: The Facts." 2010.

Swanson, J., et al. "The Socio-Environmental Context of Violent Behavior in Persons Treated for Severe Mental Illness." *American Journal of Public Health* 92, no. 9 (September 2002): 1523–1531.

Szasz, Thomas S. *The Myth of Mental Illness: Foundations of a Theory of Personal Conduct.* New York: Harper and Row, 1974.

Tabak, R. J. "Capital Punishment." In *The State of Criminal Justice 2010*, edited by Myrna Raeder. Washington, D.C.: American Bar Association, Criminal Justice Section, 2011.

Taleb, Nassim N. *The Black Swan: The Impact of the Highly Improbable.* New York: Random House, 2009.

Tanielian, T., and L. H. Jacox, eds. *Invisible Wounds of War: Psychological and Cognitive Injuries, Their Consequence, and Services to Assist Recovery.* Santa Monica, CA: Rand Center for Military Health Policy Research, 2008.

Taylor v. Taintor, 83 U.S. 366 (1872).

Teo, A. R., S. R. Holley, M. Leary, and D. E. McNiel. "The Relationship between Level of Training Accuracy and Accuracy of Violence Risk Assessment." *Psychiatric Services* 63 (November 2012): 1089–1094.

Teplin, L. A. "Police Discretion and Mentally Ill Persons." *National Institute of Justice Journal*, July 2000: 8–15.

———. "The Prevalence of Severe Mental Disorder among Male Urban Jail Detainees: Comparison with Epidemiologic Catchment Area Program." *American Journal of Public Health* 80, no. 6 (June 1990): 663–669.

Teplin, L. A., et al. "Psychiatric Disorders in Juvenile Detention." *Archives of General Psychiatry* 59 (2002): 1133–1143.

Texas Defender Service. "Deadly Speculation: Misleading Texas Capital Juries with False Predictions of Future Dangerousness." March 2004.

Timmer, J. "Incrementalism and Policymaking on Television Violence." *Communication Law and Policy* 9 (Summer 2004): 351.

Torrey, E. Fuller. *The Insanity Offense: How America's Failure to Treat the Seriously Mentally Ill Endangers Its Citizens.* New York: W. W. Norton, 2008.

———. *Out of the Shadows: Confronting America's Mental Illness Crisis.* New York: John Wiley, 1996.

Tsesis, A. "Due Process in Civil Commitments." *Washington and Lee Law Review* 68 (2011): 253.

Twining, W. "Taking Facts Seriously—Again." *Journal of Legal Education* 55 (September 2005): 360.

United States v. Booker, 543 U.S. 220 (2005).

United States v. Comstock, 130 S. Ct. 1949 (2010).

United States v. Georgia, 546 U.S. 151 (2006).

U.S. General Accounting Office. *Returning the Mentally Disabled to the Community: Government Needs to Do More.* Washington, D.C.: U.S. Accounting Office, 1977.

U.S. House Committee on the Judiciary. *The Impact of the Mentally Ill on the Criminal Justice System*. U.S. House of Representatives, September 21, 2001.

U.S. House of Representatives. "Incarceration of Youth Who Are Waiting for Community Mental Health Services in the United States." Committee on Government Reform—Minority Staff Special Investigation, July 2004.

U.S. Senate Committee on the Judiciary. "Children, Violence, and the Media: A Report for Parents and Policy Makers." September 1999.

VanNostrand, M., and G. Keebler. "Pretrial Risk Assessment in Federal Court." *Federal Probation* 73, no. 2 (September 2009).

Pope, K., and M. Vasquez. *Ethics in Psychotherapy and Counseling: A Practical Guide*. 4th ed. Hoboken, NJ: Wiley, 2011.

Viano, D. C., I. R. Casson, and E. J. Pellman. "Concussions in Professional Football: Biomechanics of the Struck Player—Part 14." *Neurosurgery* 61, no. 2 (2007): 313–327.

Viano, D. C., et al. "Concussions in Professional Football: Comparisons with Boxing Head Impacts–Part 10." *Neurosurgery* 57, no. 6 (2005): 1154–1172.

Vitek v. Jones, 445 U.S. 480 (1980).

Wakefield, J. C. "False Positives in Psychiatric Diagnoses: Implications for Human Freedom." *Theoretical Medicine and Bioethics* 31 (2010): 9.

Wald, Patricia. "Basic Personal and Civil Rights." In *The Mentally Retarded Citizen and the Law*, edited by Michael Kindred et al. New York: Free Press, 1976.

Washington State Institute for Public Policy. *Comparison of State Laws Authorizing Involuntary Commitment of Sexually Violent Predators: 2006 Update*. Olympia: Washington State Institute for Public Policy, August 2007.

Washington v. Harper, 494 U.S. 210 (1990).

Wexler, D. B. "Therapeutic Jurisprudence and Changing Conceptions of Legal Scholarship." *Behavioral Science and Law* 11 (1993): 17.

Wexler, D. B., and B. J. Winick. "Therapeutic Jurisprudence and Criminal Justice Mental Health Issues." *Mental and Physical Disability Law Reporter* 16, no. 2 (1992): 225.

Wexler, D. B., and S. E. Scoville. "Special Project: The Administration of Psychiatric Justice: Theory and Practice in Arizona." *Arizona Law Review* 13 (1971): 96.

Winick, Bruce. "Civil Commitment." In *Encyclopedia of Psychology and Law*, edited by Brian L. Cutler. Los Angeles: Sage, 2008.

Wolff, N. "Courts as Therapeutic Agents: Thinking Past the Novelty of Mental Health Courts." *Journal of the American Academy of Psychiatry and Law* 30, no. 3 (November 2002): 431.

Wollert, R. "Low Base Rates Limit Expert Certainty When Current Acturials Are Used to Identify Sexually Violent Predators: An Application of Bayes's Theorem." *Psychology, Public Policy and Law* 12, no. 1 (2006): 56–85.

Worzeletal, H. "Crisis in the Treatment of Incompetence to Stand Trial: Harbinger of a Systemic Illness." *Journal of American Academy of Psychiatry and Law* 35, no. 3 (2007): 357.

Xuetal, Xiaojing. "Do You Feel My Pain? Racial Group Membership Modulates Empathic Neural Responses." *Journal of Neuroscience* 29, no. 26 (July 2009): 8525–8529.

Zgoba, K. M., and L. M. Simon. "Recidivism Rates of Sexual Offenders Up to 7 Years Later: Does Treatment Matter?" *Criminal Justice Review* 30, no. 2 (September 2005): 155.

Zitoetal, J. M. "Psychotropic Medication Patterns among Youths in Foster Care." *Pediatrics* 121, no. 1 (2008): 157–163.

INDEX

ABOUT THE AUTHOR

John Weston Parry is the former director of the American Bar Association's Commission on Mental and Physical Disability Law (1982–2012) and editor/editor-in-chief of the *Mental and Physical Disability Law Reporter* (1979–2011). Since 1977 he has published numerous books and articles on mental disability law and the rights of persons with mental disabilities. In 1987, he received the Manfred Guttmacher Award from the American Psychiatric Association and the American Academy of Psychiatry and Law.